C. DAVID MEAD

Professor of English, Michigan State Univers

ADVISORY EDITOR TO DODD, MEAD & COMPANY

The Liberating Form

*A Handbook-Anthology of English
and American Poetry*

The Liberating Form

A *Handbook-Anthology of English*
and American Poetry

BERT C. BACH
Millikin University

WILLIAM A. SESSIONS
Georgia State University

WILLIAM WALLING
Rutgers, The State University

Dodd, Mead & Company
NEW YORK 1972 TORONTO

ISBN: 0–396–06483–3
Library of Congress Catalog Card Number: 77–175314

ACKNOWLEDGMENTS

THE BOBBS-MERRILL COMPANY, INC. for *The Faerie Queene*, edited by Robert Kellogg and Oliver Steele. Copyright © 1965, by The Odyssey Press, Inc. Reprinted by permission of The Bobbs-Merrill Company, Inc.

CHATTO AND WINDUS LTD for "Arms and the Boy" from *The Collected Poems of Wilfred Owen*. Reprinted by permission of Mr. Harold Owen and Chatto and Windus.

THE CLARENDON PRESS, OXFORD, for "Eros" from *Robert Bridges: Poetry and Prose*, ed. John Sparrow. Reprinted by permission of The Clarendon Press.

CORNELL UNIVERSITY PRESS for "Corsons Inlet" from A. R. Ammons: *Corsons Inlet*. Copyright © 1965 by Cornell University Press. Used by permission of Cornell University Press.

J. M. DENT & SONS LTD for Dylan Thomas's "Dawn Raid" and "A Refusal to Mourn the Death, by Fire, of a Child in London." Used by permission of J. M. Dent & Sons Ltd and the Trustees for the Copyrights of the late Dylan Thomas.

DODD, MEAD & COMPANY, INC. for "Heaven" from *The Collected Poems of Rupert Brooke*. Copyright 1915 by Dodd, Mead & Company. Copyright renewed 1943 by Edward Marsh. Reprinted by permission of Dodd, Mead & Company, Inc.

DOUBLEDAY & COMPANY, INC. for "Elegy for Jane," copyright 1950 from *Collected Poems of Theodore Roethke*. Reprinted by permission of Doubleday & Company, Inc.

FABER AND FABER LIMITED for "The Love Song of J. Alfred Prufrock" from T. S. Eliot: *Collected Poems 1909–1962*. Reprinted by permission of Faber and Faber Ltd.

FARRAR, STRAUS & GEROUX, INC. for "Skunk Hour" from *Life Studies* by Robert Lowell. Copyright © 1958 by Robert Lowell. Reprinted by permission of Farrar, Straus & Giroux, Inc.

GROVE PRESS, INC. for "Oread" and "Along the Yellow Sand" from *H. D.*

Selected Poems. Copyright © 1957 by Norman Holmes Pearson. Reprinted by permission of Grove Press, Inc.

HARCOURT BRACE JOVANOVICH, INC. for "The Beautiful Changes" from *The Beautiful Changes and Other Poems,* copyright 1947, by Richard Wilbur./ For "The Love Song of J. Alfred Prufrock" from *Collected Poems 1909–1962* by T. S. Eliot, copyright © 1936, 1964, by T. S. Eliot./For "Mind" from *Things of This World,* © 1956, by Richard Wilbur./For "l" from *95 Poems,* © 1958 by E. E. Cummings./For "The Scales" from *Collected Poems of William Empson,* copyright, 1949, by William Empson./For "Christmas Eve Under Hooker's Statute" and "The North Sea Undertaker's Complaint" from *Lord Weary's Castle,* copyright, 1946, by Robert Lowell./All selections reprinted by permission of Harcourt Brace Jovanovich, Inc.

HARPER & ROW, PUBLISHERS, INC. for "Yet Do I Marvel" from *On These I Stand* by Countee Cullen. Copyright, 1925 by Harper & Brothers; renewed, 1953 by Ida M. Cullen. Reprinted by permission of Harper & Row, Publishers.

HARVARD UNIVERSITY PRESS for Poem 67, "Success is Counted Sweetest," and Poem 301, "I Reason, Earth is Short," by Emily Dickinson. Reprinted by permission of the publishers and the Trustees of Amhert College from Thomas H. Johnson, Editor, *The Poems of Emily Dickinson,* Cambridge Mass.: The Belknap Press of Harvard University Press, Copyright 1951, 1955, by The President and Fellows of Harvard College.

HOLT, RINEHART AND WINSTON, INC. for "Grass" from *Cornhuskers* by Carl Sandburg. Copyright 1918 by Holt, Rinehart and Winston, Inc. Copyright 1946 by Carl Sandburg./For "Desert Places," "Stopping by Woods on a Snowy Evening," "The Tuft of Flowers," "Birches," "Mowing," "Mending Wall," and "The Road Not Taken" from *Complete Poems of Robert Frost.* Copyright 1916, 1923, 1930, 1934, 1939, by Holt, Rinehart and Winston, Inc. Copyright 1936, 1944, 1951, © 1958, 1962 by Robert Frost. Copyright © 1964, 1967 by Lesley Frost Ballantine. All selections reprinted by permission of Holt, Rinehart and Winston, Inc.

HOUGHTON MIFFLIN COMPANY for "On a Soldier Fallen in the Philippines" from *The Poems and Plays of William Vaughn Moody,* ed. John M. Manly, 1912. Reprinted by permission of Houghton Mifflin Company.

ALFRED A. KNOPF, INC. for "Havana Dreams" from *Fields of Wonder* by Langston Hughes. Copyright 1947 by Langston Hughes./For "Sunday Morning" from *The Collected Poems of Wallace Stevens.* Copyright 1923 and renewed 1951 by Wallace Stevens./For "Of Modern Poetry" from *The Collected Poems of Wallace Stevens.* Copyright 1942 by Wallace Stevens./ For "Piazza Piece" and "Blue Girls" from *Selected Poems,* revised edition, by John Crowe Ransom. Copyright 1927 by Alfred A. Knopf, Inc. and renewed 1955 by John Crowe Ransom./For "Captain Carpenter" from *Selected Poems,* revised edition, by John Crowe Ransom. Copyright 1924 and renewed 1952 by John Crowe Ransom./All selections reprinted by permission of Alfred A. Knopf, Inc.

LIVERIGHT PUBLISHING CORPORATION for "At Melville's Tomb" from *The Complete Poems and Selected Letters and Prose of Hart Crane.* Copyright 1933, 1956, 1966 by Liveright Publishing Corporation. Reprinted by permission of Liveright Publishing Corporation.

THE STERLING LORD AGENCY, INC. for "An Agony As Now" from *The Dead Lecturer.* Copyright 1964 by LeRoi Jones. Reprinted by permission of The Sterling Lord Agency, Inc.

Acknowledgments   v

Robinson Jeffers./"To the Stone Cutters" from *Selected Poetry of Robinson Jeffers.* Copyright 1924 and renewed 1952 by Robinson Jeffers./All selections reprinted by permission of Random House, Inc.

CHARLES SCRIBNER'S SONS for "Ode to the Confederate Dead" and "Sonnets at Christmas II" from *Poems* by Allen Tate./"Luke Havergal" and "Credo" from *The Children of the Night,* by Edwin Arlington Robinson, 1897./ "Miniver Cheevy" from *The Town Down the River* by Edwin Arlington Robinson. Copyright 1907 by Charles Scribner's Sons; renewal copyright 1935./All selections reprinted by permission of Charles Scribner's Sons.

TWAYNE PUBLISHERS, INC. for "The Negro's Tragedy" from *Selected Poems of Claude McKay.* Copyright Twayne Publishers and reprinted with their permission.

VANGUARD PRESS, INC. for "The Little Ghost who Died for Love" from *The Collected Poems of Edith Sitwell.* Copyright, 1954 by Edith Sitwell. Reprinted by permission of Vanguard Press, Inc.

Preface

This text aims to serve teachers and students who approach poetry through particular forms and who desire as well some apparatus which will direct them to a deeper reading of individual poems. Its introductory chapter, "The Nature of Poetry," furnishes a relatively simple discussion of terms and concepts that recur in later chapter introductions and exercises. The nine succeeding chapters provide a brief discussion of the forms under consideration; a selection of poems—organized, for the most part, chronologically—that demonstrates the characteristics and evolution of the forms; and a series of exercises designed in various ways to recall the concepts and terms that have been presented, citing their relevance to particular poems, and to introduce pertinent new considerations.

The terms *form*, *kind*, and *genre* are not synonymous. Moreover, a sonnet is clearly not a form in the same sense as blank verse, nor is blank verse a form in the same sense as an ode. Why, then, have we devised a table of contents which seems to employ different definitions of form and an overlapping structure that does not exhaust the possibilities of any single theory of literary form? And, finally, why conclude the book with a seemingly anomalous chapter entitled "Modern Poetry"? In organizing the book, we hoped to suggest—as opposed to encompass—the possibilities for poetic creation implicit in each of several concepts of form. The book's thesis is twofold: first, that all poetry of worth has form; and, second, that form—no matter how traditional—is potentially liberating. Accepting these principles, we could not compile an anthology both representative of the finest English and American poetry and characterized by reasonable brevity unless the concept of form were expanded to include its several implications for poetic creation. Moreover, a separate consideration of modern poetry (even though modern poems appear in various chapters) is justified to counter the pervasive myth that modern poets comprise a cult of formlessness. Modern poetry has characteristically evolved forms all its own, forms built on certain frequently recurring qualities, but nevertheless clearly organic and often completely developed for the individual poem.

Our choice of organization was also influenced by the alternatives evidenced in the congeries of poetry anthologies already available. Most of these follow one of four organizational principles. The most popular is chronological, the *Beowulf* to Ginsberg approach. Such an organization has meaning only if the instructor discusses the new forms which emerge in differing epochs, extracting from those forms the characteristics that contribute to a continuum of poetic experience. A more recent approach is rigidly analytical. This piecemeal method may begin with a lengthy description of connotative language, present (twenty or thirty pages later) an analysis of figures of speech, and finally (another thirty pages later) discuss tone and sound devices. Such fragmentation is surely unnatural. While analysis must serve any approach to poetry, its particular emphasis in many anthologies tends, at worst, to dehumanize art. A third approach is thematic. Furnishing ample opportunity for discussion of material either tangential or irrelevant to the study of poetry, it groups poems—often with procrustean ingenuity—under such categories as "Man and God" or "Man in Search of Himself." Such an approach directs the student away from the poem as an aesthetic expression and proposes, rather, that he consider it a religious, social, or political tract. A fourth method is simply to provide an ample group of poems without critical apparatus. All too often this editorial procedure leads to disorganized and directionless courses.

Our expanded concept of form implies a desire for pedagogical relevancy; it provides a meaningful basis for organizing a poetry anthology which addresses itself to students in introductory poetry courses. All men feel grief, or injustice, or pain, or disgust. But in describing emotions few of us go beyond such vapid statements as these: "The Senator's death made me sad." "That noise is giving me a headache." "That kind of behavior makes me sick." The poet experiencing an emotion, on the other hand, expresses it in a form calculated to enhance our response to its effect. Thus the study of forms clarifies the particular experience which the poet recreates and provides a context for discussing the personal value of poetry. As the Shakespearean critic A. C. Bradley argues in "Poetry for Poetry's Sake," substance and form cannot be separated: "The true critic in speaking of these apart does not really think of them apart; the whole, the poetic experience, of which they are but aspects, is always in his mind; and he is always aiming at a richer, truer, more intense repetition of that experience."

A note concerning our method of annotation is also necessary. Wherever knowledge of the historical or social milieu of a poem or group of poems is relevant, that information is provided either in the appropriate section introduction or exercises. When annotations appear in exercises rather than in introductions or vocabulary glosses, they do so to urge the student to form a response rather than simply to recognize a denotative meaning. Our rule of thumb concerning vocabulary glosses is this: if the word can be found in a standard desk dictionary, we do not provide a note. On the other hand, archaic expressions—especially those in early texts—are glossed at the end of the poem, as are foreign expressions and names of relevant persons or places. All texts are either taken from original sources or have been collated with authentic sources.

Bert C. Bach
William A. Sessions
William Walling

Contents

Contents — Poetry

The Liberating Form

*A Handbook-Anthology of English
and American Poetry*

Chapter 1

The Nature of Poetry

The medium of poetry is language in motion. Like the movement of music and dancing, the movement of poetry develops its meaning. And that meaning may comprise the feelings that the poet records or salutes, the thoughts that the mind comprehends, or the order that the imagination perceives. A poem does not stand still like a statue. The sounds of poetry are heard consecutively rather than concurrently. Thus a poet's handling of sound quantity, quality, tempo, and meaning constitutes his art. Even when the poem appears as a printed text, the printing symbols show sounds moving in sequence. This time-action, or rhythm, *becomes poetry* as it builds up purpose and direction.

One way to get at the poet's purpose is to see the form he uses to build up or control his time-action. To approach that shape or form is to see what it puts together. The introductory chapter you are reading concerns the basic elements of poetry that a form puts together, the elements that keep moving in time, sometimes one right after the other and sometimes all together. The chapter starts with the most basic element, words, and ends with the larger, more abstract elements of progression, tone, and theme. In it and succeeding chapters, you will discover that in reading a poem you are joining with the poet in creating a form. That is, you are taking that poet's controlled and directed time-action and, in a very real sense, doing the dance yourself. Learning the steps of the dance, of the form, is what this book is about; and what makes up the dance steps (not how they go) is the material of this first chapter. Each of the remaining chapters concerns a certain form that experienced poets have used to show these steps to best advantage. If you study these forms and all their variations, you will learn much about the nature of poetry everywhere. Best of all, you will begin to participate in the poetic act. You will join in a very ancient and very new dance, one of the most satisfying to human beings.

If—as Plato says—poetry "comes nearer to vital truth than history," you certainly may ask: what is its truth and purpose? Asking such large questions is a good way to begin a study of forms and what they put together:

1. Is poetry merely a *mimetic* art? That is, is its goal—in Aristotle's terms—simply "modes of imitation" of man's action? If so, our primary critical preoccupation should be with the accuracy of the image created in the poem, whether it be an image of a finite object or of the soul's quest for truth and beauty.

2. Is poetry a *pragmatic* art? Is its imitative nature incidental and subordinate to effects it may have on the reader? The Roman poet Horace, for example, argued that a poem's success depends on the degree of pleasure the reader derives from it. Dr. Samuel Johnson, the most influential English critic of the eighteenth century, argued for another effect, instruction, saying that "it is always a writer's duty to make the world better." Such a view centers on the craft of poetry, on "rules" that poetic traditions have formulated.

3. Is poetry an *inspired* art? The ancient critic Longinus said: "Sublimity is the echo of a great soul." In this view, poetry grows *without* foreseen ends, developing what Coleridge described as expressions of unrealized feeling and desire. Such poetry, in its emotional climax, is called by Wordsworth a "spontaneous overflow of powerful feeling."

4. Is poetry a *corporeal* art? Is the poem a self-contained phenomenon, a "thing" distinct from philosophy, sociology, politics, ethics, history, and the poet's biography? In this view, the little world of the poem is not to be related to the social, intellectual, or personal milieu of the poet himself. The poem, as so many

New Critics have argued, is an aesthetic whole whose real values are internally rather than externally defined.

As you study the forms of poetry in the following chapters, you will do well to recall these few suggestions about the truth of poetry. As general as they are, they represent in brief what living traditions of the Western world have been saying about poetry for almost three thousand years.

Yet whatever the truth of poetry, the poet, unlike the painter, employs a medium vulgarized by everyone's use. As Dr. Johnson observed, common language just does not fit word to thought and thought to object. The result is that—for most speakers—"if anything rocks at all, . . . it rocks like a cradle." But the language of poetry demands transcendence over everyday usage. Poetic language is more precise, more economical, more suggestive, and more rhythmical. For these reasons, poetry most readily reveals intense moments of human experience.

DICTION

"Words, words, words" screams a character in a popular musical comedy. A poet must feel the same way when he faces the task before him of relating the words in conversation, newspapers, and television to the language of *King Lear*, "Ode on a Grecian Urn," and "Four Quartets." A poet, however, must use a special brand of language, either created especially by him for his work or inherited from other poets, speakers, and writers. Probably he will use a combination of both. This special brand of language, called *diction*, has been at the heart of much poetic controversy. For the poet's selection of language determines in part the audience's response to his poem, and poets of different eras evidence widely differing bases for selection.

For example, in the eighteenth century, Dr. Samuel Johnson believed that diction "drawn from nature ennobles art," whereas diction "drawn from art degrades nature." When Johnson looked at the diction of Thomas Gray, a poet of his own time, he was horrified by Gray's "words arbitrarily compounded [e.g., 'many-twinkling']." Such a flexible, even conversational use of diction was just right for Wordsworth who, in his famous preface to the *Lyrical Ballads* (second ed.,

1800), wrote: "There will also be found in these volumes little of what is usually called poetic diction; as much pains has been taken to avoid it as is ordinarily taken to produce it. . . ." Wordsworth's use of the expression *poetic diction* is obviously pejorative. By it he means the stock epithets (e.g., "sylvan maids," "Fair Nymphs"), circumlocutions (e.g., "finny tribe" for fish or "liquid ambient" for water), archaisms, and ornamental allusions which had characterized much of the language of English poetry—especially that of such poets as Pope, Gray, and Thomson in the eighteenth century.

Yet in the same preface, Wordsworth spoke of "a selection of the language really spoken by men" and of "ideas . . . expressed in language fitted to their respective importance." Poetic diction does therefore exist. Moreover, even a Wordsworth must choose words to control the rhythm, or time-action, of his language. Coleridge, the friend of Wordsworth, in his *Biographia Literaria*, gave a clear statement of the levels of such selected language: "Every man's language varies according to the extent of his knowledge, the activity of his faculties, and the depth or quickness of his feelings. Every man's language has, first, its *individuality*; secondly, the common properties of the *class* to which he belongs; and thirdly, words and phrases of *universal* use."

Coleridge further felt that poetic diction because of its passionate nature ("the appropriate effect of strong excitement") was closer to universal expression than to everyday speech. One of the best modern definitions of poetic language, that by Owen Barfield in his *Poetic Diction: A Study in Meaning* (1928), stresses this arousing of the imagination: "When words are selected and arranged in such a way that their meaning either arouses, or is obviously intended to arouse, aesthetic imagination, the result may be described as *poetic diction*. Imagination is recognizable as aesthetic, when it produces pleasure merely by its proper activity." *

Although these historical attitudes toward poetic diction help you to place its meaning, only in the actual analysis of a poem can you see its function. Other than figurative language (see p. 14), what aspects of a poet's diction do you look for? Here are some questions that will help you in the looking:

---

* (New York: McGraw-Hill Book Company, 1964), p. 41; first published by Faber and Gwyer in 1928.

1. Is the diction *general* or *concrete*—that is, does it create a vague or a graphically realized sensory response in the reader?
2. Does the diction consist of words easily recognized by a heterogeneous group of readers; or is the appeal to a particular interest, age, profession, locale, or educational level?
3. Is the level of diction consistent?
4. Does the poet rely more heavily on *denotation* (dictionary definitions of words) or *connotation* (shades of meaning associated with words)? What associations do the words with connotative meanings evoke?
5. Is the diction fitting to the mood or subject matter of the poem? (The critical term *decorum* implies a careful attention to mutually appropriate action, character, style, and language. For example, Pope is discussing decorum when he makes the following evaluation of *The Iliad*: "The *Speeches* are to be considered as they flow from the characters, being perfect or defective as they agree or disagree with the manners of those who utter them.")
6. Does the poet's diction reveal constructive use of *poetic license* (the right of the poet to deviate from the diction, grammatical rules, and subjects of prose discourse)?
7. Does the poet use *archaisms* (antiquated words of an earlier period) or "literary" words? If so, what effect do they have?
8. Is the poem rich in *allusions* (direct or indirect references to events, mythology, other literary works)? If so, are the allusions primarily functional or decorative?
9. Does the poet sacrifice sense for sound; that is, in order to achieve certain sound effects (see p. 60), does he employ words or phrases inappropriate to the sense of the poem?

QUESTIONS – DICTION

MATTHEW ARNOLD (1822–88)

Dover Beach

> The sea is calm tonight,
> The tide is full, the moon lies fair

Upon the straits;—on the French coast the light
Gleams and is gone; the cliffs of England stand,
Glimmering and vast, out in the tranquil bay.   5
Come to the window, sweet is the night-air!
Only, from the long line of spray
Where the sea meets the moon-blanched land,
Listen! you hear the grating roar
Of pebbles which the waves draw back, and fling,   10
At their return, up the high strand,
Begin, and cease, and then again begin,
With tremulous cadence slow, and bring
The eternal note of sadness in.

Sophocles long ago   15
Heard it on the Aegean, and it brought
Into his mind the turbid ebb and flow
Of human misery; we
Find also in the sound a thought,
Hearing it by this distant northern sea.   20

The Sea of Faith
Was once, too, at the full, and round earth's shore
Lay like the folds of a bright girdle furled.
But now I only hear
Its melancholy, long, withdrawing roar,   25
Retreating, to the breath
Of the night-wind, down the vast edges drear
And naked shingles of the world.

Ah, love, let us be true
To one another! for the world, which seems   30
To lie before us like a land of dreams,
So various, so beautiful, so new,
Hath really neither joy, nor love, nor light,
Nor certitude, nor peace, nor help for pain;
And we are here as on a darkling plain   35
Swept with confused alarms of struggle and flight,
Where ignorant armies clash by night.

1. What words employed by Arnold are rich in connotation? What
associations do the words evoke? In a sentence or two, describe the
scene evoked by the first stanza.

2. Explain possible meanings for the allusion to Sophocles.

3. How does the "Sea of Faith" resemble the literal sea described in the first stanza? To answer, write a brief essay.

4. Is the diction appropriate to the mood of the poem? Comment especially on the following: "Glimmering and vast," "grating roar," "tremulous cadence slow," "turbid ebb and flow," "melancholy, long, withdrawing roar."

5. Is the diction consistent? For example, are there any words or phrases that create effects strikingly dissimilar from the effect created by most of the language? Explain.

HART CRANE (1899–1932)

At Melville's Tomb

Often beneath the wave, wide from this ledge
The dice of drowned men's bones he saw bequeath
An embassy. Their numbers as he watched,
Beat on the dusty shore and were obscured.

And wrecks passed without sound of bells,   5
The calyx of death's bounty giving back
A scattered chapter, lived hieroglyph,
The portent wound in corridors of shells.

Then in the circuit calm of one vast coil,
Its lashings charmed and malice reconciled,   10
Frosted eyes there were that lifted altars;
And silent answers crept across the stars.

Compass, quadrant and sextant contrive
No farther tides . . . High in the azure steeps
Monody shall not wake the mariner.   15
This fabulous shadow only the sea keeps.

1. Look up the following words and explain their appropriate meaning in the poem: *dice, embassy, calyx, hieroglyph, portent, compass, quadrant, sextant, monody.* For several of these words the dictionary provides more than one definition. Be prepared to defend the particular definition that you think appropriate to each word.

2. A number of words in the poem are nautical terms. Are these words richly connotative? Explain. Why are such words appropriate in a poem entitled "At Melville's Tomb"?

3. Does Crane's diction reveal use of poetic license? For example, a critic once asked Crane how a portent could be "wound" in a shell and how a compass, quadrant, and sextant could "contrive" tides. Assuming that the critic was scientifically correct, do his questions necessarily establish flaws in Crane's poem? Write an essay to explain your answer.

IMAGERY AND FIGURATIVE LANGUAGE

Imagery

"At Melville's Tomb" is a poem that constantly appeals to our senses. Like all elements of poetry, diction and imagery keep working together until, as in a good poem like Hart Crane's, it is hard to separate them. What we can best say about them is that they are alive and one, like each moment of experience. Certainly this experience is no dry fact, such as the statement "I went to the office" (which implies movement but is so general and inexact as to be unbelievable at any level deeper than the telephone book).

From King David, Aristotle, Thomas Aquinas, to Herbert Read and other modern critics, there is a common principle that all art begins in appeals to the bodily senses. This appeal distinguishes the particularized image of art from the conceptual language of a business letter, for example, and calls attention to the experience of life. *Imagery* may thus be defined as the poet's re-creation of the experience of life in all its sensuality through the medium of language.

Imagery may be either *literal* or *figurative*. It may literally reproduce experience by fully-rendered appeals to our seeing, hearing, tasting, touching, smelling, and moving. It may also figuratively reproduce the experience of life through comparison. In either case, literal or figurative, poetic imagery is more than a recitation of facts or details. At its best, as in "At Melville's Tomb," it is an imaginative interpretation of details which contributes to a greater exactness of statement.

But what about a business letter, you may ask? What could offer a more exact statement than a telephone bill? But is it exact *enough*?

This "enoughness" is the difference. Poetic imagery lets in more experience of life. Because nonintellectual, as well as intellectual, phenomena enter the world of poetic imagery, it gives a more complete truth about our existence.

The following expressions illustrate this difference. Although you might find Shelley's poetic statement too rhetorical for modern tastes, its very fanciness shows possibilities utterly lacking in the first statement:

FACT: The length of time in which man has suffered cannot be comprehended.

IMAGE: Unfathomable Sea! whose waves are years,
Ocean of Time, whose waters of deep woe
Are brackish with the salt of human tears!   (*Shelley*)

The first statement is a concept; the second is an experience. When you have grasped this distinction, you are well on the way to reading a poem.

Shelley's lines build on images that compare with each other. Such comparisons are not only at the very heart of poetry, but of any kind of "play" or relating activity, in which one must search for—or sense —a comparison by which he can define an emotional response. Some poetic imagery, however, is less figurative and more literal than this. For example, the following poem, called by Ezra Pound a "perfect" Imagist poem, reveals the power that imagery has for making physical detail more alive. Note that the basic image is the same as Shelley's but that the central comparison—the waves of the sea and pine trees —does not develop beyond a sharpening of sensual details. As in much modern poetry, the sharpening of the physical details—a "thingness"—is in itself a philosophical statement.

H[ILDA] D[OOLITTLE] (1886–1961)

Oread

Whirl up, sea—
whirl your pointed pines,
splash your great pines
on our rocks,

hurl your green over us,
cover us with your pools of fir.

Literal or figurative, however, all imagery begins in the senses. The following sensory categories illustrate the most common types of poetic images built on the five senses. Classifying images, or even poems, according to their appeal to the individual senses is a good device for learning to recognize the value of an individual image. To be too categorical is, of course, to forget we experience life as one. Even though images are predominantly visual, all our sensory responses tend to merge, as poets like Rimbaud have shown. For example, the quotation from Shakespeare below is classified as olfactory, but is it only that? What other senses are involved? And are these categories in themselves sufficient? What about *kinesthetic* imagery (denoting motion) or *organic* (denoting bodily processes like the heartbeat and breathing)? The purpose of this classification, then, is to help you learn the primary sensory values of an image and to encourage you, after that, to go back to the poem itself where they function.

1. *Visual* (sight)

   I dress a wound in the side, deep, deep,
   But a day or two more, for see the frame all wasted and sinking,
   And the yellow-blue countenance see.   (*Whitman*)

2. *Auditory* (hearing)

   And when they list, their lean and flashy songs
   Grate on their scrannel Pipes of wretched straw.   (*Milton*)

3. *Tactile* (touch)

   Fear death?—to feel the fog in my throat,
      The mist in my face,
   When the snows begin, and the blasts denote
      I am nearing the place,
   The power of the night, the press of the storm,
      The post of the foe. . . .   (*Browning*)

4. *Olfactory* (smell)

> Nay, but to live
> In the rank sweat of an enseamed bed,
> Stew'd in corruption, honeying and making love
> Over the nasty sty,— (*Shakespeare*)

> Hard Berg (methought), so cold, so vast,
> With mortal damps self-overcast;
> Exhaling still thy dankish breath— (*Melville*)

5. *Gustatory* (taste)

> Ay, in the very temple of Delight
>   Veil'd Melancholy has her sovran shrine,
>   Though seen of none save him whose strenuous tongue
> Can burst Joy's grape against his palate fine. . . . (*Keats*)

Having learned to recognize certain kinds of images, you are now ready to see them in a poem. The following poems illustrate how abstract concepts are made concrete and alive through imagery. In both poems the abstract themes of success and ambition are made sensual experiences.

PERCY BYSSHE SHELLEY (1792–1822)

Ozymandias

> I met a traveler from an antique land
> Who said: "Two vast and trunkless legs of stone
> Stand in the desert . . . Near them, on the sand,
> Half sunk, a shattered visage lies, whose frown,
> And wrinkled lip, and sneer of cold command,   5
> Tell that its sculptor well those passions read
> Which yet survive, stamped on these lifeless things,
> The hand that mocked them, and the heart that fed:
> And on the pedestal these words appear:
> 'My name is Ozymandias, king of kings: 10
> Look on my works, ye Mighty, and despair!'
> Nothing beside remains. Round the decay

Of that colossal wreck, boundless and bare
The lone and level sands stretch far away."

EMILY DICKINSON (1830–86)

[*Success Is Counted Sweetest*]

Success is counted sweetest
By those who ne'er succeed.
To comprehend a nectar
Requires sorest need.

Not one of all the purple host   5
Who took the flag today
Can tell the definition,
So clear of victory

As he, defeated—dying—
On whose forbidden ear   10
The distant strains of triumph
Burst agonized and clear!

In "Ozymandias," the expression "shattered visage"—which re-
mains alone to recall the self-termed "king of kings"—stands in vivid
contrast to the "frown, / And wrinkled lip, and sneer of cold com-
mand" that had ironically revealed the king's unjustified assurance.
Likewise, in Miss Dickinson's poem, a simple comment—that the
man who fails appreciates success more than he who succeeds—is
rendered poetic by the contrasting images of victory (in the second
quatrain) and those of defeat (in the third).

Besides suggesting individual, concrete sensory appeals or use of
figurative comparisons, *image* may be used in a slightly different sense.
When individual images in a poem accumulate so as to evoke a total
sensory response, the expression *image* (or sometimes, in a special
sense, *symbol*) denotes that unified response. Thus, for example, one
may say that Keats creates an image of autumn in "To Autumn" and
that Emerson creates an image of the fulfillment of life through
beauty in "The Rhodora."

JOHN KEATS (1795–1821)

To Autumn

Season of mists and mellow fruitfulness,
  Close bosom-friend of the maturing sun;
Conspiring with him how to load and bless
  With fruit the vines that round the thatch-eves run;
To bend with apples the mossed cottage-trees,   5
  And fill all fruit with ripeness to the core;
    To swell the gourd, and plump the hazel shells
  With a sweet kernel; to set budding more,
And still more, later flowers for the bees,
Until they think warm days will never cease,   10
    For Summer has o'er-brimmed their clammy cells.

Who hath not seen thee oft amid thy store?
  Sometimes whoever seeks abroad may find
Thee sitting careless on a granary floor,
    Thy hair soft-lifted by the winnowing wind;   15
Or on a half-reaped furrow sound asleep,
    Drowsed with the fume of poppies, while thy hook
    Spares the next swath and all its twinèd flowers:
And sometimes like a gleaner thou dost keep
  Steady thy laden head across a brook;   20
    Or by a cyder-press, with patient look,
    Thou watchest the last oozings hours by hours.

Where are the songs of Spring? Ay, where are they?
  Think not of them, thou hast thy music too,—
While barrèd clouds bloom the soft-dying day,   25
  And touch the stubble-plains with rosy hue;
Then in a wailful choir the small gnats mourn
  Among the river sallows, borne aloft
    Or sinking as the light wind lives or dies;
And full-grown lambs loud bleat from hilly bourn;   30
  Hedge-crickets sing; and now with treble soft
    The red-breast whistles from a garden-croft;
    And gathering swallows twitter in the skies.

RALPH WALDO EMERSON (1803–82)

The Rhodora:
On Being Asked, Whence Is the Flower?

In May, when sea-winds pierced our solitudes,
I found the fresh Rhodora in the woods,
Spreading its leafless blooms in a damp nook,
To please the desert and the sluggish brook.
The purple petals, fallen in the pool,   5
Made the black water with their beauty gay;
Here might the red-bird come his plumes to cool,
And court the flower that cheapens his array.
Rhodora! if the sages ask thee why
This charm is wasted on the earth and sky,   10
Tell them, dear, that if eyes were made for seeing,
Then Beauty is its own excuse for being:
Why thou wert there, O rival of the rose!
I never thought to ask, I never knew:
But, in my simple ignorance, suppose   15
The self-same Power that brought me there brought you.

Figurative Language

The use of imagery in this fashion leads to a special set of expressions called *figures of speech*. Such figures—which clarify the abstract, theoretical, or obscure by comparing them with the concrete—are illustrated by the following:

> A Sonnet is a moment's monument,—
> Memorial from the Soul's eternity
> To one dead deathless hour. (*D. G. Rossetti*)

> Our Garrick's a salad; for in him we see
> Oil, vinegar, sugar, and saltness agree! (*Goldsmith*)

> My life is like a stroll upon the beach,
> As near the ocean's edge as I can go. (*Thoreau*)

> The dome of thought, the palace of the soul. (*Byron*)

In poetic, as in daily language, these expressions are the natural growth of the poet's desire to get more life into his poem, to create more images of experience. Figurative imagery and figurative language are thus outgrowths of one another. Even literal imagery can be strengthened by the use of figurative language, as a careful analysis of Emerson's "The Rhodora" will prove.

Relating or "play" activity, as we have noted, is at the very heart of poetic language. Nowhere is this "play" clearer than in such expressions in our daily language as "It's hard as a rock" or "You're blind as a bat" or, in older days, "I might as well fly to the moon." Our basic language is filled with expressions, like these, that exaggerate or give more life, with the result that even a casual remark is transformed into something more alive and permanent.

Most of the figurative expressions in daily language are comparisons (but not all, as the above examples show). Indeed, all daily language, one famous poet has said, is a graveyard for comparisons that have lost the levels of "play" they once had in a poem. Keeping these levels in a poem is what good poets do; and the result is a richer language, both for the poet and for everybody else. This is what the French Symbolist poet Stephen Mallarmé meant when he said that poets "purify the dialect of the tribe," to give T. S. Eliot's version of this famous definition.

It is natural, then, that in certain periods of English and American literature, conventional comparisons have been greatly admired, while in others—notably the early seventeenth century and the modern period—poets have sought to employ elaborate or startling comparisons. All of them have been purifying "the dialect" of our "tribe," the daily language of journalism and business.

Figurative language is thus an important part of the transforming process that goes on in a poem. As a consequence, there have been many different types of figurative expressions; and from ancient Greece to Renaissance England, schoolboys had to learn whole lists of them. Comparisons, however, are the most basic figurative expressions. In fact, the term *metaphor* is sometimes used generically to include all figurative expression, although it is but one type of figurative comparison.

The two most frequently encountered figures of speech, then, are the comparisons simile and metaphor. *Simile* expresses comparison indirectly by using *like*, *as*, or *than*; metaphor states the comparison directly. In both cases, the comparison relates entities or "things" from different groups. In one brief moment, the poet shows the reader how two dissimilar "things" are similar. The result of this joining together in a kind of game is heightened life.

In the following similes, Spenser is expressing the beauty of his bride:

> Her cheeks like apples which the sun hath rudded,
> Her lips like cherries charming men to bite,
> Her breast like to a bowl of cream uncrudded . . .

T. S. Eliot, in what is probably the most famous simile in modern poetry, creates the same sense of living experience but with a different effect:

> Let us go, then, you and I,
> When the evening is spread out against the sky
> Like a patient etherized upon a table.

Whether in similes like these or in metaphors, the comparison of the two dissimilar "things" must be relevant and appropriate to the poem itself—to the motion, rhythm, or time-action that develop its meaning. In the comparisons in both the Spenser and Eliot lines, this appropriateness builds on the grammatical term *like*. Yet *like* introduces two entirely different experiences. The point is that in both poems the grammatical term makes the comparison clear and explicit; *like* tells the reader that the elements being compared ("lips" to "cherries" or "evening" to "etherized patient") are similar but not synonymous. They are related but not the same.

A *metaphor* shows this same relationship of comparison, but more dramatically. Like the simile, it does not confuse identities but shows two separate entities sharing one aspect of their being. In fact, the more powerful the metaphor, the greater difference in the identities of the two parts. Consider, for example, the following passage from a Shakespearean sonnet:

> O how shall summer's honey breath hold out
> Against the wreckful siege of battering days.

The poet's trick is to pull these together, and all at once. Metaphor lacks a joining grammatical term like *like*; the result is that the joining evokes a stronger sensory response because of its directness. Without that grammatical term, the identities tend to merge and the poet's trick, at this point of balancing the two identities, is to see that they do and, at the same time, do not. The inclusive nature of metaphor, therefore, makes its effects more dramatic than those of the simile and certainly more complex. Compare the following metaphors with the similes from Spenser and Eliot:

> Yet all experience is an arch wherethrough
> Gleams that untraveled world whose margin fades
> Forever and forever when I move. (*Tennyson*)

> England hath need of thee: she is a fen
> Of stagnant waters. . . . (*Wordsworth*)

> . . . (Inside his books, his fingers. They
> are withered yellow flowers and were never
> beautiful). (*LeRoi Jones*)

A simple way to keep the two parts of either simile or metaphor separate is to use the modern critic I. A. Richards' well-known terms, *tenor* and *vehicle*. In the line from Robert Burns, "O, my luve is like a red, red rose"—in which the speaker compares his girlfriend to a rose—"luve" is the "thing" being compared, the tenor or main idea. "Rose" carries the comparison; it is the vehicle by which the two identities of love and rose are related.

Figurative language, as you have seen, can produce a clarity that daily language seldom achieves. But one way to understand the virtues of figurative language is to see how it can be used badly. For example, Elizabeth Barrett Browning has a well-known simile in the line: "I love thee freely, as men strive for Right." The analogy is false. Men have seldom striven for right "freely"; rather, they have endured countless obstacles in their quest for right. Both sides of the comparison are inappropriate, and the result is unbelief, fatal for the experience of a poem.

Such inappropriate comparisons unfortunately abound in our language. Here are four frequently recurring types of weak figurative comparison:

Decorative metaphor. Such expressions as "the long arm of the law," "the ship of state," and "the face of the nation" do not increase clarity or intensity of expression. They are little more than ornamental synonyms for police, government, and the national image.

Dead metaphor. Such expressions as "the leg of the table" or "the body of the car" have so often been used that they have become literal rather than figurative expressions.

Cliché metaphor. Such expressions as "Business is the lifeblood of the nation" and "He is the hottest item in the entertainment world" have ceased to be vivid because of their frequent use.

Mixed metaphor. If the two parts of the metaphor are logically incompatible, the metaphor loses its effectiveness and may be classified as mixed. This is true of the following expressions: "The ship of state will have to make a forced landing" and "The road to success is full of waves and billows."

A particular simile or metaphor may appear in only one or two lines of a poem, or it may run throughout several lines, a stanza, or an entire poem. If the last of these occurs, the figurative comparison is called an *extended figure.* In the following poem Blake establishes a metaphor in line 4 (that wrath is a tree that grows) that runs through the rest of the poem.

WILLIAM BLAKE (1757–1827)

A Poison Tree

I was angry with my friend:
I told my wrath, my wrath did end.
I was angry with my foe:
I told it not, my wrath did grow.

And I watered it in fears,   5
Night and morning with my tears;
And I sunnèd it with smiles,
And with soft deceitful wiles.

And it grew both day and night
Till it bore an apple bright;   10
And my foe beheld it shine,
And he knew that it was mine,

And into my garden stole
When the night had veiled the pole:
In the morning glad I see   15
My foe outstretched beneath the tree.

As noted before, there have developed over the centuries many different types of figurative expressions. Besides simile and metaphor, here are seven most frequently encountered in the discussion of poetry:

1. *Overstatement and understatement.* Overstatement (or hyperbole) is a figure in which the poet exaggerates in order to achieve particular effects. When the lover says he dies for his beloved or burns with despair, he is employing this figure. Conversely, *understatement* achieves its effects because the poet says less than the situation apparently demands. For example, in *Beowulf*, the poet—after relating the king's great success, riches, and homage by his neighbors —simply adds: "þaet wœs god cynig" (that was a good king). Similarly, in *Paradise Lost*, when Satan stands on the edge of Hell ready for his terrible journey across Chaos, Milton quietly states: ". . . for no narrow frith/ He had to cross."

Whereas overstatement draws attention to a subject or emotion by overtly elevating it, understatement elicits attention because the reader expects more than the poet furnishes. Compare the effects of exaggeration in the following poem by Suckling and the bland understatement of the last verse of Frost's "The Road Not Taken" (p. 32):

SIR JOHN SUCKLING (1609–42)

Out Upon It! I Have Lov'd

Out upon it! I have lov'd
    Three whole days together;
And am like to love three more,
    If it prove fair weather.

Time shall moult away his wings,   5
    Ere he shall discover
In the whole wide world again
    Such a constant lover.

But the spite on 't is, no praise
   Is due at all to me: 10
Love with me had made no stays,
   Had it any been but she.

Had it any been but she,
   And that very face,
There had been at least ere this   15
   A dozen dozen in her place.

2. *Metonymy and synecdoche.* Metonymy and synecdoche denote figures so similar that it is probably hairsplitting to worry about distinguishing one from the other. In *metonymy* the actual name for something is omitted and another expression, resembling or standing in close relationship to it, is substituted. For example, to describe a prince as being "of noble blood," to call a soldier one who "took up arms," or to say "give me a smoke" instead of "give me a cigarette" all illustrate uses of metonymy. *Synecdoche,* on the other hand, denotes a figure in which either a word signifying the whole is used to signify a part or a word signifying a part is used to signify the whole. For example, one who refers to an advertising executive as "Madison Avenue" is using synecdoche (whole for part), as is one who says "three guns will protect you" instead of "three policemen will protect you" or who refers to elephants as "ivory" (part for whole). Writers use metonymy and synecdoche either to gain emphasis or to gain certain vivid connotations that literal equivalents do not evoke. The following excerpt illustrates numerous uses of both metonymy and synecdoche:

JAMES SHIRLEY (1596–1666)

from Ajax and Ulysses

The glories of our blood and state
   Are shadows, not substantial things,
There is no armor against fate,
   Death lays his icy hand on kings,
      Scepter and crown   5
      Must tumble down,

And in the dust be equal made,
With the poor crooked scythe and spade.

Some men with swords may reap the field,
 And plant fresh laurels where they kill,   10
But their strong nerves at last must yield,
 They tame but one another still;
   Early or late,
   They stoop to fate,
And must give up their murmuring breath,   15
When they pale captives creep to death.

The garlands wither on your brow,
 Then boast no more your mighty deeds,
Upon Death's purple altar now,
 See where the victor-victim bleeds,   20
   Your heads must come
   To the cold tomb;
Only the actions of the just
Smell sweet, and blossom in their dust.

3. *Apostrophe.* Apostrophe is a figure in which the dead are addressed as though alive (from Wordsworth, "Milton! thou shoudst be living at this hour"); the absent as though present; abstractions or inanimate objects as though present, alive, and able to understand (from Tennyson, "Ring out, wild bells"). The Greek root of "apostrophe" denotes "a turning away," and this idea carries over into its poetic application. When a poet employs apostrophe—usually in order to express intense emotion—he is turning from simple presentation of his poetical ideas to a form of personal address. If successful, great immediacy of effect is attained; however, apostrophe is the figure most often abused and most easily parodied. Note, for example, the disparity between Waller's successful use of the figure and the false elegance of James Grainger's:

EDMUND WALLER (1606–87)

Go, Lovely Rose

Go, lovely rose—
Tell her that wastes her time and me

That now she knows,
When I resemble her to thee,
How sweet and fair she seems to be.   5

Tell her that's young,
And shuns to have her graces spied,
That hadst thou sprung
In deserts where no men abide,
Thou must have uncommended died.   10

Small is the worth
Of beauty from the light retired:
Bid her come forth,
Suffer herself to be desired,
And not blush so to be admired.   15

Then die—that she
The common fate of all things rare
May read in thee:
How small a part of time they share
That are so wondrous sweet and fair.   20

JAMES GRAINGER (1721?–66)

from Solitude. An Ode

O Solitude, romantic maid,
Whether by nodding towers you tread,
Or haunt the desart's trackless gloom,
Or hover o'er the yawning tomb,
Or climb the Andes' clifted side,   5
Or by the Nile's coy source abide,
Or starting from your half-year's sleep
From Hecla view the thawing deep,
Or Tadmor's marble wastes survey,
Or in yon roofless cloyster stray;   10
    You, Recluse, again I woo,
    And again your steps pursue.

4. *Personification.* Personification is a figure of speech in which abstractions or inanimate objects are endowed with human charac-

teristics or sensibilities. Whereas indiscriminate attributing of human characteristics to inanimate objects may—contrary to the poet's desire—create humorous effects, judicious use of personification often stimulates an effective sensory response. In the following poem, for example, note that the first six lines personify the "Days" as deities who provide man with all the blessings of life:

RALPH WALDO EMERSON (1803–82)

Days

Daughters of Time, the hypocritic Days,
Muffled and dumb like barefoot dervishes,
And marching single in an endless file,
Bring diadems and fagots in their hands.
To each they offer gifts after his will,   5
Bread, kingdoms, stars, and sky that holds them all.
I, in my pleached garden, watched the pomp,
Forgot my morning wishes, hastily
Took a few herbs and apples, and the Day
Turned and departed silent. I, too late,   10
Under her solemn fillet saw the scorn.

5. *Paradox and irony.* Paradox and irony are related figures of speech. *Paradox* is a statement that at first appears self-contradictory, but on closer examination is seen to be either valid or true. For example, Shakespeare's line "Cowards die many times before their deaths" appears self-contradictory; however, the truth embodied in the line (i.e., frequently fearing death constitutes one's frequently experiencing death mentally) becomes clear on closer reading. Some modern critics, the most notable being Cleanth Brooks, argue that paradox is a kind of literary indirection characteristic of all poetry. The following lines from Shakespeare's *Romeo and Juliet* embody several paradoxes:

Alas! that love, whose view is muffled still
Should, without eyes, see pathways to his will . . .
Here's much to do with hate, but more with love:
Why then, O brawling love! O loving hate!

O any thing! of nothing first create.   5
O heavy lightness! serious vanity!
Mis-shapen chaos of well-seeming forms!
Feather of lead, bright smoke, cold fire, sick health!
Still-waking sleep, that is not what it is!
This love feel I, that feel no love in this!   10
Dost thou not laugh?

The term *irony* embodies at least four distinct concepts. *Dramatic irony* denotes a theatrical device in which a character's statements have a hidden—or suggestive—meaning that he does not himself understand. *Irony of situation* denotes a seemingly fateful situation quite the opposite of what might be anticipated from the circumstances. *Socratic irony* involves a person's assuming ignorance as a device for leading an opponent into a trap. Like paradox, *figurative irony* (or *irony of statement*) requires the reader to apprehend a meaning that lies beneath surface statement. As a figure of speech, it implies a statement in which the actual meaning is opposite to the apparent surface meaning. If a poet says the opposite of what he means, or praises when he actually means to belittle, his statement is twofold: first, there is a written statement and, second, there is an unspoken—or ironic—comment. Note, for example, the contrast between Blake's apparent praise and his actual condemnation in the following epigram:

Her whole life is an Epigram, smart, smooth and neatly pen'd,
Platted quite neat to catch applause with a sliding noose at the end.

QUESTIONS – IMAGERY AND FIGURATIVE LANGUAGE

WILFRED OWEN (1893–1918)

Arms and the Boy

Let the boy try along this bayonet-blade
How cold steel is, and keen with hunger of blood;
Blue with all malice, like a madman's flash;
And thinly drawn with famishing for flesh.

Lend him to stroke these blind, blunt bullet-heads   5
Which long to nuzzle in the hearts of lads,
Or give him cartridges of fine zinc teeth,
Sharp with the sharpness of grief and death.

For his teeth seem for laughing round an apple.
There lurk no claws behind his fingers supple;   10
And god will grow no talons at his heels,
Nor antlers through the thickness of his curls.

1. The poems of Wilfred Owen, written against the backdrop of
World War I, characteristically revealed the brutal enigma and
enormity of war. How does the imagery in "Arms and the Boy" sub-
stantiate these themes? Which images are literal and which figura-
tive? Is the elaborate personification in the first stanza justified? Ex-
plain.

2. Line 8 employs a tactile image to present a view of grief and
death. Is the image of cutting appropriate to the context in the poem?
Explain in a paragraph.

3. The third stanza presents an ironic commentary on man's be-
havior in war. Explain the meaning of the three negative statements
(ll. 10–12) in relation to line 9.

4. Does the poem contain a cumulative image of youth and war?
Explain in a brief essay.

WALT WHITMAN (1819–92)

To a Locomotive in Winter

Thee for my recitative,
Thee in the driving storm even as now, the snow, the winter-day de-
    clining,
Thee in thy panoply, thy measur'd dual throbbing and thy beat con-
    vulsive,
Thy black cylindric body, golden brass and silvery steel,
Thy ponderous side-bars, parallel and connecting rods, gyrating, shuttling
    at thy sides,   5
Thy metrical, now swelling pant and roar, now tapering in the distance,
Thy great protruding head-light fix'd in front,
Thy long, pale, floating vapor-pennants, tinged with delicate purple,

The dense and murky clouds out-belching from thy smoke-stack,
Thy knitted frame, thy springs and valves, the tremulous twinkle of thy
    wheels,   10
Thy train of cars behind, obedient, merrily following,
Through gale or calm, now swift, now slack, yet steadily careering;
Type of the modern—emblem of motion and power—pulse of the
    continent,
For once come serve the Muse and merge in verse, even as here I see thee,
With storm and buffeting gusts of wind and falling snow,   15
By day thy warning ringing bell to sound its notes,
By night thy silent signal lamps to swing.

Fierce-throated beauty!
Roll through my chant with all thy lawless music, thy swinging lamps at
    night,
Thy madly-whistled laughter, echoing, rumbling like an earthquake,
    rousing all,   20
Law of thyself complete, thine own track firmly holding,
(No sweetness debonair of tearful harp or glib piano thine,)
Thy trills of shrieks by rocks and hills return'd,
Launch'd o'er the prairies wide, across the lakes,
To the free skies unpent and glad and strong.   25

    1. Identify the visual, auditory, and tactile images in the first twelve lines of the poem. The "Type of the modern" (l. 13) is an "emblem of motion and power." How effectively do lines 1–12 establish this emblem? Explain in a long paragraph.

    2. Compare "To a Locomotive in Winter" with Shakespeare's "Sonnet 73" (p. 106). Which contains a greater number of figurative expressions? Does the difference suggest a major characteristic of Whitman's poetic method? Explain.

    3. The poet invokes the emblematic locomotive to "come serve the Muse and merge in verse" (l. 14). What service does the poet request? How do the images in lines 18–25 clarify and explain the invocation?

    4. What words in Whitman's poem are drawn from the vocabulary of music or music criticism? What is their significance?

SYMBOLISM AND ALLEGORY

Symbolism

Perhaps the most often used—and abused—type of modern literary criticism is symbol hunting. The journey of Coleridge's mariner, Melville's whale or Blake's tiger, Beckett's single-dimensioned characters: acts and objects like these in literary works provide fertile ground for those readers who take pleasure in deciphering symbols and searching for obscure meanings. Yet *symbolism* is more easily identified than defined. A *symbol* may best be understood as an implicit metaphor in which a physical object or act represents something, usually immaterial, beyond itself. In other words, the object or act is to be understood on two levels (as with all metaphor), the literal and the figurative (or symbolic). Consider, for example, Whitman's locomotive (p. 25). On the one hand, it is a literal black steam engine pulling a train of cars on a winter day. But on another level it is a physical object that represents something immaterial and beyond its literal definition. It is "Type of the modern—emblem of motion and power—pulse of the continent." It symbolizes the temper of the new American who, even against great obstacles, sets out to conquer a new continent.

Much argument (usually futile and at times useless) has concerned itself with where a metaphor ends and a symbol begins. Melville (in describing the relationship of Captain Ahab to the White Whale) employs metaphor when he says that all visible objects are pasteboard masks which limit and obscure man's perception; yet Moby-Dick, the visible object who embodies obscurity in the protagonist's eyes, is a symbol. Where then does the difference lie? Once the distinction between metaphorical vehicle and tenor (see p. 17) is diminished, leaving the reader to perceive a unified physical representation of an abstraction, then metaphor has become symbol. Consider, for example, this brief poem of Longfellow's:

HENRY WADSWORTH LONGFELLOW (1807–82)

The Tide Rises, the Tide Falls

The tide rises, the tide falls,
The twilight darkens, the curlew calls;

Along the sea-sands damp and brown
The traveller hastens toward the town,
  And the tide rises, the tide falls.   5

Darkness settles on roofs and walls,
But the sea, the sea in the darkness calls;
The little waves, with their soft, white hands,
Efface the footprints in the sands,
  And the tide rises, the tide falls.   10

The morning breaks; the steeds in their stalls
Stamp and neigh, as the hostler calls;
The day returns, but nevermore
Returns the traveller to the shore,
  And the tide rises, the tide falls.   15

    In the first stanza, the tide is just a tide, a part of an overall portrait of a seashore scene. But as the poem continues, it becomes clear that time is a major concern (the first stanza is set at twilight, the second at night, and the third at morning). Moreover, the tide acts in relation to man, the "traveller" (l. 4) who hastens about his business, like the "hostler" (l. 12). The tide is eternal (note that it appears in line 1 and that its presence in the refrain closes each stanza); it *is* the tide, but it is also a symbol of the expanse of time that actively obliterates all human achievement, that will inevitably "Efface the footprints in the sands" (l. 9) of time. Furthermore, the symbol is a unified physical representation of an abstract idea; that is, we are not drawn to recognize the two separate parts of a figurative relationship and to interpret the tenor.

    Though it is impossible to specify the particular extent to which this is so, all symbols are *complex* representations. In other words, a symbol differs from a sign by some degree of complexity. When a baseball umpire raises his right arm after a pitch, the sign clearly and irrevocably establishes the pitch as a strike. A red light is an unquestionable sign to stop and a green light to go. Yet these signs are not true symbols; they are not complex, nor do they require any great concentration by the observer. To understand the distinction, contrast their simplicity with the concentration required to decipher specifically what Blake's tiger represents:

WILLIAM BLAKE (1757–1827)

The Tyger

Tyger! Tyger! burning bright
In the forests of the night,
What immortal hand or eye
Could frame thy fearful symmetry?

In what distant deeps or skies   5
Burnt the fire of thine eyes?
On what wings dare he aspire?
What the hand dare seize the fire?

And what shoulder, & what art,
Could twist the sinews of thy heart?   10
And when thy heart began to beat,
What dread hand? & what dread feet?

What the hammer? what the chain?
In what furnace was thy brain?
What the anvil? what dread grasp   15
Dare its deadly terrors clasp?

When the stars threw down their spears,
And water'd heaven with their tears,
Did he smile his work to see?
Did he who made the Lamb make thee?   20

Tyger! Tyger! burning bright
In the forests of the night,
What immortal hand or eye,
Dare frame thy fearful symmetry?

Symbols are of two kinds, *traditional* or *nonce*. A traditional symbol (e.g., the cross, a serpent, a lamb) generates response both because of its particular use in the poem and because it has traditionally been employed to elicit particular responses. A nonce symbol has no traditional associations; it must generate response by its single use in the context of a given poem. For example, compare and contrast Blake's building the nonce symbol of the tiger with the traditional associations he draws on in the following poem:

The Lamb

Little Lamb, who made thee?
Dost thou know who made thee?
Gave thee life, and bid thee feed,
By the stream and o'er the mead:
Gave thee clothing of delight,   5
Softest clothing, wooly, bright;
Gave thee such a tender voice,
Making all the vales rejoice?
    Little Lamb, who made thee?
    Dost thou know who made thee?   10

Little Lamb, I'll tell thee,
Little Lamb, I'll tell thee:
He is callèd by thy name,
For he calls himself a Lamb.
He is meek, and he is mild;   15
He became a little child.
I a child, and thou a lamb,
We are callèd by his name.
    Little Lamb, God bless thee!
    Little Lamb, God bless thee!   20

Allegory

An *allegory* is an extended narrative which carries a second meaning along with its literal story. That is, an allegorical narrative contains characters, setting, and situations that are interesting both as narrative elements and as symbolic representations that come together to present an abstract statement in concrete terms. Consider, for example, Bunyan's *Pilgrim's Progress*. A character named Christian (who stands for the process of Christian salvation) journeys through such symbolic places as the Slough of Despond and Vanity Fair to his ultimate destination, the Celestial City—meeting on the way such figures as Mr. Worldly Wiseman and Giant Despair. Or consider the English morality play *Everyman*. In almost a thousand lines of verse, the play recounts how Everyman (after being called by a character named Death) is deserted by his supposed friends Beauty, Strength, Discretion, and Worldly Goods and is only accompanied on his journey to Death by Good Deeds. Allegory, which occurs most frequently in longer forms, may take the form of a prose narrative, a play, or a verse narrative. Perhaps the best English example of the latter is Edmund Spenser's *Faerie Queene* (p. 248).

Since action generally reveals intention, the symbols in an allegory are usually less subtle or less elaborate than in a purely symbolic poem. Thus, for example, it is seldom difficult to analyze the symbolic actions in a parable, fable, or beast epic (each of which is usually allegorical). This apparent lack of profundity has often led critics to denigrate all allegory, as in, for example, T. S. Eliot's charge that Hawthorne "was forever trailing off into the fanciful, even the allegorical, which is a lazy substitute for profundity." But allegory often achieves effects which suggest that the form need not be considered inferior. Note, for example, the systematic comparison—which leads to further comparison—that appears in the first quatrain of George Herbert's poem:

GEORGE HERBERT (1593–1633)

The Quip

The merrie world did on a day
With his train-bands and mates agree
To meet together, where I lay,
And all in sport to geere at me.

First Beautie crept into a rose,   5
Which when I pluckt not, Sir, said she,
Tell me, I pray, Whose hands are those?
But thou shalt answer, Lord, for me.

Then Money came, and chinking still,
What tune is this, poore man? said he: 10
I heard in Musick you had skill.
But thou shalt answer, Lord, for me.

Then came brave Glorie puffing by
In silks that whistled, who but he?
He scarce allow'd me half an eie.   15
But thou shalt answer, Lord, for me.

Then came quick Wit and Conversation
And he would needs a comfort be,
And, to be short, make an Oration.
But thou shalt answer, Lord, for me. 20

Yet when the houre of thy designe
To answer these fine things shall come;
Speak not at large; say, I am thine:
And then they have their answer home.

Each of the following poems is obviously symbolic. For each write
a full paragraph in which you cite and interpret the symbols. If you
feel that one of the poems has allegorical characteristics, write a
paragraph in which you distinguish, trace, and interpret the allegory.

ROBERT FROST (1874–1963)

The Road Not Taken

Two roads diverged in a yellow wood,
And sorry I could not travel both
And be one traveler, long I stood
And looked down one as far as I could
To where it bent in the undergrowth; 5

Then took the other, as just as fair,
And having perhaps the better claim,
Because it was grassy and wanted wear;
Though as for that the passing there
Had worn them really about the same, 10

And both that morning equally lay
In leaves no step had trodden black.
Oh, I kept the first for another day!
Yet knowing how way leads on to way,
I doubted if I should ever come back. 15

I shall be telling this with a sigh
Somewhere ages and ages hence:
Two roads diverged in a wood, and I—
I took the one less traveled by,
And that has made all the difference.   20

WALT WHITMAN (1819–92)

A Noiseless Patient Spider

A noiseless patient spider,
I marked where on a little promontory it stood isolated,
Marked how to explore the vacant vast surrounding,
It launched forth filament, filament, filament, out of itself,
Ever unreeling them, ever tirelessly speeding them.   5

And you O my soul where you stand,
Surrounded, detached, in measureless oceans of space,
Ceaselessly musing, venturing, throwing, seeking the spheres to connect
    them,
Till the bridge you will need be formed, till the ductile anchor hold,
Till the gossamer thread you fling catch somewhere, O my soul.   10

WILLIAM BUTLER YEATS (1865–1939)

The Hawk

"Call down the hawk from the air:
Let him be hooded or caged
Till the yellow eye has grown mild,
For larder and spit are bare,
The old cook enraged,   5
The scullion gone wild."

"I will not be clapped in a hood,
Nor a cage, nor alight upon wrist,
Now I have learnt to be proud
Hovering over the wood   10
In the broken mist
Or tumbling cloud."

"What tumbling cloud did you cleave,
Yellow-eyed hawk of the mind,
Last evening? that I, who had sat   15
Dumbfounded before a knave,
Should give to my friend
A pretence of wit."

PERSONA AND PROGRESSION

Persona

A poem is a composition. Like prose composition, it implies a speaker and an audience. However, although audiences are well disciplined in deriving the personality of a speaker from the spoken word, a reader who considers all composition to be autobiographically informative accepts an obvious fallacy. By denying that the composer can create a speaking (or narrating) personality outside himself, he in fact forgets the creative qualities of the imagination. Recent trends in criticism of fiction have so concerned themselves with narrative point of view that few students make the mistake of equating Mark Twain with his narrator Huck Finn or Henry James with Lambert Strether (in *The Ambassadors*); however, the same emphasis has not been evident in criticism of poetry. It is not unusual for a student to concern himself that Emily Dickinson, lying on her deathbed, was obsessed by a fly's buzzing, simply because Dickinson wrote a poem titled "I heard a Fly buzz—when I died—."

The term *persona* in poetry criticism corresponds to *narrator* in fiction criticism. It denotes a voice, other than that of the poet, which is heard in the poem. In *The Rhetoric of Fiction* (1961), a book of tremendous impact, Wayne Booth asserts that even the most subjective fiction has a conceived narrator, an alter ego used so that the novelist may gain perspective or distance. Likewise, even the most subjective poetry (e.g., romantic lyrics) employs a persona to some extent. For example, the *I* in Wordsworth's "I Wandered Lonely as a Cloud" is not really William Wordsworth, but a projection of Wordsworth into another person, even though the incident used in the poem is autobiographical and occurred in 1802 while Wordsworth walked with his sister Dorothy to Dove Cottage.

The persona in a poem may be either dramatized or undramatized;

that is, it may be an actual character—either fully or partially described—who plays a part in the action recounted, or it may be a mere voice. Note, for example, the partially dramatized persona in Tennyson's poem, the fully dramatized personae in Hardy's dialogue, and the undramatized voice in Blake's poem:

ALFRED, LORD TENNYSON (1809–92)

Flower in the Crannied Wall

Flower in the crannied wall,
I pluck you out of the crannies,
I hold you here, root and all, in my hand,
Little flower—but *if* I could understand
What you are, root and all, and all in all,   5
I should know what God and man is.

THOMAS HARDY (1840–1928)

By Her Aunt's Grave

"Sixpence a week," says the girl to her lover,
"Aunt used to bring me, for she could confide
In me alone, she vowed. 'Twas to cover
The cost of her headstone when she died.
And that was a year ago last June;   5
I've not yet fixed it. But I must soon."

"And where is the money now, my dear?"
"O, snug in my purse . . . Aunt was so slow
In saving it—eighty weeks, or near.". . .
"Let's spend it," he hints. "For she won't know   10
There's a dance to-night at the Load of Hay."
She passively nods. And they go that way.

WILLIAM BLAKE (1757–1827)

The Sick Rose

O Rose, thou art sick!
The invisible worm
That flies in the night,
In the howling storm,

Has found out thy bed   5
Of crimson joy,
And his dark secret love
Does thy life destroy.

Progression

In modern usage the term *rhetoric* has become an expression of
disparaging evaluation. On one hand, it has been used to suggest ex-
pression containing more manner than matter, while, on the other, it
has become a synonym for oratory. Nevertheless, from Plato and
Aristotle on, critics have recognized that rhetoric concerns matters
common to all forms of expression, whether poetry or prose. The
two most obvious are organization (which is handled at length in this
text in chapters on various poetic forms) and movement (or progres-
sion from one part of an organizational pattern to another). Assum-
ing that the sense of a poem is not generally presented in a random
fashion, you will find that this movement or progression in a poem
is governed by such factors as grammar, syntax, rhythm or time-
action, and, as we shall be seeing, the traditions of poetic forms. You
will also find that this movement has certain characteristic patterns
of progression.

The rhetoric of poetry, like the rhetoric of prose, may be consid-
ered in five modes of progression: (1) *static forms*, such as descrip-
tion and definition; (2) *temporal forms*, such as narration and proc-
ess; (3) *mimetic forms*, such as monologue, dialogue, and drama;
(4) *associational forms*, such as reverie; and (5) *argumentative
forms*, such as didactic poetry and satire. Although successful poems
of pure description or definition are relatively infrequent—at least
when compared to the frequency of success in other modes—descrip-

tive progression is often used subordinately in poems organized primarily according to other modes.

The following poems illustrate this essential element of progression, so often missed in poetic analysis.

1. *Static forms.* In "The Bull," William Carlos Williams evidences a preoccupation with arrangement of descriptive details. Note, however, that the bull becomes a symbol, an "Olympian Commentary on the bright passage of days"; thus pictorial details are not presented simply for description's sake:

WILLIAM CARLOS WILLIAMS (1883–1963)

The Bull

It is in captivity—
ringed, haltered, chained
to a drag
the bull is godlike

Unlike the cows   5
he lives alone, nozzles
the sweet grass gingerly
to pass the time away

He kneels, lies down
and stretching out   10
a foreleg licks himself
about the hoof

then stays
with half-closed eyes,
Olympian commentary on   15
the bright passage of days.

—The round sun
smooths his lacquer
through
the glossy pinetrees   20

his substance hard
as ivory or glass—

through which the wind
yet plays—
                    milkless   25

he nods
the hair between his horns
and eyes matted
with hyacinthine curls.

2. *Temporal forms.* In Hardy's "The Convergence of the Twain,"
a poem based on the maiden-voyage sinking of the supposedly inde-
structible *Titanic,* narration provides firm organization for the poem.
The first five stanzas furnish an ironically imaginative rendering of
the sunken ship, which lies far away "from human vanity" (1. 2).
The rest of the poem presents the irony of the consummation, that
is, the humanly unpredictable collision of the Immanent Will's crea-
tion (the Iceberg) and man's (the ship):

THOMAS HARDY (1840–1928)

The Convergence of the Twain
(*Lines on the loss of the "Titanic"*)

I

In a solitude of the sea
Deep from human vanity,
And the Pride of Life that planned her, stilly couches she.

II

Steel chambers, late the pyres
Of her salamandrine fires,   5
Cold currents thrid, and turn to rhythmic tidal lyres.

III

Over the mirrors meant
To glass the opulent
The sea-worm crawls—grotesque, slimed, dumb, indifferent.

IV

Jewels in joy designed   10
To ravish the sensuous mind
Lie lightless, all their sparkles bleared and black and blind.

V

Dim moon-eyed fishes near
Gaze at the gilded gear
And query: "What does this vaingloriousness down here?". . . 15

VI

Well: while was fashioning
This creature of cleaving wing,
The Immanent Will that stirs and urges everything

VII

Prepared a sinister mate
For her—so gaily great—   20
A Shape of Ice, for the time far and dissociate.

VIII

And as the smart ship grew
In stature, grace, and hue,
In shadowy silent distance grew the Iceberg too.

IX

Alien they seemed to be: 25
No mortal eye could see
The intimate welding of their later history,

X

Or sign that they were bent
By paths coincident
On being anon twin halves of one august event,   30

XI

Till the Spinner of the Years
Said "Now!" And each one hears,
And consummation comes, and jars two hemispheres.

3. *Mimetic forms* are in most cases poetic imitations of man's actions and speech. Monologues, dialogues, and poetic dramas all illustrate such imitation. In the following poem, Marvell attains organizational unity through clear representation of persona (the persuading lover) and audience (his "coy mistress") in a syllogistic argument of three parts:

ANDREW MARVELL (1621–78)

To His Coy Mistress

Had we but world enough, and time,
This coyness, lady, were no crime.
We would sit down, and think which way
To walk, and pass our long love's day.
Thou by the Indian Ganges' side   5
Should'st rubies find: I by the tide
Of Humber would complain. I would
Love you ten years before the Flood.
And you should, if you please, refuse
Till the conversion of the Jews.   10
My vegetable love should grow
Vaster than empires, and more slow.
An hundred years should go to praise
Thine eyes, and on thy forehead gaze:
Two hundred to adore each breast: 15
But thirty thousand to the rest;
An age at least to every part,
And the last age should show your heart.
For, lady, you deserve this state,
Nor would I love at lower rate.   20
   But at my back I always hear
Time's wingéd chariot hurrying near:
And yonder all before us lie
Deserts of vast eternity.
Thy beauty shall no more be found;   25
Nor, in thy marble vault, shall sound
My echoing song; then worms shall try
That long-preserved virginity,
And your quaint honor turn to dust,
And into ashes all my lust.   30

The grave's a fine and private place,
But none, I think, do there embrace.
   Now, therefore, while the youthful hue
Sits on thy skin like morning dew,
And while thy willing soul transpires   35
At every pore with instant fires,
Now let us sport us while we may;
And now, like amorous birds of prey,
Rather at once our Time devour,
Than languish in his slow-chapt power.   40
Let us roll all our strength and all
Our sweetness up into one ball,
And tear our pleasures with rough strife
Thorough the iron gates of life.
Thus, though we cannot make our sun   45
Stand still, yet we will make him run.

4. *Associational forms.* After condemning Whitman's sensuality, an early critic of *Leaves of Grass* charged the poet with being "as unacquainted with art as a hog is with mathematics." Certainly one of the reasons for this attack—as well as for many others—was that the coherence of Whitman's poetry escaped his critics. Often unity in Whitman's poetry—as with many later modern poets (see p. 351)— rests on free association, that is, on the free linking of ideas and sensations. This method obviously stands in sharp contrast to the traditional temporal, mimetic, or argumentative forms. In many cases the individual lines of Whitman's poetry constitute vignettes, brief pictures or images which are complete in themselves. The vignettes are —by association—combined into "catalogues," which create a cumulative impression. The following passage illustrates this technique:

WALT WHITMAN (1819–92)

from "Song of Myself"

Now I will do nothing but listen,
To accrue what I hear into this song, to let sounds contribute toward
    it.
I hear bravuras of birds, bustle of growing wheat, gossip of flames,
    clack of sticks cooking my meals,

I hear the sound I love, the sound of the human voice,
I hear all sounds running together, combined, fused or following, 5
Sounds of the city and sounds out of the city, sounds of the day and
    night,
Talkative young ones to those that like them, the loud laugh of
    work-people at their meals,
The angry base of disjointed friendship, the faint tones of the sick,
The judge with hands tight to the desk, his pallid lips pronouncing a
    death-sentence,
The heave'e'yo of stevedores unlading ships by the wharves, the re- 10
    frain of the anchor-lifters,
The ring of alarm-bells, the cry of fire, the whirr of swift-streaking
    engines and hose-carts with premonitory tinkles and color'd
    lights,
The steam-whistle, the solid roll of the train of approaching cars,
The slow march play'd at the head of the association marching two
    and two,
(They go to guard some corpse, the flag-tops are draped with black
    muslin.)

5. *Argumentative forms.* Obviously prose is the vehicle most fre-
quently employed for advancing a thesis and proceeding—either in-
directly or deductively—to support it. Though argumentative pro-
gression is most often employed in satire or forms of didactic poetry,
it seldom resembles matter-of-fact prose presentation. Many poems
begin either with a statement and proceed to support it or with a
series of incidents (or images) from which a conclusion is drawn.
However, the argumentative progression is often interrupted by
analogies (in the form of figurative comparisons) or by allusions. In
the following poem, the first verse establishes a thesis that is sup-
ported by the rest of the poem:

ARNA BONTEMPS (1902–)

A Black Man Talks of Reaping

I have sown beside all waters in my day.
I planted deep, within my heart the fear
That wind or fowl would take the grain away.
I planted safe against this stark, lean year.

I scattered seed enough to plant the land   5
In rows from Canada to Mexico
But for my reaping only what the hand
Can hold at once is all that I can show.

Yet what I sowed and what the orchard yields
My brother's sons are gathering stalk and root,   10
Small wonder then my children glean in fields
They have not sown, and feed on bitter fruit.

GEORGE GORDON, LORD BYRON (1788–1861)

When We Two Parted

When we two parted
In silence and tears,
Half broken-hearted
To sever for years,
Pale grew thy cheek and cold,   5
Colder thy kiss;
Truly that hour foretold
Sorrow to this.

The dew of the morning
Sunk chill on my brow—   10
It felt like the warning
Of what I feel now.
Thy vows are all broken,
And light is thy fame:
I hear thy name spoken,   15
And share in its shame.

They name thee before me,
A knell to mine ear;
A shudder comes o'er me—
Why wert thou so dear?   20
They know not I knew thee,
Who knew thee too well:
Long, long shall I rue thee,
Too deeply to tell.

In secret we met— 25
  In silence I grieve,
That thy heart could forget,
  Thy spirit deceive.
If I should meet thee
  After long years, 30
How should I greet thee?
  With silence and tears.

1. The title announces that the persona in the poem has separated from his lover. From reading the poem, how would you characterize the persona? What are his values? How—apparently—do his values differ from those of his former lover? What precisely is his response to the behavior of his lover since their parting? Is the subject (or theme) of mutability only evident in the last stanza? Explain.

2. Describe the mode of progression employed in the poem. Does that mode satisfactorily provide unity? Explain in a long paragraph.

LEROI JONES (1934–)

An Agony. As Now.

I am inside someone
who hates me. I look
out from his eyes. Smell
what fouled tunes come in
to his breath. Love his 5
wretched women.

Slits in the metal, for sun. Where
my eyes sit turning, at the cool air
the glance of light, or hard flesh
rubbed against me, a woman, a man, 10
without shadow, or voice, or meaning.

This is the enclosure (flesh,
where innocence is a weapon. An
abstraction. Touch. (Not mine.
Or yours, if you are the soul I had 15
and abandoned when I was blind and had

my enemies carry me as a dead man
(if he is beautiful, or pitied.

It can be pain. (As now, as all his
flesh hurts me.) It can be that. Or   20
pain. As when she ran from me into
that forest.
            Or pain, the mind
silver spiraled whirled against the
sun, higher than even old men thought   25
God would be. Or pain. And the other. The
yes. (Inside his books, his fingers. They
are withered yellow flowers and were never
beautiful.) The yes. You will, lost soul, say
'beauty.' Beauty, practiced, as the tree. The   30
slow river. A white sun in its wet sentences.

Or, the cold men in their gale. Ecstasy. Flesh
or soul. The yes. (Their robes blown. Their bowls
empty. They chant at my heels, not at yours.) Flesh
or soul, as corrupt. Where the answer moves too quickly.   35
Where the God is a self, after all.)

Cold air blown through narrow blind eyes. Flesh,
white hot metal. Glows as the day with its sun.
It is a human love. I live inside. A bony skeleton
you recognize as words or simple feeling.   40

But it has no feeling. As the metal, is hot, it is not,
given to love.

It burns the thing
inside it. And that thing
screams.   45

1. In this poem Jones's major theme concerns the problem of
identity. Paraphrase the first verse paragraph. (Whereas the term
stanza denotes a group of visually separate and rhymed verses that
recur in a consistent order throughout a poem, *verse paragraph* de-
notes a visually separate unit that does not consistently recur. Though
technically distinguishable, the terms are frequently used interchange-

ably.) What attitude—or reaction—does the persona define in himself? Who is the "someone who hates me" (ll. 1–2)?

2. Even though Jones has become a symbol of the black militant movement and has charged that black writers should be "missionaries of Blackness," his own poems are neither characteristically didactic nor preoccupied redundantly with a sameness of theme. Is the race problem an overt theme in this poem? If not overt, how does it furnish a milieu for understanding the conflict which the poem embodies? Explain in a short essay.

3. Describe the mode of progression employed. How are associations connected in the poem (i.e., by logic, by image, by chronology, by spatial arrangement, etc.)? Does this method of connection furnish a unified structure for the poem? Explain.

4. What is the "agony" cited in the title? How is a sense of enclosure and pain realized in the poem? Cite specific images that contribute to that realization. Would you describe the poem as rich in imagery (compare the number of images with those in Williams' "The Bull")? Explain. How graphic are the images?

5. Describe the diction in the poem. In a statement of literary—and cultural—self-reliance, Jones once charged that "we can get nothing from England." How is a freedom from poetic conventions exemplified by Jones's diction? What weaknesses, if any, would you cite in that diction?

6. What kinds of figurative language occur in the poem? Cite particular figures and explain their function. Which figures are strikingly original? Which, if any, are vague, cliché, or (and this must obviously be a subjective judgment) needlessly ambiguous?

METER AND SCANSION

The term *prosody* embodies any study of versification, including meter, rhyme, rhythm, and verse forms; and that study directs us to the transformed language of the poem. If poetry is language in motion, as we said at the very beginning of this chapter, creating its own time-action or rhythm, the basis of that *rhythm* has traditionally been related to the concept of meter. Meter, therefore, is one of the most important elements necessary to transform our daily language into the poetic language that, at its best, keeps all the levels of "play" in balance. Controlling the rhythm of that balance is the main purpose of meter, and the result of meter (at its best) is a richer life in the poem, a transformed language.

The whole question of meter in our time is complex. Before you begin any study of traditional meters, therefore, you should be aware of the various types of rhythm to be found in modern poetry (for a full discussion of these, see p. 354 ff.); these modern experiments in meter have made critics turn back and review old classifications. The result has been the kind of creative interplay that always occurs when the modern and the traditional are viewed in the perspective of each other. Yet certain basic facts remain, and the discussion of meter here will lead you not only to a greater appreciation of most of English and American poetry, in which traditional meters have been used, but also to a deeper understanding of rhythm in any poem.

The English language, like all Germanic languages, is heavily accentual; that is, the syllables in English words and sentences receive varying degrees of stress or emphasis. Even in English prose, stressed syllables are clearly distinguished from those unstressed. In the following sentence, for example, only syllables receiving stress are marked:

$$\text{I róde to tówn in a cár.}$$

The alternation of stressed and unstressed syllables is called *rhythm*. Certain patterns of alternation have—by their recurrent use in poetic expression—become recognizable and have been labeled. When rhythm is measurable and can be seen to follow a recognizable pattern of alternation, it is called *meter*. The recognizable pattern itself is called a *metrical foot*.

Studies of prosody have distinguished numerous types of metrical feet; however, the student of English poetry will need to recognize only six. They are:

1. *iamb* (iambic foot). Example: mỹ hoúse, hotél
   An iambic foot contains two syllables, the first unstressed and the second stressed. It is by far the most common metrical foot in all English poetry. The following lines of poetry illustrate its use:

Whose woods these are I think I know. (*Frost*)
Come live with me and be my love. (*Marlowe*)
Had we but world enough and time. (*Marvell*)

2. *trochee* (trochaic foot). Example: walking
   A trochaic foot contains two syllables, the first stressed and the second unstressed.

   Double, double, toil and trouble (*Shakespeare*)
   Trochee trips from long to short. (*Coleridge*)
   For the rare and radiant maiden whom the angels name Lenore.
                                                          (*Poe*)

3. *anapest* (anapestic foot). Example: interrupt
   An anapestic foot contains three syllables, the first two unaccented and the third accented.

   Like a child from the womb, like a ghost from the tomb.
                                                        (*Shelley*)
   The Assyrians come down like a wolf on the fold (*Byron*)
   With a leap and a bound the swift Anapests throng (*Coleridge*)

4. *dactyl* (dactylic foot). Example: lovingly
   A dactylic foot contains three syllables, the first stressed and the succeeding two unstressed.

   Ever to come up with Dactyl trisyllable (*Coleridge*)
   Dripping their snow on the green grass (*Ransom*)
   Once when the snow of the year was beginning to fall (*Frost*)

5. *spondee* (spondaic foot). Example: heartbreak
   A spondaic foot contains two syllables, each of which is stressed. Though Coleridge (in the example below) uses the spondee as dominant meter for a line, the spondaic foot is almost always used simply for variation in a line based on another meter.

   Slow Spondee stalks; strong foot! (*Coleridge*)
   Roll on, thou deep and dark blue Ocean—roll! (*Byron*)

6. *pyrrhic* (pyrrhic foot)

A pyrrhic foot contains two syllables, neither of which is stressed. Like the spondee, the pyrrhic is commonly used for varying a line based on another meter.

Through caverns measureless to man   (*Coleridge*)

To tread the dreary paths without a guide   (*Johnson*)

Description of meter (*scansion*) involves not only defining types of metrical feet which either dominate or vary poetic lines; it also requires determining of line length. To do this, one simply counts the number of feet in the line, using the following designations: *monometer* (1), *dimeter* (2), *trimeter* (3), *tetrameter* (4), *pentameter* (5), *hexameter* (6), *heptameter* (7), *octameter* (8). The hexameter line (or *alexandrine*) is often used to vary a metrical pattern.

In describing meter, a reader can lose sight of his proper function, can begin to implant rather than to describe, thus becoming prescriptive rather than descriptive. Properly, however, scansion is a descriptive rather than a prescriptive process. Few poetic lines—particularly good poetic lines—are entirely regular; and the poet establishes a meter so that his variations from it will draw attention. Likewise, the poet varies meter, substituting feet freely, to avoid monotony and false emphasis. Natural expression consists of units determined by logic and by necessity for breath pauses, and these two requisites often run counter to regular meter. Likewise, grammatical units (e.g., prepositional phrases, nouns and their modifiers, verb clusters)—usually corresponding to logical sentence breaks—demand pauses which may cause alterations in metrical pattern. Note, for example, the following units into which Tennyson's lines from "The Lady of Shalott" fall:

Willows whiten, aspens quiver,

Little breezes dusk and shiver

Through the wave that runs forever

By the island in the river

Flowing down to Camelot.

Prosodists use the term *caesura* to indicate a pause within the poetic line. Because the grammatical nature of English causes most lines to have some pause near the middle (note the unit breaks in each of Tennyson's lines), it is wise to employ the term only when the pause is meaningful. For example, only the first line of the Tennyson excerpt has caesura, and that pause is indicated by internal punctuation.

In certain periods of English literature (most notably, the eighteenth century) there has been a tendency also to have a syntactical break, indicated by some form of punctuation, at the end of most poetic lines. A line with a syntactical break at the end is called *end-stopped*; a line not end-stopped is called *run-on*; and the presence in a poem of run-on lines is called *enjambment*. In periods where enjambment is common (e.g., the Romantic, Victorian, and Modern periods), a freedom and variation in rhythm leads poetry to appear more flowing and, at times, less artificially regular. The following poems demonstrate the contrasting effects of end-stopped and run-on lines:

MATTHEW PRIOR (1664–1721)

A Dutch Proverb

Fire, Water, Woman, are Man's Ruin;
Says wise Professor VANDER BRÜIN.
By Flames a House I hir'd was lost
Last Year: and I must pay the Cost.
This Spring the Rains o'erflowed my Ground: 5
And my best Flanders Mare was drown'd.
A Slave I am to CLARA's Eyes:
The Gipsey knows her Pow'r, and flies.
Fire, Water, Woman, are My Ruin:
And great Thy Wisdom, VANDER BRÜIN.   10

RICHARD WILBUR (1921–   )

The Beautiful Changes

One wading a Fall meadow finds on all sides
The Queen Anne's Lace lying like lilies
On water; it glides
So from the walker, it turns

Dry grass to a lake, as the slightest shade of you   5
Valleys my mind in fabulous blue Lucernes.

The beautiful changes as a forest is changed
By a chameleon's tuning his skin to it;
As a mantis, arranged
On a green leaf, grows   10
Into it, makes the leaf leafier, and proves
Any greenness is deeper than anyone knows.

Your hands hold roses always in a way that says
They are not only yours; the beautiful changes
In such kind ways,   15
Wishing ever to sunder
Things and things' selves for a second finding, to lose
For a moment all that it touches back to wonder.

Learning to Scan

The point has been made that scansion is a descriptive rather than
a prescriptive process. When you scan a poem, you use visual symbols
to represent kinds of sound sequences, recurrence of sound sequences,
and caesura. These commonly employed symbols are the most useful:

⌣ for syllables unstressed in their context
/ for syllables stressed in their context
| for division between poetic feet
|| for caesura

For purpose of illustration, we shall use the first stanza of Gray's
"Elegy Written in a Country Church-Yard":

The Cur|few tolls | the knell | of part|ing day, |
The low|ing herd | wind slow|ly o'er | the lea, |
The plow|man home|ward plods | his wear|y way, |
And leaves | the world | to dark|ness and | to me. |

Scanning the stanza reveals that it is unusually regular iambic pen-
tameter (since each line has five feet and only three of the twenty
feet are substitutions) and that it is free of strong caesura, even
though each line is end-stopped.

Learning how to scan a line of poetry is not difficult. In fact, if you use the following steps, you will find how natural the whole process of scansion is.

1. Read the passage aloud, being careful not to implant on it your own preconceived idea of the poem's rhythm. Then mark the accented and unaccented syllables:

   I met a Lady in the meads

   Full beautiful, a fairy's child:

   Her hair was long, her foot was light,

   And her eyes were wild. (*Keats*)

After marking the passage, read it aloud again to be sure you have not marked an accent where none is deserved. Then note whether the passage is in *rising meter* (iambic and anapestic), in which the voice rises from an unaccented to an accented syllable, or whether it is in *falling meter* (trochaic and dactyllic), in which the voice falls from an accented to an unaccented syllable.

2. By examining your markings, determine the type of metrical foot (see p. 47) that predominates; then place symbols to separate the feet:

   I met | a La|dy in | the meads |

   Full beaut|iful, | a fair|y's child; |

   Her hair | was long, | her foot | was light, |

   And her eyes | were wild. |

Obviously the dominant meter is iambic, though pyrrhics vary the first and second lines and an anapest the fourth. Though the first three lines are tetrameter and the fourth dimeter, only the third line is an entirely regular iambic tetrameter line.

3. A caesura may occur at any point in the poetic line. If it occurs near the beginning, it is called *initial caesura*; if near the middle, *medial caesura*; and, if near the end, *terminal caesura*. Poetry of some periods (especially the eighteenth century) stresses medial caesura as a structural device; however, in other periods caesura occurs as a more subtle and flexible device for varying lines.

By again reading the passage aloud, determine whether there is caesura in one or more lines. If the caesura does not correspond to the end of a metrical foot, enter the double-bar symbol to indicate its presence. If the caesura does correspond to the end of a metrical foot, add a bar to the one you have already placed.

I met | a La|dy in | the meads |
Full beaut|iful, || a fair|y's child; |
Her hair | was long, || her foot | was light, |
And her eyes | were wild. |

Here we have two instances of strong medial caesura, which rhetorically balances the lines.

Reasons for Scansion

Too often scansion is thought to be either a meaningless game or a lame excuse for quibbling over whether a given syllable in a poem is stressed or unstressed. Why, after all, should one who wishes to understand a poem or one who wants a few minutes of pleasure from a poem bother to scan it at all? The reason, of course, is that scansion answers a number of questions which can be answered in no other way. With regards to the value of scansion, the following observations may be helpful:

First, it is often observed that there is more than one legitimate reading—and scansion—of a poem. Reader X may with reason simply be unable to accept an accented syllable in Reader Y's scansion. However, though they do not agree, both Readers X and Y have—by process of scanning the poem—forced themselves to concentrate on the sounds of the poem more than if they had casually read it.

Scansion, since it usually defines rhythm, aids the reader in determining whether a poet's rhythm is appropriate to his sense. In reading poetry, one very early notices that certain metrical patterns are associated not only with particular structural forms (e.g., sonnet, heroic verse, poetic drama), but also with particular subjects and themes. For example, it is now a commonplace that the exact rhyme and trochaic tetrameter meter of Longfellow's "A Psalm of Life" are inappropriate to a poem which has as its theme a philosophical and religious celebration of life.

Scansion leads one to recognize the source of monotony (if no variations appear), a common cause for a particular poem's inability to retain a reader's attention. Metrical incompetence is not only evident in the poet whose devotion to rhyme keeps him from establishing a meter; it is also evident in the poet who establishes exact metrical regularity in the first verse and proceeds to maintain it vigorously. Note, for example, the effect of metrical monotony in the following excerpt from a poem of Timothy Dwight:

> Thou pay'st the tax, the rich man will not pay;
> Thou feed'st the poor, the rich man drives away.
> Thy sons, for freedom, hazard limbs, and life,
> While pride applauds, but shuns the manly strife:

By visually emphasizing variations in established metrical patterns, scansion draws attention to the variations and demands that the reader interpret them. Why, for example, may a poet wish to slow a line by excessive use of caesura? Or, why are particular lines end-stopped in a poem in which most lines are run-on? In other words, a poet may use meter for gaining emphasis and guiding the reader.

QUESTIONS – METER AND SCANSION

Scan each of the following poems in order to answer these questions (the last three in short essays).

1. What is the dominant meter?

2. What variations in the dominant meter occur? What, if any, is the significance of these variations?

3. Is the meter appropriate to the subject or theme? Why, or why not?

4. What is the effect of caesura and of end-stopped and/or run-on lines?

WILLIAM BLAKE (1757–1827)

London

I wander thro' each charter'd street,
Near where the charter'd Thames does flow,
And mark in every face I meet
Marks of weakness, marks of woe.

In every cry of every Man,   5
In every Infant's cry of fear,
In every voice, in every ban,
The mind-forg'd manacles I hear.

How the Chimney-sweeper's cry
Every black'ning Church appalls;   10
And the hapless Soldier's sigh
Runs in blood down Palace walls.

But most thro' midnight streets I hear
How the youthful Harlot's curse
Blasts the new born Infant's tear,   15
And blights with plagues the Marriage hearse.

ROBERT LOWELL (1917–   )

The North Sea Undertaker's Complaint

Now south and south and south the mallard heads,
His green-blue bony hood echoes the green
Flats of the Weser, and the mussel beds
Are sluggish where the webbed feet spanked the lean
Eel grass to tinder in the take-off. South   5
Is what I think of. It seems yesterday
I slid my hearse across the river mouth
And pitched the first iced mouse into the hay.
Thirty below it is. I hear our dumb
Club-footed orphan ring the Angelus   10
And clank the bell-chain for St. Gertrude's choir
To wail with the dead bell the martyrdom

Of one more blue-lipped priest; the phosphorous
Melted the hammer of his heart to fire.

SOUND DEVICES

When Pope charged that in poetry "the sound must seem an echo
to the sense," he identified both the inherent strength and weakness
of poetic sound devices. However, technical competence in the use of
such devices as rhyme, alliteration, and assonance is not an end in it-
self. When it becomes a virtuoso performance contributing nothing
to the poem's progression, mood, or theme, it will likely lead to the
kind of situation in which the architecture is perfect but the building
falls. The following are sound devices which poets commonly employ:

Rhyme

The most familiar kind of rhyme is *end rhyme*—that is, the repeti-
tion of vowel and consonant sounds at the ends of poetic lines.
Though the following list makes no attempt to be comprehensive, it
includes several of the most common kinds of rhyming sounds:

1. *whole words:* day, hay
2. *last syllables of words:* recall, appall
3. *identical sounding words of different meaning:* week, weak
   (called *identical rhyme, rich rhyme,* or *rime riche*)
4. *groups of words:* walked to school, stalked to school
5. *last syllable of words followed by whole words:* recall it, befall it
6. *three consecutive matching syllables:* intel*lectual*, henp*ecked
   you all*

In addition to exact rhyme (which is sometimes called complete,
full, or true rhyme), critics have also coined such terms as *near rhyme,
half rhyme, slant rhyme,* or *approximate rhyme* to describe rhymed
sounds that are phonetically similar but not corresponding. *Slant
rhyme* patterns words in which vowel sounds merely resemble each
other but final consonant sounds are identical (e.g., sun-loon, skip-
nap), while *half rhyme* patterns vowels even more disparate (e.g.,
night-bought, foot-boat). Rhyming sounds in which the end of a

word is ignored are called *apocapated rhyme* (e.g., row-showgirl).

An important distinction between types of end rhyme is that between masculine and feminine. A *masculine rhyme* is one in which rhyming syllables ending a poetic line are metrically stressed (e.g., intent-repent), and a *feminine rhyme* is one in which they are unstressed. In *quatrains* (four-line stanzas) rhyming *abab* (see pp. 304–306), a master like Herrick can quite effectively make the *a* rhyme masculine and the *b* feminine:

ROBERT HERRICK (1591–1674)

To the Virgins, to Make Much of Time

Gather ye rose-buds while ye may,
   Old Time is still a-flying;
And this same flower that smiles today
   Tomorrow will be dying.

The glorious lamp of heaven, the Sun,   5
   The higher he's a-getting;
The sooner will his race be run,
   And nearer he's to setting.

That age is best which is the first,
   When youth and blood are warmer;   10
But being spent, the worse, and worst
   Times, still succeed the former.

Then be not coy, but use your time;
   And while ye may, go marry;
For having lost but once your prime,   15
   You may for ever tarry.

Besides end rhyme, two significant kinds of rhyme are internal rhyme and leonine rhyme. Rather than occurring at the ends of two or more lines, *internal rhyme* occurs within a single line (from Swinburne, "Villon, our sad bad glad mad brother's name"). Its presence often unifies the line and makes it euphonious. A type of internal rhyme, *leonine rhyme*, is present when the word before a caesura rhymes with the final word in the line (from Joaquin Miller, "Breath of balm, in a field of brown"). Although less frequent than either end rhyme or internal rhyme, poets sometimes employ *initial rhyme*, that is, rhyme that occurs in the first words of poetic lines. In addition to end rhyme, the following lines from Thomas Hood illustrate initial rhyme:

> Mad from life's history,
> Glad to death's mystery.

Alliteration and Assonance

Alliteration and assonance are types of internal rhymes. *Alliteration* is the repetition of consonantal sound in two or more words of a line of poetry. The following lines from poets of different periods illustrate the use of alliteration:

In a somer seson. Whan soft was the sonne   (*Langland*)

Thy lust and liking is from thee gone.   (*Skelton*)

To the low last edge of the long lone land.   (*Swinburne*)

Bones built in me, flesh filled, blood brimmed the curse   (*Hopkins*)

Although usually distinguished in single lines of poetry, alliteration may also provide structural linkage between one line and another or between one stanza and another. In the following poem, the seventeenth century metaphysical poet Vaughan uses alliteration effectively:

HENRY VAUGHAN (1622–95)

The Waterfall

> With what deep murmurs through time's silent stealth
> Doth thy transparent, cool, and watery wealth
>   Here flowing fall,
>   And chide, and call,
> As if his liquid, loose retinue stayed
> Lingering, and were of this steep place afraid,
>   The common pass   5

Where, clear as glass,
All must descend—
Not to an end,   10
But, quickened by this deep and rocky grave,
Rise to a longer course more bright and brave.

Dear stream! dear bank, where often I
Have sat and pleased my pensive eye,
Why, since each drop of thy quick store   15
Runs thither whence it flowed before,
Should poor souls fear a shade or night,
Who came, sure, from a sea of light?
Or since those drops are all sent back
So sure to thee, that none doth lack,   20
Why should frail flesh doubt any more
That what God takes he'll not restore?

O useful element and clear!
My sacred wash and cleanser here,
My first consigner unto those   25
Fountains of life where the Lamb goes!
What sublime truths and wholesome themes
Lodge in thy mystical, deep streams—
Such as dull man can never find,
Unless that Spirit lead his mind   30
Which first upon thy face did move,
And hatched all with His quickening love.
As this loud brook's incessant fall
In streaming rings restagnates all,
Which reach by course the bank and then   35
Are no more seen, just so pass men.
O my invisible estate,
My glorious liberty, still late!
Thou art the channel my soul seeks,
Not this with cataracts and creeks.   40

Assonance is the repetition of identical or similar vowel sounds, most often occurring on stressed syllables within words. For example, note these uses:

Along the heath and near his favorite tree   (*Gray*)

Out of the old and new, out of the square entirely divine   (*Whitman*)

Like alliteration, assonance contributes to metrical effect by providing a sensory basis for unity. One naturally assumes that vowels made in the same part of the vocal mechanism are related to each other. Note, for example, that unity in Browning's poem results not only from dominant masculine end rhymes, but also from lavish use of both alliteration and assonance:

ROBERT BROWNING (1812–89)

Home-Thoughts, from The Sea

Nobly, nobly Cape Saint Vincent to the Northwest died away;
Sunset ran, one glorious blood-red, reeking into Cadiz Bay;
Bluish 'mid the burning water, full in face Trafalgar lay;
In the dimmest North-east distance dawned Gibraltar grand and gray;
"Here and here did England help me: how can I help England?"—say,   5
Whoso turns as I, this evening, turn to God to praise and pray,
While Jove's planet rises yonder, silent over Africa.

Onomatopoeia and Sound by Association

Onomatopoeia is a sound device in which the poet selects (or occasionally coins) words which imitate the sound associated with the object or action denoted. For example, the words *hiss, boom,* and *purr* denote sounds which pronunciation of the words themselves imitates. By employing words which associate sound with sense meaning, the poet may create a unified impression; however, if onomatopoeia appears for its own sake in a virtuoso performance, the sounds of the poem may be intrusive and the poem flat and meaningless. This is true, for example, of the following selection from "The Bells":

EDGAR ALLAN POE (1809–49)

from The Bells
I

Hear the sledges with the bells—
Silver bells!

What a world of merriment their melody foretells!
How they tinkle, tinkle, tinkle,
In the icy air of night!   5
While the stars that oversprinkle
All the heavens, seem to twinkle
With a crystalline delight;
Keeping time, time, time,
In a sort of Runic rhyme,   10
To the tintinnabulation that so musically wells
From the bells, bells, bells, bells,
Bells, bells, bells—
From the jingling and the tinkling of the bells.

Besides the sound created by a word and its resemblance to an object
or action, *onomatopoeia* is also used to denote words which evoke
predictable emotional responses. For example, the word *dreary* or
dash evokes by its sound a sense of depression or vigor. Note Poe's use
of this device in the first stanza of "Ulalume":

from Ulalume

The skies they were ashen and sober:
The leaves they were crispèd and sere—
The leaves they were withering and sere:
It was night, in the lonesome October
Of my most immemorial year: 5
It was hard by the dim lake of Auber,
In the misty mid region of Weir—
It was down by the dank tarn of Auber,
In the ghoul-haunted woodland of Weir.

Repetition, assonance, alliteration, and slowing or speeding of lines by
carefully placed caesura often work in conjunction with onomato-
poetic effects to evoke a strong sensory response. For example, observe
the use of these devices in the following poem:

WILLIAM VAUGHN MOODY (1869–1910)

On a Soldier Fallen in the Philippines

Streets of the roaring town,
Hush for him, hush, be still!

He comes, who was stricken down
Doing the word of our will.
Hush! Let him have his state,
Give him his soldier's crown.
The grists of trade can wait
Their grinding at the mill,
But he cannot wait for his honor, now the trumpet has been blown;
Wreathe pride now for his granite brow, lay love on his breast of
    stone.

Toll! Let the great bells toll
Till the clashing air is dim.
Did we wrong this parted soul?
We will make it up to him.
Toll! Let him never guess
What work we set him to.
Laurel, laurel, yes;
He did what we bade him do.
Praise, and never a whispered hint but the fight he fought was good;
Never a word that the blood on his sword was his country's own
    heart's-blood.

A flag for the soldier's bier
Who dies that his land may live;
O, banners, banners here,
That he doubt not nor misgive!
That he heed not from the tomb
The evil days draw near
When the nation, robed in gloom,
With its faithless past shall strive.
Let him never dream that his bullet's scream went wide of its island
    mark,
Home to the heart of his darling land where she stumbled and sinned
    in the dark.

QUESTIONS – SOUND DEVICES

Read the following poems carefully and, in short essays, answer
these questions:

1. What is the rhyme scheme? What kinds of end rhyme are em-
ployed? Is the rhyme scheme effective? Why, or why not?

2. Does the poet employ masculine or feminine rhyme? What ef-
fect does this have on the way the poem is read? Explain.

3. What types of internal rhyme are employed? What is their ef-
fect?

4. How effectively does the poet employ sound association? What
particular words are onomatopoetic? Are caesura and repetition used
effectively? Cite particular examples.

ROBERT FROST (1874–1963)

Desert Places

Snow falling and night falling fast, oh, fast
In a field I looked into going past,
And the ground almost covered smooth in snow,
But a few weeds and stubble showing last.

The woods around it have it—it is theirs.   5
All animals are smothered in their lairs.
I am too absent-spirited to count;
The loneliness includes me unawares.

And lonely as it is that loneliness
Will be more lonely ere it will be less—   10
A blanker whiteness of benighted snow
With no expression, nothing to express.

They cannot scare me with their empty spaces
Between stars—on stars where no human race is.
I have it in me so much nearer home   15
To scare myself with my own desert places.

GERARD MANLEY HOPKINS (1844–89)

The Sea and the Skylark

On ear and ear two noises too old to end
    Trench—right, the tide that ramps against the shore;

With a flood or a fall, low lull-off or all roar,
Frequenting there while moon shall wear and wend.

Left hand, off land, I hear the lark ascend,   5
   His rash-fresh re-winded new-skeinèd score
   In crisps of curl off wild winch whirl, and pour
And pelt music, till none's to spill nor spend.

How these two shame this shallow and frail town!
   How ring right out our sordid turbid time,   10
Being pure! We, life's pride and cared-for crown,

   Have lost that cheer and charm of earth's past prime:
   Our make and making break, are breaking, down
   To man's last dust, drain fast towards man's first slime.

EMILY DICKINSON (1830–86)

[I Reason, Earth is Short]

I reason, Earth is short—
And Anguish—absolute—
And many hurt,
But, what of that?

I reason, we could die—   5
The best Vitality
Cannot excel Decay,
But, what of that?

I reason, that in Heaven—
Somehow, it will be even—   10
Some new Equation, given—
But, what of that?

THEME AND TONE

Theme

The *theme* of a poem is the idea expressed about the subject. It is
the natural synthesis of all the elements we have been discussing in
this chapter. However, like the poetic elements that express it and
develop it, the theme has been transformed. It has become a precise

verbal statement, with a precise form to express it—traditional or otherwise—and it is therefore impossible to isolate discussion of theme from such collateral formal elements as diction, imagery, symbolism, figurative language, tone, and sound devices. The theme *is* the form and its elements; and the form, the theme. We may isolate one from the other for purposes of analysis, but it is the total phenomenon of the poem that counts. When a baseball pitcher pitches or a dancer dances, the entire action is one.

It is a misconception, then, to think that theme equals moral. To employ the term *moral* (or *message*) in this sense implies a lesson-teaching maxim grafted onto the structure of the poem by a didactic poet. Usually such a moral is simple enough to be summarized in a phrase or sentence. Theme, on the other hand, implies a complexity embodied in—not grafted onto—the form and structure of the poem, all the elements discussed in this chapter. In good poems the critic must abstract the theme from the poem rather than depend on the poet to state it explicitly. For example, the theme of Hardy's "The Convergence of the Twain" (p. 38), abstracted, is that there is an inherent vanity in all human aspirations. That theme, however, exists *only* in the ironic tone, the images and figures of the ill-fated *Titanic*, in short, in the elements that make up the form.

Tone

Theme is thus no simple message, but a subtle relating or "play" of elements in a unique verbal form. Obviously, then, one of the best ways to discover theme is through tone. *Tone* helps to establish the level of this play of elements; it denotes *the poet's attitude toward his subject and his audience.* Just as any person may feel joy, sorrow, arrogance, humility, and numerous other emotions, so the poet—whose aim is precise statement—may employ a tone that is serious, sentimental, sarcastic, playful, or any one of many possible attitudes.

One of the worst mistakes, however, for a reader to make at this stage of synthesizing all the elements of poetry is to assume that tone is autobiographical. It may or may not reflect the poet's personal concerns. What is absolutely certain is that this tone, like the theme it is developing, exists *only* in the poem, insofar as it is tone. Tone is therefore dependent on the other elements of the poem, the structure of which it is a part, for its very existence. The form of the poem has transformed the personal concerns of the poet into something living, concrete, but impersonal. Consider, for example, a brief poem of Emerson's:

RALPH WALDO EMERSON (1803–82)

Grace

How much, preventing God, how much I owe
To the defences thou hast round me set;
Example, custom, fear, occasion slow,—
These scornéd bondmen were my parapet.
I dare not peep over this parapet   5
To gauge with glance the roaring gulf below,
The depths of sin to which I had descended,
Had not these me against myself defended.

If one considers Emerson an unqualified exponent of individualism and man's innate Goodness, he will have difficulty rationalizing the theme of this poem. Here the poet, in a prayerful, reverential tone (note the effect of the inversions in ll. 1–2 and 8, and the religious use of "thou" in l. 2) renders thanks to God for the unmerited love and favor (that is, grace) of His divine influence. That moral strength, the poet asserts, has taken the form of "Example, custom, fear, occasion slow" (l. 3). The tone is strengthened by the poet's heavy use of metaphoric language (e.g., "scornéd bondmen," "parapet," "roaring gulf," "depths of sin"), a common feature of all prayer.

QUESTIONS – THEME AND TONE

HERMAN MELVILLE (1819–91)

The Berg
(A Dream)

I saw a ship of martial build
(Her standards set, her brave apparel on)

Directed as by madness mere
Against a stolid iceberg steer,
Nor budge it, though the infatuate ship went down.   5
The impact made huge ice-cubes fall
Sullen, in tons that crashed the deck;
But that one avalanche was all—
No other movement save the foundering wreck.

Along the spurs of ridges pale,   10
Not any slenderest shaft and frail,
A prism over glass-green gorges lone,
Toppled; nor lace of traceries fine,
Nor pendant drops in grot or mine
Were jarred, when the stunned ship went down.   15

Nor sole the gulls in cloud that wheeled
Circling one snow-flanked peak afar,
But nearer fowl the floes that skimmed
And crystal beaches, felt no jar.
No thrill transmitted stirred the lock   20
Of jack-straw needle-ice at base;
Towers undermined by waves—the block
Atilt impending—kept their place.
Seals, dozing sleek on sliddery ledges
Slipt never, when by loftier edges   25
Through very inertia overthrown,
The impetuous ship in bafflement went down.

Hard Berg (methought), so cold, so vast,
With mortal damps self-overcast;
Exhaling still thy dankish breath—   30
Adrift dissolving, bound for death;
Though lumpish thou, a lumbering one—
A lumbering lubbard loitering slow,
Impingers rue thee and go down,
Sounding thy precipice below,   35
Nor stir the slimy slug that sprawls
Along thy dead indifference of walls.

1. Explain the meaning of "infatuate ship" (1. 5). Of "stunned
ship" (1. 15). Of "impetuous ship" (1. 27). Are these personifica-
tions decorative or functional? How do they contribute to establish-
ing theme? Answer in a long paragraph.

2. Is the tone of the poem one of sadness, irony, seriousness, or some more specific designation? Do meter (especially caesura placement in the last stanza), sound devices, and particularly graphic images contribute to theme? Explain.

3. Compare the tone, imagery, and theme of "The Berg" with Hardy's "The Convergence of the Twain" (p. 38).

4. In one or two paragraphs, abstract the theme of "The Berg" and discuss the contributions of all characteristics of poetry to establishing that theme.

EDWIN ARLINGTON ROBINSON (1869–1935)

Luke Havergal

Go to the western gate, Luke Havergal,
There where the vines cling crimson on the wall,
And in the twilight wait for what will come.
The leaves will whisper there of her, and some,
Like flying words, will strike you as they fall;   5
But go, and if you listen she will call.
Go to the western gate, Luke Havergal—
Luke Havergal.

No, there is not a dawn in eastern skies
To rift the fiery night that's in your eyes;   10
But there, where western glooms are gathering,
The dark will end the dark, if anything:
God slays Himself with every leaf that flies,
And hell is more than half of paradise.
No, there is not a dawn in eastern skies—   15
In eastern skies.

Out of a grave I come to tell you this,
Out of a grave I come to quench the kiss
That flames upon your forehead with a glow
That blinds you to the way that you must go.   20
Yes, there is yet one way to where she is,
Bitter, but one that faith may never miss.
Out of a grave I come to tell you this—
To tell you this.

There is the western gate, Luke Havergal,   25
There are the crimson leaves upon the wall.
Go, for the winds are tearing them away,—
Nor think to riddle the dead words they say,
Nor any more to feel them as they fall;
But go, and if you trust her she will call.   30
There is the western gate, Luke Havergal—
Luke Havergal.

1. Who is the speaker in the poem? Do lines 1–3 clarify his relationship to Luke Havergal? Explain.

2. Who is the "she" of lines 6, 21, and 30? What is her relation to Luke Havergal?

3. In which stanza of the poem is paradox used extensively? What is the meaning of the paradoxical statements? Does that meaning clarify the theme of the entire poem? Explain.

4. Describe the tone of the poem. Do the rhythm and rhyme of the poem contribute to or detract from that tone? Explain.

5. Is the poem rich in graphic imagery? In figurative language? Does Robinson depend more heavily on the denotation or connotation of words and expressions? Explain.

6. What is the theme of the poem? Is it stated explicitly?

Chapter 2

The Ballad

THE TRADITIONAL BALLAD

As a descriptive term for a literary type, *ballad* denotes simply a song that tells a story. More than merely a song, however, a ballad is a folk-song—that is, it belongs not to an individual personality (an "author") but to a region or a nation. For that reason, a ballad possesses certain characteristics which make it unique among the forms presented in this book.

A ballad is usually anonymous. Much as with the wheel, shared by all but about whose invention we can only speculate, the original version of any one ballad is lost to us somewhere in the past. All that remains are the one or more variants which have descended, through oral transmission, from some unknown original. Furthermore, none of these multiple versions (if there are multiple versions) has more authenticity than any other version of the same ballad. A brief example should make this peculiarity of the ballad clear.

"Willie and Lady Maisry" is a ballad which survives in two versions. The first (A) was recited to a collector, probably in the west of Scotland, by an old woman who remembered hearing it from her grandmother. The second (B) was printed by a different collector from researches he had conducted farther to the north. Following is the opening stanza of each:

Willie was a widow's son,
 And he wore a milk-white weed, O
And weel could Willie read and write,
 Far better ride on steed, O   (70 A)*

Sweet Willie was a widow's son,
 And milk-white was his weed;
It sets him weel to bridle a horse,
 And better to saddle a steed, my dear,
 And better to saddle a steed.   (70 B)

Obviously there are significant differences between the two stanzas. Yet despite these differences (and despite the possible conviction that one is artistically superior to the other), the fact remains that A and B are exactly parallel in one essential respect: both represent a variation on an unknown original ballad. Or, to put it somewhat differently, we can say that each version of a ballad which survives in print is an artificially final record of what was in actuality only a single performance of a potentially infinite number of variant performances.

The central point to understand about the ballad, then, is that it is usually preliterary. It has flourished best either in those times or in those areas relatively untouched by the sophistication of the printed page (e.g., in rural England and Scotland from roughly the late eleventh to the early seventeenth century, and in culturally isolated areas, such as the mountains of the United States). Those specimens which have been preserved in print (often by mere chance) are like flies in amber: what gave them their actual life—the voice of the performer as he sang them and the tune which was their accompaniment—are necessarily lost to us now that we study them on the printed page as poetry. And yet as abstracted and as artificial as such an approach necessarily must be, the literary study of the ballad is valuable for laying bare some of the essential ways in which literature can work upon its audience.

Consider, for example, the remarkable similarity of technique which ballads share. It is not merely that they tell a story: almost all of them tell it in a peculiarly typical fashion. As a result, in ballad after ballad we find the stress placed almost at once on the crucial situation (as a number of critics have remarked, ballads usually begin in the fifth act). Note these openings:

* Numbers and letters refer to the arrangement of ballads in Francis James Child's monumental collection of 1882–98, *English and Scottish Popular Ballads*.

"Rise up, rise up, now, Lord Douglas," she says,
　　"And put on your armour so bright;
Let it never be said that a daughter of thine
　　Was married to a lord under night."　(7 B)

There came a ghost to Margret's door,
　　With many a grievous groan,
And ay he tirled at the pin,
　　But answer made she none.　(77 A)

The knight stands in the stable-door,
　　And he was for to ryde,
When out then came his fair lady,
　　Desiring him to byde.　(88 A)

In addition to swift focusing upon a single situation, ballads also share a typical device for development: the episode around which the ballad is usually centered is presented almost totally in terms of action and dialogue. That is, the technique of the ballad is highly dramatic, and it may be helpful to think of the typical ballad as a short, intensified play that opens on the very edge of its climax. Indeed, so marked is this concentration upon dramatic presentation that often the technique of the ballad reflects a pronounced fragmentation of time. Here, for example, are the first three stanzas of "Sir Patrick Spens":

The king sits in Dumferling toune,
　　Drinking the blude-reid wine:
"O whar will I get guid sailor,
　　To sail this schip of mine?"

Up and spak an eldern knicht,
　　Sat at the kings richt kne:
"Sir Patrick Spence is the best sailor
　　That sails upon the se."

The king has written a braid letter,
　　And signed it wi his hand,
And sent it to Sir Patrick Spence,
　　Was walking on the sand.　(58 A)

The dramatic emphasis has prescribed an extraordinarily sharp change of scene in the third stanza, from the king's writing the letter to Sir Patrick's "walking on the sand." In many ballads this device can be called "cinematic," that is, the story is told in flashes of vivid scenes with little attention to connecting links between them. At least one critic has likened the technique of the ballad to the practice of montage in the film.

This highly dramatized technique has led to another striking feature of the ballad—its impersonality. The events which occur and the dialogue which is spoken are almost invariably allowed to create their own effect. Rarely, probably never in the best ballads, does a commentator or a nondramatized reflection interpret the significance of the story. In this respect the anonymous balladeer has reached something very close to the complete aesthetic detachment described in James Joyce's *Portrait of the Artist as a Young Man:* "The artist, like the God of the creation, remains within or behind or beyond or above his handiwork, invisible, refined out of existence, indifferent, paring his fingernails."

But there are also other specialized characteristics of the ballad. For one, it unfolds through a stanzaic pattern. And although at least eight major types of stanza have been described by critics, one is so prevalent that it has earned for itself the title of "ballad stanza." This is a quatrain in alternating four- and three-stress lines with a rhyme scheme of *abcb*. The following are representative examples of the ballad stanza:

> There lived a wife at Usher's Well,
>   And a wealthy wife was she;
> She had three stout and stalwart sons,
>   And sent them oer the sea.   (79 A)

> Lady Alice was sitting in her bower-window,
>   Mending her midnight quoif,
> And there she saw as fine a corpse
>   As ever she saw in her life.   (85 A)

Many ballads characteristically make use of a refrain, such as this from "The Twa Sisters":

> There were two sisters, they went playing,
>   With a hie downe downe a downe-a

To see their father's ships come sayling in.
With a hy downe downe a downe-a   (10 A)

Or this, from "Willie's Lyke-Wake":

"Willie, Willie, I'll learn you a wile,"
And the sun shines over the valleys and a'
"How this pretty fair maid ye may beguile."
Amang the blue flowrs and the yellow and a'   (25 A)

Moreover, this device of the refrain—of a line or lines that are repeated within a poem—is rather closely related to still another characteristic of many ballads, the technique that has been called "incremental repetition." What this phrase means can be shown by the first two stanzas of "Lord Randal":

"O where ha you been, Lord Randal, my son?
And where ha you been, my handsome young man?"
"I ha been at the greenwood; mother, mak my bed soon,
For I'm wearied wi huntin, and fain wad lie down."

"An wha met ye there, Lord Randal, my son?   5
An wha met you there, my handsome young man?"
"O I met wi my true-love; mother, mak my bed soon,
For I'm wearied wi huntin, an fain wad lie down."   (12 A)

Note that there is a great deal of repetition from stanza to stanza, but note too the incremental nature of it: it is not merely repetition, but rather repetition employed in such a way that the action advances in a curiously intense and effective manner.

QUESTIONS – THE TRADITIONAL BALLAD

The Three Ravens

There were three rauens sat on a tree,
   Downe a downe, hay down, hay downe
There were three rauens sat on a tree,
   With a downe

There were three rauens sat on a tree,   5
They were as blacke as they might be.
    With a downe derrie, derrie, derrie, downe, downe

The one of them said to his mate,
"Where shall we our breakefast take?"

"Downe in yonder greene field,   10
There lies a knight slain vnder his shield.

"His hounds they lie downe at his feete,
So well they can their master keepe.

"His haukes they flie so eagerly,
There's no fowle dare him come nie."   15

Downe there comes a fallow doe,
As great with yong as she might goe.

She lift vp his bloudy hed,
And kist his wounds that were so red.

She got him vp vpon her backe,   20
And carried him to earthen lake.

She buried him before the prime,
She was dead herselfe ere euen-song time.

God send euery gentleman,
Such haukes, such hounds, and such a leman.   25

leman (25): lover.

1. In many ballads, the refrain is printed only for the first stanza. In an actual performance of this text, how would the second stanza most likely be presented?

2. What does the refrain contribute to this ballad? Would it be more effective without the refrain? Explain.

3. Where in this ballad does there seem to be the record of some folk belief or tradition which is no longer clear to us?

4. Aside from folk belief, what else is there in this ballad which is left unexplained? Does this lack of explicitness detract from or increase the effectiveness of "The Three Ravens"? Explain in a short essay.

5. Describe the progression (see p. 36) employed in this ballad. How does the progression differ from that of "The Bull" (p. 37)?

6. Would you describe the poem as being rich in imagery? Explain. If not, what compensates for a lack of imagery? Write several paragraphs to explain your answer.

The Twa Corbies

As I was walking all alane,
I heard twa corbies making a mane;
The tane unto the t'other say,
"Where sall we gang and dine to-day?"

"In behint yon auld fail dyke,   5
I wot there lies a new slain knight;
And naebody kens that he lies there,
But his hawk, his hound, and lady fair.

"His hound is to the hunting gane,
His hawk to fetch the wild-fowl hame,   10
His lady's ta'en another mate,
So we may mak our dinner sweet.

"Ye'll sit on his white hause-bane,
And I'll pike out his bonny blue een;
Wi ae lock o his gowden hair   15
We'll theek our nest when it grows bare.

"Mony a one for him makes mane,
But nane sall ken where he is gane;
Oer his white banes, when they are bare,
The wind sall blaw for evermair."   20

Title: The Two Ravens. *mane* (2): moan. *tane* (3): one. *gang* (4): go. *auld fail dyke* (5): old turf wall. *hause-bane* (13): neck bone. *een* (14): eyes. *gowden* (15): golden. *theek* (16): thatch. *ken* (18): know.

1. This ballad was published by Sir Walter Scott in 1803 as a "counterpart" rather than a "copy" of "The Three Ravens." In what significant ways does it differ from "The Three Ravens"? Which is the more effective poem? Which is the more effective ballad? Explain.

Edward

"Why dois your brand sae drap wi bluid,
　　　　Edward, Edward,
Why dois your brand sae drap wi bluid,
　　And why sae sad gang yee O?"　　　　　　　　　5
"O I hae killed my hauke sae guid,
　　　　Mither, mither,
O I hae killed my hauke sae guid,
　　And I had nae mair bot hee O."

"Your haukis bluid was nevir sae reid,
　　　　Edward, Edward,　　　　　　　　　　　10
Your haukis bluid was nevir sae reid,
　　My deir son I tell thee O."
"O I hae killed my reid-roan steid,
　　　　Mither, mither,
O I hae killed my reid-roan steid,　　　　　　　15
　　That erst was sae fair and frie O."

"Your steid was auld, and ye hae gat mair,
　　　　Edward, Edward,
Your steid was auld, and ye hae gat mair,
　　Sum other dule ye drie O."　　　　　　　　20
"O I hae killed my fadir deir,
　　　　Mither, mither,
O I hae killed my fadir deir,
　　Alas, and wae is mee O!"

"And whatten penance wul ye drie for that,　　25
　　　　Edward, Edward?
And whatten penance will ye drie for that?
　　My deir son, now tell me O."
"Ile set my feit in yonder boat,
　　　　Mither, mither,　　　　　　　　　　　30
Ile set my feit in yonder boat,
　　And Ile fare ovir the sea O."

"And what wul ye doe wi your towirs and your ha,
　　　　Edward, Edward?
And what wul ye doe wi your towirs and your ha,　35
　　That were sae fair to see O?"

"Ile let thame stand tul they doun fa,
　　　　Mither, mither,
Ile let thame stand tul they doun fa,
　　For here nevir mair maun I bee O." 　　　　　　　40

"And what wul ye leive to your bairns and your wife,
　　　　Edward, Edward?
And what wul ye leive to your bairns and your wife,
　　Whan ye gang ovir the sea O?"
"The warldis room, late them beg thrae life, 　　　　45
　　　　Mither, mither,
The warldis room, late them beg thrae life,
　　For thame nevir mair wul I see O."

"And what wul ye leive to your ain mither deir,
　　　　Edward, Edward? 　　　　　　　　　　　50
And what wul ye leive to your ain mither deir?
　　My deir son, now tell me O."
"The curse of hell frae me sall ye beir,
　　　　Mither, mither,
The curse of hell frae me sall ye beir, 　　　　　　55
　　Sic counseils ye gave to me O."

dois (1): does. *brand* (1): sword. *gang* (4): go. *erst* (16): once. *frie* (16): spirited. *dule* (20): sorrow. *drie* (20): suffer. *ha* (33): hall. *fa* (37): fall. *maun* (41): must. *bairns* (42): children. *warldis* (45): world's. *thrae* (45): through. *sic* (56): such.

1. There are two climaxes in this ballad; where do they occur? How does incremental repetition serve to intensify the overall effect of the ballad? Suppose, for example, the second and the sixth lines of each stanza were to be omitted. What would be lost?

2. Explain as fully as you can Edward's motivation for his crime. Do lines 45–48 suggest that Edward's wife and children were accomplices?

3. Why does Edward lie at first to his mother? What do her responses to his first two answers reveal about her? What is further revealed about the mother by the series of questions she begins to ask from line 35 onward? by her repetitive use of "My deir son"?

4. What is left unexplained in this ballad? Do you think "Edward" needs more detail to be fully effective? Why, or why not?

5. Is there a narrative progression here? If so, trace its steps in a

long paragraph. In longer traditional ballads, we may even divide the
the ballad into acts as in a drama. Are the steps of narrative progres-
sion here (as in "The Three Ravens" and "The Twa Corbies") like
acts of a drama? Or is it easier to think of them as separate scenes of a
movie flowing together?

6. Describe the tone (see p. 65) of the poem. Is it noticeably dif-
ferent from that of "The Twa Corbies"? Why, or why not?

7. In the introduction to this section, the point is made that the
balladeer rarely becomes a commentator on the significance of his
story. Is this true in "Edward"? If so, does the ballad still contain a
theme (see p. 64)? Explain.

Son Davie

"What bluid's that on thy coat lap,
    Son Davie, son Davie?
What bluid's that on thy coat lap?
    And the truth come tell to me."

"It is the bluid of my great hawk,   5
    Mother lady, mother lady:
It is the bluid of my great hawk,
    And the truth I have told to thee."

"Hawk's bluid was neer sae red,
    Son Davie, son Davie: 10
Hawk's bluid was neer sae red,
    And the truth come tell to me."

"It is the bluid of my greyhound,
    Mother lady, mother lady:
It is the bluid of my greyhound,
    And it wadna rin for me."   15

"Hound's bluid was neer sae red,
    Son Davie, son Davie:
Hound's bluid was neer sae red,
    And the truth come tell to me."   20

"It is the bluid o my brither John,
    Mother lady, mother lady:

It is the bluid o my brither John,
  And the truth I have told to thee."

"What about did the plea begin,   25
  Son Davie, son Davie?"
"It began about the cutting of a willow wand
  That would never been a tree."

"What death dost thou desire to die,
  Son Davie, son Davie?   30
What death dost thou desire to die?
  And the truth come tell to me."

"I'll set my foot in a bottomless ship,
  Mother lady, mother lady:
I'll set my foot in a bottomless ship,   35
  And ye'll never see mair o me."

"What wilt thou leave to thy poor wife,
  Son Davie, son Davie?"
"Grief and sorrow all her life,
  And she'll never see mair o me."   40

"What wilt thou leave to thy old son,
  Son Davie, son Davie?"
"I'll leave him the weary world to wander up and down,
  And he'll never get mair o me."

"What wilt thou leave to thy mother dear,   45
  Son Davie, son Davie?"
"A fire o coals to burn her, wi hearty cheer,
  And she'll never get mair o me."   (13 A)

plea (25): quarrel.

Lord Randal

"O where ha you been, Lord Randal, my son?
And where ha you been, my handsome young man?"
"I ha been at the greenwood; mother, mak my bed soon,
For I'm wearied wi hunting, and fain wad lie down."

"An wha met ye there, Lord Randal, my son?   5
An wha met you there, my handsome young man?"
"O I met wi my true-love; mother, mak my bed soon,
For I'm wearied wi huntin, an fain wad lie down."

"And what did she give you, Lord Randal, my son?
And what did she give you, my handsome young man?"   10
"Eels fried in a pan; mother, mak my bed soon,
For I'm wearied wi huntin, and fain wad lie down."

"And wha gat your leavins, Lord Randal, my son?
And what gat your leavins, my handsom young man?"
"My hawks and my hounds; mother, mak my bed soon,   15
For I'm wearied wi hunting, and fain wad lie down."

"And what becam of them, Lord Randal, my son?
And what becam of them, my handsome young man?"
"They stretched their legs out an died; mother, mak my bed soon,
For I'm wearied wi hunting, and fain wad lie down."   20

"O I fear you are poisoned, Lord Randal, my son!
I fear you are poisoned, my handsome young man!"
"O yes, I am poisoned; mother, mak my bed soon,
For I'm sick at the heart, and I fain wad lie down."

"What d'ye leave to your mother, Lord Randal, my son?   25
What d'ye leave to your mother, my handsome young man?"
"Four and twenty milk kye; mother, mak my bed soon,
For I'm sick at the heart, and I fain wad lie down."

"What d'ye leave to your sister, Lord Randal, my son?
What d'ye leave to your sister, my handsome young man?"   30
"My gold and my silver; mother, mak my bed soon,
For I'm sick at the heart, an I fain wad lie down."

"What d'ye leave to your mother, Lord Randal, my son?
What d'ye leave to your brother, my handsome young man?"
"My houses and my lands; mother, mak my bed soon,   35
For I'm sick at the heart, and I fain wad lie down."

"What d'ye leave to your true-love, Lord Randal, my son?
What d'ye leave to your true-love, my handsome young man?"

"I leave her hell and fire; mother, mak my bed soon,
For I'm sick at the heart, and I fain wad lie down." (12 A) 40

kye (27): cows

Child Waters

Childe Watters in his stable stoode,
  And stroaket his milke-white steede;
To him came a ffaire young ladye
  As ere did weare womans weede.

Saies, "Christ you saue, good Chyld Waters!   5
  Sayes, Christ you saue and see!
My girdle of gold, which was too longe,
  Is now to short ffor mee.

"And all is with one chyld of yours,
  I ffeele sturre att my side;   10
My gowne of greene, it is to strayght;
  Before it was to wide."

"If the child be mine, Faire Ellen," he sayd,
  "Be mine, as you tell mee,
Take you Cheshire and Lancashire both,   15
  Take them your owne to bee.

"If the child be mine, Ffaire Ellen," he said,
  Be mine, as you doe sweare,
Take you Cheshire and Lancashire both,
  And make that child your heyre."   20

Shee saies, "I had rather haue one kisse.
  Child Waters, of thy mouth,
Then I wold haue Cheshire and Lancashire both,
  That lyes by north and south.

"And I had rather haue a twinkling,   25
  Child Waters, of your eye,
Then I wold haue Cheshire and Lancashire both,
  To take them mine oune to bee."

"To-morrow, Ellen, I must forth ryde
  Soe ffarr into the north countrye;   30
The ffairest lady that I can ffind,
  Ellen, must goe with mee."
"And euer I pray you, Child Watters,
  Your ffootpage let me bee!"

"If you will my ffootpage be, Ellen,   35
  As you doe tell itt mee,
Then you must cutt your gownne of greene
  An inche aboue your knee.

"Soe must you doe your yellow lockes,
  Another inch aboue your eye;   40
You must tell noe man what is my name;
  My ffootpage then you shall bee."

All this long day Child Waters rode,
  Shee ran bare ffoote by his side;
Yett was he neuer soe curteous a knight   45
  To say, Ellen, will you ryde?

But all this day Child Waters rode,
  Shee ran barffoote thorow the broome;
Yett he was neuer soe curteous a knight
  As to say, Put on your shoone.   50

"Ride softlye," shee said, "Child Waters;
  Why doe you ryde soe ffast?
The child which is no mans but yours
  My bodye itt will burst."

He says, "Sees thou yonder water, Ellen,   55
  That fflowes from banke to brim?"
"I trust to God, Child Waters," shee said,
  "You will neuer see mee swime."

But when shee came to the waters side,
  Shee sayled to the chinne: 60
"Except the lord of heauen be my speed,
  Now must I learne to swimme."

The salt waters bare vp Ellens clothes,
    Our Ladye bare vpp her chinne,
And Child Waters was a woe man, good Lord,   65
    To ssee Faire Ellen swime.

And when shee ouer the water was,
    Shee then came to his knee:
He said, "Come hither, Ffaire Ellen,
    Loe yonder what I see!   70

"Seest thou not yonder hall, Ellen?
    Of redd gold shine the yates;
There's four and twenty ffayre ladyes,
    The ffairest is my wordlye make.

"Seest thou not yonder hall, Ellen?   75
    Of redd gold shineth the tower;
There is four and twenty ffaire ladyes,
    The fairest is my paramoure."

"I doe see the hall now, Child Waters,
    That of redd gold shineth the yates;   80
God giue good then of your selfe,
    And of your wordlye make!

"I doe see the hall now, Child Waters,
    That of redd gold shineth the tower;
God giue good then of your selfe,   85
    And of your paramoure!"

There were four and twenty ladyes,
    Were playing att the ball,
And Ellen, was the ffairest ladye,
    Must bring his steed to the stall.   90

There were four and twenty faire ladyes
    Was playing att the chesse;
And Ellen, shee was the ffairest ladye,
    Must bring his horsse to grasse.

And then bespake Child Waters sister,   95
    And these were the words said shee:

You haue the prettyest ffootpage, brother,
   That euer I saw with mine eye;

"But that his belly it is soe bigg,
   His girdle goes wonderous hye;   100
And euer I pray you, Child Waters,
   Let him goe into the chamber with mee."

"It is more meete for a little ffootpage,
   That has run through mosse and mire,
To take his supper vpon his knee   105
   And sitt downe by the kitchin fyer,
Then to goe into the chamber with any ladye
   That weares soe rich attyre."

But when the had supped euery one,
   To bedd they took the way: 110
He sayd, "Come hither, my little footpage,
   Harken what I doe say.

"And goe thee downe into yonder towne,
   And low into the street;
The ffairest ladye that thou can find,   115
   Hyer her in mine armes to sleepe,
And take her vp in thine armes two,
   For filinge of her ffeete."

Ellen is gone into the towne,
   And low into the streete;   120
The fairest ladye that shee cold find
   Shee hyred in his armes to sleepe,
And tooke her in her armes two,
   For filing of her ffeete.

"I pray you now good Child Waters,   125
   That I may creepe in att your bedds feete;
For there is noe place about this house
   Where I may say a sleepe."

This night and itt droue on affterward
   Till itt was neere the day: 130
He sayd, "Rise vp, my litle ffoote-page,
   And giue my steed corne and hay;

And soe doe thou the good blacke oates,
    That he may carry me the better away."

And vp then rose Ffaire Ellen,   135
    And gaue his steed corne and hay,
And soe shee did and the good blacke oates,
    That he might carry him the better away.

Shee layned her backe to the manger side,
    And greiuouslye did groane;   140
And that beheard his mother deere,
    And heard her make her moane.

Shee said, "Rise vp, thou Child Waters,
    I thinke thou art a cursed man;
For yonder is a ghost in thy stable,   145
    That greiuouslye doth groane,
Or else some woman laboures of child.
    Shee is soe woe begone."

But vp then rose Child Waters,
    And did on his shirt of silke;   150
Then he put on his other clothes
    On his body as white as milke.

And when he came to the stable-dore,
    Full still that hee did stand,
That hee might heare now Faire Ellen,   155
    How shee made her monand.

Shee said, "Lullabye, my owne deere child!
    Lullabye, deere child, deere!
I wold thy father were a king,
    Thy mother layd on a beere!"   160

"Peace now," he said, "good Faire Ellen,
    And be of good cheere, I thee pray,
And the bridall and the churching both,
    They shall bee vpon one day."   (63 A)

Childe (1): young man. *weede* (4): clothing. *shoone* (50): shoes. *woe* (65):
unhappy. *yates* (72): gates. *make* (82): mate. *monand* (156): moaning.

86   *The Ballad*

1. Since a ballad tells a story, there will be found in it a narrative progression from beginning to end. At the same time, as we have seen, the ballad frequently dramatizes its narrative as fully as possible. Divide "Child Waters" into five "acts" and point out the places where there are breaks in narrative continuity for the sake of keeping the dramatic level at a high pitch. Where does this impulse to focus on scenes lead to problems in clarity or to bits of material which remain undeveloped? How important are such occurrences to the overall effect of "Child Waters"?

2. What does "Child Waters" reveal about the folk attitude towards women and marriage? What, for example, are we to think of Child Waters himself? Are we to admire him? despise him? think of him as a good fellow? What are we to think about Ellen?

3. A variant of "Child Waters"—"Burd Ellen" (63 B)—begins with this stanza:

> "I warn ye all, ye gay ladies,
>   That wear scarlet an brown,
> That ye dinna leave your father's house,
>   To follow young men frae town."

What would be the effect of such an opening on "Child Waters"? Would it make the story clearer? Would it increase the ballad's significance? Would it be an improvement or a weakening of the total impression? Explain.

QUESTIONS – THE AMERICAN BALLAD

Frankie and Johnny

Frankie and Johnny were lovers, O, how that couple could love.
Swore to be true to each other, true as the stars above.
He was her man, but he done her wrong.

Frankie she was his woman, everybody knows.
She spent one hundred dollars for a suit of Johnny's clothes.   5
He was her man, but he done her wrong.

Frankie and Johnny went walking, Johnny in his bran' new suit,
"O good Lawd," says Frankie, "but don't my Johnny look cute?"
He was her man, but he done her wrong.

Frankie went down to Memphis; she went on the evening train.   10
She paid one hundred dollars for Johnny a watch and chain.
He was her man, but he done her wrong.

Frankie went down to the corner, to buy a glass of beer;
She says to the fat bartender, "Has my loving man been here?
He was my man, but he done me wrong."   15

"Ain't going to tell you no story, ain't going to tell you no lie,
I seen your man 'bout an hour ago with a girl named Alice Fry.
If he's your man, he's doing you wrong."

Frankie went back to the hotel, she didn't go there for fun,
Under her long red kimono she toted a forty-four gun.   20
He was her man, but he done her wrong.

Frankie went down to the hotel, looked in the window so high,
There was her lovin' Johnny a-lovin' up Alice Fry;
He was her man, but he done her wrong.

Frankie threw back her kimono; took out the old forty-four;   25
Roota-toot-toot, three times she shot, right through that hotel door.
She shot her man, 'cause he done her wrong.

Johnny grabbed off his Stetson. "O good Lawd, Frankie, don't shoot."
But Frankie put her finger on the trigger, and the gun went roota-toot-
  toot.
He was her man, but she shot him down.   30

"Roll me over easy, roll me over slow,
Roll me over easy, boys, 'cause my wounds are hurting me so,
I was her man, but I done her wrong."

With the first shot Johnny staggered; with the second shot he fell;
When the third bullet hit him, there was a new man's face in hell.   35
He was her man, but he done her wrong.

Frankie heard a rumbling away down under the ground.
Maybe it was Johnny where she had shot him down.
He was her man, and she done him wrong.

"Oh, bring on your rubber-tired hearses, bring on your rubber-tired
     hacks,   40
They're takin' my Johnny to the buryin' groun' but they'll never bring
     him back.
He was my man, but he done me wrong."

The judge he said to the jury, "It's plain as plain can be.
This woman shot her man, so it's murder in the second degree.
He was her man, though he done her wrong."   45

Now it wasn't murder in the second degree, it wasn't murder in the third.
Frankie simply dropped her man, like a hunter drops a bird.
He was her man, but he done her wrong.

"Oh, put me in that dungeon. Oh, put me in that cell.
Put me where the northeast wind blows from the southeast corner of
     hell.   50
I shot my man 'cause he done me wrong."

Frankie walked up to the scaffold, as calm as a girl could be,
She turned her eyes to heaven and said, "Good Lord, I'm coming to thee.
He was my man, and I done him wrong."

1. This ballad is American in origin. In what significant ways does
it differ from the traditional ballads of England and Scotland?

2. What structural part does the refrain play in "Frankie and
Johnny"?

3. A noted student of the traditional ballad, G. H. Gerould, has
remarked that although American ballads "are often vigorous in
action" and "tend to present an incident in sharp focus, . . . they
have not the restrained emotional tensity or the unconsciously poetic
language of the traditional ballad in its better state. They are senti-
mental instead of being poignant with feeling." Based on reading
"Frankie and Johnny," do you agree with this judgment? Why, or
why not? Be as specific as you can, referring to significant elements
both in the traditional English (and Scottish) ballads and in the
American one.

4. Describe the meter of this ballad. Does the meter detract from
the theme? Explain. To what degree does the oral nature of the
ballad make this question relevant—or irrelevant?

5. Describe the diction (see p. 5) in "Frankie and Johnny." How
does it contribute to or detract from the theme?

THE LITERARY BALLAD

But enough has been said to indicate that the traditional ballad possesses sufficient characteristics of its own to merit treatment as a type. Indeed, many of these characteristics have been employed by sophisticated poets in the writing of *literary ballads*, a term used to describe poems which are deliberate and conscious imitations of the traditional ballad. (Significantly, it was not until the eighteenth century that literary ballads first came into prominence—that is, at a time when the traditional ballad had become largely a museum piece.)

Probably the Romantic period in England was the time of greatest flowering of the literary ballad. Then, at any rate, Coleridge wrote his *Rime of the Ancient Mariner*; Scott, his "Proud Maisie"; and Keats, his "La Belle Dame Sans Merci." But all through the nineteenth century elements of the traditional ballad continued to exert a significant influence on poets so diverse as Alfred, Lord Tennyson, Dante Gabriel Rossetti, William Morris, Oliver Wendell Holmes, and Algernon Swinburne. And in our own century some of the poets who have written literary ballads are Ezra Pound, John Crowe Ransom, William Butler Yeats, and Robert Penn Warren. In short, although the traditional ballad has led a most precarious existence since the advent of widespread printing, its form has continued to make itself felt down to the present time.

QUESTIONS – THE LITERARY BALLAD:
KEATS · DAVIDSON · RANSOM

JOHN KEATS (1795–1821)

La Belle Dame Sans Merci

O what can ail thee, Knight at arms,
    Alone and palely loitering?
The sedge has withered from the Lake
    And no birds sing!

O what can ail thee, Knight at arms,
    So haggard, and so woebegone?
The squirrel's granary is full
    And the harvest's done.

I see a lily on thy brow
    With anguish moist and fever dew,
And on thy cheeks a fading rose
    Fast withereth too.

I met a Lady in the Meads,
    Full beautiful, a faery's child,
Her hair was long, her foot was light
    And her eyes were wild.

I made a Garland for her head,
    And bracelets too, and fragrant Zone;
She looked at me as she did love
    And made sweet moan.

I set her on my pacing steed
    And nothing else saw all day long,
For sidelong would she bend and sing
    A faery's song.

She found me roots of relish sweet,
    And honey wild, and manna dew,
And sure in language strange she said
    "I love thee true."

She took me to her elfin grot
    And there she wept and sighed full sore,
And there I shut her wild wild eyes
    With kisses four.

And there she lulléd me asleep,
    And there I dreamed, Ah Woe betide!
The latest dream I ever dreamt
    On the cold hill side.

I saw pale Kings, and Princes too,
    Pale warriors, death-pale were they all;

5

10

15

20

25

30

35

They cried, "La belle dame sans merci
Thee hath in thrall!"   40

I saw their starved lips in the gloam
With horrid warning gapéd wide,
And I awoke, and found me here
On the cold hill's side.

And this is why I sojourn here,   45
Alone and palely loitering;
Though the sedge is withered from the Lake
And no birds sing.

Title: The Beautiful Lady Without Pity. *latest* (35): last.

1. At first glance, Keats seems to have kept to the traditional ballad stanza in the writing of his poem: each stanza is a quatrain, and the rhyme scheme is *abcb* throughout. Yet if we examine the fourth line of each stanza more closely, we will discover that Keats has effected a variation on the traditional ballad form. What is that variation? How does it help to create the peculiar effect of "La Belle Dame Sans Merci"?

2. Note that the melodic quality (or euphony) of the poem results largely from Keats's use of rich vowel sounds and liquid consonants (that is, *l* and *r* sounds). What other sound devices (see p. 56 ff.) does he employ? How do they cumulatively contribute to the overall atmosphere of the poem? Explain in a few paragraphs.

3. Describe the mode of progression (see p. 36) employed in the poem. How does it differ from that in most of the traditional ballads?

JOHN DAVIDSON (1857–1909)

A Ballad of Hell

"A letter from my love to-day!
Oh, unexpected, dear appeal!"
She struck a happy tear away,
And broke the crimson seal.

"My love, there is no help on earth,   5
No help in heaven; the dead-man's bell

Must toll our wedding; our first hearth
  Must be the well-paved floor of hell."

The colour died from out her face,
  Her eyes like ghostly candles shone;   10
She cast dread looks about the place,
  Then clenched her teeth and read right on.

"I may not pass the prison door;
  Here must I rot from day to day,
Unless I wed whom I abhor,   15
  My cousin, Blanche of Valencay.

"At midnight with my dagger keen
  I'll take my life; it must be so.
Meet me in hell to-night, my queen,
  For weal and woe."   20

She laughed although her face was wan,
  She girded on her golden belt,
She took her jewelled ivory fan,
  And at her glowing missal knelt.

Then rose, "And am I mad?" she said: 25
  She broke her fan, her belt untied;
With leather girt herself instead,
  And stuck a dagger at her side.

She waited, shuddering in her room,
  Till sleep had fallen on all the house.   30
She never flinched; she faced her doom:
  They two must sin to keep their vows.

Then out into the night she went,
  And stooping crept by hedge and tree;
Her rose-bush flung a snare of scent,   35
  And caught a happy memory.

She fell, and lay a minute's space;
  She tore the sward in her distress;
The dewy grass refreshed her face;
  She rose and ran with lifted dress.   40

She started like a morn-caught ghost
   Once when the moon came out and stood
To watch; the naked road she crossed,
   And dived into the murmuring wood.

The branches snatched her streaming cloak;   45
   A live thing shrieked; she made no stay!
She hurried to the trysting-oak—
   Right well she knew the way.

Without a pause she bared her breast,
   And drove her dagger home and fell,   5c
And lay like one that takes her rest,
   And died and wakened up in hell.

She bathed her spirit in the flame,
   And near the centre took her post;
From all sides to her ears there came,   55
   The dreary anguish of the lost.

The devil started at her side,
   Comely, and tall, and black as jet.
"I am young Malespina's bride;
   Has he come hither yet?"   60

"My poppet, welcome to your bed."
   "Is Malespina here?"
"Not he! To-morrow he must wed
   His cousin Blanche, my dear!"

1. John Davidson (1857–1909) was one of the most successful practitioners of the literary ballad about the turn of the century. In his "A Ballad of Hell," how effective is he in the attempt to dramatize his story as fully as possible? Does he rely as drastically upon the cinematic technique (see the introduction to this chapter) as do the older ballads? or does his use of figurative language—for example, lines 10, 35–36, 41—and of unnecessary narrative detail impede the action? Is any of his narrative detail actually unnecessary? Explain.

2. What is there in the theme of "A Ballad of Hell" which might suggest that Davidson belongs to the modern world? Is there anything in "Captain Carpenter" (below) that designates it as modern? Explain.

JOHN CROWE RANSOM (1888–   )

Captain Carpenter

Captain Carpenter rose up in his prime
Put on his pistols and went riding out
But had got wellnigh nowhere at that time
Till he fell in with ladies in a rout.

It was a pretty lady and all her train   5
That played with him so sweetly but before
An hour she'd taken a sword with all her main
And twined him of his nose for evermore.

Captain Carpenter mounted up one day
And rode straightway into a stranger rogue   10
That looked unchristian but be that as may
The Captain did not wait upon prologue.

But drew upon him out of his great heart
The other swing against him with a club
And cracked his two legs at the shinny part   15
And let him roll and stick like any tub.

Captain Carpenter rode many a time
From male and female took he sundry harms
He met the wife of Satan crying "I'm
The she-wolf bids you shall bear no more arms."   20

Their strokes and counters whistled in the wind
I wish he had delivered half his blows
But where she could have made off like a hind
The bitch bit off his arms at the elbows.

And Captain Carpenter parted with his ears   25
To a black devil that used him in this wise
O Jesus ere his threescore and ten years
Another had plucked out his sweet blue eyes.

Captain Carpenter got up on his roan
And sallied from the gate in hell's despite   30

I heard him asking in the grimmest tone
If any enemy yet there was to fight?

"To any adversary it is fame
If he risk to be wounded by my tongue
Or burnt in two beneath my red heart's flame   35
Such are the perils he is cast among.

"But if he can he has a pretty choice
From an anatomy with little to lose
Whether he cut my tongue and take my voice
Or whether it be my round red heart he choose."   40

It was the neatest knave that ever was seen
Stepping in perfume from his lady's bower
Who at this word put in his merry mien
And fell on Captain Carpenter like a tower.

I would not knock old fellows in the dust   45
But there lay Captain Carpenter on his back
His weapons were the old heart in his bust
And a blade shook between rotten teeth alack.

The rogue in scarlet and grey soon knew his mind
He wished to get his trophy and depart   50
With gentle apology and touch refined
He pierced him and produced the Captain's heart.

God's mercy rest on Captain Carpenter now
I thought him Sirs an honest gentleman
Citizen husband soldier and scholar enow   55
Let jangling kites eat of him if they can.

But God's deep curses follow after those
That shore him of his goodly nose and ears
His legs and strong arms at the two elbows
And eyes that had not watered seventy years.   60

The curse of hell upon the sleek upstart
Who got the Captain finally on his back
And took the red red vitals of his heart
And made the kites to whet their beaks clack clack.

Chapter 3

The Sonnet

"Scorn not the Sonnet," says the Romantic poet Wordsworth, and it is difficult to see how any student of poetry could. As Wordsworth goes on to say in his sonnet on the sonnet, this form has challenged the greatest poets from Dante and Petrarch to Shakespeare, Spenser, and Milton. He might have added himself, Shelley, Keats, Arnold, Hopkins, Baudelaire, Rilke, E. A. Robinson, W. H. Auden, Allen Tate, Robert Frost, and Dylan Thomas—to name only a few who have used the form successfully since Wordsworth. In sheer bulk the sonnet lays claim to being one of the most popular of all poetic forms in English.

What is the challenge of this brief form? Ultimately it consists both of the limitation of the fourteen lines—the challenge to say something important in a little space—and the required strict interweaving of rhymes that are so very difficult in English. The Roman poet Horace, whose view of poetry was pragmatic (see p. 2), understood this practical value of limitation ("much in little" as he called it), and saw a value in it. Length restrictions of the sonnet, indeed, work not as disadvantages, but actually provide the poet a means to sharpen and to deepen his ideas. "Nuns fret not at their narrow convent room," says Wordsworth in another sonnet on the form of the sonnet; even as the convent is no prison for the nun, but the very means by which she can sharpen and define her understanding of reality, so the restrictions of the sonnet result in a clearer definition that one might lack altogether if he did not have the value of limitation.

ITALIAN AND ENGLISH SONNETS

The sonneteer accepts more rigid prescriptions than the poet who employs other poetic forms. In English the sonnet has two intricate rhyme schemes: the *Italian,* and the *English* or *Shakespearean.* The Italian, as its name implies, is closer to the original Petrarchan mode of sonnet writing. (Petrarch [1304–74] was an Italian poet whose sonnets to Laura began the whole chain of writing sonnets to a beautiful woman; a series of sonnets written in this manner came to be called a *sonnet sequence.*) The Italian sonnet has the following rhyme scheme: *abba abba cde cde.* Each letter stands for a certain sound, and if the letter repeats in the rhyme scheme, the sound which the letter indicates is repeated (see p. 56 ff.). The first *quatrain* of Milton's sonnet illustrates:

> Avenge, O Lord, thy slaughtered saints, whose bones
> Lie scattered on the Alpine mountains cold,
> Even them who kept thy truth so pure of old
> When all our fathers worshipped stocks and stones . . .

In this quatrain, *bones* is *a, cold* is *b, old* is *b,* and *stones* is *a* again. The Italian rhyme scheme is difficult in English because Italian, unlike English, has a very large vocabulary of words that rhyme. This scheme has only five sounds (i.e., *a, b, c, d, e*) that repeat; that is, only five rhymes appear in the entire fourteen lines. Yet even with this rhyme restriction, some of the greatest sonnets in English have been written in the Italian rhyme scheme.

The English (or Shakespearean) sonnet has a much easier rhyme scheme than the Italian, allowing more rhymes and thus suiting itself more easily to the difficulty of finding rhymes in English. Its rhyme scheme is *abab cdcd efef gg.* Note that the last two verses of the English sonnet form a couplet (see p. 134). It is one of the great achievements of English poetry that this couplet, serving to conclude an intricate rhyme scheme, has yielded some of our most memorable poetic lines:

So shalt thou feed on Death, that feeds on men,
And Death once dead, there's no more dying then.

Various critics have called this couplet the "whip" of the sonnet because, as in Shakespeare's sonnets, it provides a comment on the whole twelve lines of the poem preceding it. The couplet lashes back, in other words. It is also important to remember that many English sonneteers combine the Italian rhyme scheme and the couplet, with rhyme schemes like the following: *abba abba cdcd ee.*

THE ROLE OF STRUCTURE

What functions do these two rhyme schemes perform? First, note that both the Italian and English rhyme schemes have distinct breaks, that certain rhymes are used in particular places and not in others. Primarily these breaks are an attempt to furnish the poem with circumscribed areas in which to think and speak. The Italians, who wrote most of the first sonnets, called the first eight lines of any sonnet the *octet* or *octave* and the last six lines the *sestet*. The first eight lines, the octet, are themselves broken down into two quatrains; but together the eight lines form one main thought. This main thought is usually centered around the problem that the sonnet poses, the question that it asks, or the situation for which it seeks a response. The last six lines, or sestet, resolve the problem, answer the question, or respond to the initial situation. The English sonnet also builds on the octet and sestet, but it has many variations as well—such as three quatrains and a couplet, with breaks occurring between each of the four units; or octet, quatrain, and couplet, with the break occurring between each of the three units. Through this blending of octet and sestet and variations, the sonnet as a form gains its unity.

When all these elements are placed together—the rhythmic patterns, the rhyme schemes, the divisions of octet and sestet—what unique structure has been created? That is, how should one consider the sonnet as a whole? In the Elizabethan age, a time of some of the world's greatest sonnets, Sir John Harrington said that the sonnet and the *epigram* were alike, only that one was "sweet" and the other "salt." This analogy of sonnet to epigram is appropriate, for it emphasizes the brevity, the sharp turns of thought and phrase, the concentration of idea and form in both. Viewing the sonnet as a type of verse letter is likewise appropriate; it suggests the tone of familiarity found in the best sonnets, a tone which allows for sublime comments as well as personal response.

THE EVOLUTION OF THE SONNET

The great Petrarchan sonnets in English have this quality of the verse letter; and in the first period of the sonnet in our language—that is, from the translations of Wyatt to the sonnet cycles of Sidney, Spenser, and Shakespeare (roughly, the sixteenth century)—the Petrarchan mode of writing is the dominant one. Actually Chaucer wrote the first sonnet in English, a translation of Petrarch in *Troilus and Cressida*. But it was not until the time of Henry VIII (reigned 1509–47) that the sonnet as a popular form emerged, and then it was Wyatt's personal variation of the Petrarchan original. The form developed and achieved its greatest popularity during the age of Elizabeth (reigned 1558–1603).

The Petrarchan original is essentially a long love poem, a series of sonnets dating from the fourteenth century and addressed to Laura, an Italian noblewoman. The sonnets do not have any settled *narrative* or story, but they do reflect the ups and downs of a man who is desperately in love with a beautiful woman (quite unattainable, of course). There is no story, but there are always two principal characters: the lover and the beloved, or the frustrated man and the disdainful woman (the beautiful Laura). Rather than episodes in a narrative, the sonnet cycle has themes that repeat as the man has his ups and downs. These themes have their own variations, just as in great symphonies. Essentially the recurrent themes of the Petrarchan original concern the man's love for the woman and his failure to achieve that love. This failure, however, does not destroy him; rather, it inspires him by providing in the woman an ideal for his existence. That is, in true neoplatonic fashion, the woman's beauty of body and soul gives direction to the man's suffering life. She has "formed" his soul and therefore the direction of his life. It should be pointed out, however, that during this first period in England, in the sixteenth century, Petrarch's original themes and conventions were not slavishly imitated; indeed, they were used with fascinating differences by all the great sonneteers.

In the seventeenth century, the Petrarchan experience was completely displaced. Individual sonneteers, more noticeably distinct from one another than had been many sonneteers of the previous century, rejected Petrarch's increasingly formalized themes and, instead, used the sonnet as a vehicle for more personal experience, usually religious. While these writers formed no closely knit school, they shared disdain for the conventions or traditions of the Petrarchan model. The most notable sonneteers of this period are Donne and Milton.

As a form, the sonnet virtually disappeared with the advent of neoclassicism. Neither its Petrarchan idealization in the sixteenth century or its personal tone in the seventeenth century was amenable to the "rationality" of Dryden and Pope. It was not until the Romantics that the sonnet found favor again. This third phase included the sonnets of Wordsworth, Shelley, and Keats; the influence here was clearly the sonnet of the seventeenth century and of Shakespeare. Also in this third phase are the Victorian attempts of Elizabeth Barrett Browning, Matthew Arnold, Dante Gabriel Rossetti, and the variations of George Meredith, to name a few. Finally, the few good sonnets of modern British and American literature fit this same phase: they are largely personal revelations and fit no prescribed mode, as the old Petrarchan. But what is fascinating to study in modern poetry is the adaptation of the old sonnet form to modern themes and the discovery again of how, even in the modern world, limitation in form has a way of freeing content.

There are three broad periods, then, of the sonnet in English: (1) the sixteenth century, especially the age of Elizabeth; (2) the seventeenth century; and (3) the Romantic, Victorian, and Modern periods. The tremendous achievement of the sonnet in the Renaissance left an indelible mark on English and American poetry; and it is very true that, as a result, most young poets of all periods have tried their hands at this form. In this way, the sonnet, with its limitations and its challenge, has continued to intrigue generations of readers and writers of poetry.

SIR THOMAS WYATT (1503–42)

My Galley Chargéd with Forgetfulness

My galley chargéd with forgetfulness
Thorough sharp seas, in winter nights doth pass
'Tween rock and rock; and eke mine enemy, alas,
That is my lord, steereth with cruelness.
And every oar a thought in readiness,   5
As though that death were light in such a case.
An endless wind doth tear the sail apace
Of forcéd sighs and trusty fearfulness.
A rain of tears, a cloud of dark disdain,
Hath done the wearied cords great hinderance,   10
Wreathéd with error and eke with ignorance.
The stars be hid that led me to this pain,
Drownéd is reason that should me consort,
And I remain despairing of the port.

galley (1): ship. *Thorough* (2): through. *eke* (3): also. *consort* (13): escort.

1. This early sonnet is Wyatt's own translation of one of Petrarch, and already the English *tone* (see p. 65) differs from the Italian original. Wyatt here, as the critic Sergio Baldi has pointed out, explores his own pessimism and does not find in his love any inspiration or idealization. Wyatt has made his own personal variation on the Petrarchan original (see introduction to this chapter). The entire poem is an *extended metaphor* (see p. 18) for his passion, a love leading to despair. What are the *tenor* and *vehicle* (see p. 17) of the metaphor?

2. Having established the basic terms of the extended metaphor, discuss in a long paragraph the manner in which Wyatt has made a point-by-point comparison of his passion or love to the effects of the storm on the ship.

3. Allowing for the difference in pronunciation today, note that the octet of this poem has a regular Italian rhyme scheme. The sestet, however, has a varied pattern, one of the many variations allowed in an Italian sestet. Describe the rhyme scheme of the entire poem.

SIR PHILIP SIDNEY (1554–86)

Sonnet 49 *(from Astrophel and Stella)*

I on my horse, and Love on me, doth try
Our horsemanships, while by strange work I prove
A horseman to my horse, a horse to Love,
And now man's wrongs in me, poor beast, descry.
The reins wherewith my rider doth me tie   5
Are humbled thoughts, which bit of reverence move,
Curbed in with fear, but with gilt boss above
Of hope, which makes it seem fair to the eye.
The wand is will; thou, fancy, saddle art,
Girt fast by memory; and while I spur   10
My horse, he spurs with sharp desire my heart;
He sits me fast, however I do stir;
And now hath made me to his hand so right
That in the manage myself takes delight.

fancy (9): imagination.

1. Like the Wyatt sonnet, this poem builds on an extended metaphor. What are the tenor and vehicle?

2. In Wyatt's sonnet, one must envision the kind of ships in the days of Henry VIII. In Sidney's, one must imagine the Renaissance sport of horsemanship. Terms like *bit, boss, wand,* and *manage* are therefore important to know. But primarily one must envision the essential analogy between loving and horsemanship. Explain each step in the analogy.

3. In Sidney's sonnet sequence, *Astrophel and Stella,* the theme of "sincere" overpowering love recurs often. In this sonnet, how does the extended metaphor develop that theme? What effect results from Sidney's identifying the *persona* (see p. 34) of his sonnet cycle—Astrophel—with the horse? What is the effect of using abstract diction like *hope, will, fancy,* and *memory?*

4. Renaissance psychology held that moral action could result only when reason controlled passion and therefore directed the will toward a proper end. But what happens to reason in the sonnets by Wyatt and Sidney? How does this knowledge of Renaissance psychology give an added emotional impact to the poem? Does it contribute to understanding Sidney's concept of "sincerity"? Explain.

5. Describe the rhyme scheme. Is it Italian or English? What is the effect of the final couplet? Does this *irony* (see p. 24) help in developing the "sincerity" of Astrophel? Explain. How does irony help to make the sonnet epigrammatic?

6. Sidney is a master of figurative language (see p. 14). Note the use of *apostrophe* and, in the last line, *paradox*. In Renaissance grammar schools the rhetoric of Latin and Greek formed the basis of all study; thus, use of figurative expressions became second nature for all great poets of the age. Poetic devices also blended with these figures of rhetoric. Identify examples of *alliteration* and *assonance* (see p. 58 ff.); then discuss any implications they may have for the expression of Astrophel's love.

7. Scan line 12 (see p. 49). Is the meter regular? For example, does the second foot appear more of a spondee than an iamb? It is important to note that few lines are purely iambic, especially where (as here) the poet intends a personal and conversational tone. What is the effect of the caesura? Does it, like other sound devices, enhance the "sincerity" of Astrophel, the lover whose personal revelation is the sonnet itself? Explain in a short essay showing how such formal devices can develop content.

EDMUND SPENSER (1552?–99)

Sonnet 75 (from Amoretti)

One day I wrote her name upon the strand,
But came the waves and washéd it away:
Agayne I wrote it with a second hand,
But came the tyde, and made my paynes his pray.
"Vayne man," sayd she, "that doest in vaine assay,   5
A mortall thing so to immortalize,
For I my selve shall lyke to this decay,
And eek my name bee wypéd out lykewize."
"Not so," quod I, "let baser things devize
To dy in dust, but you shall live by fame: 10
My verse your vertues rare shall eternize,
And in the hevens wryte your glorious name.
Where whenas death shall all the world subdew,
Our love shall live, and later life renew."

pray (4): prey; victim. *eek* (8): also. *quod* (9): said.

1. Spenser's sonnet sequence *Amoretti* (which can be translated as "little love letters"), unlike Sidney's sequence *Astrophel and Stella*, creates more psychological interest in the woman and her nature than in the conflicts of the lover himself. The man in these sonnets celebrating courtship wins his admired lady, just as Spenser himself married Elizabeth Boyle and then wrote another poem (*Epithalamion*) celebrating his wedding day. Spenser's interests are also larger, more discursive, and less dramatic than Sidney's or Wyatt's. For example, in this sonnet Spenser presents a philosophical theme common in the Renaissance. That theme holds that the poet's art—his poem—will outlast time and, in fact, will give immortality to the beloved. Read the sonnet carefully and then discuss in a short essay how a philosophical theme—the Renaissance concept of mutability—contributes to the idealization of the woman, that is, to Spenser's own variation on the Petrarchan original.

2. Is there a narrative in this sonnet? How does this episode differ from those in the sonnets of Wyatt and Sidney? The poem is composed almost entirely of literal language; lacking the extended metaphors of Wyatt's and Sidney's sonnets, it is built on an illustration rather than an analogy. What is the effect in tone? Compare the despair of Wyatt's persona and the "sincerity" of Astrophel with the remarks of the speaker here. Is the speaker's language, which is literal, less poetic? Explain.

3. Why is the division of the octet and sestet important in the meaning of this sonnet? How do the two parts relate? How does the couplet reinforce the shift in meaning that comes with the sestet? In the octet, what is the relationship of the two quatrains? How do these technical relationships—demanded by the rigors of the sonnet form—develop the content of the sonnet?

4. The rhyme scheme here is neither Italian nor English, for Spenser invented a scheme of his own for the *Amoretti*, one closer to the intimate interlocking of *rhyme royal* (see p. 323). What dramatic effect in lines 8 and 9 results from this interlocking?

5. Is the iambic pentameter in this sonnet more or less regular than in Wyatt's or Sidney's? What is the tonal effect of regularity in the last line? Also in the last line, what effect results from caesura, alliteration, and a series of short vowels in accented syllables?

WILLIAM SHAKESPEARE (1564–1616)

Sonnet 29

When, in disgrace with fortune and men's eyes,
I all alone beweep my outcast state,
And trouble deaf heaven with my bootless cries,
And look upon myself, and curse my fate,
Wishing me like to one more rich in hope,   5
Featured like him, like him with friends possessed,
Desiring this man's art and that man's scope,
With what I most enjoy contented least;
Yet in these thoughts myself almost despising,
Haply I think on thee—and then my state,   10
Like to the lark at break of day arising
From sullen earth, sings hymns at heaven's gate;
For thy sweet love remembered such wealth brings
That then I scorn to change my state with kings.

bootless (3): profitless. *haply* (10): by chance.

Sonnet 73

That time of year thou mayst in me behold
When yellow leaves, or none, or few, do hang
Upon those boughs which shake against the cold,
Bare ruined choirs, where late the sweet birds sang.
In me thou see'st the twilight of such day   5
As after sunset fadeth in the west;
Which by and by black night doth take away,
Death's second self, that seals up all in rest.
In me thou see'st the glowing of such fire,
That on the ashes of his youth doth lie,   10
As the deathbed whereon it must expire,
Consumed with that which it was nourished by.
This thou perceiv'st, which makes thy love more strong,
To love that well which thou must leave ere long.

ere (14): before.

Sonnet 116

Let me not to the marriage of true minds   3.5
Admit impediments. Love is not love
Which alters when it alteration finds,
Or bends with the remover to remove:
Oh, no! it is an ever-fixéd mark,   5
That looks on tempests and is never shaken;
It is the star to every wandering bark,
Whose worth's unknown, although his height be taken.
Love's not Time's fool, though rosy lips and cheeks
Within his bending sickle's compass come;   10
Love alters not with his brief hours and weeks,
But bears it out even to the edge of doom.
If this be error and upon me proved,
I never writ, nor no man ever loved.

Sonnet 129

Th' expense of spirit in a waste of shame
Is lust in action; and till action, lust
Is perjured, murderous, bloody, full of blame,
Savage, extreme, rude, cruel, not to trust,
Enjoyed no sooner but despiséd straight;   5
Past reason hunted; and no sooner had,
Past reason hated, as a swallowed bait,
On purpose laid to make the taker mad:
Mad in pursuit, and in possession so;
Had, having, and in quest to have, extreme;   10
A bliss in proof, and proved, a very woe;
Before, a joy proposed; behind, a dream.
All this the world well knows; yet none knows well
To shun the heaven that leads men to this hell.

Sonnet 130

My mistress' eyes are nothing like the sun;
Coral is far more red than her lips' red;
If snow be white, why then her breasts are dun;
If hairs be wires, black wires grow on her head.

I have seen roses damasked, red and white,   5
But no such roses see I in her cheeks;
And in some perfumes is there more delight
Than in the breath that from my mistress reeks.
I love to hear her speak, yet well I know
That music hath a far more pleasing sound;   10
I grant I never saw a goddess go,
My mistress, when she walks, treads on the ground.
And yet, by heaven, I think my love as rare
As any she belied with false compare.

dun (3): dull brown. *damasked* (5): richly patterned.

1. The preceding five sonnets are part of an untitled sonnet sequence published in 1609, although they were probably written in the early 1590's, when the other great sonnet sequences (Sidney's *Astrophel and Stella* in 1591, and Spenser's *Amoretti* in 1595) were published. The most remarkable characteristic of this sequence of 154 sonnets centers in Shakespeare's power to transform the tritest of events, the most commonplace emotions, the simplest ideas, creating from them something so alive and original that the force of these poems has been renewed in each generation since his day. More specifically, in his sonnet sequence Shakespeare took the Petrarchan patterns and turned them upside down. The Petrarchan idealization of a woman became an idealization of a young man, with this important difference: the older man—the persona of the sonnets—"educates" the young man to the perennial truths of life, such as the force of mutability, the need for plenitude in life, and the necessity of the open and constant heart. Shakespeare develops these themes in 126 sonnets and then appends twenty-eight more in which he tells of a "dark lady" who provides him with a realistic love quite different from the idealized beauty and inspiration of the young man. Contrast the first three sonnets here (29, 73, 116) with the last two (129, 130). What are the thematic differences between these two loves that occur here? For example, how do the couplets that end Sonnets 29 and 129 present a distinction between the young man and the dark lady?

2. What is the lesson that the older man teaches in Sonnet 116? How can that lesson be contrasted to the sexual anguish of Sonnet 129 or to the frank acceptance of Sonnet 130? Write a short essay to explain that contrast. In Sonnet 73 the persona teaches the effect of

mutability on human existence and then relates his idealized love to this destructive effect; in Sonnet 129 this very effect of change produces a loveless horror and despair. What does such mutability mean in each sonnet? Do the concepts differ? Contrast the images and rhythms of Sonnets 73 and 129. How do these techniques of verse reinforce the thematic differences? Write a short essay exploring this relationship of form and content in Sonnets 73 and 129.

3. The development of Sonnet 29 moves downward and then, through reversal, rises abruptly. How do sound devices reinforce this development? Contrast auditory images in the octet with those in the sestet.

4. The octet of Sonnet 29 is built on hyperbole. How does the vocabulary, the choice of diction, develop this figure of speech?

5. Though the sestet, like the octet, of Sonnet 29 is built on hyperbole, the exaggeration in the sestet is one of joy, not despair. Note the pivotal use of the word "haply" and of caesura in line 9. However, what contributes to the tonal effect of hyperbolic reversal in the sestet is a subtle technical effect. In order to discover this effect, note the uses of literal and figurative language in the sonnet. Where is the first marked use of metaphoric language? Does a change in rhythm occur at the same place? What is the effect of enjambment? of the use of feminine rhyme? Does the couplet act as a "whip" responding to the rest of the sonnet, or does it merely finish out the hyperbole of the sestet? Explain. Finally, contrast the hyperbole of the first and last lines to see the kind of unity that the sonnet achieves.

6. Sonnet 73 is rhetorically organized around an ingenious use of parallelism. Instead of the conventional octet and sestet, it contains three quatrains and a couplet, or 4 + 4 + 4 + 2. Each quatrain parallels the other in that each is built on an implied metaphor. What common function do these metaphors carry out? Explain. Note that each of the quatrains becomes progressively complex so that the third ends in line 12 with a philosophical statement about man's ambiguous condition in a mutable and destructive world. Explain in an essay how this progression results in an emphatic organization for the sonnet.

7. Sonnet 116 begins with a famous metaphor, the source of which can be found in the Book of Common Prayer of the Anglican Church. Is the connotation of the marriage service relevant to the theme of the sonnet? What is the tonal effect of the caesura in line 2? To evaluate the importance of inversion, contrast line 3 with line 1 of

Sonnet 73. As in Sonnet 73, Shakespeare here uses parallel metaphors, but not in quatrains. Similarly, these metaphors are unlike those of Sonnet 73 in that they are *explicit*. Describe each of the metaphors. What is the use of *personification* (see p. 22) in lines 9 and 10? Why is "rosy lips and cheeks" an example of *metonymy* (see p. 20)? How does the couplet function in this sonnet?

8. The emotions of Sonnet 129 arise from a rather literal description of the older man's attitude toward the sexual act. The woman, in Shakespeare's transformation of Petrarch, does not liberate the man; the beauty and "sweet love" of the young man does that, as evidenced by Sonnet 29 and others. Yet the "dark lady"—so unlike the blonde Stella and the chaste heroine of *Amoretti*—is a necessity. How does the description in Sonnet 130 distinguish Shakespeare's heroine from the Petrarchan goddess? Does this suggest that the persona takes less delight in his lady? Explain. The feeling of genuine horror in Sonnet 129 results from the persona's recognition that surrender to physical passions requires the anguish of spiritual loss. How does the lack of metaphorical language contribute to this feeling? What other poetic devices contribute to this effect?

QUESTIONS – DONNE · HERBERT

JOHN DONNE (1573–1631)

Holy Sonnet 7

At the round earths imagin'd corners, blow
Your trumpets, Angells, and arise, arise
From death, you numberlesse infinities
Of soules, and to your scattred bodies goe,
All whom the flood did, and fire shall o'erthrow,   5
All whom warre, dearth, age, agues, tyrannies,
Despaire, law, chance, hath slaine, and you whose eyes,
Shall behold God, and never tast deaths woe.
But let them sleepe, Lord, and mee mourne a space,
For, if above all these, my sinnes abound,   10
'Tis late to ask abundance of thy grace,
When wee are there; here on this lowly ground,

Teach mee how to repent; for that's as good
As if thou'hadst seal'd my pardon, with thy blood.

agues (6): fevers.

1. To appreciate a Donne sonnet, one must first consider the speaking voice. While in the sonnets of the sixteenth century, there was certainly a voice speaking—often in anguished accents about love —the strongly personal voice is a unique characteristic of metaphysical poetry. It is equally important to consider the dramatic situation with which a metaphysical poem opens and in which the voice speaks. As the modern critic Helen Gardner has said, "the moment of dramatic experience" is one of the three main characteristics of such early seventeenth-century poetry. In this sonnet, where has Donne imagined himself? Why is the situation more dramatic and more personal than any found in sonnets of the sixteenth century? Explain in a long paragraph.

2. Donne's sonnets are also called "Divine Meditations." As critics have shown, he probably patterned their very structure on the three parts of the formal meditation that Ignatius Loyola devised for his order of Catholic priests, the Jesuits. These three parts appealed to the memory or imagination, the understanding, and the will or prayer. Examine the octet here and see which of the three parts of an Ignatian meditation is evoked. The sestet is clearly a prayer. But what is its relation to the octet? What function is served by the clear break between the octet and sestet? What is the paradoxical effect of this reversal? Explain.

3. This sonnet, written about 1609, is clearly distinguishable from the Petrarchan sonnet. Does the form follow a regular sonnet rhyme scheme? What irregularities in the rhythm appear? What is the dramatic result of this irregularity within the tight form of the sonnet? How does this rhythmic effect develop a subject matter differently from the Petrarchan sonnets? Donne's attitude toward his subject is obviously not so formal or ceremonious as that found in the conventional Petrarchans. Is the difference in attitude evidenced by powerful metrical stresses? Explain. Finally, although the colloquy in this poem is obviously not between the lover and his mistress, the voice speaking is like the Petrarchan lover's. To whom, however, is the voice speaking in the sestet?

4. How is the effect of the voice enhanced by the use of caesura and enjambment? What is the result of the tight rhyme scheme within this conversational prose rhythm? What is the effect in line 9 of the assonance of "sleepe" and "mee"? Find uses of alliteration in lines 10 and 11. What do these words have in common? Why are they related? How does this tying together of diction through alliteration emphasize the whole meaning of the sestet?

5. Donne avoids the storehouse of figurative language employed by Petrarchan sonneteers. How does this deliberate attempt to avoid mannered figurative language correspond to Donne's conversational rhythms and irregular iambic pentameter? Does it support a specific attitude toward his subject? What, for example, is the difference between his concept of "sincerity" and Sir Philip Sidney's? Explain in a short essay.

Holy Sonnet 9

If poisonous minerals, and if that tree
Whose fruit threw death on else immortal us,
If lecherous goats, if serpents envious
Cannot be damned, alas, why should I be?
Why should intent or reason, born in me,   5
Make sins, else equal, in me more heinous?
And mercy being easy and glorious
To God, in His stern wrath why threatens He?
But who am I, that dare dispute with Thee,
O God? Oh, of Thine only worthy blood   10
And my tears, make a heavenly Lethean flood,
And drown in it my sins' black memory.
That Thou remember them, some claim as debt;
I think it mercy, if Thou wilt forget.

Holy Sonnet 14

Batter my heart, three-personed God; for you
As yet but knock, breathe, shine, and seek to mend;
That I may rise and stand, o'erthrow me, and bend
Your force to break, blow, burn, and make me new.
I, like an usurped town t'another due,   5

Labor t'admit you, but oh, to no end.
Reason, your viceroy in me, me should defend,
But is captived, and proves weak or untrue.
Yet dearly I love you, and would be lovèd fain,
But am betrothed unto your enemy;   10
Divorce me, untie or break that knot again;
Take me to you, imprison me, for I,
Except you enthrall me, never shall be free,
Nor ever chaste, except you ravish me.

GEORGE HERBERT (1593–1633)

Prayer (I)

Prayer, the church's banquet, angels' age,
   God's breath in man returning to his birth,
   The soul in paraphrase, heart in pilgrimage,
The Christian plummet sounding heaven and earth;

Engine against th' Almighty, sinner's tower,   5
   Reversèd thunder, Christ-side-piercing spear,
   The six-days' world transposing in an hour,
A kind of tune, which all things hear and fear;

Softness, and peace, and joy, and love, and bliss,
   Exalted manna, gladness of the best,   10
   Heaven in ordinary, man well dressed,
The Milky Way, the bird of Paradise,

   Church bells beyond the stars heard, the soul's blood,
   The land of spices; something understood.

1. Before Herbert became an Anglican priest, he was the public orator at Cambridge. Therefore he was a master of rhetorical effects. Like Donne, he could throw away obvious figurative language in order to gain the appearance of directness. Directness is particularly important in this sonnet, since something so personal as meditation reaches into one's deepest resources. Here, therefore, as in Donne's sonnets, one must listen for the speaking voice. To emphasize the effect of that voice, Herbert uses a brilliant manipulation of syntax.

What is this manipulation? How do the series of phrases in the sonnet dramatize the "sincerity" of the speaking voice? If the sonnet were filled with complete statements, rational concepts about the subject would be developed. Why are short phrases more appropriate for this subject? Explain in a short paragraph.

2. What kind of sonnet is this? What is its rhyme scheme? In the final couplet, there is a building of phrases to what appears an anti-climax. But why is the phrase "something understood" more truly a climax to the poem than, for example, the exotic "land of spices"? Is this an example of understatement?

3. The poem is built on contrasts in diction and rhythm. Comparing "birth" and "breath" in line 2, distinguish their relationship in content as well as in sound. "Christ-side-piercing spear" (l. 6) with its spondees contributes to conversational rhythms; yet the phrase evokes the very action it describes. The result is something like Gerard Manley Hopkins' phrasing (see "God's Grandeur," p. 127). Look for other examples of this compounding of diction which Sir Philip Sidney, in his *Apology for Poetry*, calls one of the glories of the English language. Note that after the jagged rhythms of lines 5, 6, and 7 (where these compound epithets abound) the lines return to the most fluid iambic pentameter. What effect is Herbert aiming at? Finally, note that there is only one clause in the entire poem. Where is it? What does its use at that particular juncture help to mark?

4. Metaphysical poetry builds largely on connotative values of diction, not on limited denotative language. Employing a phrase like "man well dressed" (l. 11) as a metaphor for prayer is indeed stretching the connotation of a phrase so that one may feel, as Dr. Johnson felt about the metaphysicals, that "the most heterogeneous ideas are by violence yoked together." However, examining the metaphor carefully in terms of Herbert's religious premises will make its relevance clear. Explain this relevance in a paragraph. Moreover, all of the poem is not built on connotation; rather, it is built on contrast. What lines or phrases are clearly denotative and lack any resonance of meaning? How does this contrast contribute to the directness of the voice speaking?

JOHN MILTON (1608–74)

Sonnet 18

Avenge, O Lord, thy slaughtered saints, whose bones
  Lie scattered on the Alpine mountains cold;
  Even them who kept thy truth so pure of old
  When all our fathers worshipped stocks and stones,
Forget not: in Thy book record their groans   5
  Who were Thy sheep and in their ancient fold
  Slain by the bloody Piemontese, that rolled
  Mother with infant down the rocks. Their moans
The vales redoubled to the hills, and they
  To Heaven. Their martyred blood and ashes sow   10
  O'er all th' Italian fields where still doth sway
The triple tyrant: that from these may grow
  A hundred-fold, who having learnt Thy way
  Early may fly the Babylonian woe.

Sonnet 19

When I consider how my light is spent
  Ere half my days in this dark world and wide,
  And that one talent which is death to hide
  Lodged with me useless, though my soul more bent
To serve therewith my Maker, and present   5
  My true account, lest He returning chide;
  "Doth God exact day-labor, light denied?"
  I fondly ask. But Patience, to prevent
That murmur, soon replies, "God doth not need
  Either man's work or His own gifts. Who best   10
  Bear His mild yoke, they serve Him best. His state
Is kingly: Thousands at His bidding speed,
  And post o'er land and ocean without rest;
  They also serve who only stand and wait."

The Evolution of the Sonnet   115

Sonnet 23

Methought I saw my late espousèd saint
   Brought to me like Alcestis from the grave,
   Whom Jove's great son to her glad husband gave,
   Rescued from death by force though pale and faint.
Mine, as whom washed from spot of child-bed taint   5
   Purification in the Old Law did save,
   And such, as yet once more I trust to have
   Full sight of her in Heaven without restraint,
Came vested all in white, pure as her mind:
   Her face was veiled, yet to my fancied sight,   10
   Love, sweetness, goodness, in her person shined
So clear, as in no face with more delight.
   But O, as to embrace me she inclined,
   I waked, she fled, and day brought back my night.

Old Law (6): Jewish scriptures.

1. Milton's sonnets can be roughly divided into two kinds, the personal (e.g., Sonnets 19 and 23) and the occasional (e.g., Sonnet 18). But even in the sonnets written for some public occasion or responding, as in Sonnet 18, to an historical event, there is a prevailing personal tone. Always, as with Donne and Herbert, there is the sense of a voice speaking in its own personal accents. The majority of Milton's sonnets were written as immediate personal utterances in a period when, as Latin Secretary of State in Cromwell's government, he had little time for writing poetry. Thus, unlike the Petrarchan sonnets and even unlike the meditations of Donne, there is no formalization of sequence from sonnet to sonnet. Each sonnet is a complete entity; there are no relationships so tight as those between the Shakespearean sonnets. Lacking this unity of sequence, Milton was required to do a great deal in each sonnet, to pursue diligently the concentration required by the Horatian dictum "multum in parvo." It was natural, then, that Milton would use a device that he had already used so magnificently in *Lycidas* (see p. 341): allusion. Through skillful use of allusions to mythology, the personal is enlarged into the impersonal and therefore made accessible to an audience. In each of these three sonnets, there is at least one allusion to Greek mythology or to the Christian Bible. Identify each and then,

in an essay, discuss how Milton enlarges, by the use of myth, the dimensions of his subjects: the Italian massacre, his anguish over his blindness, and the dream about his wife. In this same essay, you should also note how, in the limited space of a sonnet, use of allusions contributes to the development of vast themes. Finally, contrast Milton's use of allusion with Herbert's phrase "exalted Manna" in "Prayer (I)."

2. What is the rhyme scheme of each sonnet? What kind of rhyme does Milton use (see p. 56)? Milton's sonnets are often called *verse paragraphs*, the term that is also used to describe metrical units in *Paradise Lost*. Is that term a good one for each of these sonnets? Why? If so, what happens to the division between the octet and sestet in each? Is there a second part that answers the first part? One technical achievement of Miltonic verse that allows us to think of it in terms of verse paragraphs is his command of the caesura; the real breaks in the rhythmic pattern come in the middle as often as at the end of the lines. But, as analysis of the rhyme schemes of these sonnets shows, Milton also has a highly effective and tight handling of rhymes. What is the result? Toward which breaks (caesura or rhymes) is our greatest attention drawn? Why? Explain in a paragraph.

3. In Sonnet 18, find each of the caesuras and then decide, line by line, where the most effective breaks occur—at the caesura or at the rhymes? Pace is very important in the reading of any poem, and it is often determined by what makes the reader stop as well as what makes him move along. The powerful phrase "thy slaughtered Saints" (1. 1) is the first deterrent to speed. Here the reader must remember that Italian Protestants had been murdered by the government of the Italian Piedmont at the instigation, hints Milton, of the Pope, "the triple tyrant" (1. 12), who resides in Rome or "Babylon." What other phrases determine the pace of the poem, either through the force of allusion or through historical fact? How do the myth of Cadmus and the Parable of the Sower (Matthew 13:8) contribute to the poem's meaning?

4. In Sonnet 19, both the allusion to the talent and other references, such as "Thousands" (of angels) in line 12, are clearly Biblical. What is the pun on "talent"? Noting seventeenth-century diction, distinguish what Milton meant by "fondly" and "prevent" (1. 8). Certain words have connotations beyond the context of the poem.

For example, what does Milton mean by "wait," the last word of the poem? In a short essay, explain how this choice of diction summarizes the theme (see p. 64) of the poem.

5. The allusion in Sonnet 23 is clear. Like the Biblical allusion in Sonnet 19, the directness and ease of reference is a counterbalance to Milton's intensely personal references, particularly to his blindness. The word "saint" here (l. 1) indicates simply one in heaven. If the "saint" is Milton's beloved second wife, Katherine Woodcock, the mention of "Purification" (l. 6) reveals the fact that both she and her son died in childbirth or shortly thereafter. Milton was blind when he married her, which may explain the description in line 9, although the context of the dream is important at all times in the poem. How important are these biographical details for understanding the sonnet? Could it be read successfully without them? Explain.

6. Describe the distinctive tone (see p. 65) in each of these sonnets. What dramatizes this tone for us? How is the tone of each sonnet consistent with its subject matter? Explain in an essay.

QUESTIONS – THE ROMANTICS

WILLIAM WORDSWORTH (1770–1850)

The World Is Too Much with Us

The world is too much with us; late and soon,
Getting and spending, we lay waste our powers:
Little we see in Nature that is ours;
We have given our hearts away, a sordid boon!
This Sea that bares her bosom to the moon;   5
The winds that will be howling at all hours,
And are up-gathered now like sleeping flowers;
For this, for everything, we are out of tune;
It moves us not.—Great God! I'd rather be
A Pagan suckled in a creed outworn;   10
So might I, standing on this pleasant lea,
Have glimpses that would make me less forlorn;
Have sight of Proteus rising from the sea;
Or hear old Triton blow his wreathèd horn.

boon (4): gift. *lea* (11): field.

1. Much has been written about the Romantic revolution in poetry that Wordsworth and others were so instrumental in achieving. This poem reflects that revolution on two levels: (1) in its subject matter and (2) in its return to the form of the sonnet. In the latter case, this return was to the personal voice of the seventeenth-century sonnets, not to the formalized figurative language of the earlier period. The subject of the Romantic sonnet is a spontaneous one, spontaneously perceived. In fact, almost all of the sonnets by the Romantic poets have specific titles, even specific dates. For these poets, the form of the sonnet presented an established means of personal utterance that was sanctioned by a truer past than the immediate past of the "mechanized" eighteenth century. Wordsworth's theme, the loss of vitality in the modern world, is also a Romantic one. How does the structure of the sonnet develop this theme? What is the relationship of the octet to the sestet? What is the effect of the interjection? Explain the evocation. Who were Proteus and Triton? What are the effects of these allusions? Do these Greek deities formalize and develop the qualities given in lines 5, 6, and 7? If so, how?

2. What is the rhyme scheme of the poem? How firmly is the prosody based on iambic pentameter? Show how Wordsworth's rhymes, metrical irregularities, and placement of caesura combine to approximate a conversational tone. Is the tone consistent with diction like "suckled" (1. 10) and "wreathèd" (1. 14)? Is the diction colloquial? Compare the sonnet with Milton's Sonnet 19 or Shakespeare's Sonnet 116. Is Wordsworth's more or less artificial? Explain in a short essay.

London, 1802

Milton! thou shouldst be living at this hour:
England hath need of thee: she is a fen
Of stagnant waters: altar, sword, and pen,
Fireside, the heroic wealth of hall and bower,
Have forfeited their ancient English dower   5
Of inward happiness. We are selfish men;
Oh! raise us up, return to us again;
And give us manners, virtue, freedom, power.
Thy soul was like a star, and dwelt apart;
Thou hadst a voice whose sound was like the sea: 10

Pure as the naked heavens, majestic, free,
So didst thou travel on life's common way,
In cheerful godliness; and yet thy heart
The lowliest duties on herself did lay.

Scorn Not the Sonnet

Scorn not the Sonnet; Critic, you have frowned,
Mindless of its just honours; with this key
Shakspeare unlocked his heart; the melody
Of this small lute gave ease to Petrarch's wound;
A thousand times this pipe did Tasso sound;   5
With it Camöens soothed an exile's grief;
The Sonnet glittered a gay myrtle leaf
Amid cypress with which Dante crowned
His visionary brow: a glow-worm lamp,
It cheered mild Spenser, called from Faeryland   10
To struggle through dark ways; and, when a damp
Fell round the path of Milton, in his hand
The Thing became a trumpet; whence he blew
Soul-animating strains—alas, too few!

PERCY BYSSHE SHELLEY (1792–1822)

Sonnet: England in 1819

An old, mad, blind, despised, and dying king,—
Princes, the dregs of their dull race, who flow
Through public scorn,—mud from a muddy spring,—
Rulers who neither see, nor feel, nor know,
But leech-like to their fainting country cling,   5
Till they drop, blind in blood, without a blow,—
A people starved and stabbed in the untilled field,—
An army, which liberticide and prey
Makes as a two-edged sword to all who wield
Golden and sanguine laws which tempt and slay;   10
Religion Christless, Godless—a book sealed;
A Senate,—Time's worst statute unrepealed,—
Are graves, from which a glorious Phantom may
Burst, to illumine our tempestuous day.

GEORGE GORDON, LORD BYRON (1788–1824)

Sonnet on Chillon

Eternal Spirit of the chainless Mind!
Brightest in dungeons, Liberty! thou art,
For there thy habitation is the heart—
The heart which love of thee alone can bind;
And when thy sons to fetters are consigned—   5
To fetters, and the damp vault's dayless gloom,
Their country conquers with their martyrdom,
And Freedom's fame finds wings on every wind.
Chillon! thy prison is a holy place,
And thy sad floor an altar—for 'twas trod,   10
Until his very steps have left a trace
Worn, as if thy cold pavement were a sod,
By Bonnivard!—May none those marks efface!
For they appeal from tyranny to God.

Chillon (title): a Swiss castle used as a political prison. *Bonnivard* (13): a controversial hero and ardent reformer who was imprisoned for six years at Chillon.

JOHN KEATS (1795–1821)

On First Looking into Chapman's Homer

Much have I travell'd in the realms of gold,
And many goodly states and kingdoms seen;
Round many western islands have I been
Which bards in fealty to Apollo hold.
Oft of one wide expanse had I been told   5
That deep-brow'd Homer ruled as his demesne;
Yet did I never breathe its pure serene
Till I heard Chapman speak out loud and bold:
Then felt I like some watcher of the skies
When a new planet swims into his ken;   10
Or like stout Cortez when with eagle eyes
He star'd at the Pacific—and all his men
Look'd at each other with a wild surmise—
Silent, upon a peak in Darien.

fealty (4): loyalty. *demesne* (6): country. *serene* (7): serenity.

1. While the Romantic poets may have neglected the rich rhetorical storehouse of the Renaissance poets, they certainly understood the nature of metaphor. Keats's sonnet on first reading a translation of Homer by the Renaissance poet George Chapman is a superb example of sustained metaphor. The two similes composing the clearly marked sestet are merely a tightening or formalization of the implicit metaphor dominating the octet. Distinguish and explain the tenor and vehicle of the octet's metaphor. What, for example, are "the realms of gold" (l. 1) and the "many western islands" (l. 3) that are "in fealty to Apollo" (l. 4)? What does "travell'd" mean in terms of the basic metaphor? Geographical discoveries in previous centuries had often been made for strict commercial purposes. How does the metaphor establish a truer relationship—at least according to Romantic teachings—between Wordsworth's "world" and "the realms of gold"? Where, says Keats, are the best discoveries?

2. This poem builds on a narrative like Shelley's "Ozymandias" (see p. 11), but it does not seem as fabled because of the two similes in the sestet. Even though Keats mistakenly substituted Cortez for Balboa, a sense of the real historical world included in Keats's own spiritual discovery is not lessened. How does this kind of allusion enlarge the experience of the poem? It is significant that both Wordsworth (in "The World Is Too Much with Us") and Keats use allusion at the end of their poems to create a picture for their readers; thus there is a moment of fixity at the end of both sonnets. Moreover, both present a picture obviously meant for meditation. So too is the final scene in "Ozymandias"—but what are the advantages of Wordsworth's more detailed mythological picture and Keats's historical one over Shelley's rather vague scene? What effect is Shelley aiming at?

3. The first verse of Keats's sonnet resembles in diction the conversational tone of a child's story. Is conversational diction maintained throughout? Explain. By marking the rhyme scheme, distinguish the sonnet form Keats has employed. To what extent is this form consistent with the control of the entire poem? Is Keats's sonnet more or less artificial than those of the Renaissance? Explain your answer in a long paragraph.

When I Have Fears

When I have fears that I may cease to be
Before my pen has glean'd my teeming brain,
Before high-piled books, in charact'ry,
Hold like rich garners the full ripen'd grain;
When I behold, upon the night's starr'd face,   5
Huge cloudy symbols of a high romance,
And think that I may never live to trace
Their shadows, with the magic hand of chance;
And when I feel, fair creature of an hour,
That I shall never look upon thee more,   10
Never have relish in the faery power
Of unreflecting love!—then on the shore
Of the wide world I stand alone, and think
Till Love and Fame to nothingness do sink.

Bright Star! Would I Were Steadfast as Thou Art

Bright star! would I were steadfast as thou art—
    Not in lone splendor hung aloft the night,
And watching, with eternal lids apart,
    Like nature's patient sleepless Eremite,
The moving waters at their priestlike task   5
    Of pure ablution round earth's human shores,
Or gazing on the new soft-fallen mask
    Of snow upon the mountains and the moors—
No—yet still steadfast, still unchangeable,
    Pillowed upon my fair love's ripening breast,   10
To feel for ever its soft fall and swell,
    Awake for ever in a sweet unrest,
Still, still to hear her tender-taken breath,
And so live ever—or else swoon to death.

Eremite (4): recluse.

EDGAR ALLAN POE (1809–49)

To Science

Science! true daughter of Old Time thou art!
　Who alterest all things with thy peering eyes.
Why preyest thou thus upon the poet's heart,
　Vulture, whose wings are dull realities?
How should he love thee? or how deem thee wise?　　5
　Who wouldst not leave him in his wandering
To seek for treasure in the jewelled skies,
　Albeit he soared with an undaunted wing?
Hast thou not dragged Diana from her car?
　And driven the Hamadryad from the wood　　10
To seek a shelter in some happier star?
　Hast thou not torn the Naiad from her flood,
The Elfin from the green grass, and from me
The summer dream beneath the tamarind tree?

HENRY WADSWORTH LONGFELLOW (1807–82)

Divina Commedia (I)

Oft have I seen at some cathedral door
A laborer, pausing in the dust and heat,
Lay down his burden, and with reverent feet
Enter, and cross himself, and on the floor
Kneel to repeat his paternoster o'er;　　5
Far off the noises of the world retreat;
The loud vociferations of the street
Become an undistinguishable roar.
So, as I enter here from day to day,
And leave my burden at this minster gate,　　10
Kneeling in prayer, and not ashamed to pray,
The tumult of the time disconsolate

To inarticulate murmurs dies away,
While the eternal ages watch and wait.

Milton

I pace the sounding sea-beach and behold
How the voluminous billows roll and run,
Upheaving and subsiding, while the sun
Shines through their sheeted emerald far unrolled,
And the ninth wave, slow gathering fold by fold   5
All its loose-flowing garments into one,
Plunges upon the shore, and floods the dun
Pale reach of sands, and changes them to gold.
So in majestic cadence rise and fall
The mighty undulations of thy song,   10
O sightless bard, England's Maeonides!
And ever and anon, high over all
Uplifted, a ninth wave superb and strong,
Floods all the soul with its melodious seas.

Maeonides (11) : Homer.

HENRY TIMROD (1828–67)

Most Men Know Love

Most men know love but as a part of life;
They hide it in some corner of the breast,
Even from themselves; and only when they rest
In the brief pauses of that daily strife,
Wherewith the world might else be not so rife,   5
They draw it forth (as one draws forth a toy
To soothe some ardent, kiss-exacting boy)
And hold it up to sister, child, or wife.
Ah me! why may not love and life be one?
Why walk we thus alone, when by our side,   10
Love, like a visible God, might be our guide?
How would the marts grow noble! and the street,
Worn like a dungeon-floor by weary feet,
Seem then a golden court-way of the Sun!

MATTHEW ARNOLD (1822–88)

Shakespeare

Others abide our question. Thou art free.
We ask and ask—Thou smilest and art still,
Out-topping knowledge. For the loftiest hill,
Who to the stars uncrowns his majesty,

Planting his steadfast footsteps in the sea,   5
Making the heaven of heavens his dwelling place,
Spares but the cloudy border of his base
To the foiled searching of mortality;
And thou, who didst the stars and sunbeams know,
Self-schooled, self-scanned, self-honored, self-secure,   10
Didst tread on earth unguessed at.—Better so!

All pains the immortal spirit must endure,
All weakness which impairs, all griefs which bow,
Find their sole speech in that victorious brow.

ELIZABETH BARRETT BROWNING (1806–61)

from Sonnets from the Portuguese (43)

How do I love thee? Let me count the ways.
I love thee to the depth and breadth and height
My soul can reach, when feeling out of sight
For the ends of Being and ideal Grace.
I love thee to the level of everyday's   5
Most quiet need, by sun and candle light.
I love thee freely, as men strive for Right;
I love thee purely, as they turn from Praise.
I love thee with the passion put to use
In my old griefs, and with my childhood's faith.   10
I love thee with a love I seemed to lose
With my lost saints—I love thee with the breath,
Smiles, tears, of all my life!—and, if God choose,
I shall but love thee better after death.

GEORGE MEREDITH (1828–1909)

Lucifer in Starlight

On a starred night Prince Lucifer uprose.
Tired of his dark dominion swung the fiend
Above the rolling ball in cloud part screened,
Where sinners hugged their spectre of repose.
Poor prey to his hot fit of pride were those.   5
And now upon his western wing he leaned,
Now his huge bulk o'er Afric's sands careened,
Now the black planet shadowed Arctic snows.
Soaring through wider zones that pricked his scars
With memory of the old revolt from Awe,   10
He reached a middle height, and at the stars,
Which are the brain of heaven, he looked, and sank.
Around the ancient track marched rank on rank,
The army of unalterable law.

GERARD MANLEY HOPKINS (1844–89)

God's Grandeur

The world is charged with the grandeur of God.
    It will flame out, like shining from shook foil;
    It gathers to a greatness, like the ooze of oil
Crushed. Why do men then now not reck his rod?
Generations have trod, have trod, have trod;   5
    And all is seared with trade; bleared, smeared with toil;
    And wears man's smudge and shares man's smell: the soil
Is bare now, nor can foot feel, being shod.

And for all this, nature is never spent;
    There lives the dearest freshness deep down things;   10
And though the last lights off the black West went
    Oh, morning, at the brown brink eastward, springs—
Because the Holy Ghost over the bent
    World broods with warm breast and with ah! bright wings.

1. What kinds of rhymes does Hopkins employ (see p. 56 ff.)?
How is the rhythm varied? Cite examples of assonance, alliteration,

and caesura. What cumulative effect do these devices create? Explain.

2. Hopkins greatly admired Milton, especially what he called Milton's "sequence of phrase." How might Milton's sonnets furnish a context for understanding "God's Grandeur," especially lines 4, 5, 13, and 14? In a short essay, relate the technical effects described in question one to your answer.

3. Hopkins was also remarkable for his original images. What is startling about the first two similes? How effective are these similes for establishing the meaning of the octet? Notice that much of the poem is composed of literal language. What effect does this create? Compare the language of this sonnet with Herbert's "Prayer (II)."

4. This sonnet is built on contrast. As with the early sonneteers, Hopkins marks his change in content with the natural break of the octet and sestet. What is the contrast in meaning? There are two kinds of renewal at the end of the poem. What are they?

5. On p. 63, you will find another sonnet by Hopkins. Does it have a similar theme of renewal? How does its theme differ from "God's Grandeur"? Compare in a long essay the themes of both sonnets by Hopkins with that of Wordsworth's "The World Is Too Much with Us." How does Hopkins' diction create a greater sense of renewal or change? Or does it? Would you consider Hopkins a Romantic poet? Why?

EDWIN ARLINGTON ROBINSON (1869–1935)

Credo

I cannot find my way: there is no star
In all the shrouded heavens anywhere;
And there is not a whisper in the air
Of any living voice but one so far
That I can hear it only as a bar   5
Of lost, imperial music, played when fair
And angel fingers wove, and unaware,
Dead leaves to garlands where no roses are.
No, there is not a glimmer, nor a call,
For one that welcomes, welcomes when he fears,   10
The black and awful chaos of the night;

For through it all—above, beyond it all—
I know the far-sent message of the years,
I feel the coming glory of the Light.

ROBERT FROST (1874–1963)

Mowing

There was never a sound beside the wood but one,
And that was my long scythe whispering to the ground.
What was it it whispered? I knew not well myself;
Perhaps it was something about the heat of the sun,
Something, perhaps, about the lack of sound—   5
And that was why it whispered and did not speak.
It was no dream of the gift of idle hours,
Or easy gold at the hand of fay or elf:
Anything more than the truth would have seemed too weak
To the earnest love that laid the swale in rows,   10
Not without feeble-pointed spikes of flowers
(Pale orchises), and scared a bright green snake.
The fact is the sweetest dream that labor knows
My long scythe whispered and left the hay to make.

make (14): dry.

CLAUDE McKAY (1891–1948)

The Negro's Tragedy

It is the Negro's tragedy I feel
Which binds me like a heavy iron chain,
It is the Negro's wounds I want to heal
Because I know the keenness of his pain,
Only a thorn-crowned Negro and no white   5
Can penetrate into the Negro's ken,
Or feel the thickness of the shroud of night
Which hides and buries him from other men.

So what I write is urged out of my blood.
There is no white man who could write my book,   10

Though many think their story should be told
Of what the Negro people ought to brook.
Our statesmen roam the world to set things right.
This Negro laughs and prays to God for light!

COUNTEE CULLEN (1903–46)

Yet Do I Marvel

I doubt not God is good, well-meaning, kind.
And did He stoop to quibble could tell why
The little buried mole continues blind,
Why flesh that mirrors Him must some day die,
Make plain the reason tortured Tantalus   5
Is baited by the fickle fruit, declare
If merely brute caprice dooms Sisyphus
To struggle up a never-ending stair.
Inscrutable His ways are, and immune
To catechism by a mind too strewn   10
With petty cares to slightly understand
What awful brain compels His awful hand.
Yet do I marvel at this curious thing:
To make a poet black, and bid him sing!

1. Both Claude McKay and Countee Cullen were Negro writers of the Harlem Renaissance during the early decades of this century. Unlike several other Negro writers associated with that movement (most notably, Langston Hughes), McKay and Cullen employed conventional poetic rhythms and forms. In the two sonnets above, each poet views a particular aspect of the black writer's dilemma in a white society. Compare the views in a short essay.

2. Cullen recognized Keats as a significant influence on his work. What devices characteristically employed by Keats in his sonnet "On First Looking into Chapman's Homer" are also employed by Cullen in "Yet Do I Marvel"? Do those devices intensify the personal, romantic tone of Cullen's sonnet? How? What purposes do the allusions serve? Does the poem follow a conventional sonnet rhyme scheme? Explain.

3. Compare the diction of the two sonnets by McKay and Cullen. How does the difference reinforce the distinct tones?

JOHN CROWE RANSOM (1888–)

Piazza Piece

—I am a gentleman in a dustcoat trying
To make you hear. Your ears are soft and small
And listen to an old man not at all,
They want the young men's whispering and sighing.
But see the roses on your trellis dying   5
And hear the spectral singing of the moon;
For I must have my lovely lady soon,
I am a gentleman in a dustcoat trying.

—I am a lady young in beauty waiting
Until my truelove comes, and then we kiss.   10
But what grey man among the vines is this
Whose words are dry and faint as in a dream?
Back from my trellis, Sir, before I scream!
I am a lady young in beauty waiting.

1. The theme of Death and the Maiden is very old, and it is often
viewed as a kind of wooing. This wooing and its dialogue remind us
of the Petrarchan sonnet which, ironically, this poem imitates in form.
The form, therefore, acts as a kind of irony within which the rest of
the poem operates. How does the use of rhyme, for example, drama-
tize the ironic situation of the poem? What is the thematic signifi-
cance of using feminine rhyme (see p. 57) in key lines?

2. The Southern locale of the poem (note the use of "piazza," the
old-fashioned Southern word for porch) adds to this irony and recalls
a whole tradition of modern literature. How does this sonnet, for
example, reflect an atmosphere similar to that of William Faulkner's
short story "A Rose for Emily"?

ALLEN TATE (1899–)

Sonnets at Christmas (II)

Ah, Christ, I love you rings to the wild sky
And I must think a little of the past:
When I was ten I told a stinking lie

That got a black boy whipped; but now at last
The going years, caught in an accurate glow,   5
Reverse like balls englished upon green baize—
Let them return, let the round trumpets blow
The ancient crackle of the Christ's deep gaze.
Deafened and blind, with senses yet unfound,
Am I, untutored to the after-wit   10
Of knowledge, knowing a nightmare has no sound;
Therefore with idle hands and head I sit
In late December before the fire's daze
Punished by crimes of which I would be quit.

1. In this sonnet Allen Tate also uses the Southern background in
that he makes a personal allusion to his Kentucky boyhood. How
does the allusion in the octet develop the final scene before the fire
in the sestet? What theme is developed? How does this personal
theme relate to the universal figure of Christ and the season?

2. Compare the tone of the speaking voice here with that in Rob-
ert Lowell's sonnet "The North Sea Undertaker's Complaint" (p.
55). Does the religious attitude in each produce joy in the speaker?
Why not? Which is more clearly a dramatic monologue (see p.
204)? Why? Both poems, like most modern poetry, use objects or
"things" to create a seemingly objective, even naturalistic world. How
do these "things" relate to the religious meditation of each speaker?
Explain in a short essay and then relate this "thingness" to the re-
ligious sonnets of Hopkins.

3. Line 6 has a startling simile. Explain it. What is its source?
What does its use here tell us about the persona's attitude toward his
"going years" (l. 5)? Compare this sonnet with Shakespeare's Son-
net 73 and note any similarities in theme. What are the differences?
Are there similarities to the devotional sonnets of the seventeenth
century? Compare and contrast in a short essay.

DYLAN THOMAS (1914–53)

Among Those Killed in the Dawn Raid Was a Man
Aged a Hundred

When the morning was waking over the war
He put on his clothes and stepped out and he died,

The locks yawned loose and a blast blew them wide,
He dropped where he loved on the burst pavement stone
And the funeral grains of the slaughtered floor.   5
Tell his street on its back he stopped a sun
And the craters of his eyes grew springshoots and fire
When all the keys shot from the locks, and rang.
Dig no more for the chains of his grey-haired heart.
The heavenly ambulance drawn by a wound   10
Assembling waits for the spades' ring on the cage.
O keep his bones away from that common cart,
The morning is flying on the wings of his age
And a hundred storks perch on the sun's right hand.

1. Here again is a contemporary subject—using the kind of specific title that the Romantics emphasized. Yet it finds its fullest expression, oddly enough, in the limitation of an old form. Thomas uses the sonnet's brevity and conciseness to express his grief over the death of the old man. Like Donne and Keats, Thomas gives an almost narrative account in the octet—a great deal of the language devoted to a literal description of the event itself. Identify this literal language, inverted though it may be. What is the basic dramatic situation of the poem?

2. Thomas' elaborate use of metaphor dominates the very pace of the poem. What, for example, is the meaning of "grey-haired heart" (1. 9) and the double meaning of "keys" (1. 8)? This kind of yoking together of images reminds us of the metaphysical sonnets. Cite other points of identity with the seventeenth century, especially with the associative imagery of "Prayer (I)."

3. In the final line there are clearly symbols or allusions that are not like Donne's metaphors or Herbert's images. How, for example, does the reference to the "hundred storks" or to "the sun's right hand" enlarge our experience of the death of the anonymous old man? The last three lines of the poem, in fact, constitute a shift in tone. They build in a kind of rhapsody that affirms the eternity of the old man. How do these allusions strengthen that affirmation?

Chapter 4

The Couplet

The *couplet,* two lines of verse in any meter rhyming *aa,* is one of the most obvious and recurrent rhyme schemes in English poetry. It is used principally in two contexts: as a form in long poetic compositions and as an integral part of other stanzaic forms, for example, ottava rima (see p. 331), rhyme royal (see p. 323), and the English sonnet (see p. 98). In these frameworks, poets as diverse in talent and theme as Chaucer, Shakespeare, Marlowe, Milton, Donne, Marvell, Butler, Dryden, Pope, Keats, Coleridge, and Browning have found the couplet usable.

CLOSED AND OPEN COUPLETS

Couplets fall into two generic classes: closed and open. A *closed couplet* is one in which the first line is grammatically unified (i.e., it consists of a complete modifier, a complete dependent phrase or clause, or a complete independent clause) and the second line is slowed or stopped at the end by major punctuation. Not only grammatically unified, a closed couplet also contains a complete thought which—though contributing to the total sense of the poem—is meaningful in itself. The following are examples of closed couplets:

Even I, a dunce of more renown than they,
Was sent before but to prepare thy way: (*Dryden*)

By thee was Pluto charm'd so well
While rapture seiz'd the sons of hell—   (*Freneau*)

And therefore I have sailed the seas and come
To the holy city of Byzantium.   (*Yeats*)

Each of these couplets demonstrates a different kind of grammatical unity. In the Dryden couplet, the first verse contains the subject and appositive phrase; the second, the verb and its modifiers. In the Freneau couplet, the first verse contains the independent main clause, while the second contains a dependent adverbial clause. And in the Yeats couplet, the first verse contains the subject and its two verbs, while the second contains a prepositional phrase used adverbially. Note too that each of the couplets, even though excerpted from a long poem, contains a complete and independent expression.

An *open couplet* contains neither a complete expression nor a complete syntactical unit. Rather, it depends on verses which precede and / or follow it to complete both its thought and the grammatical unit of which it is a part. When a poet employs this device, his couplets move from one into another through a series of enjambments (see p. 50). Since neither of the verses making up the couplet is necessarily end-stopped and since the rhyming syllables often occur in the middle of grammatical units, the rhyme scheme of the open couplet is less ostentatious than that of the closed. It provides unity and metrical pleasure, but does not detract from sense by forcefully calling attention to itself. The following are examples of open couplets:

Bifel that in that seson on a day,
In Southwerk at the Tabard as I lay
Redy to wenden on my pylgrimage
To Canterbury with ful devout corage,
At nyght was come into that hostelrye
Wel nyne and twenty in a compaignye,   (*Chaucer*)

That's my last Duchess painted on the wall,
Looking as if she were alive. I call
That piece a wonder, now: Frà Pandolf's hands
Worked busily a day, and there she stands.   (*Robert Browning*)

I, Deborah, in my long cloak of brown,
Like the small nightingale that dances down
The cherried boughs, creep to the doctor's bare
Booth . . . cold as ivy in the air, (*Edith Sitwell*)

THE HISTORY OF THE ENGLISH COUPLET

In English poetry, most couplets are either of tetrameter or pentameter length (see p. 49). Couplet form was employed in early European poetry, but its frequent use in English poetry did not come until the Anglo-Norman period (1066–1350). Though the tetrameter (sometimes called "short" or octosyllabic) couplet was not used widely until the seventeenth century, the pentameter couplet, used first by Chaucer as a major vehicle for his *Canterbury Tales*, has been used both frequently and successfully since the fifteenth century. In the late seventeenth and eighteenth centuries, indeed, it was the form most rigorously held to by poets who adhered to prescriptive prosodic theory and practice. Why, the reader may ask, did such a seemingly uncomplicated rhyme scheme achieve such popularity and success as a poetic form?

The popularity of the couplet may be explained partially by the fact that consecutive rhyme heightens or intensifies certain poetic tones and effects which neither alternate rhyme nor the absence of rhyme can properly do. Foremost among these effects is the mnemonic, or memory-assisting, character of the couplet. Since rhymes occur so close together, we tend to recall not only rhyming syllables, but also the grammatical units of which they are a part. The following lines are easily recalled not because they embody unusually original thought, but because the poet cast them in couplet form:

Double, double toil and trouble;
Fire burn and cauldron bubble. (*Shakespeare*)

True wit is nature to advantage dress'd,
What oft was thought, but ne'er so well express'd. (*Pope*)

Listen, my children, and you shall hear,
Of the midnight ride of Paul Revere, (*Longfellow*)

Combined with this mnemonic effect, the brevity of the couplet—leaving out the wordiness often cluttering other forms—leads to a unique aphoristic quality. Many of our best known adages and precepts appear in couplet form.

The juxtaposed rhymes of the couplet also render it useful for establishing antitheses. In most couplets the *pace* (i.e., speed with which a verse * may be read) of the first verse contrasts to some degree with that of the second. Note, for example, that monosyllables in the first verse of T. S. Eliot's couplet require a leisurely reading entirely inappropriate to the second verse:

> In the room the women come and go
> Talking of Michelangelo.

This contrasting pace—suggesting movement and countermovement—reinforces through sound association the presentation of thesis and antithesis, climax and anticlimax, comparison and contrast, and alternative reaction. Consider the following couplets:

> Spare diet is the cause love lasts,
> For surfeits sooner kill than fasts.   (*Suckling*)

> The dream is a cocktail at Sloppy Joe's—
> (Maybe—nobody knows.)   (*Langston Hughes*)

Suckling's couplet presents a contrast between man's emotional reaction to abstinence and to overindulgence; its verses contrast only slightly in pace because the monosyllables and terminal alliteration in the first verse tend to compensate for an extra syllable in the second. Hughes's couplet contrasts a striking affirmation in the first verse with a notable qualification in the second; the ten syllables in the first verse and six in the second cause a greater contrast in pace between his verses than is evident in Suckling's.

Since the couplet form is so often associated with eighteenth-century satire, philosophical verse, and *vers de société*, we often forget its potential as a vehicle for concentrated lyric effects. Nevertheless,

---

* The term *verse* denotes a single metrical line of poetry; however, it is also used loosely (some would say inaccurately) to denote a stanza of poetry and, less frequently, a short section of any writing (as the verses into which the chapters of the Bible are divided).

the form is much more versatile than we sometimes assume. In the Prologue to the *Canterbury Tales* and in many of the tales themselves, Chaucer (1343?–1400) used an open, five-stressed iambic couplet as a device for relating narrative. The form, characterized by numerous enjambments, permitted the narrative to flow from one verse to another without hindrance from metrical prescriptions. Though the form was popular in the fifteenth and sixteenth centuries, it underwent numerous mutations. In the poetry of Christopher Marlowe (1564–93), we witness not only mastery of blank verse, but also subtle innovations in two couplet forms: (1) the relatively end-stopped octosyllabic couplet (two of which compose his quatrains) in "The Passionate Shepherd to his Love" and (2) the iambic pentameter couplet (less open than Chaucer's) in "Hero and Leander." By comparing the following couplets from "The Passionate Shepherd" with a couplet by Thomas Dekker, a near contemporary of Marlowe, we may recognize a basic difference between the octosyllabic and the pentameter ideal:

> Come live with me, and be my love
> And we will all the pleasures prove
> That hills and valleys, dales and fields,
> Woods or steepy mountain yields.   (*Marlowe*)

> This age thinks better of a gilded fool
> Than of a threadbare saint in wisdom's school.   (*Dekker*)

In the two Marlowe couplets, there are—exclusive of articles and possessive pronouns—only one adjective and no adverbs, whereas in the single Dekker couplet there are an adverb and three adjectives. From this example, we may deduce what actually happens when an octosyllabic couplet is expanded to pentameter length: adjectives, adverbs, euphemisms, and—at times—circumlocutions provide the additional length. Thus the two types of couplet deal in different basic styles of language: the octosyllabic is more general and lean, since it cannot metrically afford the discrimination which modifiers provide, and the pentameter is more precise and subtle, since it can.

During the last half of the seventeenth century and throughout most of the eighteenth, the couplet experienced its greatest popularity in English poetry. Though Milton, Marvell, the "Metaphysical Poets" (Donne, Crashaw, Herbert), and others had used couplets either before or near the mid-seventeenth century, they failed to establish a dominant tradition which appealed to poets after the Restoration of Charles II (1660). Edmund Waller (1606–87), on the other hand, a parliamentarian and court poet who wrote panegyrics on such figures as Charles I and Oliver Cromwell, established that tradition. Turning from the metrical freedom in such poets as Donne and Marvell, Waller adopted the closed pentameter couplet—a form which eventually came to be called the *heroic couplet*. In the following couplets, the character of his innovation is evident:

> "You must sit down," says Love, "and taste my meat."
> So I did sit and eat. (*Herbert*)

> Though she were true,·when you met her,
> And last, till you write your letter,
>   Yet she
>   Will be
> False, ere I come, to two, or three. (*Donne*)

> Illustrious acts high raptures do infuse,
> And every conqueror creates a muse. (*Waller*)

> Madam, new years may well expect to find
> Welcome from you, to whom they are so kind; (*Waller*)

Note that the closed pentameter regularity in Waller contrasts vividly with Herbert, whose couplet joins pentameter and trimeter lines, and with Donne, whose couplet and triplet are in widely disparate meters.

When John Dryden (1631–1700) charged that the "excellence and dignity of rhyme were never fully known till Mr. Waller taught it" and Alexander Pope (1688–1744) judged poetry before Waller as "that former savagery," they dissociated themselves from the metrical experimentation characteristic of the early seventeenth century and epitomized a new mood. The closed pentameter couplet which they espoused earned the name "heroic couplet" because of its association with heroic and epic subjects, notably the heroic plays and translations of Homer and Virgil. In accordance with that association, the heroic couplet characteristically contains elevated diction, elaborate figures of speech, imaginative inversions, and bold use of allusions. The following excerpt from Dryden's "To the Memory of Mr. Oldham" is typical:

The History of the English Couplet 139

Farewel, too little and too lately known,
Whom I began to think and call my own;
For sure our Souls were near ally'd, and thine
Cast in the same Poetick mould as mine.
One common Note on either Lyre did strike,
And Knaves and Fools we both abhorr'd alike:
To the same Goal did both our Studies drive,
The last set out the soonest did arrive.
Thus *Nisus* fell upon the slippery place,
Whilst his young Friend perform'd and won the Race.

Because the heroic couplet was inextricably linked with elevated subject matter, it provided ample opportunities for the satirist. Specifically, the substitution of "low" subject matter into a metrical framework which itself suggested elegance created an ironic tone appropriate for satire. Note, for example, the irony resulting from Dryden's comic deflation of the poet Thomas Shadwell:

All human things are subject to decay,
And when Fate summons, monarchs must obey.
This Flecknoe found, who, like Augustus, young
Was call'd to empire, and had govern'd long:
In prose and verse, was own'd, without dispute,
Thro' all the realms of *Nonsense* absolute.

In the seventeenth century Samuel Butler (1600–80) published a long poem, *Hudibras*, which concerned various topical controversies of church and state. Not only did the poem contrast with earlier poets' treatment of these subjects by employing coarse imagery and diction; it also featured an original use of the couplet form which more closely filled Butler's needs than earlier traditions in couplet form would have done. The result was that English poetry inherited a new form: the *Hudibrastic couplet*. The Hudibrastic couplet is well suited for satire; its rapid octosyllabic pace, its feminine rhymes which often juxtapose incongruous words, its accents falling in ludicrous places—all provide an admirable union of sound and sense. That is, the laughably absurd sound of the poem reinforces the idea that the subject is itself absurd. The following excerpt from *Hudibras* illustrates how it contrasted with the heroic couplet:

He knew the seat of Paradise,
Could tell in what degree it lies,

And, as he was disposed, could prove it
Below the moon, or else above it;
What Adam dreamt of when his bride
Came from her closet in his side;
Whether the devil tempted her
By a High Dutch interpreter;
If either of them had a navel;
Who first made music malleable;
Whether the serpent at the Fall
Had cloven feet, or none at all.

After the mid-eighteenth century, the heroic couplet and the Hudibrastic couplet began to lose favor and eventually gave way to less restricted forms. Each might appear as a variation inserted into other metrical patterns, but poets in the nineteenth and twentieth centuries used them sparingly. Why did the heroic couplet, which achieved such eminence in its own time, lose ground so quickly and irrevocably? At least part of the explanation lies in the poetic needs of particular frames of mind and historical periods. After the mid-eighteenth century, poets who sought to achieve lyric effects and to present narrative or dramatic situations soon recognized limitations in the heroic couplet. Like multicolored bricks in an immense wall, couplets contributed to a cumulative effect yet also insisted on their own individual identities. Likewise, in long poems—especially those written by poets less gifted than Dryden and Pope—couplets presented a relatively undifferentiated quality which soon became boring. The obvious metrical response was the running or open couplet. In this form, the couplet became an important vehicle for Romantic, Victorian, and modern poems.

QUESTIONS – CHAUCER

GEOFFREY CHAUCER (1343?–1400)

from Prologue to the Canterbury Tales

Whan that Aprille with his shoures soote
The droghte of March hath perced to the roote,

And bathed every veyne in swich licour
Of which vertu engendred is the flour;
Whan Zephirus eek with his sweete breeth   5
Inspired hath in every holt and heeth
The tendre croppes, and the yonge sonne
Hath in the Ram his half cours yronne,
And smale fowles maken melodye,
That slepen al the nyght with open eye   10
(So priketh hem nature in hir corages):
Than longen folk to goon on pilgrymages,
And palmeres for to seken straunge strondes,
To ferne halwes, kouthe in sondry londes;
And specially from every shires ende   15
Of Engelond to Caunterbury they wende,
The holy blisful martir for to seke,
That hem hath holpen what that they were seeke.
     Bifel that, in that sesoun on a day,
In Southwerk at the Tabard as I lay   20
Redy to wenden on my pilgrymage
To Caunterbury with ful devout corage,
At nyght was come into that hostelrye
Wel nyne and twenty in a compaignye,
Of sondry folk, by aventure yfalle   25
In felaweshipe, and pilgrymes were they alle,
That toward Caunterbury wolden ryde.
The chambres and the stables weren wyde,
And wel we weren esed atte beste.
And shortly, whan the sonne was to reste,   30
So hadde I spoken with hem everichon,
That I was of hir felaweshipe anon,
And made forward erly for to ryse,
To take oure wey ther as I yow devyse.
     But nathelees, whil I have tyme and space,   35
Er that I ferther in this tale pace,
Me thynketh it acordant to resoun
To telle yow al the condicioun
Of ech of hem, so as it semed me,
And whiche they weren, and of what degree,   40
And eek in what array that they were inne:
And at a Knyght than wol I first bigynne.

---

soote (1): sweet. *swich* (3): such. *Zephirus* (5): the West Wind. *eek* (5): also.
Ram (8): the zodiacal sign of the constellation Aries. *priketh* (11): inspires.

hem (11): them. *palmeres* (13): pilgrims who have been to Jerusalem. *straunge strondes* (13): foreign shores. *ferne halwes* (14): distant shrines. *kouthe* (14): known. *shires* (15): counties. *wende* (16): go. *martir* (17): St. Thomas à Becket. *holpen* (18): help. *hostelrye* (23): inn. *esed* (29): treated. *everichon* (31): every one. *devyse* (34): relate.

1. This selection from the "Prologue" is an expository passage that precedes a series of character sketches. What function does this exposition serve? Summarize in a long paragraph the details furnished by the passage.

2. Describe Chaucer's pentameter couplet. Are the couplets primarily open or closed? Put an "x" by each couplet which you judge to be closed; then state the *complete thought* which each contains. In the open couplets, do rhymes usually occur at the end or in the middle of syntactical units?

QUESTIONS – MARLOWE • DONNE

CHRISTOPHER MARLOWE (1564–93)

The Passionate Shepherd to His Love

Come live with me and be my Love,
And we will all the pleasures prove
That valleys, groves, hills, and fields,
Woods, or steepy mountains yields.

And we will sit upon the rocks   5
Seeing the shepherds feed their flocks,
By shallow rivers, to whose falls
Melodious birds sing madrigals.

And I will make thee beds of roses,
And a thousand fragrant posies,   10
A cap of flowers, and a kirtle
Embroidered all with leaves of myrtle;

A gown made of the finest wool,
Which from our pretty lambs we pull;

Fair linèd slippers for the cold,   15
With buckles of the purest gold;

A belt of straw and ivy buds
With coral clasps and amber studs:
And if these pleasures may thee move,
Come live with me, and be my Love.   20

The shepherd swains shall dance and sing
For thy delight each May morning:
If these delights thy mind may move,
Then live with me and be my Love.

kirtle (11): dress.

JOHN DONNE (1573–1631)

The Bait

Come live with me, and be my love,
And we will some new pleasures prove
Of golden sands, and crystal brooks:
With silken lines, and silver hooks.

There will the river whispering run   5
Warm'd by thy eyes, more than the Sun;
And there the enamour'd fish will stay,
Begging themselves they may betray.

When thou wilt swim in that live bath,
Each fish, which every channel hath,   10
Will amorously to thee swim,
Gladder to catch thee, than thou him.

If thou to be so seen be'st loath
By Sun, or Moon, thou dark'nest both,
And if myself have leave to see,   15
I need not their light, having thee.

Let others freeze with angling reeds,
And cut their legs with shells and weeds,

Or treacherously poor fish beset,
With strangling snare, or windowy net: 20

Let coarse bold hands, from slimy nest
The bedded fish in banks out-wrest;
Or curious traitors, sleave-silk flies,
Bewitch poor fishes' wand'ring eyes.

For thee, thou need'st no such deceit,   25
For thou thyself art thine own bait;
That fish that is not catch'd thereby,
Alas, is wiser far than I.

The Flea

Mark but this flea, and mark in this
How little that which thou deny'st me is;
Me it suck'd first, and now sucks thee,
And in this flea our two bloods mingled be;
Confess it: this cannot be said   5
A sin, or shame, or loss of maidenhead;
   Yet this enjoys before it woo,
    And pamper'd swells with one blood made of two,
   And this, alas, is more than we would do.

Oh stay, three lives in one flea spare,   10
Where we almost, nay, more than married are.
This flea is you and I, and this
Our marriage bed, and marriage temple is;
Though parents grudge, and you, we're met
And cloister'd in these living walls of jet.   15
   Though use make you apt to kill me,
    Let not to that, self-murder added be,
   And sacrilege, three sins in killing three.

Cruel and sudden, hast thou since
Purpled thy nail in blood of innocence?   20
In what could this flea guilty be,
Except in that drop which it suck'd from thee?
Yet thou triumph'st, and say'st that thou
Find'st not thyself, nor me, the weaker now:

'Tis true; then learn how false fears be: 25
Just so much honour, when thou yield'st to me,
Will waste, as this flea's death took life from thee.

1. In each of these three poems the couplet is used as an integral part of a stanzaic form. Marlowe's quatrains (see p. 304) are composed of two relatively end-stopped octosyllabic couplets, as are Donne's in "The Bait." In "The Flea," each of Donne's stanzas is composed of three couplets and a triplet (see p. 294). With specific reference to these poems, would you agree with the assertion made in this chapter (p. 138) that the octosyllabic couplet is more general and lean than the pentameter couplet? Explain.

2. Many poems were written in reply to Marlowe's "Passionate Shepherd to His Love." Donne's "The Bait" is one of them. How do the two poems differ in tone (see p. 65)? Which seems to you more sincere? Does the difference in imagery help to establish a difference in tone? Explain in a long paragraph.

3. "The Flea" is one of the best examples of "metaphysical" poetry to be found in literature (see p. 111). This kind of poetry tended to work toward the brevity of an epigram and therefore used the couplet, particularly the octosyllabic, as a form that would express, according to Dr. Johnson, "the most heterogeneous ideas . . . by violence yoked together." Is such "violence" evidenced in the two parts of the metaphor here? To what is the flea compared? Is there a persuasive or argumentative purpose here? What would you call the progression (see p. 36) of this poem? Does the tightness in the rhymes of the couplets, opening to the freedom of the triplets, help this progression? Explain in a paragraph.

HENRY VAUGHAN (1622–95)

The World

I saw Eternity the other night,
Like a great Ring of pure and endless light,

All calm, as it was bright;
And round beneath it, Time in hours, days, years,
  Driven by the spheres,   5
Like a vast shadow moved: in which the world
  And all her train were hurled.
The doting lover in his quaintest strain
  Did there complain;
Near him, his lute, his fancy, and his flights,   10
  Wit's sour delights,
With gloves, and knots, the silly snares of pleasure,
  Yet his dear treasure,
All scattered lay, while he his eyes did pore
  Upon a flower.   15

The darksome statesman, hung with weights and woe,
Like a thick midnight-fog, moved there so slow,
  He did not stay, nor go;
Condemning thoughts—like sad eclipses—scowl
  Upon his soul,   20
And clouds of crying witnesses without
  Pursued him with one shout.
Yet digged the mole, and lest his ways be found,
  Worked under ground,
Where he did clutch his prey; but one did see   25
  That policy;
Churches and altars fed him; perjuries
  Were gnats and flies;
It rained about him blood and tears; but he
  Drank them as free.   30

The fearful miser on a heap of rust
Sate pining all his life there, did scarce trust
  His own hands with the dust,
Yet would not place one piece above, but lives
  In fear of thieves.   35
Thousands there were as frantic as himself
  And hugged each one his pelf;
The downright epicure placed heaven in sense,
  And scorned pretence;
While others, slipped into a wide excess,   40
  Said little less;
The weaker sort slight, trivial wares enslave,
  Who think them brave;

The History of the English Couplet

And poor, despisèd Truth sat counting by
    Their victory.   45

Yet some, who all this while did weep and sing,
And sing, and weep, soared up into the Ring;
    But most would use no wing.
O fools (said I) thus to prefer dark night
    Before true light!   50
To live in grots and caves, and hate the day
    Because it shows the way,
The way, which from this dead and dark abode
    Leads up to God,
A way where you might tread the sun, and be   55
    More bright than he.
But as I did their madness so discuss,
    One whispered thus,
"This Ring the Bridegroom did for none provide,
    But for His bride."   60

John, Cap. 2, Ver. 16, 17.

*All that is in the world, the lust of the flesh, the lust of the eyes, and
the pride of life, is not of the father, but is of the world.*

*And the world passeth away, and the lusts thereof, but he that doth
the will of God abideth for ever.*

1. This poem is also metaphysical, but its subject—instead of seduc-
tion—is religious. Look back to Chapter 3 and the discussion of
John Donne's "Holy Sonnets" to see how religious poetry can also
be metaphysical. Here, as in "The Flea," the use of the couplet
varies with the triplet to bring forth a particular experience, and
once more the form liberates the experience. What is the relation-
ship of the triplet beginning each stanza to the couplets in each?
How does this differ from Donne's use of the couplets?

2. The poem begins with a striking statement and two elaborate
similes. Explain the extended similes that begin in lines 2 and 6. Do
they seem to fit Dr. Johnson's definition for metaphysical poetry (see
p. 146)? What is the major contrast in the poem? Explain in a long
paragraph.

3. How does the contrasting pace (see p. 137) of the two verses
that comprise Vaughan's couplets contribute to the development of

the poem's basic theme? Does sound association reinforce his presentation of thesis and antithesis? climax and anticlimax? comparison and contrast? alternative reaction? Explain. By scanning the first fifteen lines of the poem, describe the particular contrast in pace that exists.

4. Does the poem maintain the level of the brilliant image at the beginning? Compare the images at the beginning and at the end of the poem. Is the quality of the couplets also uneven? Does this relationship of form and content affect the total experience of the poem? Explain your answer in a short essay, using both "The Flea" and "The World" as illustrations of your answers.

5. "The World" is a striking example of the metrical freedom and restriction simultaneously imposed by pentameter couplets. How metrically regular are these couplets? Does Vaughan take greater metrical liberties in the first or second verse of his couplets? How do these couplets contrast, for example, with Marlowe's in "The Passionate Shepherd to His Love" (p. 143)?

QUESTIONS – DRYDEN

JOHN DRYDEN (1631–1700)

Prologue to Aureng-Zebe

> Our author, by experience, finds it true,
> 'Tis much more hard to please himself than you;
> And out of no feign'd modesty, this day
> Damns his laborious trifle of a play:
> Not that it's worse than what before he writ, 5
> But he has now another taste of wit;
> And, to confess a truth, (though out of time,)
> Grows weary of his long-lov'd mistress, Rhyme.
> Passion's too fierce to be in fetters bound,
> And nature flies him like enchanted ground. 10
> What verse can do, he has perform'd in this,
> Which he presumes the most correct of his;
> But spite of all his pride, a secret shame
> Invades his breast at Shakespeare's sacred name:

Aw'd when he hears his godlike Romans rage,   15
He, in a just despair, would quit the stage;
And to an age less polish'd, more unskill'd,
Does, with disdain, the foremost honours yield.
As with the greater dead he dares not strive,
He would not match his verse with those who live: 20
Let him retire, betwixt two ages cast,
The first of this, and hindmost of the last.
A losing gamester, let him sneak away;
He bears no ready money from the play.
The fate which governs poets thought it fit   25
He should not raise his fortunes by his wit.
The clergy thrive, and the litigious bar;
Dull heroes fatten with the spoils of war:
All southern vices, Heav'n be prais'd, are here;
But wit's a luxury you think too dear.   30
When you to cultivate the plant are loath,
'Tis a shrewd sign 'twas never of your growth;
And wit in northern climates will not blow,
Except, like orange trees, 'tis hous'd from snow.
There needs no care to put a playhouse down,   35
'Tis the most desert place of all the town:
We and our neighbours, to speak proudly, are
Like monarchs, ruin'd with expensive war;
While, like wise English, unconcern'd you sit,
And see us play the tragedy of wit.   40

1. In 1675 Dryden produced *Aureng-Zebe*, the last of several rhymed heroic plays which he wrote during the dramatic revival which followed the Restoration of Charles II (1660). In the "Prologue" here reprinted, what attitude does Dryden express toward his "long-lov'd mistress, Rhyme" (l. 8)? What is the significance of his reflection on the relationship between passionate subject matter and the metrical prescription of rhyme (l. 9)? Does the rest of the "Prologue" clarify that reflection? Explain.

2. Disregarding the fact that the "Prologue" is composed of closed pentameter couplets, what characteristics of diction, figurative language, syntax, and allusions suggest that these are heroic couplets? Explain.

3. Compare and contrast Dryden's couplets with those employed by Vaughan in "The World." What virtue does Dryden derive from

the extra syllables at his command? Does he sacrifice anything? Explain.

4. How does the pace of Dryden's couplets differ from that in "The World"? Scan verses 1–10. How regular are the pentameter couplets? Does placement of caesura provide adequate metrical contrast? What is the effect of metrical regularity (or irregularity) in this poem?

from Mac Flecknoe

All human things are subject to decay,
And when Fate summons, monarchs must obey,
This Flecknoe found, who, like Augustus, young
Was call'd to empire, and had govern'd long:
In prose and verse, was own'd, without dispute,   5
Thro' all the realms of *Nonsense,* absolute.
This aged prince, now flourishing in peace,
And blest with issue of a large increase,
Worn out with business, did at length debate
To settle the succession of the State;   10
And, pond'ring which of all his sons was fit
To reign, and wage immortal war with wit,
Cried: " 'T is resolv'd; for Nature pleads, that he
Should only rule, who most resembles me.
Sh—— alone my perfect image bears,   15
Mature in dulness from his tender years:
Sh—— alone of all my sons is he
Who stands confirm'd in full stupidity,
The rest to some faint meaning make pretense,
But Sh—— never deviates into sense.   20
Some beams of wit on other souls may fall,
Strike thro', and make a lucid interval;
But Sh——'s genuine night admits no ray,
His rising fogs prevail upon the day.
Besides, his goodly fabric fills the eye,   25
And seems design'd for thoughtless majesty:
Thoughtless as monarch oaks that shade the plain,
And, spread in solemn state, supinely reign.

Mac Flecknoe (title): son of Flecknoe, that is, Richard Flecknoe, a terrible poet and playwright who had recently died. *Sh——* (15): Thomas Shadwell, a poet and playwright who was a contemporary of Dryden.

1. "Mac Flecknoe" is subtitled "A Satire upon the True-Blue-Protestant Poet, T[homas]. S[hadwell]." The form of the poem is that of the mock heroic. Why are heroic couplets, since they are usually associated with elevated subject matter, particularly appropriate for satire? For example, why are the first six lines of the poem satirically effective?

2. If "Mac Flecknoe" is a mock heroic, what characteristics usually associated with the heroic couplet are mocked in this excerpt?

QUESTIONS – SWIFT

JONATHAN SWIFT (1667–45)

On Critics
In Imitation of Anacreon

Let 'em Censure: what care I?
The Herd of Criticks I defie.
Let the Wretches know, I write
Regardless of their Grace, or Spight.
No, no: the Fair, the Gay, the Young   5
Govern the Numbers of my Song.
All that They approve is sweet:
And All is Sense, that They repeat.
  Bid the warbling Nine retire:
Venus, String thy Servant's Lyre: 10
Love shall be my endless Theme:
Pleasure shall triumph over Fame:
And when these Maxims I decline,
Apollo, may Thy Fate be Mine:
May I grasp at empty Praise;   15
And lose the Nymph, to gain the Bays.

Numbers (6): metrical rhythm. *Bays* (16): a token of honor for poets.

A Description of the Morning

Now hardly here and there an hackney-coach
Appearing, showed the ruddy morn's approach.

Now Betty from her master's bed had flown,
And softly stole to discompose her own;
The slip-shod 'prentice from his master's door   5
Had pared the dirt, and sprinkled round the floor.
Now Moll had whirled her mop with dexterous airs,
Prepared to scrub the entry and the stairs.
The youth with broomy stumps began to trace
The kennel-edge, where wheels had worn the place.   10
The small-coal man was heard with cadence deep,
Till drowned in shriller notes of chimney-sweep:
Duns at his lordship's gate began to meet;
And brickdust Moll had screamed through half the street.
The turnkey now his flock returning sees.   15
Duly let out a-nights to steal for fees:
The watchful bailiffs take their silent stands,
And schoolboys lag with satchels in their hands.

1. Compare the kind of couplets used by Swift in "On Critics" with that in "A Description of the Morning." What different effects do they create?

2. Compare the diction employed in the two poems. How does the diction affect the tone?

3. In "A Description of the Morning," how effective is Swift's imagery?

QUESTIONS – BROWNING AND THE MODERNS

Each of the following poems is in couplets; yet the form here reveals liberties (or, at least, differences) that distinguish it from the earlier couplets illustrated in this section. "My Last Duchess" is a dramatic monologue (see p. 204), and it is perhaps the most outstanding nineteenth-century success in couplet form. The remaining four poems reveal the modern poet's use of couplet form. As you read the poems, note characteristics of the couplets that distinguish them from their predecessors in English literature. At the same time, note differences in diction, imagery, tone, and theme.

ROBERT BROWNING (1812–89)

My Last Duchess

FERRARA

That's my last Duchess painted on the wall,
Looking as if she were alive. I call
That piece a wonder, now: Frà Pandolf's hands
Worked busily a day, and there she stands.
Will't please you sit and look at her? I said   5
"Frà Pandolf" by design, for never read
Strangers like you that pictured countenance,
The depth and passion of its earnest glance,
But to myself they turned (since none puts by
The curtain I have drawn for you, but I)   10
And seemed as they would ask me, if they durst,
How such a glance came there; so, not the first
Are you to turn and ask thus. Sir, 'twas not
Her husband's presence only, called that spot
Of joy into the Duchess' cheek; perhaps   15
Frà Pandolf chanced to say, "Her mantle laps
Over my lady's wrist too much," or "Paint
Must never hope to reproduce the faint
Half-flush that dies along her throat": such stuff
Was courtesy, she thought, and cause enough   20
For calling up that spot of joy. She had
A heart—how shall I say?—too soon made glad,
Too easily impressed: she liked whate'er
She looked on, and her looks went everywhere.
Sir, 'twas all one! My favour at her breast,   25
The dropping of the daylight in the West,
The bough of cherries some officious fool
Broke in the orchard for her, the white mule
She rode with round the terrace—all and each
Would draw from her alike the approving speech,   30
Or blush, at least. She thanked men,—good! but thanked
Somehow—I know not how—as if she ranked
My gift of a nine-hundred-years-old name
With anybody's gift. Who'd stoop to blame
This sort of trifling? Even had you skill   35
In speech—(which I have not)—to make your will
Quite clear to such an one, and say, "Just this

Or that in you disgusts me; here you miss,
Or there exceed the mark"—and if she let
Herself be lessoned so, nor plainly set   40
Her wits to yours, forsooth, and made excuse,
—E'en then would be some stooping; and I choose
Never to stoop. Oh sir, she smiled, no doubt,
Whene'er I passed her; but who passed without
Much the same smile? This grew; I gave commands;   45
Then all smiles stopped together. There she stands
As if alive. Will't please you rise? We'll meet
The company below, then. I repeat,
The Count your master's known munificence
Is ample warrant that no just pretence   50
Of mine for dowry will be disallowed;
Though his fair daughter's self, as I avowed
At starting, is my object. Nay, we'll go
Together down, sir. Notice Neptune, though,
Taming a sea-horse, thought a rarity,   55
Which Claus of Innsbruck cast in bronze for me!

Ferrara (subtitle): After the untimely death of his young first wife, the Duke of
Ferrara began bargaining through an agent to marry the niece of a prominent
nobleman. In this poem, the Duke is speaking to the agent of the Count, who is
the father of his potential bride. *Frà Pandolf* (3): a painter. *Claus of Innsbruck*
(56): a sculptor.

1. Describe the tone of the poem. How does the contrast between
the Duke's view of himself and the reader's view of him contribute
to establishing tone? In the dramatic situation, how does the Duke's
apparent intention—his relationship to his audience—furnish a con-
text in which the poem's tone must be judged? Answer these ques-
tions in a brief essay.

2. Describe the mode of progression (see p. 36) in the poem. Is
the mode uninterrupted, or are there digressions? How does the
dramatic situation explain any digressions that may appear?

3. How do the open couplets contribute to the increasing emo-
tional tempo in the poem? Do the enjambments contribute to that
tempo? How do caesura and the contrasting pace of the couplets aid
in characterizing the Duke? Write a long essay answering these ques-
tions.

4. Compare "My Last Duchess" with Robinson's "The Prodigal
Son" (p. 157). Are both dramatic monologues? Are the two poets

equally adept at evoking a dramatic scene? Explain. Does the effect of Browning's poem result from the mere revelation of a single mind —as in any monologue—or from the tension created by a dramatic situation? What of Robinson's poem? How closely do Robinson's couplets resemble Browning's? Do they function with equal effectiveness in liberating the subject? Explain in a brief essay.

RUPERT BROOKE (1887–1915)

Heaven

Fish (fly-replete, in depth of June
Dawdling away their wat'ry noon)
Ponder deep wisdom, dark or clear,
Each secret fishy hope or fear.
Fish say, they have their Stream and Pond;   5
But is there anything Beyond?
This life cannot be All, they swear,
For how unpleasant, if it were!
One may not doubt that, somehow, good
Shall come of Water and of Mud;   10
And, sure, the reverent eye must see
A Purpose in Liquidity.
We darkly know, by Faith we cry,
The future is not Wholly Dry.
Mud unto Mud!—Death eddies near—   15
Not here the appointed End, not here!
But somewhere, beyond Space and Time,
Is wetter water, slimier slime!
And there (they trust) there swimmeth One
Who swam ere rivers were begun,   20
Immense, of fishy form and mind,
Squamous, omnipotent, and kind;
And under that Almighty Fin
The littlest fish may enter in.
Oh! never fly conceals a hook,   25
Fish say, in the Eternal Brook,
But more than mundane weeds are there,
And mud, celestially fair;
Fat caterpillars drift around,
And Paradisal grubs are found;   30

Unfading moths, immortal flies,
And the worm that never dies.
And in that Heaven of all their wish,
There shall be no more land, say fish.

EDWIN ARLINGTON ROBINSON (1869–1935)

The Prodigal Son

You are not merry, brother. Why not laugh,
As I do, and acclaim the fatted calf?
For, unless ways are changing here at home,
You might not have it if I had not come.
And were I not a thing for you and me   5
To execrate in anguish, you would be
As indigent a stranger to surprise,
I fear, as I was once, and as unwise.
Brother, believe as I do, it is best
For you that I'm again in the old nest—   10
Draggled, I grant you, but your brother still,
Full of good wine, good viands, and good will.
You will thank God, some day, that I returned,
And may be singing for what you have learned,
Some other day; and one day you may find   15
Yourself a little nearer to mankind.
And having hated me till you are tired,
You will begin to see, as if inspired,
It was fate's way of educating us.
Remembering then when you were venomous,   20
You will be glad enough that I am gone,
But you will know more of what's going on;
For you will see more of what makes it go,
And in more ways than are for you to know.
We are so different when we are dead,   25
That you, alive, may weep for what you said;
And I, the ghost of one you could not save,
May find you planting lentils on my grave.

LANGSTON HUGHES (1902-67)

Havana Dreams

The dream is a cocktail at Sloppy Joe's—
(Maybe—nobody knows.)

The dream is the road to Batabano.
(But nobody knows if that is so.)

Perhaps the dream is only her face—
Perhaps it's a fan of silver lace—
Or maybe the dream's a Vedado rose—
(*Quien sabe?* Who really knows?)

ROBERT FROST (1874-1963)

The Tuft of Flowers

I went to turn the grass once after one
Who mowed it in the dew before the sun.

The dew was gone that made his blade so keen
Before I came to view the leveled scene.

I looked for him behind an isle of trees;   5
I listened for his whetstone on the breeze.

But he had gone his way, the grass all mown,
And I must be, as he had been,—alone,

"As all must be," I said within my heart,
"Whether they work together or apart."   10

But as I said it, swift there passed me by
On noiseless wing a bewildered butterfly,

Seeking with memories grown dim o'er night
Some resting flower of yesterday's delight.

And once I marked his flight go round and round,   15
As where some flower lay withering on the ground.

And then he flew as far as eye could see,
And then on tremulous wing came back to me.

I thought of questions that have no reply,
And would have turned to toss the grass to dry;   20

But he turned first, and led my eye to look
At a tall tuft of flowers beside a brook,

A leaping tongue of bloom the scythe had spared
Beside a reedy brook the scythe had bared.

I left my place to know them by their name,   25
Finding them butterfly-weed when I came.

The mower in the dew had loved them thus,
By leaving them to flourish, not for us,

Nor yet to draw one thought of ours to him,
But from sheer morning gladness at the brim.   30

The butterfly and I had lit upon,
Nevertheless, a message from the dawn,

That made me hear the wakening birds around,
And hear his long scythe whispering to the ground,

And feel a spirit kindred to my own;   35
So that henceforth I worked no more alone;

But glad with him, I worked as with his aid,
And weary, sought at noon with him the shade;

And dreaming, as it were, held brotherly speech
With one whose thought I had not hoped to reach.   40

"Men work together," I told him from the heart,
"Whether they work together or apart."

Chapter 5

Blank Verse: The Drama

Blank verse is the common term for unrhymed iambic pentameter. The following excerpt from Shakespeare's *Richard III* illustrates regular blank verse:

> Wh̆y dŏ | yŏu lóok | ŏn ús, | ănd sháke | yŏur héad, |
> Ănd cáll | ŭs ŏr|phăns, wrĕt|chĕs, cást|ăwáys, |
> Ĭf thăt | ŏur nó|blĕ fá|thĕr wĕre | ălíve? |

In terms of sheer volume, it is the dominant metrical form in English poetry. A recent writer on poetic meter, for example, estimates that "about three-quarters of all English poetry is in blank verse." * Moreover, in almost every period of English poetry some of the greatest achievements have been in blank verse. These include the dramas of the Shakespearean era, Milton's *Paradise Lost* (1667), Wordsworth's *Prelude* (1804–05, 1850), Browning's *Ring and the Book* (1869), Frost's "Birches" (1916), and Stevens' "Sunday Morning" (1923).

Such a combination of volume and excellence suggests a strong correlation between English used in intensified utterance (one essential feature of poetry) and the nature of blank verse. This conclu-

---

* Paul Fussell, Jr., *Poetic Meter and Poetic Form* (New York: Random House, 1965), p. 75.

sion is reinforced by a suggestive coincidence: blank verse, which as such dominated the greatest period of English national expression—poetic drama in the late sixteenth and early seventeenth centuries—can still be found lurking in the pages of those nineteenth and twentieth-century novelists (e.g., Dickens, Melville, Faulkner, and Thomas Wolfe) who especially strove for effects through a highly rhetorical prose.

What is the secret of this pervasive dominance? Why, for example, did blank verse become the medium for an unrivaled poetic achievement within a half-century of its introduction to England? The answers lie partially in the nature of the form itself. But to understand the form we should first know something of its development.

BEGINNINGS OF BLANK VERSE IN ENGLISH

Not until the middle of the sixteenth century (in 1554) did the first example of unrhymed pentameter verse appear in England. In that year the Earl of Surrey published a blank verse translation of Book IV of Virgil's *Aeneid*. Seven years later the first English drama in blank verse, *The Tragedy of Gorbodoc*, was performed. Here is a passage from that historically important play, in which Philander, an aged counselor, argues for the division of Gorboduc's kingdom between his two sons:

> The mo the stronger, if they gree in one.
> The smaller compass that the realm doth hold,
> The easier is the sway thereof to weld
> The nearer justice to the wronged poor,
> The smaller charge, and yet enough for one.   (I. ii.)

mo (1): more. *gree* (1): agree. *weld* (3): wield.

In this very stiff and extraordinarily regular blank verse (for discussion of metrical monotony, see p. 54), every line contains exactly ten syllables and every foot is accented on the second syllable. Furthermore, unlike the passage from Shakespeare cited above, the lack of flow within and between the lines is quite noticeable. Indeed, the metrical monotony of *Gorboduc* suggests nothing so much as that the two men who collaborated on it (Thomas Sackville and Thomas

Norton) wrote as if they were composing rhymed pentameter couplets and simply dispensing with the rhyme.

The tentative use of blank verse in *Gorboduc* reveals a striking feature of the form. Because it fails to rhyme, blank verse departed (and in a sense still departs) from certain common assumptions about the nature of poetry written in English. Rhyme *is* one of our more or less automatic associations with the term *poetry*. For that reason, Dr. Johnson could approve the remark of a friend that "blank verse seems to be verse only to the eye" and then go on to add in his own voice: "Poetry may subsist without rhyme, but English poetry will not often please; nor can rhyme ever be safely spared but when the subject is able to support itself. Blank verse . . . has neither the easiness of prose nor the melody of numbers [that is, what Dr. Johnson would consider "true" verse], and therefore tires by long continuance." That Dr. Johnson is wrong—and, in fact, outrageously wrong, as perhaps only a great critic can be—is not the point. Rather, he ironically implies the great virtue of blank verse: through its very failure to rhyme, it has a potential freedom from conspicuous artifice that may explain its dominant role in English poetry, especially that written for the stage. By departing from the "bondage of rhyming" (to use Milton's phrase), blank verse may attain a greater naturalness and flexibility than forms confined by rhyme; moreover, it may sound like the flow of ordinary speech, while at the same time keeping the potential for statements far more intense.

THE INCREASE OF ACCENTUAL VARIATION

As we have seen in its first appearance in *Gorboduc*, blank verse was neither flexible nor intense. Here, however, is a contrasting passage from *Tamburlaine the Great*, Part I (1587), written by Christopher Marlowe, the first great poet to use blank verse for the stage:

> I hold | the Fates | bound fast | in i|ron chains, |
> And with | my hand | turn For|tune's wheel | about; |
> And soon|er shall | the sun | fall from | his sphere |
> Than Tam|burlaine | be slain | or o|vercome. | (I. ii.)

Clearly this blank verse is superior to the passage from *Gorboduc*.
And while it is undeniable that part of its greater intensity springs
from the spirit of the poet himself (indeed, Marlowe is noted for his
"mighty line"), we should also recognize how accentual variation
contributes to the total effect. In the first line, for example, the third
foot ("bound fast") is a spondee; thus the double stress serves to in-
dicate more surely the depth of Tamburlaine's conviction that he
truly does control his own fate. In the same light, the fourth foot of
the third line ("fall from") substitutes a trochee for an iamb. This
pattern is perfectly appropriate for the image and emotion con-
veyed by Tamburlaine's words ("sooner shall the sun fall"), for
the rhythm of the foot itself is falling from an unaccented
syllable.

DRAMATIC BLANK VERSE

Like the authors of *Gorboduc*, Marlowe also confined himself to a
pattern of end-stopped lines (see p. 50), each of which contains ten
syllables. Now consider a final example of dramatic blank verse, a
passage from Shakespeare. Hamlet is describing to Horatio his steal-
ing of the sealed commission Rosencrantz and Guildenstern were
carrying with them on the voyage to England (only the accents are
indicated in this passage):

> HAMLET.   Up from my cabin,
> My sea-gown scarf'd about me, in the dark
> Grop'd I to find out them; had my desire,
> Finger'd their packet, and in fine withdrew
> To my own room again; making so bold . . .

Here, although the understood pattern is that of blank verse, no line
is regular. Instead, we have a poetic utterance of complete dramatic
authenticity; the poetry is infused within the rhythms of a voice ex-
pressing impetuosity, a sense of danger, and an uncertainty over
what may possibly be discovered. Thus the first line, with its five
syllables and opening accent on *up*, increases our sense of the sudden-
ness with which Hamlet has decided to act. Furthermore, there is

an enjambment (see p. 50) in both the second and fourth lines. The carry-over in meaning from the second to the third line increases our sense of Hamlet's uncertainty and danger; the carry-over from the fourth to the fifth emphasizes the safe return to his own quarters, since the initial danger has ended. Moreover, the third line has eleven syllables (the eleventh being the unaccented one at the end of *desire*); this feminine ending (see p. 57) is fairly common in late Elizabethan blank verse. And, still further, the final line begins with a pyrrhic (see p. 49) that fulfills a characteristic function, that of heightening the sense of rapid movement in verse. All this is to say that in dramatic poetry of this proficiency the regular pattern of blank verse is largely understood as an underlying scheme upon which the dramatist is performing a variation to intensify his effects.

From this brief summary we can indicate three stages in the development of dramatic blank verse: (1) a beginning, such as in *Gorboduc*, where the verse adheres closely to the basic pattern of iambic pentameter and the lines are end-stopped; (2) a growing intensification of the individual line in Marlowe's early verse, which takes the form of greater subtlety of accentual variation, although at first he too confined himself largely to the end-stopped line; and (3) a remarkable flexibility and freedom, best exemplified in Shakespeare's mature and late blank verse, with a recurrent use of enjambment and feminine endings.

By the time of Shakespeare's death in 1616, dramatic blank verse had already begun to disintegrate into excessive laxity, and the decline of the form continued until the Puritan Revolution closed the theaters in 1642. Yet the achievement in the years from approximately 1585 to 1620 was so great that dramatic blank verse written during this period has remained the standard for virtually every subsequent attempt to compose a poetic drama in English. Thus John Dryden's *All for Love* (1678), Thomas Otway's *The Orphan* (1680) and *Venice Preserved* (1682), Nicholas Rowe's *The Fair Penitent* (1703), Joseph Addison's *Cato* (1713), Samuel Johnson's *Irene* (1749), William Wordsworth's *The Borderers* (1796–97), Percy Bysshe Shelley's *The Cenci* (1819), Robert Browning's *A Blot on the Scutcheon* (1843) and *Colombe's Birthday* (1853), Alfred, Lord Tennyson's *Harold* (1876) and *Becket* (1884), Maxwell Anderson's *Elizabeth the Queen* (1930) and *Winterset* (1935)—all of these works demonstrate that major authors have chosen blank verse as the most fitting metrical form for poetry intended for the stage. Even

T. S. Eliot, himself a radical experimenter in poetic drama during our own century, has confessed: "I have found, in trying to write dramatic verse, that however different a metre from blank verse I was working with, whenever my attention has relaxed, or I have gone sleepy or stupid, I will wake up to find that I have been writing bad Shakespearean blank verse."

QUESTIONS – MARLOWE

Faustus, near the beginning of Marlowe's *Doctor Faustus* (c. 1590), sells his soul to the devil in return for twenty-four years of pleasure. All too quickly the years pass; and, in the play's final scene, as the clock strikes eleven, Faustus realizes that his last hour of the twenty-four years has come. At midnight he must fulfill his part of the bargain:

> *The clock strikes eleven.*
> FAUSTUS. Ah, Faustus,
> Now hast thou but one bare hour to live,
> And then thou must be damned perpetually!
> Stand still, you ever-moving spheres of heaven,
> That time may cease, and midnight never come!   5
> Fair Nature's eye, rise, rise again and make
> Perpetual day; or let this hour be but
> A year, a month, a week, a natural day,
> That Faustus may repent and save his soul!
> *O lente, lente, currite, noctis equi!*   10
> The stars move still, time runs, the clock will strike,
> The devil will come, and Faustus must be damned.
> O, I'll leap up to my God! Who pulls me down?
> See, see where Christ's blood streams in the firmament!
> One drop would save my soul—half a drop. Ah, my Christ!   15
> Ah, rend not my heart for naming of my Christ!
> Yet will I call on him! O, spare me, Lucifer!—
> Where is it now? 'Tis gone; and see where God
> Stretcheth out his arm, and bends his ireful brows!
> Mountains and hills, come, come and fall on me,   20
> And hide me from the heavy wrath of God!

O lente . . . (10): Run slowly, slowly, horses of night.

1. While every reader will not agree as to which syllables in this excerpt demand accent, there are still definite standards to be recognized. For example, consider the second line:

$$\text{N}\breve{\text{o}}\text{w h}\acute{\text{a}}\text{st} \mid \text{th}\breve{\text{o}}\text{u b}\acute{\text{u}}\text{t} \mid \text{o}\breve{\text{n}}\text{e b}\acute{\text{a}}\text{re} \mid \text{h}\breve{\text{o}}\acute{\text{u}}\text{r} \mid \text{t}\breve{\text{o}} \text{ l}\acute{\text{i}}\text{ve.} \mid$$

Such a strictly "regular" reading is clearly an unnatural one. In fact, the only indisputable iamb in the entire line is the last foot ("to live"). Now consider an alternative reading:

$$\text{N}\breve{\text{o}}\text{w h}\acute{\text{a}}\text{st} \mid \text{th}\breve{\text{o}}\text{u b}\acute{\text{u}}\text{t} \mid \text{o}\acute{\text{n}}\text{e b}\acute{\text{a}}\text{re} \mid \text{h}\acute{\text{o}}\breve{\text{u}}\text{r} \mid \text{t}\breve{\text{o}} \text{ l}\acute{\text{i}}\text{ve.} \mid$$

This is more nearly in accord both with the prose sense of the line and with the rhythms of spoken English. Note that the two irregular feet (the third is a spondee and the fourth a trochee) throw heaviest stress on the very point uppermost in Faustus' mind, that is, the "one bare hour" left to him. Now consider a third reading:

$$\text{N}\breve{\text{o}}\text{w h}\acute{\text{a}}\text{st} \mid \text{th}\breve{\text{o}}\text{u b}\acute{\text{u}}\text{t} \mid \text{o}\breve{\text{n}}\text{e b}\acute{\text{a}}\text{re} \mid \text{h}\breve{\text{o}}\text{ur} \mid \text{t}\breve{\text{o}} \text{ l}\acute{\text{i}}\text{ve.} \mid$$

Is this a more accurate description of a natural reading of the line? Does it help to dramatize the central starkness of Faustus' obsession with time? Explain in a long paragraph.

2. As the excerpt from *Hamlet* (p. 163) revealed, one effect of enjambment is to throw into heightened emphasis the material of the second line, which completes the meaning suspended at the end of the first. Find the first two occurrences of genuine enjambment in this excerpt from *Doctor Faustus*; then explain how each helps to convey more effectively the state of Faustus' mind.

3. What is Nature's eye (1. 6)? How might the wish expressed in lines 6–7 psychologically justify line 14?

4. Beginning at line 11 and continuing to the end of the passage, describe each stage of Faustus' attitude towards his impending doom. How many concepts of God does he have? What are they? Answer in a brief essay.

5. Based on your response to question 4, how might the Latin quotation in line 10 be shown to play an important part in the effect of the entire passage?

Near the end of Shakespeare's *King Lear* (1605), the suffering Lear experiences a final agony. His beloved Cordelia, the only daughter (as he discovers too late) who actually loves him, is killed before his eyes. As he holds her body in his arms, he breaks out in a cry of anguish:

> LEAR.   And my poor fool is hang'd! No, no, no life!
> Why should a dog, a horse, a rat, have life,
> And thou no breath at all? Thou'lt come no more,
> Never, never, never, never, never!
> Pray you, undo this button. Thank you, sir.   5

poor fool (1): Cordelia. Lear uses the phrase in the affectionate fashion of a parent speaking of a small child.

1. Mark the accented syllables in the first line. On what idea does the heaviest emphasis fall?

2. Mark the accented and unaccented syllables in lines 2 and 3; then divide the lines into feet. How regular is the blank verse of these two lines? Now mark the accented and unaccented syllables of line 4 and divide them into feet. What is peculiar about this line? How has the rhythm of lines 2 and 3 helped to create a heightened effect in line 4? What is the effect of line 4?

3. George Lyman Kittredge once remarked that Lear "always and everywhere" acts like a king. What is there in line 5 that bears this out?

Near the conclusion of Shakespeare's *Henry IV*, Part I (1597), Henry Percy (or "Hotspur") meets Prince Hal (or Harry) on the field of battle. Throughout the play the two have provided a contrast to each other: Hotspur, the outspoken romantic idealist, always intent on the personal glory that may redound to him; and Harry, the apparently wayward son of Henry IV, determined to rescue his name from the reputation that stains it. At last the two fight, and Hotspur —mortally wounded by Harry—falls to the ground:

> HOTSPUR.   O Harry, thou hast robb'd me of my youth!
> I better brook the loss of brittle life

Than those proud titles thou hast won of me.
They wound my thoughts worse than thy sword my flesh.
But thought's the slave of life, and life time's fool,   5
And Time, that takes survey of all the world,
Must have a stop. O, I could prophesy,
But that the earthy and cold hand of death
Lies on my tongue. No, Percy, thou art dust,
And food for—   [*Dies.*]   10

1. In what line is alliteration used most prominently? How effectively does it heighten the effect of the prose meaning of the line?
2. A spondee occurs in line 3. Where is it? How does it help to clarify the nature of Hotspur's regret?
3. What scale of values is suggested by the comparison in line 4? Explain.
4. Explain lines 5–7. How is personification used there?
5. Because they were on the edge of eternity, dying men were sometimes thought to have the power to see into the future. This is why Hotspur, in line 7, refers to his ability to "prophesy." What device of figurative language follows this reference to prophecy? How would you justify the poet's use of "earthy"? of "cold"? Answer in a brief essay.

QUESTIONS – WEBSTER

In the following excerpt from John Webster's *The Duchess of Malfi* (c. 1613), the Duchess (aware that she is about to be murdered) bids farewell to her serving woman, Cariola. Waiting near are executioners under the direction of Bosola, who is himself a hireling of Ferdinand, Duke of Calabria, the Duchess' twin brother. The motive for murder lies in a combination of the Duke's selfish attitudes: avarice (if his widowed sister does not remarry, her wealth will revert to him), outraged family pride (the Duchess has given birth to three children without having publicly remarried), and desire to revenge himself because his sister has refused to be completely dominated.

DUCHESS.   Farewell, Cariola.
    In my last will I have not much to give:

A many hungry guests have fed upon me; 3
Thine will a poor reversion.
CARIOLA.   I will die with her. 4
DUCHESS.   I pray thee, look thou giv'st my little boy 5
Some syrup for his cold, and let the girl
Say her prayers ere she sleep.
          (CARIOLA *is forced out by the* EXECUTIONERS)
                              Now what you please. 7
What death?
BOSOLA.   Strangling; 8
Here are your executioners.
DUCHESS.   I forgive them: 9
The apoplexy, catarrh, or cough o' th' lungs, 10
Would do as much as they do.
BOSOLA.   Doth not death fright you?
DUCHESS.   Who would be afraid on 't,
Knowing to meet such excellent company
In th' other world?
BOSOLA.   Yet, methinks,
The manner of your death should much afflict you: 15
This cord should terrify you.
DUCHESS.   Not a whit.
What would it pleasure me to have my throat cut
With diamonds? Or to be smothered
With cassia? Or to be shot to death with pearls?
I know death hath ten thousand several doors 20
For men to take their exits, and 'tis found
They go on such strange geometrical hinges,
You may open them both ways. Any way, for heaven sake,
So I were out of your whispering. Tell my brothers
That I perceive death, now I am well awake, 25
Best gift is they can give or I can take.
I would fain put off my last woman's fault,
I'd not be tedious to you.
EXECUTIONER.   We are ready.
DUCHESS.   Dispose of my breath how please you, but my body
Bestow upon my women, will you?
EXECUTIONER.   Yes. 30
DUCHESS.   Pull, and pull strongly, for your able strength
Must pull down heaven upon me—
Yet stay; heaven-gates are not so highly arched
As princes' palaces; they that enter there

Must go upon their knees (*Kneels*). Come, violent death.   35
Serve for mandragora to make me sleep!
Go tell my brothers, when I am laid out,
They then may feed in quiet.   (*They strangle her*)
BOSOLA.   Where's the waiting woman?
Fetch her: some other strangle the children.   40
    (*Exeunt* EXECUTIONERS, *some of whom return with* CARIOLA)
Look you, there sleeps your mistress.
CARIOLA.   Oh, you are damned
Perpetually for this! My turn is next.
Is 't not so ordered?
BOSOLA.   Yes, and I am glad
You are so well prepared for 't.
CARIOLA.   You are deceived, Sir,
I am not prepared for 't, I will not die;   45
I will first come to my answer, and know
How I have offended.
BOSOLA.   Come, dispatch her.
You kept her counsel; now you shall keep ours.
CARIOLA.   I will not die, I must not; I am contracted
To a young gentleman.
EXECUTIONER.   Here's your wedding-ring.   50
CARIOLA.   Let me but speak with the duke; I'll discover
Treason to his person.
BOSOLA.   Delays! Throttle her.
EXECUTIONER.   She bites and scratches.
CARIOLA.   If you kill me now,
I am damned; I have not been at confession
This two years.   55
BOSOLA.   When!
CARIOLA.   I am quick with child.
BOSOLA.   Why, then,
Your credit's saved.   (*They strangle* CARIOLA)
        Bear her into th' next room;
Let this lie still.
    (*Exeunt the* EXECUTIONERS *with the body of* CARIOLA)
       (*Enter* FERDINAND)
FERDINAND.   Is she dead?
BOSOLA.   She is what
You'd have her. But here begin your pity.   60
    (*Shows the Children strangled*)
Alas, how have these offended?

FERDINAND.   The death
Of young wolves is never to be pitied.
BOSOLA.   Fix
Your eye here.
FERDINAND.   Constantly.
BOSOLA.   Do you not weep?
Other sins only speak; murder shrieks out:
The element of water moistens the earth,   65
But blood flies upwards and bedews the heavens.
FERDINAND.   Cover her face; mine eyes dazzle: she died young.
BOSOLA.   I think not so; her infelicity
Seemed to have years too many.
FERDINAND.   She and I were twins;
And should I die this instant, I had lived   70
Her time to a minute.
BOSOLA.   It seems she was born first:
You have bloodily approved the ancient truth,
That kindred commonly do worse agree
Than remote strangers.
FERDINAND.   Let me see her face
Again. Why didst not thou pity her? What   75
An excellent honest man mightst thou have been,
If thou hadst borne her to some sanctuary!

reversion (4): reverting. cassia (18): cinnamon. fault (27): talkativeness. man-
dragora (36): sleeping potion. children (40): the Duchess' son and daughter
are killed at once. When! (56): an outburst of impatience directed at the execu-
tioners.

1. There has recently been much discussion of "black" humor, one
aspect of which is the evocation of laughter from situations that a
conventional point of view might find desperate, terrifying, or tragic.
What is there in this excerpt that might be called black humor? Do
such instances detract from or increase the effectiveness of the scene?
Explain.

2. Define the attitude toward death held by each character. Whose
attitude appears most complex? Why?

3. In terms of the entire scene, what is the artistic function of the
Duchess' request in lines 6–8?

4. Locate the accented syllables in line 67. How does this pattern
of accents reinforce the prose sense of the line? What does the line re-
veal about Ferdinand's emotional state? What image, for example, is

implicit there? What overall impression does Ferdinand make?
5. Is Bosola a convincing character in this scene? Explain in several
paragraphs by relating the language of his speeches and his actions.

QUESTIONS – JONSON

In Ben Jonson's *The Alchemist* (1610), Face (alias "Lungs" be-
cause he supposedly blows on the coals in the alchemist's furnace)
proceeds to swindle Sir Epicure Mammon, one of the many dupes in
the play. Mammon has been led to believe that the alchemist (the
"master" of line 1, a swindler called "Subtle") is near success in
achieving the alchemist's dream—that is, discovery of the philoso-
pher's *stone* (1. 8), which would transmute all baser metals into gold,
as well as the creation of the *elixir vitae* (1. 10), which would confer
eternal youth on the possessor. As is natural for one so gullible, Mam-
mon believes he alone will reap the benefits of the alchemist's success:

MAMMON.	Where's master?	
FACE.	At's prayers, sir, he;	1
Good man, he's doing his devotions		
For the success.		
MAMMON.	Lungs, I will set a period	3
To all thy labors; thou shalt be the master		4
Of my seraglia.		
FACE.	Good, sir.	
MAMMON.	But do you hear?	5
I'll geld you, Lungs.		
FACE.	Yes, sir.	
MAMMON.	For I do mean	6
To have a list of wives and concubines		7
Equal with Salomon, who had the *stone*		
Alike with me; and I will make me a back		
With the *elixir*, that shall be as tough		10
As Hercules, to encounter fifty a night.—		
Thou'rt sure thou saw'st it blood?		12
FACE. Both *blood and spirit*, sir.		
MAMMON. I will have all my beds blown up, not stuff'd;		
Down is too hard. And then, mine oval room		15
Fill'd with such pictures as Tiberius took		
From Elephantis, and dull Aretine		
But coldly imitated. Then, my glasses		

Cut in more subtle angles to disperse
And multiply the figures, as I walk
Naked between my succubae. My mists   20
I'll have of perfume, vapor'd 'bout the room,
To lose ourselves in, and my baths like pits
To fall into, from whence we will come forth,
And roll us dry in gossamer and roses.—
Is it arrived at ruby?—Where I spy   25
A wealthy citizen or rich lawyer
Have a sublim'd pure wife, unto that fellow
I'll send a thousand pound to be my cuckold.
FACE.   And I shall carry it?
MAMMON.   No, I'll ha' no bawds
But fathers and mothers. They will do it best.   30

succubae (21): concubines.

1. Why are the names of the two characters particularly appropriate?

2. Note that lines 5 and 6 are each broken into three parts. Note too that the medial foot of both lines is a remark by Face. At first glance—and considered in isolation—the two remarks are almost identical. Consider now the two lines in the context of lines 3–11 and discuss the comic effect Jonson creates by the apparently very slight change in the medial foot of line 6 from the medial foot of line 5.

3. How many wives and concubines did Solomon (i.e., "Salomon," l. 8) have? Why is this reference both appropriate—and comically inappropriate—for the rest of Mammon's remarks in the passage?

4. The references to colors (e.g., "blood" in l. 12, *"blood and spirit"* in l. 13, and "ruby" in l. 26) are descriptions of the supposed changes in the alchemist's formula as he nears successful completion. As such, they are clearly parts of the whole comical structure of hocus-pocus that is being used to swindle Mammon. How else do the references to color function in the entire passage?

5. Beginning at line 13 and continuing to line 24, distinguish each image in Mammon's speech. What is the total effect of the vision he is presenting? How does this relate to the "fifty" of line 11? fifty of what?

6. What are the implications of Mammon's final remarks in the passage, from line 25 to the end? How do they underscore the significance of his name?

Both following passages (A is from Marlowe's *Edward II* and B from Shakespeare's *Richard II*) are drawn from plays of the 1590's. They also embody a similar subject—that is, a king is being deposed (in passage B, the king-to-be is Bolingbroke, cousin of Richard). Read both passages before answering the questions that follow.

(A)

EDWARD.   Here, take my crown—the life of Edward too;
                        [*Takes off the crown.*]
  Two kings in England cannot reign at once.
  But stay awhile; let me be king till night,
  That I may gaze upon this glittering crown.
  So shall my eyes receive their last content,   5
  My head, the latest honor due to it,
  And jointly both yield up their wished right.
  Continue ever, thou celestial sun;
  Let never silent night possess this clime.
  Stand still, you watches of the element;   10
  All times and seasons, rest you at a stay,
  That Edward may be still fair England's king!
  But day's bright beams doth vanish fast away,
  And needs I must resign my wished crown.
  Inhuman creatures, nurs'd with tiger's milk,   15
  Why gape you for your sovereign's overthrow—
  My diadem, I mean, and guiltless life?
  See, monsters, see, I'll wear my crown again!
                       [*Puts on the crown.*]
  What, fear you not the fury of your king?
  But hapless Edward, thou art fondly led;   20
  They pass not for thy frowns as late they did,
  But seeks to make a new-elect'd king;
  Which fills my mind with strange, despairing thoughts,
  Which thoughts are martyred with endless torment,
  And, in this torment, comfort find I none,   25
  But that I feel the crown upon my head;
  And therefore let me wear it yet awhile.

watches of the element (10): celestial bodies. *fondly* (20): foolishly. *pass* (21): care.

(B)

RICHARD. Give me the crown. Here, cousin, seize the crown.
Here cousin,
On this side my hand, and on that side yours.
Now is this golden crown like a deep well
That owes two buckets, filling one another,   5
The emptier ever dancing in the air,
The other down, unseen, and full of water.
That bucket down and full of tears am I,
Drinking my griefs whilst you mount up on high.
BOLINGBROKE.   I thought you had been willing to resign.   10
RICHARD.   My crown I am, but still my griefs are mine.
You may my glories and my state depose,
But not my griefs. Still am I king of those.
BOLINGBROKE.   Part of your cares you give me with your crown.
Your cares set up do not pluck my cares down.   15
My care is loss of care, by old care done;
Your care is gain of care, by new care won.
The cares I give I have, though given away;
They tend the crown, yet still with me they stay.

owes (5): owns.

1. Describe the fluctuations of Edward's emotions in Passage A. How many lines beginning with "But" serve to indicate changes of direction in his thought? What is that change of direction in each case? What other changes in emotion take place? Explain in a paragraph.

2. Study lines 20–27 in Passage A. What is the implicit metaphor in lines 23–24? How does this metaphor increase the effectiveness of these particular eight lines?

3. Characterize Edward. Does he appear weak? Why, or why not?

4. Explain the image in lines 4–9 in Passage B. Does it appear an appropriate analogy for the situation? Why?

5. What does the image of lines 4–9 reveal about Richard—particularly in lines 8–9?

6. Note that in Passage B Richard concludes his first speech with a rhyme (ll. 8–9). Then, after Bolingbroke's short answer, Richard resumes by having his first line rhyme with Bolingbroke's reply. What might this indicate about Richard's character in the context of the seriousness of his situation? Does Bolingbroke's use of rhyme (ll. 14–19) seem any different from Richard's? Explain.

7. Compare the reactions of Edward and Richard to their respective situations.

8. Which passage seems more effective *dramatically*? Why?

9. Which passage seems more effective *poetically*? Why?

10. Based on these two passages, do you think there is any inherent conflict between dramatic effectiveness and poetic effectiveness? That is, does it seem necessary for a writer to sacrifice something of one in order to achieve the other more fully? Using specific lines as examples, explain in a short essay.

QUESTIONS – SHELLEY • SHAKESPEARE

As we have seen in several earlier passages, some of the greatest dramatic poetry concerns a character confronting his own impending death. In Shelley's tragedy, *The Cenci* (1819), we again find a character compelled to recognize the finiteness of physical life. Beatrice Cenci has contributed to the slaying of her father, a brutal and nearly insane tyrant who has forced her into a sexual relationship. Expecting a pardon from the Pope for her role in the death, Beatrice instead learns from Camillo that the Pope desires the sentence of death to be imposed upon her as swiftly as possible:

BEATRICE.   I hardly dare to fear
    That thou bring'st other news than a just pardon.
CAMILLO.   May God in heaven be less inexorable
    To the Pope's prayers, than he has been to mine.
    Here is the sentence and the warrant.
BEATRICE (*wildly*).   O   5
    My God! Can it be possible I have
    To die so suddenly? So young to go
    Under the obscure, cold, rotting, wormy ground!
    To be nailed down into a narrow place;
    To see no more sweet sunshine; hear no more   10
    Blithe voice of living thing; muse not again
    Upon familiar thoughts, sad, yet thus lost—
    How fearful! to be nothing! Or to be . . .
    What? Oh, where am I? Let me not go mad!
    Sweet Heaven, forgive weak thoughts! If there should be   15
    No God, no Heaven, no Earth in the void world;

The wide, gray, lampless, deep, unpeopled world!
If all things then should be . . . my father's spirit,
His eye, his voice, his touch surrounding me;
The atmosphere and breath of my dead life!   20
If sometimes, as a shape more like himself,
Even the form which tortured me on earth,
Masked in gray hairs and wrinkles, he should come
And wind me in his hellish arms, and fix
His eyes on mine, and drag me down, down, down!   25
For was he not alone omnipotent
On Earth, and ever present? Even though dead,
Does not his spirit live in all that breathe,
And work for me and mine still the same ruin,
Scorn, pain, despair? Who ever yet returned   30
To teach the laws of Death's untrodden realm?
Unjust perhaps as those which drive us now,
Oh, whither, whither?

In writing this passage, Shelley probably had in mind a similar
passage from a well-known play written about 1604, during the golden
age of poetic drama. In the excerpt drawn from this earlier play
(Shakespeare's *Measure for Measure*), the two speakers (Claudio and
Isabella) are brother and sister. Claudio, in prison, is under sentence
of death. As the passage begins, Isabella has just informed her brother
that he will be freed if she will submit to a dishonorable act:

ISAB.   What says my brother?
CLAUD.   Death is a fearful thing.
ISAB.   And shamed life a hateful.
CLAUD.   Ay, but to die, and go we know not where;
    To lie in cold obstruction and to rot;
    This sensible warm motion to become   5
    A kneaded clod; and the delighted spirit
    To bathe in fiery floods, or to reside
    In thrilling region of thick-ribbed ice,
    To be imprison'd in the viewless winds
    And blown with restless violence round about   10
    The pendent world; or to be worse than worst
    Of those that lawless and incertain thought
    Imagines howling! 'Tis too horrible!
    The weariest and most loathed worldly life

That age, ache, penury, and imprisonment   15
Can lay on nature is a paradise
To what we fear of death.

1. Which passage is more successful as dramatic poetry? Which, for example, conveys more successfully the sense of a character genuinely afraid of death? Justify, with specific details, your choice.

2. Write an essay on the varying attitudes toward death found in these selections. In doing so, consider the value of blank verse as a form expressing the emotional range of such attitudes.

Chapter 6

Blank Verse: Other Than the Drama

One problem confronting the practitioner of blank verse is that the form, because of its great potential for freedom and flexibility, can easily degenerate if handled too loosely. This results all too frequently in a metrical laxity that is hardly distinguishable from prose. Here, for example, is a passage from *The Lady of Pleasure*, a play written by James Shirley in 1635, not quite twenty years after Shakespeare's death:

> I like you, sir, the better, that you do not
> Wander about, but shoot home to the meaning;
> 'Tis a confidence will make a man
> Know sooner what to trust to; but I never
> Saw you before, and I believe you come not
> With hope to find me desperate upon marriage. (*I. ii.*)

The irregularity of this is extreme, especially since not one of the lines contains exactly ten syllables. But far more important than any syllabic irregularity is the obvious loss of intensity from the blank verse that was being written during Shakespeare's lifetime. Indeed, if we reprint the passage from Shirley as prose, there seems nothing left to suggest that it was once poetry:

> I like you, sir, the better, that you do not wander about,
> but sooner shoot home to the meaning; 'tis a confidence will
> make a man know sooner what to trust to; but I never saw you
> before, and I believe you come not with hope to find me
> desperate upon marriage.

Nor is Shirley an isolated figure in the two or three decades that preceded the closing of the theaters in 1642. Everywhere around him an extremely loose blank verse was being written for the stage—so loose, in fact, that soon after the theaters were reopened in 1660, John Dryden led a short-lived attempt to create a dramatic poetry that could be written in heroic couplets (see p. 138). In this attempt, abortive as it was, we can see a circle completing itself. The earliest blank verse, such as in *Gorboduc*, was extremely stiff and revealed its descent from the pentameter couplet. Gradually, in the hands of Marlowe, Shakespeare, and others, a remarkable flexibility was developed. Yet as time passed and this flexibility degenerated into laxness, more and more writers turned back to the couplet, using rhyme to restore a form and rigor that was seemingly no longer possible in blank verse.

MILTON'S RENEWAL

Almost in conjunction with this growing use of the couplet, one of the greatest metrical artists in English poetry was evolving his own version of blank verse. In the following passage from Book II of John Milton's *Paradise Lost* (first published in 1667), only the accented syllables are indicated:

> High on | a Throne | of Roy|al State, | which far |
> Outshone | the wealth | of Or|mus and | of Ind, |
> Or where | the gor|geous East | with rich|est hand |
> Show'rs on | her Kings | Barbar|ic Pearl | and Gold, |
> Satan | exal|ted sat, | by mer|it rais'd | 5
> To that | bad em|inence; | and from | despair |
> Thus high | uplif|ted be|yond hope, | aspires |
> Beyond | thus high, | insa|tiate to | pursue |
> Vain War | with Heav'n . . . |

This is richly intense blank verse, and it is interesting to recognize the elements through which Milton achieves an effect of rigorous form that distinguishes his blank verse from Shirley's. For example, unlike Shirley, Milton is clearly basing his lines on a scheme of ten syllables each. Likewise, Milton's handling of accentual variation is far more developed than Shirley's. Although almost half the lines (the first, fourth, fifth, and ninth) begin with an accented syllable, a proportion not dissimilar to the passage from Shirley, Milton's initial accents carry much more weight because of his firmer establishment of a basic iambic rhythm (at least thirty-seven of the forty-two feet in the passage can be scanned as iambic). That is, in Milton a variation from the iambic is felt more surely *as* a variation. Furthermore, three other effects, not to be found in Shirley, distinguish Milton's mastery of accentual handling. First, his repeated use of the stressed "high" (in lines 1, 7, and 8) creates an almost incantatory sense of Satan's excessive pride. Second, he varies the accent on "beyond" in lines 7 and 8, treating it as a trochee at its first appearance, and then allowing it to fall into its customary iambic pattern two feet later. And, finally, he employs nearly identical words for the last two stresses of line 2 ("and" and "*Ind*"), thus deriving from their conjunction a peculiarly effective resonance.

In addition to his accentual mastery, Milton makes recurrent use of an enjambment that is more pronounced in its effect than Shirley's, partly because of Milton's care to end each line with a stressed syllable (the "aspires" of line 7 was almost surely conceived by Milton as receiving a pronunciation similar to "aspeers," avoiding the final weak syllable of modern pronunciation) and partly because of the greater subtlety in syntax. Indeed, in the brief note he appended to *Paradise Lost* Milton requested the reader to recognize that "the sense should be variously drawn out from one Verse into another." Thus more than half the lines in the passage quoted above hang grammatically suspended, requiring elements in the following line to fulfill the syntactical expectations aroused in the reader. In the first line, for example, the concluding dependent clause ("which far") obviously requires a verb (the "Outshone" that begins l. 2) as part of its continuation. In line 3, "East," the subject of the clause begun there, also requires a verb (the "Show'rs" that opens l. 4). The verb "rais'd" of line 5 requires some syntactical structure to complete it (the "To that bad eminence" of l. 6). Syntactical expectation is also evident in lines 7 and 8.

MILTONIC SYNTAX

In Milton's syntax we find perhaps the single most significant departure not only from Shirley, but from every other previous writer of blank verse. In the passage from Shirley, for example, the poet is attempting to simulate the rhythms of actual conversation, and so we begin at once with the most common syntactical structure in English —subject, verb, and object (e.g., "I like you")—and proceed from there through a series of uncomplicated and easily anticipated clauses. In the passage from *Paradise Lost*, on the other hand, it is not until the fifth line that we reach the subject of the entire passage (i.e., "Satan"). Until that point, for four lines, we have what is essentially an elaboration by analogy of the splendor of Satan's throne. Furthermore, in that same fifth line, the ordinary syntactical order of subject, intransitive verb, and adjective becomes, instead, "Satan exalted sat." To recognize the dramatic effect of the substitution, contrast these two sentences: "John sat elevated above the crowd" and "John elevated sat above the crowd." Similarly, the second main verb of the passage ("aspires") defeats syntactical expectations in two ways: first, by the same delaying tactic used with "Satan," and, second, by the subtle change to present tense (syntactically the core of the passage is this clause: "Satan *sat* . . . and *aspires* . . .").

While the details of Milton's syntax are almost infinitely complex, the major features to note are (1) his departure in *Paradise Lost* from the colloquial structures that poets like Shirley had been writing for the stage and (2) the establishment in their place of a form of verse paragraph better suited for inspired recitation than for dramatic performance. In this latter respect, then, Milton's blank verse for *Paradise Lost* was the first significant development in the form since Shakespeare's death in 1616. By his rather strict adherence to a ten-syllable line, by his skillful employment of accentual variation and enjambment, by his extraordinarily complex use of a nonconversational syntax, but most of all by his high poetic genius, Milton was able to distill from a form that had broken down into laxity a grandeur and power it had rarely had before him.

JOHN MILTON (1608–74)

from Book I of Paradise Lost

Of Man's First Disobedience, and the Fruit
Of that Forbidden Tree, whose mortal taste
Brought Death into the World, and all our woe,
With loss of *Eden*, till one greater Man
Restore us, and regain in blissful Seat,   5
Sing Heav'nly Muse, that on the secret top
Of *Oreb*, or of *Sinai*, didst inspire
That Shepherd, who first taught the chosen Seed,
In the Beginning how the Heav'ns and Earth
Rose out of *Chaos*: Or if *Sion* Hill   10
Delight thee more, and *Siloa's* Brook that flow'd
Fast by the Oracle of God; I thence
Invoke thy aid to my advent'rous Song,
That with no middle flight intends to soar
Above th' *Aonian* Mount, while it pursues   15
Things unattempted yet in Prose or Rhyme.
And chiefly Thou O Spirit, that dost prefer
Before all Temples th' upright heart and pure,
Instruct me, for Thou know'st; Thou from the first
Wast present, and with mighty wings outspread   20
Dove-like satst brooding on the vast Abyss
And mad'st it pregnant: What in me is dark
Illumine, what is low raise and support;
That to the highth of this great Argument
I may assert Eternal Providence,   25
And justify the ways of God to men.
    Say first, for Heav'n hides nothing from thy view
Nor the deep Tract of Hell, say first what cause
Mov'd our Grand Parents in that happy State,
Favour'd of Heav'n so highly, to fall off   30
From thir Creator, and transgress his Will
For one restraint, Lords of the World besides?
Who first seduc'd them to that foul revolt?

Miltonic Syntax   183

Th' infernal Serpent; he it was, whose guile
Stirr'd up with Envy and Revenge, deceiv'd   35
The Mother of Mankind, what time his Pride
Had cast him out from Heav'n, with all his Host
Of Rebel Angels, by whose aid aspiring
To set himself in Glory above his Peers,
He trusted to have equall'd the most High,   40
If he oppos'd; and with ambitious aim
Against the Throne and Monarchy of God
Rais'd impious War in Heav'n and Battle proud
With vain attempt. Him the Almighty Power
Hurl'd headlong flaming from th' Ethereal Sky   45
With hideous ruin and combustion down
To bottomless perdition, there to dwell
In Adamantine Chains and penal Fire,
Who durst defy th' Omnipotent to Arms.
Nine times the Space that measures Day and Night   50
To mortal men, hee with his horrid crew
Lay vanquisht, rolling in the fiery Gulf
Confounded though immortal; But his doom
Reserv'd him to more wrath; for now the thought
Both of lost happiness and lasting pain   55
Torments him; round he throws his baleful eyes
That witness'd huge affliction and dismay
Mixt with obdurate pride and steadfast hate:
At once as far as Angels ken he views
The dismal Situation waste and wild,   60
A Dungeon horrible, on all sides round
As one great Furnace flam'd, yet from those flames
No light, but rather darkness visible
Serv'd only to discover sights of woe,
Regions of sorrow, doleful shades, where peace   65
And rest can never dwell, hope never comes
That comes to all; but torture without end
Still urges, and a fiery Deluge, fed
With ever-burning Sulphur unconsum'd:
Such place Eternal Justice had prepar'd   70
For those rebellious, here thir Prison ordained
In utter darkness, and thir portion set
As far remov'd from God and light of Heav'n
As from the Center thrice to th' utmost Pole.
O how unlike the place from whence they fell!   75
There the companions of his fall, o'erwhelm'd

With Floods and Whirlwinds of tempestuous fire,
He soon discerns, and welt'ring by his side
One next himself in power, and next in crime,
Long after known in *Palestine*, and nam'd   80
Beëlzebub. To whom th' Arch-Enemy,
And thence in Heav'n call'd Satan, with bold words
Breaking the horrid silence thus began.
   If thou beest he; But O how fall'n! how chang'd
From him, who in the happy Realms of Light   85
Cloth'd with transcendent brightness didst outshine
Myriads though bright: If he whom mutual league,
United thoughts and counsels, equal hope,
And hazard in the Glorious Enterprise,
Join'd with me once, now misery hath join'd   90
In equal ruin: into what Pit thou seest
From what highth fall'n, so much the stronger prov'd
He with his Thunder: and till then who knew
The force of those dire Arms? yet not for those,
Nor what the Potent Victor in his rage   95
Can else inflict, do I repent or change,
Though chang'd in outward lustre; that fixt mind
And high disdain, from sense of injur'd merit,
That with the mightiest rais'd me to contend,
And to the fierce contention brought along   100
Innumerable force of Spirits arm'd
That durst dislike his reign, and me preferring,
His utmost power with adverse power oppos'd
In dubious Battle on the Plains of Heav'n,
And shook his throne. What though the field be lost?   105
All is not lost; the unconquerable will,
And study of revenge, immortal hate,
And courage never to submit or yield:
And what is else not to be overcome?
That Glory never shall his wrath or might   110
Extort from me. To bow and sue for grace
With suppliant knee, and deify his power
Who from the terror of this Arm so late
Doubted his Empire, that were low indeed,
That were an ignominy and shame beneath   115
This downfall; since by Fate the strength of Gods
And this Empyreal substance cannot fail,
Since through experience of this great event
In Arms not worse, in foresight much advanc't,

We may with more successful hope resolve   120
To wage by force or guile eternal War
Irreconcilable to our grand Foe,
Who now triumphs, and in th' excess of joy
Sole reigning holds the Tyranny of Heav'n.
    So spake th' Apostate Angel, though in pain,   125
Vaunting aloud, but rackt with deep despair:
And him thus answer'd soon his bold Compeer.
    O Prince, O Chief of many Throned Powers,
That led th' imbattl'd Seraphim to War
Under thy conduct, and in dreadful deeds   130
Fearless, endanger'd Heav'n's perpetual King;
And put to proof his high Supremacy,
Whether upheld by strength, or Chance, or Fate;
Too well I see and rue the dire event,
That with sad overthrow and foul defeat   135
Hath lost us Heav'n, and all this mighty Host
In horrible destruction laid thus low,
As far as Gods and Heav'nly Essences
Can perish: for the mind and spirit remains
Invincible, and vigor soon returns,   140
Though all our Glory extinct, and happy state
Here swallow'd up in endless misery.
But what if he our Conqueror, (whom I now
Of force believe Almighty, since no less
Than such could have o'erpow'rd such force as ours)   145
Have left us this our spirit and strength entire
Strongly to suffer and support our pains,
That we may so suffice his vengeful ire,
Or do him mightier service as his thralls
By right of War, whate'er his business be   150
Here in the heart of Hell to work in Fire,
Or do his Errands in the gloomy Deep;
What can it then avail though yet we feel
Strength undiminisht, or eternal being
To undergo eternal punishment?   155
Whereto with speedy words th' Arch-fiend repli'd.
    Fall'n Cherub, to be weak is miserable
Doing or Suffering: but of this be sure,
To do aught good never will be our task,
But ever to do ill our sole delight,   160
As being the contrary to his high will
Whom we resist. If then his Providence

Out of our evil seek to bring forth good,
Our labour must be to pervert that end,
And out of good still to find means of evil;   165
Which oft-times may succeed, so as perhaps
Shall grieve him, if I fail not, and disturb
His inmost counsels from thir destin'd aim.
But see the angry Victor hath recall'd
His Ministers of vengeance and pursuit   170
Back to the Gates of Heav'n: the Sulphurous Hail
Shot after us in storm, o'erblown hath laid
The fiery Surge, that from the Precipice
Of Heav'n receiv'd us falling, and the Thunder,
Wing'd with red Lightning and impetuous rage,   175
Perhaps hath spent his shafts, and ceases now
To bellow through the vast and boundless Deep.
Let us not slip th' occasion, whether scorn,
Or satiate fury yield it from our Foe.
Seest thou yon dreary Plain, forlorn and wild,   180
The seat of desolation, void of light,
Save what the glimmering of these livid flames
Casts pale and dreadful? Thither let us tend
From off the tossing of these fiery waves,
There rest, if any rest can harbour there,   185
And reassembling our afflicted Powers,
Consult how we may henceforth most offend
Our Enemy, our own loss how repair,
How overcome this dire Calamity,
What reinforcement we may gain from Hope,   190
If not what resolution from despair.
    Thus Satan talking to his nearest Mate
With Head up-lift above the wave, and Eyes
That sparkling blaz'd, his other Parts besides
Prone on the Flood, extended long and large   195
Lay floating many a rood, in bulk as huge
As whom the Fables name of monstrous size,
Titanian, or *Earth-born*, that warr'd on *Jove*,
Briareos or *Typhon*, whom the Den
By ancient *Tarsus* held, or that Sea-beast   200
Leviathan, which God of all his works
Created hugest that swim th' Ocean stream:
Him haply slumb'ring on the *Norway* foam
The Pilot of some small night-founder'd Skiff,
Deeming some Island, oft, as Seamen tell,   205

With fixed Anchor in his scaly rind
Moors by his side under the Lee, while Night
Invests the Sea, and wished Morn delays:
So stretcht out huge in length the Arch-fiend lay
Chain'd on the burning Lake, nor ever thence   210
Had ris'n or heav'd his head, but that the will
And high permission of all-ruling Heaven
Left him at large to his own dark designs,
That with reiterated crimes he might
Heap on himself damnation, while he sought   215
Evil to others, and enrag'd might see
How all his malice serv'd but to bring forth
Infinite goodness, grace and mercy shown
On Man by him seduc't, but on himself
Treble confusion, wrath and vengeance pour'd.   220
Forthwith upright he rears from off the Pool
His mighty Stature; on each hand the flames
Driv'n backward slope their pointing spires, and roll'd
In billows, leave i' th' midst a horrid Vale.
Then with expanded wings he steers his fight   225
Aloft, incumbent on the dusky Air
That felt unusual weight, till on dry Land
He lights, if it were Land that ever burn'd
With solid, as the Lake with liquid fire;
And such appear'd in hue, as when the force   230
Of subterranean wind transports a Hill
Torn from *Pelorus*, or the shatter'd side
Of thund'ring *Ætna*, whose combustible
And fuell'd entrails thence conceiving Fire,
Sublim'd with Mineral fury, aid the Winds,   235
And leave a singed bottom all involv'd
With stench and smoke: Such resting found the sole
Of unblest feet. Him follow'd his next Mate,
Both glorying to have scap't *Stygian* flood
As Gods, and by thir own recover'd strength,   240
Not by the sufferance of supernal Power.
   Is this the Region, this the Soil, the Clime,
Said then the lost Arch-Angel, this the seat
That we must change for Heav'n, this mournful gloom
For that celestial light? Be it so, since hee   245
Who now is Sovran can dispose and bid
What shall be right: fardest from him is best
Whom reason hath equall'd, force hath made supreme

Above his equals. Farewell happy Fields
Where Joy for ever dwells: Hail horrors, hail   250
Infernal world, and thou profoundest Hell
Receive thy new Possessor: One who brings
A mind not to be chang'd by Place or Time.
The mind is its own place, and in itself
Can make a Heav'n of Hell, a Hell of Heav'n.   255
What matter where, if I be still the same,
And what I should be, all but less than hee
Whom Thunder hath made greater? Here at least
We shall be free; th' Almighty hath not built
Here for his envy, will not drive us hence: 260
Here we may reign secure, and in my choice
To reign is worth ambition though in Hell:
Better to reign in Hell, than serve in Heav'n
But wherefore let we then our faithful friends,
Th' associates and copartners of our loss   265
Lie thus astonisht on th' oblivious Pool,
And call them not to share with us their part
In this unhappy Mansion, or once more
With rallied Arms to try what may be yet
Regain'd in Heav'n, or what more lost in Hell?   270
   So *Satan* spake, and him *Beëlzebub*
Thus answer'd. Leader of those Armies bright,
Which but th' Omnipotent none could have foiled,
If once they hear that voice, thir liveliest pledge
Of hope in fears and dangers, heard so oft   275
In worst extremes, and on the perilous edge
Of battle when it rag'd, in all assaults
Thir surest signal, they will soon resume
New courage and revive, though now they lie
Groveling and prostrate on yon Lake of Fire,   280
As we erewhile, astounded and amaz'd,
No wonder, fall'n such a pernicious highth.
   He scarce had ceas't when the superior Fiend
Was moving toward the shore; his ponderous shield
Ethereal temper, massy, large and round,   285
Behind him cast; the broad circumference
Hung on his shoulders like the Moon, whose Orb
Through Optic Glass the *Tuscan* Artist views
At Ev'ning from the top of *Fesole*,
Or in *Valdarno*, to descry new Lands,   290
Rivers or Mountains in her spotty Globe.

His Spear, to equal which the tallest Pine
Hewn on *Norwegian* hills, to be the Mast
Of some great Ammiral, were but a wand,
He walkt with to support uneasy steps   295
Over the burning Marl, not like those steps
On Heaven's Azure, and the torrid Clime
Smote on him sore besides, vaulted with Fire;
Nathless he so endur'd, till on the Beach
Of that inflamed Sea, he stood and call'd   300
His Legions, Angel Forms, who lay intrans't
Thick as Autumnal Leaves that strow the Brooks
In *Vallombrosa,* where th' *Etrurian* shades
High overarch't imbow'r; or scatter'd sedge
Afloat, when with fierce Winds *Orion* arm'd   305
Hath vext the Red-Sea Coast, whose waves o'erthrew
Busiris and his *Memphian* Chivalry,
While with perfidious hatred they pursu'd
The Sojourners of *Goshen,* who beheld
From the safe shore thir floating Carcasses   310
And broken Chariot Wheels, so thick bestrown
Abject and lost lay these, covering the Flood,
Under amazement of thir hideous change.
He call'd so loud, that all the hollow Deep
Of Hell resounded. Princes, Potentates,   315
Warriors, the Flow'r of Heav'n, once yours, now lost,
If such astonishment as this can seize
Eternal spirits; or have ye chos'n this place
After the toil of Battle to repose
Your wearied virtue, for the ease you find   320
To slumber here, as in the Vales of Heav'n?
Or in this abject posture have ye sworn
To adore the Conqueror? who now beholds
Cherub and Seraph rolling in the Flood
With scatter'd Arms and Ensigns, till anon   325
His swift pursuers from Heav'n Gates discern
Th' advantage, and descending tread us down
Thus drooping, or with linked Thunderbolts
Transfix us to the bottom of this Gulf.
Awake, arise, or be for ever fall'n.   330
    They heard, and were abasht, and up they sprung
Upon the wing, as when men wont to watch
On duty, sleeping found by whom they dread,

Rouse and bestir themselves ere well awake.
Nor did they not perceive the evil plight   335
In which they were, or the fierce pains not feel;
Yet to thir General's Voice they soon obey'd
Innumerable. As when the potent Rod
Of *Amram's* Son in *Egypt's* evil day
Wav'd round the Coast, up call'd a pitchy cloud   340
Of *Locusts*, warping on the Eastern Wind,
That o'er the Realm of impious *Pharaoh* hung
Like Night, and darken'd all the Land of *Nile:*
So numberless were those bad Angels seen
Hovering on wing under the Cope of Hell   345
'Twixt upper, nether, and surrounding Fires;
Till, as a signal giv'n, th' uplifted Spear
Of thir great Sultan waving to direct
Thir course, in even balance down they light
On the firm brimstone, and fill all the Plain;   350
A multitude, like which the populous North
Pour'd never from her frozen loins, to pass
Rhene or the *Danaw*, when her barbarous Sons
Came like a Deluge on the South, and spread
Beneath *Gibraltar* to the *Lybian* sands.   355
Forthwith from every Squadron and each Band
The Heads and Leaders thither haste where stood
Thir great Commander; Godlike shapes and forms
Excelling human, Princely Dignities,
And Powers that erst in Heaven sat on Thrones;   360
Though of thir Names in heav'nly Records now
Be no memorial, blotted out and ras'd
By thir Rebellion, from the Books of Life.

Oreb and *Sinai* (7): mountains intimately connected with Divine Revelation in
the Old Testament. *That Shepherd* (8): Moses. *Sion Hill* (10): near Jerusalem,
where the voice of God was heard by Hebrew prophets. *Siloa's Brook* (11): near
Jerusalem. *Aonian Mount* (15): traditional home of the Greek muses. *Spirit*
(17): the creative force of God that inspired the Hebrew prophets. *durst* (102):
past tense of *dare*. *Empyreal* (117): heavenly. *Compeer* (127): comrade.
Seraphim (129): angels. *slip* (178): let slip. *rood* (196): a space of 5½ to 8
yards. *Titanian* (198): a variant of Titan. *Briareos of Typhon* (199): two myth-
ical figures whose rebellion against Jove led to their being thrown into the under-
world. *night-founder'd* (204): caught in darkness. *Pelorus* (232) and *Aetna*
(233): volcanic mountains. *Stygian* (239): hellish. *fardest* (247): farthest.
Tuscan Artist (288): Galileo. *Fesole* (289) and *Valdarno* (290): situated above
the Arno River in Italy. *Ammiral* (294): admiral's flagship. *Marl* (296): ground.
Nathless (299): not the less. *Vallombrosa* (303): "Shady Valley," situated near

Florence. *Orion* (305): a constellation associated with storms. *Busiris* (307): a legendary Egyptian king. *Sojourners of Goshen* (309): those persecuted by Pharaoh. *Amram's Son* (339): Moses. *Cope* (345): roof. *Rhene or the Danaw* (353): Rhine or the Danube.

1. Milton belongs to two great—and apparently conflicting—movements in the intellectual and spiritual history of England. On the one hand, his wealth of classical learning and almost unrivaled mastery of an elaborate craft stamp him as one of the supreme figures of the Renaissance. On the other, his intense dedication to the Puritan cause in England and his own deeply held individual concept of Christianity place him as one of the significant figures of the Protestant Reformation. By paying especial attention to the opening sixteen lines and by noting the source of the excerpt's several allusions, point out in a long paragraph specific references to the two movements. Which appears dominant? Why?

2. An *epic* is a long narrative poem written in an exalted style and centered upon the destiny of an heroic nature. Some conventions of the epic are these: (1) the poet opens with an announcement of his theme; (2) he invokes the aid of a muse; (3) he asks the muse an epic question; (4) the reply to that question begins the action of the poem; (5) the action itself begins *in media res*, that is, in the middle of things. Show how Milton either fulfills or ignores each of these conventions in the opening of *Paradise Lost*.

3. To what myth does Milton refer in line 198? How does the allusion to Briareos and Typhon (l. 199) function in the simile Milton begins in line 196? To what line does the simile extend?

4. One of the major reasons for the elaborate syntax Milton evolved in *Paradise Lost* is the nature of his subject. That is, in a poem which deals with God, Satan, and the Biblical Fall, the rhythms of ordinary speech would strike the reader's ear as absurdly flat-footed and inappropriate. Study the sentence which runs from the middle of line 44 to the end of line 49; then in an essay point out each of the departures it takes from the more common syntactical structures of English (it may help to rewrite the sentence in a more conventional form). Some critics, while granting that *Paradise Lost* is a superb example of highly wrought art, have gone on to complain that the poem is not written in English. Based on the entire excerpt from Book I, would you agreee or disagree? Explain in your essay.

5. John Dryden, a much younger contemporary of Milton, once

declared that Milton saw nature "through the spectacles of books." Study the passage that runs from line 283 to line 313, paying especial attention to Milton's similes, and evaluate in a few paragraphs the justice of Dryden's charge. In your analysis of each simile, it will probably be helpful to use the concepts of vehicle and tenor (see p. 17).

6. Some critics have claimed that Milton miscalculated in the opening of *Paradise Lost* and made Satan—the intended "villain" of the epic—too heroic. Analyze the character of Satan as it is presented in this excerpt from Book I. Does it seem "noble" to you? Are there any traces of self-deception? of wishful thinking? of apparent dishonesty and self-contradiction? Explain.

7. Study lines 242–255. How many of the lines are exactly ten syllables? (The word "Heav'n" is almost always a one-syllable word in Milton's prosody.) Mark the accented syllables. How strongly does Milton establish an iambic pattern? Indicate three variations from the iambic in the passage and in a paragraph comment on the effectiveness of each variation. In addition to a recurrent use of enjambment, Milton is also noted for his employment of varying breaks (or caesura) within a line. That is, at some point within a line there may be a natural pause, often (but not always) suggested by a mark of punctuation. In most lines there will be one break, although in line 242 there are two (after "Region" and after "Soil"). Indicate the significant breaks in lines 242–255. How do they vary from line to line? Does the break ever occur on the same syllable of two consecutive lines? How significant are the breaks in establishing the rhythm of this passage?

POST-MILTONIC BLANK VERSE

Milton's achievement was so overwhelming that since his time only three possible choices regarding blank verse seem apparent for a poet: (1) like T. S. Eliot in our own century, he can accuse Milton of having built a "Chinese Wall" against further progress in blank verse and can avoid using the form; (2) like Wordsworth in the first half of the nineteenth century, he can use Milton as an ideal model and create his own personal blank verse based at least in part on Miltonic "paragraphs"; or (3) like Robert Browning in the Victorian period or

Robert Frost in our own time, he can write a blank verse that aims once more at restoring to the form the rhythms of an actual speaking voice, without surrendering, at the same time, the intensity of poetry.

WILLIAM WORDSWORTH (1770–1850)

Lines Composed a Few Miles Above Tintern Abbey

Five years have past; five summers, with the length
Of five long winters! and again I hear
These waters, rolling from their mountain-springs
With a soft inland murmur.—Once again
Do I behold these steep and lofty cliffs,   5
That on a wild secluded scene impress
Thoughts of more deep seclusion; and connect
The landscape with the quiet of the sky.
The day is come when I again repose
Here, under this dark sycamore, and view   10
These plots of cottage-ground, these orchard-tufts,
Which at this season, with their unripe fruits,
Are clad in one green hue, and lose themselves
'Mid groves and copses. Once again I see
These hedge-rows, hardly hedge-rows, little lines   15
Of sportive wood run wild; these pastoral farms,
Green to the very door; and wreaths of smoke
Sent up, in silence, from among the trees!
With some uncertain notice, as might seem
Of vagrant dwellers in the houseless woods,   20
Or of some hermit's cave, where by his fire
The hermit sits alone.
                              These beauteous forms,
Through a long absence, had not been to me
As is a landscape to a blind man's eye:
But oft, in lonely rooms, and 'mid the din   25
Of towns and cities, I have owed to them
In hours of weariness, sensations sweet,
Felt in the blood, and felt along the heart;

And passing even into my purer mind,
With tranquil restoration:—feelings too   30
Of unremembered pleasure: such, perhaps,
As have no slight or trivial influence
On that best portion of a good man's life,
His little, nameless, unremembered acts
Of kindness and of love. Nor less, I trust,   35
To them I may have owed another gift,
Of aspect more sublime; that blessèd mood,
In which the burthen of the mystery,
In which the heavy and the weary weight
Of all this unintelligible world,   40
Is lightened:—that serene and blessèd mood,
In which the affections gently lead us on,—
Until, the breath of this corporeal frame
And even the motion of our human blood
Almost suspended, we are laid asleep   45
In body, and become a living soul:
While with an eye made quiet by the power
Of harmony, and the deep power of joy,
We see into the life of things.
                                        If this
Be but a vain belief, yet, oh! how oft—   50
In darkness and amid the many shapes
Of joyless daylight; when the fretful stir
Unprofitable, and the fever of the world,
Have hung upon the beatings of my heart—
How oft, in spirit, have I turned to thee,   55
O sylvan Wye! thou wanderer through the woods,
How often has my spirit turned to thee!
    And now, with gleams of half-extinguished thought,
With many recognitions dim and faint,
And somewhat of a sad perplexity,   60
The picture of the mind revives again:
While here I stand, not only with the sense
Of present pleasure, but with pleasing thoughts
That in this moment there is life and food
For future years. And so I dare to hope,   65
Though changed, no doubt, from what I was when first
I came among these hills; when like a roe
I bounded o'er the mountains, by the sides
Of the deep rivers, and the lonely streams,
Wherever nature led: more like a man   70

Flying from something that he dreads than one
Who sought the thing he loved. For nature then
(The coarser pleasures of my boyish days,
And their glad animal movements all gone by)
To me was all in all. I cannot paint   75
What then I was. The sounding cataract
Haunted me like a passion: the tall rock,
The mountain, and the deep and gloomy wood,
Their colors and their forms, were then to me
An appetite; a feeling and a love,   80
That had no need of a remoter charm,
By thought supplied, nor any interest
Unborrowed from the eye.—That time is past,
And all its aching joys are now no more,
And all its dizzy raptures. Not for this   85
Faint I, nor mourn nor murmur; other gifts
Have followed; for such loss, I would believe,
Abundant recompense. For I have learned
To look on nature, not as in the hour
Of thoughtless youth; but hearing oftentimes   90
The still, sad music of humanity,
Nor harsh nor grating, though of ample power
To chasten and subdue. And I have felt
A presence that disturbs me with the joy
Of elevated thoughts; a sense sublime   95
Of something far more deeply interfused,
Whose dwelling is the light of setting suns,
And the round ocean and the living air,
And the blue sky, and in the mind of man:
A motion and a spirit, that impels   100
All thinking things, all objects of all thought,
And rolls through all things. Therefore am I still
A lover of the meadows and the woods
And mountains; and of all that we behold
From this green earth; of all the mighty world   105
Of eye, and ear,—both what they half create,
And what perceive; well pleased to recognize
In nature and the language of the sense
The anchor of my purest thoughts, the nurse,
The guide, the guardian of my heart, and soul   110
Of all my moral being.
                        Nor perchance,
If I were not thus taught, should I the more

Suffer my genial spirits to decay:
For thou art with me here upon the banks
Of this fair river; thou my dearest Friend,   115
My dear, dear Friend; and in thy voice I catch
The language of my former heart, and read
My former pleasures in the shooting lights
Of thy wild eyes. Oh! yet a little while
May I behold in thee what I was once,   120
My dear, dear Sister! and this prayer I make,
Knowing that Nature never did betray
The heart that loved her; 'tis her privilege,
Through all the years of this our life, to lead
From joy to joy: for she can so inform   125
The mind that is within us, so impress
With quietness and beauty, and so feed
With lofty thoughts, that neither evil tongues,
Rash judgments, nor the sneers of selfish men,
Nor greetings where no kindness is, nor all   130
The dreary intercourse of daily life,
Shall e'er prevail against us, or disturb
Our cheerful faith that all which we behold
Is full of blessings. Therefore let the moon
Shine on thee in thy solitary walk;   135
And let the misty mountain-winds be free
To blow against thee: and, in after years,
When these wild ecstasies shall be matured
Into a sober pleasure; when thy mind
Shall be a mansion for all lovely forms,   140
Thy memory be as a dwelling-place
For all sweet sounds and harmonies; oh! then,
If solitude, or fear, or pain, or grief,
Should be thy portion, with what healing thoughts
Of tender joy wilt thou remember me,   145
And these my exhortations! Nor, perchance—
If I should be where I no more can hear
Thy voice, nor catch from thy wild eyes these gleams
Of past existence—wilt thou then forget
That on the banks of this delightful stream   150
We stood together; and that I, so long
A worshipper of Nature, hither came
Unwearied in that service: rather say
With warmer love—oh! with far deeper zeal
Of holier love. Nor wilt thou then forget,   155

That after many wanderings, many years
Of absence, these steep woods and lofty cliffs,
And this green pastoral landscape, were to me
More dear, both for themselves and for thy sake!

roe (67): deer. *genial* (113): inborn. *dearest Friend* (115): Dorothy Words-
worth, the poet's sister, two years his junior.

1. Wordsworth wrote "Tintern Abbey" a few days after taking a walking tour there with his sister. What is the effect of the poet using the word "five" three times in the first two lines? How can "connect" (l. 7) be interpreted as the key word to the first twenty-two lines? How many "connections" are there? What, for example, is the effect of the repetitive use of "again"?

2. Why does the persona in the poem feel something of "a sad perplexity" (l. 60)? What is meant by "remoter charm" (l. 81)? What is the "abundant recompense" (l. 88) that the persona believes he has found? Explain line 91.

3. For Wordsworth, Milton was the supreme model in English poetry, and he once declared that the ideal of harmony in blank verse was attained "in the apt arrangement of pauses and cadences, and the sweep of the whole paragraphs . . . and not in the even flow, much less in the prominence or antithetical vigor of single lines, which were indeed injurious to the total effect, except where they were introduced for some specific purpose." Note that the beginnings of new verse paragraphs in "Tintern Abbey" are indicated by pronounced breaks in the appearance of the type (e.g., ll. 22, 58, 111). How do these paragraph divisions correspond to the thought divisions of the poem? Explain. Into how many paragraphs may "Tintern Abbey" be divided? How do the paragraph divisions correspond to the thought divisions of the poem?

4. Is this poem primarily about memory, Nature (l. 122), growing old, perception? some combination of these four? Explain in a short essay.

ALFRED, LORD TENNYSON (1809–92)

Ulysses

It little profits that an idle king,
By this still hearth, among these barren crags,
Matched with an agèd wife, I mete and dole
Unequal laws unto a savage race,
That hoard, and sleep, and feed, and know not me.   5
I cannot rest from travel: I will drink
Life to the lees: all times I have enjoyed
Greatly, have suffered greatly, both with those
That loved me, and alone; on shore, and when
Through scudding drifts the rainy Hyades   10
Vexed the dim sea: I am become a name;
For always roaming with a hungry heart
Much have I seen and known: cities of men
And manners, climates, councils, governments,
Myself not least, but honored of them all;   15
And drunk delight of battle with my peers,
Far on the ringing plains of windy Troy.
I am a part of all that I have met;
Yet all experience is an arch wherethrough
Gleams that untravelled world whose margin fades   20
For ever and for ever when I move.
How dull it is to pause, to make an end,
To rust unburnished, not to shine in use!
As though to breathe were life! Life piled on life
Were all too little, and of one to me   25
Little remains: but every hour is saved
From that eternal silence, something more,
A bringer of new things; and vile it were
For some three suns to store and hoard myself,
And this gray spirit yearning in desire   30
To follow knowledge like a sinking star,
Beyond the utmost bound of human thought.
   This is my son, mine own Telemachus,
To whom I leave the scepter and the isle—

Well-loved of me, discerning to fulfil   35
This labor, by slow prudence to make mild
A rugged people, and through soft degrees
Subdue them to the useful and the good.
Most blameless is he, centered in the sphere
Of common duties, decent not to fail   40
In offices of tenderness, and pay
Meet adoration to my household gods,
When I am gone. He works his work, I mine.
   There lies the port; the vessel puffs her sail:
There gloom the dark broad seas. My mariners,   45
Souls that have toiled, and wrought, and thought with me—
That ever with a frolic welcome took
The thunder and the sunshine, and opposed
Free hearts, free foreheads—you and I are old;
Old age hath yet his honor and his toil.   50
Death closes all: but something ere the end,
Some work of noble note, may yet be done,
Not unbecoming men that strove with Gods.
The lights begin to twinkle from the rocks:
The long day wanes: the slow moon climbs: the deep   55
Moans round with many voices. Come, my friends,
'Tis not too late to seek a newer world.
Push off, and sitting well in order smite
The sounding furrows; for my purpose holds
To sail beyond the sunset, and the baths   60
Of all the western stars, until I die.
It may be that the gulfs will wash us down:
It may be we shall touch the Happy Isles,
And see the great Achilles, whom we knew.
Though much is taken, much abides; and though   65
We are not now that strength which in old days
Moved earth and heaven, that which we are, we are:
One equal temper of heroic hearts,
Made weak by time and fate, but strong in will
To strive, to seek, to find, and not to yield.   70

Hyades (10): a group of stars whose rising is associated with rain. *Happy Isles*
(63): paradise.

1. Ulysses is the Latin name for Odysseus, the hero of Homer's
Odyssey. As Tennyson conceives him, Ulysses (having returned to
Ithaca after ten years of wandering following the fall of Troy) is un-
able to rest or remain in one place, even though his age and past ex-

ploits would seem to merit for him a well-earned retirement. How are we to interpret this unrest of Ulysses? As something noble? as mere wanderlust? as emotional insecurity? (Cite specific passages in the poem to support your conclusion.) Some critics have interpreted the poem as a depiction of an egocentric figure who is always looking off into the distance and consistently ignoring the realities at hand. Do you agree? Why, or why not? Tennyson himself remarked of this poem that it reflected his own "need of going forward and braving the struggle of life" after the death of his very close friend, Arthur Hallam. How important is an author's own statement of intention about his work? Does it rule out other conflicting interpretations? Discuss.

2. Using the concepts of vehicle and tenor, analyze the metaphor in lines 18–21. What is the implicit metaphor in line 23? What figures of speech are to be found in lines 47–49? Are these figures purposeful or merely decorative? Explain.

3. Study the blank verse of lines 54–70. How is the effect of slowness achieved in lines 55–56? by extra syllables? by accentual variation? by vowel manipulation? Explain. Why is the extreme metrical regularity of line 70 especially appropriate?

ROBERT BROWNING (1812–89)

The Bishop Orders His Tomb at Saint Praxed's Church

ROME, 15—

Vanity, saith the preacher, vanity!
Draw round my bed: is Anselm keeping back?
Nephews—sons mine . . . ah God, I know not! Well—
She, men would have to be your mother once,
Old Gandolf envied me, so fair she was!   5
What's done is done, and she is dead beside,
Dead long ago, and I am Bishop since,
And as she died so must we die ourselves,
And thence ye may perceive the world's a dream.
Life, how and what is it? As here I lie   10
In this state-chamber, dying by degrees,
Hours and long hours in the dead night, I ask,
"Do I live, am I dead?" Peace, peace seems all.
Saint Praxed's ever was the church for peace;

And so, about this tomb of mine. I fought   15
With tooth and nail to save my niche, ye know:
—Old Gandolf cozened me, despite my care;
Shrewd was that snatch from out the corner south
He graced his carrion with, God curse the same!
Yet still my niche is not so cramped but thence   20
One sees the pulpit o' the epistle-side,
And somewhat of the choir, those silent seats,
And up into the aery dome where live
The angels, and a sunbeam's sure to lurk:
And I shall fill my slab of basalt there,   25
And 'neath my tabernacle take my rest,
With those nine columns round me, two and two,
The odd one at my feet where Anselm stands:
Peach-blossom marble all, the rare, the ripe
As fresh-poured red wine of a mighty pulse.   30
—Old Gandolf with his paltry onion-stone,
Put me where I may look at him! True peach,
Rosy and flawless: how I earned the prize!
Draw close: that conflagration of my church
—What then? So much was saved if aught were missed!   35
My sons, ye would not be my death? Go dig
The white-grape vineyard where the oil-press stood,
Drop water gently till the surface sink,
And if ye find . . . ah God, I know not, I! . . .
Bedded in store of rotten fig-leaves soft,   40
And corded up in a tight olive-frail,
Some lump, ah God, of *lapis lazuli*,
Big as a Jew's head cut off at the nape,
Blue as a vein o'er the Madonna's breast . . .
Sons, all have I bequeathed you, villas, all,   45
That brave Frascati villa with its bath,
So, let the blue lump poise between my knees,
Like God the Father's globe on both his hands
Ye worship in the Jesu Church so gay,
For Gandolf shall not choose but see and burst!   50
Swift as a weaver's shuttle fleet our years:
Man goeth to the grave, and where is he?
Did I say basalt for my slab, sons? Black—
'Twas ever antique-black I meant! How else
Shall ye contrast my frieze to come beneath?   55
The bas-relief in bronze ye promised me,
Those Pans and Nymphs ye wot of, and perchance

Some tripod, thyrsus, with a vase or so,
The Savior at his sermon on the mount,
Saint Praxed in a glory, and one Pan   60
Ready to twitch the Nymph's last garment off,
And Moses with the tables . . . but I know
Ye mark me not! What do they whisper thee,
Child of my bowels, Anselm? Ah, ye hope
To revel down my villas while I gasp   65
Bricked o'er with beggar's moldy travertine
Which Gandolf from his tomb-top chuckles at!
Nay, boys, ye love me—all of jasper, then!
'Tis jasper ye stand pledged to, lest I grieve
My bath must needs be left behind, alas!   70
One block, pure green as a pistachio-nut,
There's plenty jasper somewhere in the world—
And have I not Saint Praxed's ear to pray
Horses for ye, and brown Greek manuscripts,
And mistresses with great smooth marbly limbs?   75
—That's if ye carve my epitaph aright,
Choice Latin, picked phrase, Tully's every word,
No gaudy ware like Gandolf's second line—
Tully, my masters? Ulpian serves his need!
And then how I shall lie through centuries,   80
And hear the blessed mutter of the mass,
And see God made and eaten all day long,
And feel the steady candle-flame, and taste
Good strong thick stupefying incense-smoke!
For as I lie here, hours of the dead night,   85
Dying in state and by such slow degrees,
I fold my arms as if they clasped a crook,
And stretch my feet forth straight as stone can point,
And let the bedclothes, for a mortcloth, drop
Into great laps and folds of sculptor's-work: 90
And as yon tapers dwindle, and strange thoughts
Grow, with a certain humming in my ears,
About the life before I lived this life,
And this life too, popes, cardinals and priests,
Saint Praxed at his sermon on the mount,   95
Your tall pale mother with her talking eyes,
And new-found agate urns as fresh as day,
And marble's language, Latin pure, discreet,
—Aha, ELUCESCEBAT quoth our friend?
No Tully, said I, Ulpian at the best!   100

Evil and brief hath been my pilgrimage.
All *lapis*, all, sons! Else I give the Pope
My villas! Will ye ever eat my heart?
Ever your eyes were as a lizard's quick,
They glitter like your mother's for my soul,   105
Or ye would heighten my impoverished frieze,
Piece out its starved design, and fill my vase
With grapes, and add a vizor and a term,
And to the tripod ye would tie a lynx
That in his struggle throws the thyrsus down,   110
To comfort me on my entablature
Whereon I am to lie till I must ask,
"Do I live, am I dead?" There, leave me, there!
For ye have stabbed me with ingratitude
To death—ye wish it—God, ye wish it! Stone—   115
Gritstone, a-crumble! Clammy squares which sweat
As if the corpse they keep were oozing through—
And no more *lapis* to delight the world!
Well go! I bless ye. Fewer tapers there,
But in a row: and, going, turn your backs   120
—Ay, like departing altar-ministrants,
And leave me in my church, the church for peace,
That I may watch at leisure if he leers—
Old Gandolf, at me, from his onion-stone,
As still he envied me, so fair she was!   125

onion-stone (31): a poor kind of marble that peels. *olive-frail* (41): a small basket for holding olives. *lapis lazuli* (42): a valuable blue stone. *travertine* (66): limestone. *mortcloth* (89): the ceremonial cloth spread over a corpse or a coffin. *term* (108): that is, Terminus, the Roman god of boundaries.

1. Browning is the acknowledged master of the *dramatic monologue,* a form which (at its most complete) possesses the following characteristics: (1) a single speaker who is presented as clearly distinct from the poet himself; (2) an audience whose presence is felt within the poem (in this, the dramatic monologue differs from the soliloquy); and (3) a situation that induces the speaker to reveal, usually unwittingly, the essence of his character. What is the speaker's condition in Browning's poem? Where is he? Who is his audience? What is the dramatic situation?

2. Characterize the Bishop. In how many ways does he use God's name? Has he been a good bishop? What is his view of eternity? How

can lines like 1 and 51–52 be explained? Why does his voice break in lines 3 and 39? Who is the "she" of lines 4 and 125? Does the description in lines 56–62 provide at least some key to the Bishop's character? Explain. "ELUCESCEBAT" (99) is a late Latin form of *elucebat*, which means "he was illustrious." Ulpian (100), as befits a writer of a period when Rome's literature had sharply declined, makes use of the corrupt form; Tully (that is, Cicero) would make use of the much chaster, "classical" word. What, then, do lines 76–79 and 98–100 reveal about the Bishop?

3. How does Browning's blank verse here differ from Milton's in the excerpt from *Paradise Lost?* Be as specific as you can.

4. Tennyson's "Ulysses" is also a dramatic monologue. Compare Browning's use of the form to Tennyson's. Which seems to you the better poem? On what grounds?

5. Although Browning wrote several blank-verse dramas for theatrical performance, his plays are now forgotten, while his dramatic monologues remain a part of world literature. What are the differences between a dramatic monologue and a play which might explain Browning's success in the one and his failure in the other?

QUESTIONS – FROST · STEVENS

ROBERT FROST (1874–1963)

Birches

When I see birches bend to left and right
Across the lines of straighter darker trees,
I like to think some boy's been swinging them.
But swinging doesn't bend them down to stay.
Ice-storms do that. Often you must have seen them   5
Loaded with ice a sunny winter morning
After a rain. They click upon themselves
As the breeze rises, and turn many-colored
As the stir cracks and crazes their enamel.
Soon the sun's warmth makes them shed crystal shells   10
Shattering and avalanching on the snow-crust—

Such heaps of broken glass to sweep away
You'd think the inner dome of heaven had fallen.
They are dragged to the withered bracken by the load,
And they seem not to break; though once they are bowed   15
So low for long, they never right themselves:
You may see their trunks arching in the woods
Years afterwards, trailing their leaves on the ground
Like girls on hands and knees that throw their hair
Before them over their heads to dry in the sun.   20
But I was going to say when Truth broke in
With all her matter-of-fact about the ice-storm
I should prefer to have some boy bend them
As he went out and in to fetch the cows—
Some boy too far from town to learn baseball,   25
Whose only play was what he found himself,
Summer or winter, and could play alone.
One by one he subdued his father's trees
By riding them down over and over again
Until he took the stiffness out of them,   30
And not one but hung limp, not one was left
For him to conquer. He learned all there was
To learn about not launching out too soon
And so not carrying the tree away
Clear to the ground. He always kept his poise   35
To the top branches, climbing carefully
With the same pains you use to fill a cup
Up to the brim, and even above the brim.
Then he flung outward, feet first, with a swish,
Kicking his way down through the air to the ground.   40
So was I once myself a swinger of birches.
And so I dream of going back to be.
It's when I'm weary of considerations,
And life is too much like a pathless wood
Where your face burns and tickles with the cobwebs   45
Broken across it, and one eye is weeping
From a twig's having lashed across it open.
I'd like to get away from earth awhile
And then come back to it and begin over.
May no fate willfully misunderstand me   50
And half grant what I wish and snatch me away
Not to return. Earth's the right place for love:
I don't know where it's likely to go better.
I'd like to go by climbing a birch tree,

And climb black branches up a snow-white trunk   55
Toward heaven, till the tree could bear no more,
But dipped its top and set me down again.
That would be good both going and coming back.
One could do worse than be a swinger of birches.

1. The following remark is Frost's attempt to describe the success-
ful poem: "It begins in delight, it inclines to the impulse, it assumes
direction with the first line laid down, it runs a course of lucky events,
and ends in a clarification of life." How revealing are these remarks
with respect to "Birches"? Answer in a long paragraph.
2. Compare the blank verse of "Birches" either to that of Brown-
ing's "The Bishop Orders His Tomb" or to that of the Stevens' poem
that follows. Be as specific as you can, using the concepts of syllabic
regularity, diction, enjambment, accentual variation, syntax, and
whatever formal devices you think relevant. You should also consider
the basic question of how a traditional form can liberate contempo-
rary content.

WALLACE STEVENS (1879–1955)

Sunday Morning

I

Complacencies of the peignoir, and late
Coffee and oranges in a sunny chair,
And the green freedom of a cockatoo
Upon a rug mingle to dissipate
The holy hush of ancient sacrifice.   5
She dreams a little, and she feels the dark
Encroachment of that old catastrophe,
As a calm darkens among water-lights.
The pungent oranges and bright, green wings
Seem things in some procession of the dead,   10
Winding across wide water, without sound.
The day is like wide water, without sound,
Stilled for the passing of her dreaming feet
Over the seas, to silent Palestine,
Dominion of the blood and sepulchre.   15

Why should she give her bounty to the dead?
What is divinity if it can come
Only in silent shadows and in dreams?
Shall she not find in comforts of the sun,
In pungent fruit and bright, green wings, or else   20
In any balm or beauty of the earth,
Things to be cherished like the thought of heaven?
Divinity must live within herself:
Passions of rain, or moods in falling snow;
Grievings in loneliness, or unsubdued   25
Elations when the forest blooms; gusty
Emotions on wet roads on autumn nights;
All pleasures and all pains, remembering
The bough of summer and the winter branch.
These are the measures destined for her soul.   30

III

Jove in the clouds had his inhuman birth.
No mother suckled him, no sweet land gave
Large-mannered motions to his mythy mind.
He moved among us, as a muttering king,
Magnificent, would move among his hinds,   35
Until our blood, commingling, virginal,
With heaven, brought such requital to desire
The very hinds discerned it, in a star.
Shall our blood fail? Or shall it come to be
The blood of paradise? And shall the earth   40
Seem all of paradise that we shall know?
The sky will be much friendlier then than now,
A part of labor and a part of pain,
And next in glory to enduring love,
Not this dividing and indifferent blue.   45

IV

She says, "I am content when wakened birds,
Before they fly, test the reality
Of misty fields, by their sweet questionings;
But when the birds are gone, and their warm fields
Return no more, where, then, is paradise?"   50
There is not any haunt of prophecy,
Nor any old chimera of the grave,

Neither the golden underground, nor isle
Melodious, where spirits gat them home,
Nor visionary south, nor cloudy palm   55
Remote on heaven's hill, that has endured
As April's green endures; or will endure
Like her remembrance of awakened birds,
Or her desire for June and evening, tipped
By the consummation of the swallow's wings.   60

V

She says, "But in contentment I still feel
The need of some imperishable bliss."
Death is the mother of beauty; hence from her,
Alone, shall come fulfilment to our dreams
And our desires. Although she strews the leaves   65
Of sure obliteration on our paths,
The path sick sorrow took, the many paths
Where triumph rang its brassy phrase, or love
Whispered a little out of tenderness,
She makes the willow shiver in the sun   70
For maidens who were wont to sit and gaze
Upon the grass, relinquished to their feet.
She causes boys to pile new plums and pears
On disregarded plate. The maidens taste
And stray impassioned in the littering leaves.   75

VI

Is there no change of death in paradise?
Does ripe fruit never fall? Or do the boughs
Hang always heavy in that perfect sky,
Unchanging, yet so like our perishing earth,
With rivers like our own that seek for seas   80
They never find, the same receding shores
That never touch with inarticulate pang?
Why set the pear upon those river-banks
Or spice the shores with odors of the plum?
Alas, that they should wear our colors there,   85
The silken weavings of our afternoons,
And pick the strings of our insipid lutes!
Death is the mother of beauty, mystical,
Within whose burning bosom we devise
Our earthly mothers waiting, sleeplessly.   90

Supple and turbulent, a ring of men
Shall chant in orgy on a summer morn
Their boisterous devotion to the sun,
Not as a god, but as a god might be,
Naked among them, like a savage source. 95
Their chant shall be a chant of paradise,
Out of their blood, returning to the sky;
And in their chant shall enter, voice by voice,
The windy lake wherein their lord delights,
The trees, like serafin, and echoing hills, 100
That choir among themselves long afterward.
They shall know well the heavenly fellowship
Of men that perish and of summer morn.
And whence they came and whither they shall go
The dew upon their feet shall manifest. 105

VIII

She hears, upon that water without sound,
A voice that cries, "The tomb in Palestine
Is not the porch of spirits lingering.
It is the grave of Jesus, where he lay."
We live in an old chaos of the sun, 110
Or old dependency of day and night,
Or island, solitude, unsponsored, free,
Of that wide water, inescapable.
Deer walk upon our mountains, and the quail
Whistle about us their spontaneous cries; 115
Sweet berries ripen in the wilderness;
And, in the isolation of the sky,
At evening, casual flocks of pigeons make
Ambiguous undulations as they sink,
Downward to darkness, on extended wings. 120

1. What is the significance of the title? What is the occasion of the poem?

2. What is the "old catastrophe" (l. 7)? How do the questions that begin stanza II grow out of the first stanza? Explain line 23.

3. How do the concepts of the third stanza grow out of the opening mention of Jove? What, for example, was the effect upon the human mind of its ability to conceive of a Jove?

4. How is the concept of immortality treated in the fourth stanza? The paradox that is stated in the fifth stanza (l. 63) provides the keynote for what might be called the resolution of the poem. In a long paragraph explain the paradox in the light of the poem's development. 5. What sort of ceremony or ritual is suggested in the seventh stanza? Is it religious? Explain. What, finally, is the "philosophy" that seems to underlie "Sunday Morning"? Does this "philosophy" seem related to the philosophical concepts in Stevens' "Of Modern Poetry" (see p. 380). Is it significant that both of these poems with quite modern content build their prosody on the old form of blank verse?

Chapter 7

The Ode

The ode is a lyric poem of ceremonious effect which embodies a complex thought or emotion. Organized by elaborate argument, illustration, or presentation, the ode is further characterized by impressive length, elevated diction, and a serious or exalted tone. Though frequently an occasional piece—that is, a piece written to honor a particular event or person (e.g., Marvell's "An Horatian Ode upon Cromwell's Return from Ireland" or Lowell's "Ode Recited at the Harvard Commemoration"), the form often serves as a mode for philosophical reflection, as with Pope's "Ode on Solitude," Shelley's "Ode to the West Wind," or the last three poems in this chapter: Allen Tate's "Ode to the Confederate Dead," William Carlos Williams' "To a Dog Injured in the Street," and Marianne Moore's "To a Steam Roller." In these last three poems the perennial vitality of the ode as a form allows for a modern celebration of surprisingly new but appropriate subjects. The result is that an old form is the expression of completely modern content.

CLASSICAL ANTECEDENTS

As a formal structure, the ode generally displays *strophic* (i.e., composed of stanzas) rather than *stichic* (i.e., verses running continuously and uninterrupted by stanzaic units) organization. Its form in English and American poetry has evolved principally from loose interpretations of two classical antecedents: Pindar (522?–443 B.C.) and Horace (65–8 B.C.). Pindar's odes, written either to be performed as choral lyrics for dramatic productions at the Greek festivals in honor of Dionysus or at gatherings in celebration of athletic victories, gave to English poetry the *triadic* (three-stanza) structure known as the Pindaric ode. Horace's odes, written to be read rather than for a public ceremony, were characterized by a placid tone more often privately reflective than occasional. They gave to English poetry the *homo-strophic* (single stanza) structure that serves as stanzaic base for a poem—sometimes called the Horatian ode—which usually features large and metrically intricate stanzas.

Pindar's odes were composed of *triads*—that is, units of three stanzas. The first stanza was called *strophe*, the second (identical metrically and in length with the first) was called *antistrophe*, and the third (featuring a different length and metrical pattern) was called *epode*. In the following English imitation of the Pindaric triad, the Renaissance poet Ben Jonson uses the English terms *turne* for strophe, *counter-turne* for antistrophe, and *stand* for epode:

THE TURNE

Brave Infant of *Saguntum*, cleare
Thy comming forth in that great yeare,
When the Prodigious *Hannibal* did crowne
His rage, with razing your immortall Towne.
Thou, looking then about,   5
E're thou wert halfe got out,
Wise child, did'st hastily returne,
And mad'st thy Mothers wombe thine urne.
How summ'd a circle didst thou leave man-kind
Of deepest lore, could we the Center find!   10

THE COUNTER-TURNE

Did wiser Nature draw thee back,
From out the horrour of that sack?
Where shame, faith, honour, and regard of right
Lay trampled on; the deeds of death, and night,
Urg'd, hurried forth, and horld   15
Upon th'affrighted world:

Sword, fire, and famine, with fell fury met;
And all on utmost ruine set;
As, could they but lifes miseries fore-see,
No doubt all Infants would returne like thee.   20

THE STAND

For, what is life, if measur'd by the space,
Not by the act?
Or masked man, if valu'd by his face,
Above his fact?
Here's one out-liv'd his Peeres,   25
And told forth fourescore yeares;
He vexed time, and busied the whole State;
Troubled both foes, and friends;
But ever to no ends:
What did this Stirrer, but die late?   30
How well at twentie had he falne, or stood!
For three of his four-score, he did no good.

In this ode to two friends (Cary and Morrison), one of whom died in
early youth, Jonson uses the first triad to draw an elaborate contrast
between the untimely death of a youth of promise and the unnec-
essary old age of those who fail to contribute meaningfully (e.g.,
Hannibal, who began the second Punic War by destroying Sagun-
tum). Note that both strophe and antistrophe are ten-line couplet
stanzas, while the epode contains twelve lines in a different rhyme
scheme.

Most of Pindar's odes contained fewer than five triads. And while
the poet initially had complete freedom of metrical choice, he re-
linquished that freedom once he had completed his first triad. For in
any given Pindaric ode, all strophes and all antistrophes of every
triad were identical metrically and in stanzaic length; likewise, all
epodes were identical. Though several English poets have sought to
adapt strictly the Pindaric form to their native tongue, few of them—
notably Jonson (1573–1637), William Collins (1721–59), and
Thomas Gray (1716–70)—have achieved any degree of success.
Gray's two Pindarics, "The Progress of Poesy" and "The Bard,"
probably represent the greatest technical competency any English
poet has reached in adapting the form.

Literary historians have provided numerous explanations for the
failure of the Pindaric as an English ode form. The most frequent is

that its formal triadic structure, though meaningful to Greek pageant audiences, appeared falsely stilted and meaningless to English readers. For the Greek audience, the basis for identical strophe and antistrophe was obvious. A choral dance with musical accompaniment moved from the altar to the right and back to the altar during the strophe; the same dance and musical accompaniment was repeated with movement to the left during the antistrophe. Identical dances, music, and distance of movement prescribed and gave meaning to identical poetic form in strophe and antistrophe. The epode, on the other hand, was sung to new music, a new dance, and was performed entirely before the altar; thus the basis for its freedom from the length and metrical prescriptions of the first two parts was rendered dramatically apparent.

Though the Horatian or—in more common usage—the homostrophic ode requires stanzas of equal length and identical meter, there is infinite variety among odes that follow these prescriptions. Compare, for example, the simple iambic quatrain of Pope's "Ode on Solitude" and Coleridge's elaborate twenty-one verse stanzas in "France: An Ode." In addition, stanzaic repetition in a homostrophic ode creates for English readers a metrical anticipation which the Pindaric—because of its long stanzas and dual pattern (i.e., one scheme for strophe and antistrophe, another for epode)—seldom achieves. The poet, cognizant that his reader must recognize and recall a single pattern, can employ greater metrical complexity and stanzaic length; at the same time, he can vary his pattern for effect and expect incremental repetition to keep his reader from losing the overall pattern.

THE ENGLISH ODE

The English ode (sometimes called the irregular ode, the Cowleyan ode, or the English Pindaric) has unlimited freedom of metrical pattern and stanzaic length. Its originator, Abraham Cowley (1618–67), partially derived his early reputation from fifteen rhymed, irregular poems that he called Pindaric odes. Later critics mistakenly asserted that Cowley did not know or understand the triadic form of the true Pindaric and thus naturally failed to imitate it; however, in truth Cowley aspired not to imitate form, but to adapt the spirit of the original Pindaric to English poetry. The result was that he began a tradition in which each stanza of a given ode differed both metrically and in length from any other stanza. Since the poet set for himself no prescriptive stanzaic pattern or rhyme scheme, he could easily adapt various stanzas to changing thoughts or emotions, thus—at least theoretically—attaining greater correspondence between sound and sense. Consider, for example, the first stanza of Cowley's "Life and Fame"

> Oh Life, thou *Nothings younger Brother!*
> So *like*, that one might take *One* for the *other!*
> What's *Some Body*, or *No Body?*
> In all the *Cobwebs* of the *Schoolmens* trade,
> We no such nice *Distinction* woven see,   5
> As 'tis *To be*, or *Not to Be.*
> *Dream* of a *Shadow!* a *Reflection* made
> From the false glories of the gay *reflected Bow*,
> Is a more *solid* thing then *Thou.*
> Vain weak-built *Isthmus*, which dost proudly rise   10
> Up betwixt *two Eternities;*
> Yet canst nor *Wave* nor *Wind* sustain,
> But *broken* and *orewhelm'd*, the endless *Oceans* meet again.

Like the selection from Jonson's Cary-Morrison ode, this passage contains elevated language, dignified rhythms, lofty thoughts of general significance, complexity of syntax and stanzaic form, and elegant apostrophe. In other words, the spirit of Cowley's ode closely resembles that of Jonson; they differ only in terms of adherence to metrical prescriptions. Acknowledged triumphs of this Cowleyan or English ode are, for example, Dryden's "Alexander's Feast, or, The Power of Musique" and "Song for St. Cecilia's Day," Wordsworth's "Ode: Intimations of Immortality," Tennyson's "Ode on the Death of the Duke of Wellington," and Allen Tate's "Ode on the Confederate Dead."

FLEXIBILITY OF THE ODE

Regardless of type, the ode is a lyric form often employed by poets who wish to present either a complex idea or emotion. The ultimate worth of a particular ode will likely be determined not by its regularity or irregularity, but by the degree to which its overall organization supports this idea or emotion. In some cases the reader will be left to deduce the idea from its implicit presentation, while in others the poet explicitly states his theme. Pope, for example, states his theme in the last stanza of "Ode on Solitude":

> Thus let me live, unseen, unknown,
> Thus unlamented let me die,
> Steal from the world, and not a stone
> Tell where I lie.

Often the serious or exalted tone of a reflective ode is introduced by efficacious use of the periodic sentence (i.e., a sentence in which the meaning and grammatical form are not completed until the end, as, for example, the sentence serving as the first section of Shelley's "Ode to the West Wind") or of elaborate apostrophe and personification (see pp. 21–23). Such use of apostrophe is evident in the first four verses of Keats's "Ode on a Grecian Urn":

> Thou still unravished bride of quietness,
> Thou foster-child of silence and slow time,
> Sylvan historian, who canst thus express
> A flowery tale more sweetly than our rhyme:

While apostrophe is especially characteristic of the patriotic ode or occasional piece, it may also be employed in less hortatory poetry, as, for example, the first stanza of Poe's "To Helen":

> Helen, thy beauty is to me
> Like those Nicean barks of yore,
> That gently, o'er a perfumed sea,
> The weary, way-worn wanderer bore
> To his own native shore.

The ode, then, is a very flexible lyric presentation. Though the form may be prescriptive—should the poet choose formal adherence to either the Pindaric or Horatian traditions—it always provides the poet with complete freedom in choice of initial stanzaic pattern. Moreover, it is the form most ideally suited to poetic presentation of a complex idea or emotion. Like the Spenserian stanza in the next

chapter, the ode offers the length necessary for the celebration or
ceremony that will express fully such complexity.

THOMAS GRAY (1716–71)

The Progress of Poesy
A Pindaric Ode

I—1

Awake, Aeolian lyre, awake,
And give to rapture all thy trembling strings.
From Helicon's harmonious springs
A thousand rills their mazy progress take;
The laughing flowers that round them blow   5
Drink life and fragrance as they flow.
Now the rich stream of music winds along,
Deep, majestic, smooth, and strong,
Through verdant vales and Ceres' golden reign;
Now rolling down the steep amain,   10
Headlong, impetuous, see it pour;
The rocks and nodding groves rebellow to the roar.

I—2

Oh! Sovereign of the willing soul,
Parent of sweet and solemn-breathing airs,
Enchanting shell! the sullen Cares   15
And frantic Passions hear thy soft control.
On Thracia's hills the Lord of War
Has curbed the fury of his car,
And dropped his thirsty lance at thy command.
Perching on the sceptered hand   20
Of Jove, thy magic lulls the feathered king,
With ruffled plumes and flagging wing;
Quenched in dark clouds of slumber lie
The terror of his beak, and lightnings of his eye.

Thee the voice, the dance, obey,   25
Tempered to thy warbled lay.
O'er Idalia's velvet-green
The rosy-crownèd Loves are seen
On Cytherea's day;
With antic Sports, and blue-eyed Pleasures,   30
Frisking light in frolic measures;
Now pursuing, now retreating,
Now in circling troops they meet,
To brisk notes in cadence beating
Glance their many-twinkling feet.   35
Slow melting strains their queen's approach declare;
Where'er she turns the Graces homage pay.
With arms sublime that float upon the air,
In gliding state she wins her easy way;
O'er her warm cheek and rising bosom move   40
The bloom of young desire and purple light of love.

II—1

Man's feeble race what ills await,
Labor, and penury, the racks of pain,
Disease, and sorrow's weeping train,
And death, sad refuge from the storms of fate!   45
The fond complaint, my song, disprove,
And justify the laws of Jove.
Say, has he given in vain the heavenly Muse?
Night, and all her sickly dews,
Her spectres wan, and birds of boding cry   50
He gives to range the dreary sky;
Till down the eastern cliffs afar
Hyperion's march they spy, and glittering shafts of war.

II—2

In climes beyond the solar road,
Where shaggy forms o'er ice-built mountains roam,   55
The Muse has broke the twilight-gloom
To cheer the shivering native's dull abode.
And oft, beneath the odorous shade
Of Chili's boundless forests laid,
She deigns to hear the savage youth repeat   60
In loose numbers wildly sweet

Their feather-cinctured chiefs and dusky loves.
Her track, where'er the goddess roves,
Glory pursue, and generous shame,
The unconquerable mind, and Freedom's holy flame. 65

II—3

Woods that wave o'er Delphi's steep,
Isles that crown the Aegean deep,
Fields that cool Ilissus laves,
Or where Maeander's amber waves
In lingering labyrinths creep, 70
How do your tuneful echoes languish,
Mute, but to the voice of anguish!
Where each old poetic mountain
Inspiration breathed around,
Every shade and hallowed fountain 75
Murmured deep a solemn sound;
Till the sad Nine in Greece's evil hour
Left their Parnassus for the Latian plains.
Alike they scorn the pomp of tyrant Power,
And coward Vice, that revels in her chains. 80
When Latium had her lofty spirit lost,
They sought, O Albion! next, thy sea-encircled coast.

III—1

Far from the sun and summer-gale,
In thy green lap was Nature's darling laid,
What time, where lucid Avon strayed, 85
To him the mighty mother did unveil
Her awful face; the dauntless child
Stretched forth his little arms, and smiled.
"This pencil take," she said, "whose colors clear
Richly paint the vernal year; 90
Thine too these golden keys, immortal boy!
This can unlock the gates of joy;
Of horror that, and thrilling fears,
Or ope the sacred source of sympathetic tears."

III—2

Nor second he that rode sublime 95
Upon the seraph-wings of ecstasy,
The secrets of the abyss to spy.
He passed the flaming bounds of place and time;

The living throne, the sapphire-blaze,
Where angels tremble while they gaze,　　　　　　　　　　100
He saw; but blasted with excess of light,
Closed his eyes in endless night.
Behold where Dryden's less presumptuous car,
Wide o'er the fields of glory bear
Two coursers of ethereal race,　　　　　　　　　　　　105
With necks in thunder clothed, and long-resounding pace.

III—3

Hark, his hands the lyre explore!
Bright-eyed Fancy, hovering o'er,
Scatters from her pictured urn
Thoughts that breathe and words that burn.　　　　　110
But ah! 'tis heard no more—
O lyre divine, what daring spirit
Wakes thee now? Though he inherit
Nor the pride nor ample pinion
That the Theban Eagle bear,　　　　　　　　　　　　115
Sailing with supreme dominion
Through the azure deep of air;
Yet oft before his infant eyes would run
Such forms as glitter in the Muse's ray
With orient hues, unborrowed of the sun;　　　　　　120
Yet shall he mount, and keep his distant way
Beyond the limits of a vulgar fate—
Beneath the good how far—but far above the great.

1. Why may "The Progress of Poesy" be termed a Pindaric ode? Compare metrical arrangement of strophe and antistrophe in each triad. Compare metrical arrangement of the epodes in each triad.

2. The ceremonious effect of the ode results largely from its elevated diction. Why would one consider the diction of "The Progress of Poesy" elevated? Does the predominance of allusion contribute largely to that elevation? Explain. Why would one consider the tone formal and serious? How do alliteration and assonance contribute to establishing tone? Note, for example, their evidence in the first and last verses of the first strophe:

> Awake, Aeolian lyre, awake,
> The rocks and nodding groves rebellow to the roar.

How does elaborate use of personification contribute to tone? At times does it distort meaning? Note, for example, "laughing flowers" (l. 5). What specifically does this image convey? Is it perhaps ambiguous or without meaning? Cite throughout the poem other similar uses of personification.

3. During the Restoration and eighteenth century, the Pindaric ode—as well as the ode in general—was often the form employed to develop themes concerning the power of music. How does Gray's ode fall into this tradition? Is the theme developed through argument, illustration, presentation, or some combination of these?

4. Is the elaborate triadic structure of Gray's poem only illustrative of his metrical versatility, or does it serve meaningfully to indicate thematic development in the poem? Explain in a paragraph. The apostrophe in line 1 addresses the "Aeolian" (i.e., exultant or festive) lyre; what different "Aeolian" effects of musical sound are elicited in the first strophe? In the antistrophe, how does the second verse (l. 14) distinguish a type of music different from that celebrated in the strophe? What different effects "of sweet and solemn-breathing airs" are distinguished? What other power of harmony is presented in the epode? Describe the subject-matter scope and total effect of the first triad. How does the subject matter of the second triad differ from that of the first? Is the "progress" of the poem's title here clearly evident? Explain. In the third triad, "Nature's darling" (l. 84) is Shakespeare, and "he that rode sublime" (l. 95) is Milton. How do allusions to particular poets in the third triad indicate thematic progression from the geographical and historical emphases of the second triad?

QUESTIONS – POPE • COLERIDGE • KEATS • POE

ALEXANDER POPE (1688–1744)

Ode on Solitude

Happy the man whose wish and care
A few paternal acres bound,

Content to breathe his native air,
  In his own ground.

Whose herds with milk, whose fields with bread,   5
  Whose flocks supply him with attire,
Whose trees in summer yield him shade,
  In winter fire.

Blest, who can unconcern'dly find
  Hours, days, and years slide soft away,   10
In health of body, peace of mind,
  Quiet by day,

Sound sleep by night; study and ease,
  Together mixt; sweet recreation;
And Innocence, which most does please   15
  With meditation.

Thus let me live, unseen, unknown,
  Thus unlamented let me die,
Steal from the world, and not a stone
  Tell where I lie.   20

1. In the introduction to this section, the point is made that odes in the Horatian tradition feature a placid tone more privately reflective than do many occasional pieces written in the Pindaric mode. Compare the diction of Pope's "Ode on Solitude" with that of Gray's "Progress of Poesy." Which is more elegant and formal? How does diction affect tone in the two poems? Explain in a paragraph.

2. Pope's quatrains rhyming *abab* evidence the most common quatrain form in all English literature. Compare the greater ease in anticipating rhyme in this poem with the relative difficulty in Coleridge's "France: An Ode." What effect does ease of anticipating rhyme have on the poem's tone?

3. Does Pope group sounds that are noticeably euphonious rather than cacophonous? From which of the following sound devices does Pope's euphony result: alliteration, assonance, omission of series of unaccented syllables, predominance of vowel sounds, omission of placing harsh consonants together, appropriate placing of accented syllables, predominance of usually pleasing liquids or semivowels (*l, m, n, r, y, w*), internal and end rhyme, line balance resulting from

caesura, appropriate meter? What effect does euphony or cacophony have on tone? Compare and contrast sound devices in the last quatrain of "Ode on Solitude" with that evident in these lines from Browning:

> A tap at the pane, the quick sharp scratch
> And blue spurt of a lighted match.

4. A common use of the poetic license is *inversion*, that is, alteration of the subject-verb-complement order that usually characterizes the English sentence. What effect does this inversion have on poetic emphasis? Is the second quatrain of "Ode on Solitude" grammatically dependent on the first? Is the fourth quatrain grammatically dependent on the third? The word "Blest" (l. 9) is part of an elliptical sentence; compare that sentence with line 1. The word "Thus" (l. 17) denotes "as a result of"; how is it structurally dependent upon the words "Happy" (l. 1) and "Blest" (l. 9)? Is progression in the poem inductive or deductive; that is, does it reason from particular facts or individual cases to a general conclusion, or does it reason vice versa? All of the foregoing questions (under number 4) concern progression; define the progression of "Ode on Solitude" by comparing it with Keats's "Ode on a Grecian Urn."

SAMUEL TAYLOR COLERIDGE (1772–1834)

France: An Ode

I

Ye Clouds! that far above me float and pause,
    Whose pathless march no mortal may controul!
Ye Ocean-Waves! that, wheresoe'er ye roll,
Yield homage only to eternal laws!
Ye Woods! that listen to the night-birds singing,   5
    Midway the smooth and perilous slope reclined,
Save when your own imperious branches swinging,
    Have made a solemn music of the wind!
Where, like a man beloved of God,
Through glooms, which never woodman trod,   10
    How oft, pursuing fancies holy,

My moonlight way o'er flowering weeds I wound,
    Inspired, beyond the guess of folly,
By each rude shape and wild unconquerable sound!
O ye loud Waves! and O ye Forests high!   15
    And O ye Clouds that far above me soared!
Thou rising Sun! thou blue rejoicing Sky!
    Yea, every thing that is and will be free!
Bear witness for me, wheresoe'er ye be,
    With what deep worship I have still adored   20
        The spirit of divinest Liberty.

II

When France in wrath her giant-limbs upreared,
    And with that oath, which smote air, earth, and sea,
    Stamped her strong foot and said she would be free,
Bear witness for me, how I hoped and feared!   25
With what a joy my lofty gratulation
    Unawed I sang, amid a slavish band:
And when to whelm the disenchanted nation,
    Like fiends embattled by a wizard's wand,
        The Monarchs marched in evil day,   30
        And Britain joined the dire array;
    Though dear her shores and circling ocean,
Though many friendships, many youthful loves
    Had swoln the patriot emotion
And flung a magic light o'er all her hills and groves;   35
Yet still my voice, unaltered, sang defeat
    To all that braved the tyrant-quelling lance,
And shame too long delayed and vain retreat!
For ne'er, O Liberty! with partial aim
I dimmed thy light or damped thy holy flame;   40
    But blessed the paeans of delivered France,
And hung my head and wept at Britain's name.

III

"And what," I said, "though Blasphemy's loud scream
    With that sweet music of deliverance strove!
    Though all the fierce and drunken passions wove   45
A dance more wild than e'er was maniac's dream!
    Ye storms, that round the dawning East assembled,
The Sun was rising, though ye hid his light!"
    And when, to soothe my soul, that hoped and trembled,
The dissonance ceased, and all seemed calm and bright;   50

When France her front deep-scarr'd and gory
Concealed with clustering wreaths of glory;
  When, insupportably advancing,
Her arm made mockery of the warrior's ramp;
  While timid looks of fury glancing,   55
Domestic treason, crushed beneath her fatal stamp,
Writhed like a wounded dragon in his gore;
  Then I reproached my fears that would not flee;
"And soon," I said, "shall Wisdom teach her lore
In the low huts of them that toil and groan!   60
And, conquering by her happiness alone,
  Shall France compel the nations to be free,
Till Love and Joy look round, and call the Earth their own."

IV

Forgive me, Freedom! O forgive those dreams!
  I hear thy voice, I hear thy loud lament,   65
  From bleak Helvetia's icy caverns sent—
I hear thy groans upon her blood-stained streams!
  Heroes, that for your peaceful country perished,
And ye that, fleeing, spot your mountain-snows
  With bleeding wounds; forgive me, that I cherished   70
One thought that ever blessed your cruel foes!
  To scatter rage, and traitorous guilt,
  Where Peace her jealous home had built;
    A patriot-race to disinherit
Of all that made their stormy wilds so dear;   75
    And with inexpiable spirit
To taint the bloodless freedom of the mountaineer—
O France, that mockest Heaven, adulterous, blind,
  And patriot only in pernicious toils!
Are these thy boasts, Champion of human kind?   80
  To mix with Kings in the low lust of sway,
Yell in the hunt, and share the murderous prey;
To insult the shrine of Liberty with spoils
  From freemen torn; to tempt and to betray?

V

  The Sensual and the Dark rebel in vain,   85
Slaves by their own compulsion! In mad game
They burst their manacles and wear the name
  Of Freedom, graven on a heavier chain!

O Liberty! with profitless endeavour
Have I pursued thee, many a weary hour;   90
  But thou nor swell'st the victor's strain, nor ever
Didst breathe thy soul in forms of human power.
  Alike from all, howe'er they praise thee,
    (Nor prayer, nor boastful name delays thee)
      Alike from Priestcraft's harpy minions,   95
  And factious Blasphemy's obscener slaves,
      Thou speedest on thy subtle pinions,
The guide of homeless winds, and playmate of the waves!
And there I felt thee!—on that sea-cliff's verge,
  Whose pines, scarce travelled by the breeze above,   100
Had made one murmur with the distant surge!
Yes, while I stood and gazed, my temples bare,
And shot my being through earth, sea, and air,
  Possessing all things with intensest love,
    O Liberty! my spirit felt thee there.   105

1. An *invocation* is a poetic device by which the poet calls on something (e.g., God, a saint, the Muse, an abstraction, an object) to bless, help, inspire, or protect. To what natural phenomena does Coleridge direct the invocation in Stanza I? How does verse 18 clarify significance of the phenomena? Why are the objects invoked appropriate to the poet's plea expressed in verses 19–21?

2. In stanza II the poet reveals that he had previously equated the French Revolution with freedom. What had been his attitude toward that Revolution and toward his native England's opposition to it?

3. In stanza III the poet suggests his early reaction to the revolutionary terrorists and blasphemers. Explain that reaction. What hopes do verses 61–63 suggest that the poet had held for the Revolution?

4. Does stanza IV show that the poet's hopes were realized? Explain his present conviction.

5. Explain the lyric effect of the apostrophe (see p. 21) in stanza V. What romantic attitude is expressed toward all forms of government? Demonstrate in a brief paragraph the relationship of the apostrophe in stanza V to those in stanza I.

6. Considering rhyme scheme, meter, and stanzaic length, would you term "France" a homostrophic ode? Does each stanza further

develop a single theme? What structural principles do you recognize in the poem (note, for example, that two of the five stanzas reveal a preponderance of nature images)?

JOHN KEATS (1795–1821)

Ode on a Grecian Urn

I

Thou still unravished bride of quietness,
    Thou foster-child of silence and slow time,
Sylvan historian, who canst thus express
    A flowery tale more sweetly than our rhyme:
What leaf-fringed legend haunts about thy shape   5
    Of deities or mortals, or of both,
        In Tempe or the dales of Arcady?
What men or gods are these? What maidens loath?
    What mad pursuit? What struggle to escape?
        What pipes and timbrels? What wild ecstasy?   10

II

Heard melodies are sweet, but those unheard
    Are sweeter; therefore, ye soft pipes, play on;
Not to the sensual ear, but, more endeared,
    Pipe to the spirit, ditties of no tone:
Fair youth, beneath the trees, thou canst not leave   15
    Thy song, nor ever can those trees be bare;
        Bold Lover, never, never canst thou kiss,
Though winning near the goal—yet, do not grieve;
    She cannot fade, though thou hast not thy bliss,
        Forever wilt thou love, and she be fair!   20

III

Ah, happy, happy boughs! that cannot shed
    Your leaves, nor ever bid the spring adieu;
And, happy melodist, unwearièd,
    Forever piping songs forever new;
More happy love! more happy, happy love!   25
    Forever warm and still to be enjoyed,
        Forever panting, and forever young;
All breathing human passion far above,

That leaves a heart high-sorrowful and cloyed,
  A burning forehead, and a parching tongue.   30

IV

Who are these coming to the sacrifice?
  To what green altar, O mysterious priest,
Lead'st thou that heifer lowing at the skies,
  And all her silken flanks with garlands dressed?
What little town by river or sea shore,   35
  Or mountain-built with peaceful citadel,
    Is emptied of this folk, this pious morn?
And, little town, thy streets forevermore
  Will silent be; and not a soul to tell
    Why thou are desolate, can e'er return.   40

V

O Attic shape! Fair attitude! with brede
  Of marble men and maidens overwrought,
With forest branches and the trodden weed;
  Thou, silent form, dost tease us out of thought
As doth eternity: Cold Pastoral!   45
  When old age shall this generation waste,
    Thou shalt remain, in midst of other woe
Than ours, a friend to man, to whom thou say'st,
  "Beauty is truth, truth beauty,—that is all
    Ye know on earth, and all ye need to know."   50

1. Review the introduction to Chapter 3, paying particular attention to the rhyme schemes of both the Petrarchan and English sonnets. Note that Keats's ten-verse stanzas combine characteristics of both patterns. What is the rhyme scheme of the first four verses? Is this scheme common (compare it with the first four verses of either the English sonnet or the Spenserian stanza)? Note the rhyme scheme of verses 5, 6, and 7 in Keats's stanza. Is it comparable to any part of the Petrarchan sonnet? How do the rhymes of verses 8, 9, and 10 in Keats's stanza relate to those of verses 5, 6, and 7? What effects result from the regularity of the final three verses in the third and fourth stanzas, when contrasted with the irregularity in the last three verses of the last stanza?

2. In the first three verses of the first stanza, apostrophe is em-

ployed three times. How does each amplify the poet's conception of the Grecian urn? What specifically is being described in the final six verses of the stanza?

3. How does the reference to "pipes and timbrels" in the first stanza provide meaningful transition to the second stanza?

4. Explain the paradox (see p. 23) of "melodies . . . unheard" and "ditties of no tone" in the second stanza. Is resolution of the paradox necessary for understanding the second, third, and fourth stanzas? Explain.

5. Explain the following comparison in the last stanza: "Thou, silent form, dost tease us out of thought / As doth eternity . . ." What is the "truth" of the urn's appeal? How does this clarify the meaning of the final two verses in the poem?

6. How does the form of the ode particularly serve Keats in this poem? In writing a paragraph to answer this question, cite particular aspects of the ode as they relate to the specific subject—or theme—of the poem.

EDGAR ALLAN POE (1809–49)

To Helen

Helen, thy beauty is to me
    Like those Nicèan barks of yore
That gently, o'er a perfumed sea,
    The weary way-worn wanderer bore
To his own native shore.   5

On desperate seas long wont to roam,
    Thy hyacinth hair, thy classic face,
Thy Naiad airs have brought me home
    To the glory that was Greece,
And the grandeur that was Rome.   10

Lo, in yon brilliant window-niche
    How statue-like I see thee stand,
    The agate lamp within thy hand,
Ah! Psyche, from the regions which
    Are holy land!   15

1. Is this poem an ode? What characteristics of the ode does it possess or lack? The question of length is obviously foremost. Is the strength of Poe's theme lessened by the brevity of the poem? Explain. What devices strengthen his poetic statement?

2. In an essay, compare the brevity of this ode with that of Marianne Moore's "To a Steam Roller" (p. 244). Is the celebration lessened in each? What exactly is the celebration in each?

QUESTIONS – DRYDEN • WORDSWORTH

JOHN DRYDEN (1631–1700)

A Song for St. Cecilia's Day, 1687

1

From harmony, from heavenly harmony
    This universal frame began:
      When Nature underneath a heap
      Of jarring atoms lay,
    And could not heave her head,   5
The tuneful voice was heard from high:
    "Arise, ye more than dead."
Then cold, and hot, and moist, and dry,
    In order to their stations leap,
      And Music's power obey.   10
From harmony, from heavenly harmony
    This universal frame began:
      From harmony to harmony
Through all the compass of the notes it ran,
The diapason closing full in man.   15

2

What passion cannot Music raise and quell!
    When Jubal struck the corded shell,
    His listening brethren stood around,
    And, wondering, on their faces fell
    To worship that celestial sound.   20
Less than a god they thought there could not dwell
    Within the hollow of that shell

That spoke so sweetly and so well.
What passion cannot Music raise and quell!

3

The trumpet's loud clangor   25
   Excites us to arms,
With shrill notes of anger,
   And mortal alarms.
The double double double beat
   Of the thundering drum   30
Cries: "Hark! the foes come;
Charge, charge, 'tis too late to retreat."

4

The soft complaining flute
In dying notes discovers
The woes of hopeless lovers,   35
Whose dirge is whispered by the warbling lute.

5

Sharp violins proclaim
Their jealous pangs, and desperation,
Fury, frantic indignation,
Depth of pains, and height of passion,   40
   For the fair, disdainful dame.

6

But O! what art can teach,
   What human voice can reach,
The sacred organ's praise?
   Notes inspiring holy love,   45
Notes that wing their heavenly ways
   To mend the choirs above.

7

Orpheus could lead the savage race;
And trees unrooted left their place,
   Sequacious of the lyre;   50
But bright Cecilia raised the wonder higher:
When to her organ vocal breath was given,
An angel heard, and straight appeared,
   Mistaking earth for heaven.

As *from the power of sacred lays*   55
   The spheres began to move,
And sung the great Creator's praise
   To all the blest above;
So, when the last and dreadful hour
This crumbling pageant shall devour,   60
The trumpet shall be heard on high,
The dead shall live, the living die,
And Music shall untune the sky.

1. Dryden's ode, like those of Cowley, is irregular and imitates no formal structure. Does Dryden attempt to adapt the spirit of the original Pindaric to his own purpose? Explain in a paragraph. Dryden's poem is an occasional piece written for a musical society's celebration of St. Cecilia's Day (St. Cecilia is the patron saint of music). Compare the tone with that of Gray's "Progress of Poesy" (p. 218).

2. In the introduction to this chapter the point is made that the irregular ode, since it accepts no prescriptive stanzaic pattern, can readily adapt various stanzas to changing thoughts or emotions. Does Dryden's poem reveal such adaptation? In what stanzas do couplets and / or triplets occur? What effect do they have on tone? Is the meter of the various stanzas appropriate to their particular subject matter? Note, for example, the accents in the first four verses of the third stanza:

The trúmpet's loúd clángor
Excítes us to arms
With shríll notes of anger
And mórtal alárms.

Do not the short lines and heavy accents actually create a "loud clangor" that corresponds to the sound of the trumpet? Contrast these lines with the iambic pentameter verse that ends the fourth stanza:

Whŏse dírge | ĭs whís|pĕr'd bý | thĕ wárb|lĭng lúte. |

Flexibility of the Ode   233

Is the latter meter more appropriate for denoting an instrument that "discovers / The woes of hopeless lovers" (ll. 34–35)? Explain.

WILLIAM WORDSWORTH (1770–1850)

Ode: Intimations of Immortality from Recollections of Early Childhood

> The Child is father of the Man;
> And I could wish my days to be
> Bound each to each by natural piety.

I

There was a time when meadow, grove, and stream,
The earth, and every common sight,
  To me did seem
  Apparelled in celestial light,
The glory and the freshness of a dream.   5
It is not now as it hath been of yore;—
  Turn wheresoe'er I may,
   By night or day,
The things which I have seen I now can see no more.

II

  The rainbow comes and goes,   10
  And lovely is the rose,
  The moon doth with delight
Look round her when the heavens are bare;
  Waters on a starry night
  Are beautiful and fair;   15
  The sunshine is a glorious birth;
  But yet I know, where'er I go,
That there hath past away a glory from the earth.

III

Now, while the birds thus sing a joyous song,
  And while the young lambs bound   20
   As to the tabor's sound,
To me alone there came a thought of grief:
A timely utterance gave that thought relief,
  And I again am strong:

The cataracts blow their trumpets from the steep;   25
No more shall grief of mine the season wrong;
I hear the echoes through the mountains throng,
The winds come to me from the fields of sleep,
        And all the earth is gay;
            Land and sea   30
        Give themselves up to jollity,
            And with the heart of May
        Doth every beast keep holiday;—
            Thou child of joy,
Shout round me, let me hear thy shouts, thou happy shepherd-boy! 35

IV

Ye blessèd creatures, I have heard the call
    Ye to each other make; I see
The heavens laugh with you in your jubilee;
    My heart is at your festival,
        My head hath its coronal,   40
The fulness of your bliss, I feel—I feel it all.
    Oh evil day! if I were sullen
    While earth herself is adorning,
        This sweet May-morning,
    And the children are culling   45
        On every side,
    In a thousand valleys far and wide,
    Fresh flowers; while the sun shines warm,
And the babe leaps up on his mother's arm:—
    I hear, I hear, with joy I hear!   50
    —But there's a tree, of many, one,
A single field which I have looked upon,
Both of them speak of something that is gone:
    The pansy at my feet
    Doth the same tale repeat: 55
Whither is fled the visionary gleam?
Where is it now, the glory and the dream?

V

Our birth is but a sleep and a forgetting:
The soul that rises with us, our life's star,
    Hath had elsewhere its setting,   60
        And cometh from afar:
    Not in entire forgetfulness,
    And not in utter nakedness,

But trailing clouds of glory do we come
From God, who is our home: 65
Heaven lies about us in our infancy!
Shades of the prison-house begin to close
Upon the growing boy,
But he beholds the light, and whence it flows,
He sees it in his joy;   70
The youth, who daily farther from the east
Must travel, still is Nature's priest,
And by the vision splendid
Is on his way attended;
At length the man perceives it die away,   75
And fade into the light of common day.

VI

Earth fills her lap with pleasures of her own;
Yearnings she hath in her own natural kind,
And, even with something of a mother's mind,
And no unworthy aim,   80
The homely nurse doth all she can
To make her foster-child, her inmate man,
Forget the glories he hath known,
And that imperial palace whence he came.

VII

Behold the child among his new-born blisses,   85
A six year's darling of a pigmy size!
See, where 'mid work of his own hand he lies,
Fretted by sallies of his mother's kisses,
With light upon him from his father's eyes!
See, at his feet, some little plan or chart,   90
Some fragment from his dream of human life,
Shaped by himself with newly-learnèd art;
A wedding or a festival,
A mourning or a funeral;
And this hath now his heart,   95
And unto this he frames his song:
Then will he fit his tongue
To dialogues of business, love, or strife;
But it will not be long
Ere this be thrown aside,   100
And with new joy and pride

The little actor cons another part;
Filling from time to time his "humorous stage"
With all the persons, down to palsied age,
That life brings with her in her equipage;   105
    As if his whole vocation
    Were endless imitation.

VIII

Thou, whose exterior semblance doth belie
    Thy soul's immensity;
Thou best philosopher, who yet dost keep   110
Thy heritage, thou eye among the blind,
That, deaf and silent, read'st the eternal deep,
Haunted for ever by the eternal mind,—
    Mighty prophet! Seer blest!
    On whom those truths do rest,   115
Which we are toiling all our lives to find,
In darkness lost, the darkness of the grave;
Thou, over whom thy immortality
Broods like the day, a master o'er a slave,
A presence which is not to be put by;   120
Thou little child, yet glorious in the might
Of heaven-born freedom on thy being's height,
Why with such earnest pains dost thou provoke
The years to bring the inevitable yoke,
Thus blindly with thy blessedness at strife?   125
Full soon thy soul shall have her earthly freight,
And custom lie upon thee with a weight,
Heavy as frost, and deep almost as life!

IX

    O joy! that in our embers
    Is something that doth live,   130
    That nature yet remembers
    What was so fugitive!
The thought of our past years in me doth breed
Perpetual benediction: not indeed
For that which is most worthy to be blest;   135
Delight and liberty, the simple creed
Of childhood, whether busy or at rest,
With new-fledged hope still fluttering in his breast:—
    Not for these I raise
    The song of thanks and praise;   140

But for those obstinate questionings
Of sense and outward things,
Fallings from us, vanishings;
Blank misgivings of a creature
Moving about in worlds not realized, 145
High instincts before which our mortal nature
Did tremble like a guilty thing surprised:
    But for those first affections,
    Those shadowy recollections,
    Which, be they what they may, 150
Are yet the fountain light of all our day,
Are yet a master light of all our seeing;
    Uphold us, cherish, and have power to make
Our noisy years seem moments in the being
Of the eternal silence: truths that wake, 155
    To perish never;
Which neither listlessness, nor mad endeavor,
    Nor man nor boy,
Nor all that is at enmity with joy,
Can utterly abolish or destroy! 160
    Hence in a season of calm weather
    Though inland far we be,
Our souls have sight of that immortal sea
    Which brought us hither,
    Can in a moment travel thither, 165
And see the children sport upon the shore,
And hear the mighty waters rolling evermore.

           x

Then sing, ye birds, sing, sing a joyous song!
    And let the young lambs bound
    As to the tabor's sound! 170
We in thought will join your throng,
    Ye that pipe and ye that play,
    Ye that through your hearts today
    Feel the gladness of the May!
What though the radiance which was once so bright 175
Be now forever taken from my sight,
    Though nothing can bring back the hour
Of splendor in the grass, of glory in the flower;
    We will grieve not, rather find
    Strength in what remains behind; 180

In the primal sympathy
Which having been must ever be;
In the soothing thoughts that spring
Out of human suffering;
In the faith that looks through death,   185
In years that bring the philosophic mind.

XI

And O, ye fountains, meadows, hills, and groves,
Forebode not any severing of our loves!
Yet in my heart of hearts I feel your might;
I only have relinquished one delight   190
To live beneath your more habitual sway.
I love the brooks which down their channels fret,
Even more than when I tripped lightly as they;
The innocent brightness of a new-born day
   Is lovely yet;   195
The clouds that gather round the setting sun
Do take a sober coloring from an eye
That hath kept watch o'er man's mortality;
Another race hath been, and other palms are won.
Thanks to the human heart by which we live,   200
Thanks to its tenderness, its joys, and fears,
To me the meanest flower that blows can give
Thoughts that do often lie too deep for tears.

1. Poetry for Wordsworth was that "spontaneous overflow of powerful feeling" which resulted from "emotion recollected in tranquillity." Theoretically, though not always in practice, Wordsworth disclaimed the ornate self-consciousness which had so distinguished eighteenth-century poetry from prose. Judging "poetic" language to be artificial, he proposed rather a "selection of the real language of men in a state of vivid sensation." In a short essay, compare Wordsworth's ode with Dryden's "A Song for St. Cecilia's Day" (p. 231) or Gray's "The Progress of Poesy" (p. 218) by paying close attention to the following: diction, allusion, figurative language, sentence inversion, rhyme, meter.

2. Into what thematic divisions does Wordsworth's poem fall? What is the primary theme of the first four stanzas? What new theme is introduced in the fifth stanza? In the ninth? With reference to the poem, Wordsworth once wrote: "Nothing was more difficult

for me in childhood than to admit the notion of death as a state applicable to my own being." How does this poem represent that he came to terms with the dilemma?

THE MODERN ODE

With the exception of Allen Tate's "Ode to the Confederate Dead," few modern odes have attained widespread critical acceptance. As you read the modern poems in this exercise, consider their relationship to the formal ode. Which characteristics of the ode do they possess, and which do they lack? How do they show the ironic fact that celebration is just as relevant today as in centuries past?

ALLEN TATE (1899–   )

Ode to the Confederate Dead

Row after row with strict impunity
The headstones yield their names to the element,
The wind whirrs without recollection;
In the riven troughs the splayed leaves
Pile up, of nature the casual sacrament   5
To the seasonal eternity of death;
Then driven by the fierce scrutiny
Of heaven to their election in the vast breath,
They sough the rumor of mortality.

Autumn is desolation in the plot   10
Of a thousand acres where these memories grow
From the inexhaustible bodies that are not
Dead, but feed the grass row after rich row.
Think of the autumns that have come and gone!—
Ambitious November with the humors of the year,   15
With a particular zeal for every slab,
Staining the uncomfortable angels that rot
On the slabs, a wing chipped here, an arm there:
The brute curiosity of an angel's stare
Turns you, like them, to stone,   20
Transforms the heaving air

Till plunged to a heavier world below
You shift your sea-space blindly
Heaving, turning like the blind crab.

    Dazed by the wind, only the wind   25
    The leaves flying, plunge

You know who have waited by the wall
The twilight certainty of an animal,
Those midnight restitutions of the blood
You know—the immitigable pines, the smoky frieze   30
Of the sky, the sudden call: you know the rage,
The cold pool left by the mounting flood,
Of muted Zeno and Parmenides.
You who have waited for the angry resolution
Of those desires that should be yours tomorrow,   35
You know the unimportant shrift of death
And praise the vision
And praise the arrogant circumstance
Of those who fall
Rank upon rank, hurried beyond decision—   40
Here by the sagging gate, stopped by the wall.

    Seeing, seeing only the leaves
    Flying, plunge and expire

Turn your eyes to the immoderate past,
Turn to the inscrutable infantry rising   45
Demons out of the earth—they will not last.
Stonewall, Stonewall, and the sunken fields of hemp,
Shiloh, Antietam, Malvern Hill, Bull Run.
Lost in that orient of the thick and fast
You will curse the setting sun.   50

    Cursing only the leaves crying
    Like an old man in a storm

You hear the shout, the crazy hemlocks point
With troubled fingers to the silence which
Smothers you, a mummy, in time.   55

                    The hound bitch
Toothless and dying, in a musty cellar
Hears the wind only.

Now that the salt of their blood
Stiffens the saltier oblivion of the sea, 60
Seals the malignant purity of the flood,
What shall we who count our days and bow
Our heads with a commemorial woe
In the ribboned coats of grim felicity,
What shall we say of the bones, unclean, 65
Whose verdurous anonymity will grow?

The ragged arms, the ragged heads and eyes
Lost in these acres of the insane green?
The gray lean spiders come, they come and go;
In a tangle of willows without light 70
The singular screech-owl's tight
Invisible lyric seeds the mind
With the furious murmur of their chivalry.

We shall say only the leaves
Flying, plunge and expire 75

We shall say only the leaves whispering
In the improbable mist of nightfall
That flies on multiple wing:
Night is the beginning and the end
And in between the ends of distraction 80
Waits mute speculation, the patient curse
That stones the eyes, or like the jaguar leaps
For his own image in a jungle pool, his victim.

What shall we say who have knowledge
Carried to the heart? Shall we take the act 85
To the grave? Shall we, more hopeful, set up the grave
In the house? The ravenous grave?
                              Leave now
The shut gate and the decomposing wall:
The gentle serpent, green in the mulberry bush,
Riots with his tongue through the hush— 90
Sentinel of the grave who counts us all!

WILLIAM CARLOS WILLIAMS (1883–1963)

To a Dog Injured in the Street

IT IS MYSELF,
      not the poor beast lying there
         yelping with pain
that brings me to myself with a start—
      as at the explosion   5
         of a bomb, a bomb that has laid
all the world waste.
      I can do nothing
         but sing about it
and so I am assuaged   10
      from my pain.

A DROWSY NUMBNESS drowns my sense
      as if of hemlock
         I had drunk. I think
of the poetry   15
      of René Char
         and all he must have seen
and suffered
      that has brought him
         to speak only of   20
sedgy rivers,
      of daffodils and tulips
         whose roots they water,
even to the freeflowing river
      that laves the rootlets   25
         of those sweet scented flowers
that people the
      milky
         way.

I REMEMBER *Norma*   30
      our English setter of my childhood
         her silky ears
and expressive eyes.
      She had a litter
         of pups one night   35
in our pantry and I kicked
      one of them

> thinking, in my alarm,
> that they
> were biting her breasts 40
> to destroy her.

> I REMEMBER also
> a dead rabbit
> lying harmlessly
> on the outspread palm 45
> of a hunter's hand.
> As I stood by
> watching
> he took a hunting knife
> and with a laugh 50
> thrust it
> up into the animal's private parts.
> I almost fainted.

> WHY SHOULD I think of that now?
> The cries of a dying dog 55
> are to be blotted out
> as best I can.
> René Char
> you are a poet who believes
> in the power of beauty 60
> to right all wrongs.
> I believe it also.
> With invention and courage
> we shall surpass
> the pitiful dumb beasts, 65
> let all men believe it,
> as you have taught me also
> to believe it.

René Char (16): French resistance fighter and poet.

MARIANNE MOORE (1887–   )

To a Steam Roller

The illustration
is nothing to you without the application.

You lack half wit. You crush all the particles down
    into close conformity, and then walk back and forth on them.

Sparkling chips of rock   5
are crushed down to the level of the parent block.
    Were not "impersonal judgment in esthetic
        matters, a metaphysical impossibility," you

might fairly achieve
it. As for butterflies, I can hardly conceive   10
    of one's attending upon you, but to question
        the congruence of the complement is vain, if it exists.

Chapter 8

The Spenserian Stanza

A primary advantage of studying poetic forms is that it takes the reader back to the very moment in which a poem is born. Nowhere is this phenomenon more evident than in studying the stanza form invented by the Renaissance poet Edmund Spenser for his epic *The Faerie Queene*. The Spenserian stanza, one of the longest in English, consists of nine lines. The first eight are in iambic pentameter, but the ninth is in the difficult iambic hexameter, a basic line of French verse that is more commonly called an alexandrine. The rhyme scheme of the stanza is equally complex: *ababbcbcc*. Seemingly burdened—one might almost say, shackled—by long and odd mixtures of rhythm and rhyme, the poets must be few who would choose such a form to express their feelings, ideas, and responses to the world about them.

But the opposite is true. The Spenserian stanza, the Renaissance vehicle for one of the few great long poems in English, experienced a complete renewal in the Romantic era and became the vehicle for three great poems of that period: Byron's "Childe Harold's Pilgrimage," Shelley's "Adonais," and Keats's "The Eve of St. Agnes." In addition, poets used the form in the seventeenth and eighteenth centuries, rather consciously imitating Spenser—and in the later nineteenth, using the Romantic renewal of the form. Although the Spenserian stanza has rarely been used in modern poetry, it has been imitated or

adapted for short lyric poems—as in the poetry of Robert Lowell—
and has resulted in fascinating combinations of old and new.

Why would any poet choose such a form? For Spenser the stanza
of nine lines was a means for carrying his narrative forward—an ab-
solute necessity in any long poem—and at the same time slowing it
down enough so that the reader can summarize his feelings toward
the material just presented. To invent such a complex form, Spenser
drew on *rhyme royal* (see p. 323), Italian *ottava rima* (see p. 331),
and the stanza form in Chaucer's *Monk's Tale* (*ababbcbc*).

ADVANTAGES OF THE FORM

All of these sources, however, could not have turned the stanza
into a functioning vehicle if Spenser had not understood the sheer
advantages of the form for his epic. First, there are only three rhymes;
and the repetition of the *b* rhymes and the ease by which the *a* and *c*
rhymes are united give an extremely tight structure to the stanza.
The placement of these rhymes provides a varied effect as well as
unity of sound, with the result that the final alexandrine—the most
significant innovation of the stanza—is blended inevitably with the
whole. Such a use of three rhymes for nine lines is no mean achieve-
ment. Secondly, the twelve syllables of the alexandrine (and with
the extra syllables often a dramatic shift in the caesura) offer the
reader a pause for summary and reflection, providing an epigram-
matic effect much like that of the final couplet of a Shakespearean
sonnet (see p. 98). At the same time the alexandrine finishes the
stanza with the dignity demanded by epic, and—in a lesson learned
by such Romantic admirers as Keats—Spenser often echoes this last
line in the first line of his next stanza:

4

A lovely Ladie rode him faire beside,
Upon a lowly Asse more white then snow,
Yet she much whiter, but the same did hide
Under a vele, that wimpled was full low,
And over all a blacke stole she did throw,
As one that inly mournd: so was she sad,
And heavie sat upon her palfrey slow:

Seeméd in heart some hidden care she had,
And by her in a line a milke white lambe she lad.

5

So pure an innocent, as that same lambe,
  She was in life and every vertuous lore,
  And by descent from Royall lynage came
  Of ancient Kings and Queenes, that had of yore
  Their scepters stretcht from East to Westerne shore,
  And all the world in their subjection held;
  Till that infernall feend with foule uprore
  Forwasted all their land, and them expeld:
Whom to avenge, she had this Knight from far compeld.

(*The Faerie Queene*, Book I, Canto 1)

Spenser's stanza is therefore an instrument that isolates and blocks off certain areas, allowing for the fullest amplitude of expression. It is also an instrument that, by its consistent stanza form, propels the reader forward.

Nevertheless, one should not assume that a long stanza provides the poet a license for prolixity. The Spenserian stanza does provide a vast area for display, and its very length has proved itself precarious for the poet who has little to say. Verbosity has led to the failure of most imitations of this stanza form. Yet, like all great poets, Spenser invented the form to better express his content or, rather, so that the two should be one. A philosophical allegory such as *The Faerie Queene* demanded a form capable of resolving in complexity all the problems of such a subject. The Spenserian stanza was a logical choice for such a work.

QUESTIONS – SPENSER

EDMUND SPENSER (1552?–99)

from Book I, Canto XI of The Faerie Queene

8

By this the dreadful beast drew nigh to hand,
Half flying and half footing in his haste,
That with his largeness measurèd much land

And made wide shadow under his huge waist,
As mountain doth the valley overcast.
Approaching nigh, he rearèd high afore
His body monstrous, horrible, and vast,
Which to increase his wondrous greatness more,
Was swollen with wrath, and poison, and with bloody gore.

9

And over, all with brazen scales was armed
Like plated coat of steel, so couchèd near
That nought mote pierce, ne might his corse be harmed
With dint of sword nor push of pointed spear.
Which as an eagle, seeing prey appear
His airy plumes doth rouse, full rudely dight,
So shakèd he that horror was to hear.
For as the clashing of an armor bright,
Such noise his rousèd scales did send unto the knight.

10

His flaggy wings, when forth he did display,
Were like two sails in which the hollow-wind
Is gathered full and worketh speedy way.
And eke the pens that did his pinions bind
Were like main yards with flying canvas lined,
With which whenas him list the air to beat,
And there by force unwonted passage find,
The clouds before him fled for terror great,
And all the heavens stood still, amazèd with his threat.

11

His huge long tail, wound up in hundred folds,
Does overspread his long brass-scaly back,
Whose wreathèd boughts whenever he unfolds
And thick entangled knots adown does slack—
Bespotted as with shields of red and black—
It sweepeth all the land behind him far,
And of three furlongs does but little lack.
And at the point two stings infixèd are,
Both deadly sharp, that sharpest steel exceeden far.

12

But stings and sharpest steel did far exceed
The sharpness of his cruel rending claws;

Dead was it sure, as sure as death in deed,
Whatever thing does touch his ravenous paws,
Or what within his reach he ever draws.
But his most hideous head my tongue to tell
Does tremble; for his deep devouring jaws
Wide gapèd like the grisly mouth of hell,
Through which into his dark abyss all ravin fell.

13

And that more wondrous was, in either jaw
Three ranks of iron teeth enrangèd were,
In which yet trickling blood and gobbets raw
Of late devourèd bodies did appear,
That sight thereof bred cold congealèd fear.
Which to increase and all at once to kill,
A cloud of smothering smoke and sulfur sear
Out of his stinking gorge forth steamèd still,
That all the air about with smoke and stench did fill.

14

His blazing eyes, like two bright shining shields,
Did burn with wrath and sparkled living fire.
As two broad beacons, set in open fields,
Send forth their flames far off to every shire,
And warning give that enemies conspire
With fire and sword the region to invade,
So flamed his eyne with rage and rancorous ire;
But far within, as in a hollow glade,
Those glaring lamps were set, that made a dreadful shade.

15

So dreadfully he towards him did pass,
Forelifting up aloft his speckled breast,
And often bounding on the bruisèd grass,
As for great joyance of his new-come guest.
Eftsoons he gan advance his haughty crest,
As chafèd boar his bristles doth uprear,
And shook his scales, to battle ready dressed—
That made the Red Cross Knight nigh quake for fear—
As bidding bold defiance to his foeman near.

16

The knight gan fairly couch his steady spear
And fiercely ran at him with rigorous might.

The pointed steel, arriving rudely there,
His harder hide would neither pierce nor bite,
But glancing by, forth passèd forward right.
Yet sore amovèd with so puissant push,
The wrathful beast about him turnèd light,
And him so rudely, passing by, did brush
With his long tail that horse and man to ground did rush.

17

Both horse and man up lightly rose again,
And fresh encounter towards him addressed;
But th' idle stroke yet back recoiled in vain,
And found no place his deadly point to rest.
Exceeding rage inflamed the furious beast
To be avengèd of so great despite;
For never felt his impierceable breast
So wondrous force from hand of living wight.
Yet had he proved the power of many a puissant knight.

18

Then with his waving wings displayèd wide,
Himself up high he lifted from the ground,
And with strong flight did forcibly divide
The yielding air, which nigh too feeble found
Her flitting parts and element unsound
To bear so great a weight. He cutting way
With his broad sails, about him soarèd round;
At last low stooping with unwieldy sway,
Snatched up both horse and man to bear them quite away.

19

Long he them bore above the subject plain,
So far as yewen bow a shaft may send,
Till struggling strong did him at last constrain
To let them down before his flight'ès end.
As haggard hawk, presuming to contend
With hardy fowl above his able might,
His weary pounces all in vain doth spend
To truss the prey too heavy for his flight;
Which coming down to ground, does free itself by fight.

20

He so disseizèd   of his gripping gross,
The knight his thrillant spear again assayed

In his brass-plated body to emboss,
And three men's strength unto the stroke he laid.
Wherewith the stiff beam quakèd as afraid,
And glancing from his scaly neck, did glide
Close under his left wing, then broad displayed.
The piercing steel there wrought a wound full wide,
That with the uncouth smart the monster loudly cried.

21

He cried as raging seas are wont to roar
When wintry storm his wrathful wreck does threat:
The rolling billows beat the ragged shore
As they the earth would shoulder from her seat,
And greedy gulf does gape as he would eat
His neighbor element in his revenge;
Then gin the blustering bretheren boldly threat
To move the world from off his steadfast hinge,
And boistrous battle make, each other to avenge.

22

The steely head stuck fast still in his flesh,
Till with his cruel claws he snatched the wood
And quite asunder broke. Forth flowèd fresh
A gushing river of black gory blood
That drownèd all the land whereon he stood;
The stream thereof would drive a water-mill.
Trebly augmented was his furious mood
With bitter sense of his deep-rooted ill,
That flames of fire he threw forth from his large nostril.

23

His hideous tail then hurlèd he about,
And therewith all enwrapped the nimble thighs
Of his froth-foamy steed, whose courage stout,
Striving to loose the knot that fast him ties,
Himself in straiter bands too rash implies,
That to the ground he is perforce constrained
To throw his rider; who can quickly rise
From off the earth with dirty blood distained,
For that reproachful fall right foully he disdained.

24

And fiercely took his trenchant blade in hand,
With which he struck so furious and so fell

That nothing seemed the puissance could withstand,
Upon his crest the hardened iron fell,
But his more hardened crest was armed so well
That deeper dent therein it would not make;
Yet so extremely did the buff him quell
That from thenceforth he shunned the like to take,
But when he saw them come, he did them still forsake.

25

The knight was wroth to see his stroke beguiled,
And smote again with more outrageous might;
But back again the sparkling steel recoiled,
And left not any mark where it did light,
As if in adamant rock it had been pight.
The beast, impatient of his smarting wound
And of so fierce and forcible despite,
Thought with his wings to sty above the ground,
But his late wounded wing unserviceable found.

26

Then full of grief and anguish vehement,
He loudly brayed, that like was never heard,
And from his wide devouring oven sent
A flake of fire, that flashing in his beard,
Him all amazed and almost made afeared.
The scorching flame sore swingèd all his face,
And through his armor all his body seared,
That he could not endure so cruel case,
But thought his arms to leave and helmet to unlace.

27

Not that great champion of the antique world,
Whom famous poets' verse so much doth vaunt
And hath for twelve huge labors high extolled,
So many furies and sharp fits did haunt,
When him the poisoned garment did enchant,
With centaur's blood and bloody verses charmed,
As did this knight twelve thousand dolors daunt,
Whom fiery steel now burnt that erst him armed,
That erst him goodly armed, now most of all him harmed.

STANZA 9: *over* (1): over his back. *so couchèd near* (2): closely arranged. *mote*
(3): might. *corse* (3): body. *rouse* (6): shake. *dight* (6): arranged.

STANZA 10: *flaggy* (1): drooping. *hollow* (2): insubstantial. *eke* (4): also. *pens* (4): quills. *pinions* (4): feathers. *list* (6): began.
STANZA 11: *boughts* (3): coils. *furlong(s)* (7): a unit of distance equal to 220 yards.
STANZA 12: *in deed* (3): in its result. *gapèd* (8): opened. *ravin* (9): prey.
STANZA 13: *that* (1): what. *enrangèd* (2): arranged in files. *gobbets* (3): lumps of meat. *sear* (7): burning.
STANZA 14: *shire* (4): county. *eyne* (7): eyes. *that* (9): which.
STANZA 15: *Eftsoons* (5): again. *chafèd* (6): angered.
STANZA 16: *couch* (1): aim. *forward right* (5): on by. *light* (7): quickly.
STANZA 17: *his* (4): its. *despite* (6): outrage. *wight* (8): creature. *proved* (9): tested.
STANZA 18: *flitting parts* (5): moving particles. *unsound* (5): weak. *unwieldy sway* (8): ponderous force.
STANZA 19: *subject plain* (1): plain below. *yewen* (2): yew. *haggard* (5): wild. *above his able might* (6): beyond his ability. *pounces* (7): claws. *truss* (8): seize.
STANZA 20: *He so disseizèd of his gripping gross* (1): freed from his formidable grip. *thrillant* (2): piercing. *assayed* (2): put to the test. *emboss* (3): plunge. *beam* (5): spear. *broad displayed* (7): spread out.
STANZA 21: *neighbor element* (6): i.e., the earth. *blustering bretheren* (7): i.e., the winds. *steadfast hinge* (8): axis.
STANZA 23: *implies* (5): entangles. *can* (7): began to. *distained* (8): stained.
STANZA 24: *quell* (7): dismay. *forsake* (9): avoid.
STANZA 25: *pight* (5): struck against. *despite* (7): powerful injury. *sty* (8): soar.
STANZA 26: *swingèd* (6): singed.
STANZA 27: *erst* (8): at first.

1. This excerpt, from the end of the first book of Spenser's epic, contains the story of the first day of battle between the Red Cross Knight and the dragon. After a vivid description of the dragon (st. 8–14), the fight begins, ending in a kind of stalemate, with both the dragon and the Red Cross Knight badly hurt. If you were to read the rest of the canto, you would discover that in the night after this battle, the Red Cross Knight falls near a well that has miraculous powers and renews his strength. He and the dragon fight the next day, resulting in the same kind of stalemate, and during that night again the Knight is renewed, this time by a Tree of Life. On the third day the Knight defeats the exhausted dragon and frees the besieged parents of Una. Limited as this excerpt is, you can see the motion of Spenser's narrative. Look especially at stanzas 15–26 and see if, at any point, you find a pause in the action. Is there a lull in the battle for meditation or reflection? What exactly does the Knight do with his weapons? How does the dragon attack? What details help you to visualize this brutal encounter?

2. What purpose is served by the alexandrine that closes each

stanza of the fight scene (st. 15–26)? How is each of these alex-
andrines united to the stanza following it? Do the alexandrines il-
lustrate Spenser's using form to increase tempo—or pace (see
p. 137)? What is the advantage of making the alexandrines in the
fight scene as smooth as possible?

3. Notice the alexandrines in the opening stanzas of the excerpt
(8–14). Do they tend to complete each stanzaic unit or to look for-
ward? Are there more caesuras in the alexandrines of this section than
in the fight scene? If so, why?

4. Stanza 18 is a good example of what the modern critic Northrup
Frye calls "imitative harmony." What Frye means is that Spenser
imitates the action of the fight through a rhetorical device that is
built on exact representation through sound (see also *onomatopoeia*,
p. 60). Give two clear examples of "imitative harmony" in stanza
18. How does the alliteration contribute to building suspense in this
stanza?

from Book VII, Canto VIII of The Faerie Queene

1

When I bethink me on that speech whilere
Of Mutability, and well it weigh,
Me seems that though she all unworthy were
Of the heaven's rule, yet very sooth to say,
In all things else she bears the greatest sway.
Which makes me loathe this state of life so tickle,
And love of things so vain to cast away;
Whose flowering pride, so fading and so fickle,
Short Time shall soon cut down with his consuming sickle.

2

Then gin I think on that which Nature said,
Of that same time when no more change shall be,
But steadfast rest of all things, firmly stayed
Upon the pillars of eternity,
That is contrair to Mutability.
For all that moveth doth in change delight;
But thenceforth all shall rest eternally

With him that is the God of Sabaoth hight.
O that great Sabaoth God, grant me that Sabbath's sight.

STANZA 1: *tickle* (6): uncertain.

1. Notice the effect of the final alexandrine in the first stanza. Specifically, what effect is caused by the spondees, monosyllables, and a word like "consuming"?
2. In the last line Spenser is punning on the words "Saboath," referring to the Hebraic "Lord of hosts," and "Sabbath," meaning simply "time of rest" (in terms of the poem, used synonymously with "pillars of eternity," stanza 2, line 4). Such wordplay is typical of Renaissance poetry. Does this pun increase or disturb your understanding of the passage? Explain.
3. These stanzas illustrate the meditative structure possible in the Spenserian stanza. Does the Spenserian stanza seem as correct for this reflection on mutability and eternity as the form did for narration and description? Why, or why not? Write a short essay remarking the different uses of the form in both Spenser selections.

THE FOLLOWERS OF SPENSER

In the Spenserian imitations of the seventeenth and eighteenth centuries, the form was used (sometimes not very aptly) in a variety of ways. James Thomson's "Castle of Indolence" (1748) develops mood and melody rather than the economy of Spenser's narrative; and in the work of this pre-Romantic—who remarkably imitated Spenser in the age of Pope and thereby preserved the form for the next century—begins the false impression that the stanza form is more suited for description than for narration or action. The stanza is brilliantly but not deeply used by William Shenstone in his mock heroic "The Schoolmistress" (1737–48) and was rather eccentrically chosen by Robert Burns for his dialect poem "The Cotter's Saturday Night" (1786).

Like Burns and Thomson, the Romantics initially found in Spenser's form an alternative to the predominant meters of their age and of the immediately preceding age. Their choice of the stanza was thus a result of one of the principles of Romanticism: that one should search for a truer past, embodied particularly in the idea of the "primitive" as truer than the immediate past. The use of the Spenserian stanza by the Romantic poets, it should be noted, was highly inventive and original. Only the originality of Byron could have conceived of the Spenserian stanza as a form for the rootless wanderings of the despairing Harold. With powerful insight, Byron understood Spenser's desire for complexity as his own. The result is a magnificent device expressing landscape (Spain, Greece, Belgium, the Rhine, Switzerland, and Italy) as character. As critics have pointed out, the *ottava rima* in the later "Don Juan" was perhaps Byron's truer form. In "Childe Harold's Pilgrimage," however, there is an interesting correspondence of form and content. For in Byron's poem, the modern "neural itch," as Auden calls it—the desire to get moving in order to find reality—finds expression in the Spenserian stanza.

> There is a very life in our despair,
> Vitality of poison,—a quick root
> Which feeds these deadly branches; for it were
> As nothing did we die; but Life will suit
> Itself to Sorrow's most detested fruit,
> Like to the apples on the Dead Sea's shore,
> All ashes to the taste: Did man compute
> Existence by enjoyment, and count o'er
> Such hours 'gainst years of life,—say, would he name threescore?
>   ("Childe Harold's Pilgrimage," Canto III, Stanza 34)

Shelley chose the form for "Adonais" because, in writing a pastoral elegy for the death of Keats, he needed a form that could both contain the artificiality of such an elegy and yet give expression to a contemporary analysis of the meaning of a poet's life. Thus, in "Adonais" the Spenserian stanza finds its greatest expression as meditative form. This original choice gave Shelley the right instrument for all the ancient pastoral conventions—almost impossible to achieve in a modern poem—and a complex form for his philosophical analysis of the prophetic role of the modern poet. As with Byron's choice of the Spenserian stanza for "Childe Harold," the very form of "Adonais" is symbolic (i.e., it echoes a past against a present) and enriches the content of the poem. The result of Shelley's choice is that "Adonais" has a rare sweep and magnificence, a success of length, of totality of expression, in all its complex units. The effect is also that the Spenserian stanza allows the great moments to appear inevitable:

> He is a portion of the loveliness
> Which once he made more lovely: he doth bear
> His part, while the one Spirit's plastic stress
> Sweeps through the dull dense world, compelling there
> All new successions to the forms they wear;
> Torturing th' unwilling dross that checks its flight
> To its own likeness, as each mass may bear;
> And bursting in its beauty and its might
> From trees and beasts and men into the Heaven's light.
>
> ("Adonais," Stanza 43)

The same originality is to be found in Keats's use of the Spenserian stanza in "The Eve of St. Agnes." Here the subject (a medieval Romeo and Juliet story with a happy ending) is also suited to the form. Again the extraordinary sensuous atmosphere of the poem, with its singularly controlled tone, demonstrates how the choice of the right form can enrich the content of a poem. Keats—like Byron and Shelley—chose a form that becomes symbolic through its proper use. Literally, for these Romantics in their use of the Spenserian stanza, the medium *is* the message, or at least a good part of it. For seldom has the complexity of sensual response and a world mingling dream and reality been so deeply realized as in Keats's poem, and this complexity clearly found the right medium in Spenser's stanza:

> Anon his heart revives: her vespers done,
> Of all its wreathéd pearls her hair she frees;
> Unclasps her warméd jewels one by one;
> Loosens her fragrant bodice; by degrees
> Her rich attire creeps rustling to her knees:
> Half-hidden, like a mermaid in sea-weed,
> Pensive awhile she dreams awake, and sees,
> In fancy, fair St. Agnes in her bed,
> But dares not look behind, or all the charm is fled.
>
> ("The Eve of St. Agnes," Stanza 26)

What happens in all three of these great Romantic poems is that the past operates in the present in the most natural of all ways, through form. The relationship of each poem to Spenser's *Faerie Queene* shows further how the form itself—in this case, the Spenserian stanza—can provide a context and richness through echoing a model of formal perfection, on the one hand, and, on the other, through echoing the very world of Spenser. In these poems, the stanza form thus operates as a kind of serious *parody* of Spenser's original. In every case, as in the eighteenth-century use of the Spenserian stanza, there was even an attempt to model diction on Spenser's very artificial diction. In the Romantic poems, the Spenserian diction was either consummately handled (as in Keats's "The Eve of St. Agnes") or abandoned entirely (as in the last two cantos of Byron's "Childe Harold's Pilgrimage").

Here the term *parody* does not imply any attempt to mimic or burlesque the original of Spenser. It is rather imitation that intends deliberately to echo a form and thereby enrich the poem being written. This kind of parody has been called "neutral parody" by Rosemond Tuve in a discussion of the poetry of George Herbert, and it seems as accurate as any term in describing what has obviously been a device of poets since the Greeks of the Alexandrian age. Furthermore, this kind of parody is perhaps all a poet can do when a previous great poet has exhausted a form that he wishes to employ. No one after Milton, for example, could ever use blank verse for an epic in English without producing a parodic effect. But the achievement of Byron, Shelley, and Keats is that each understood the concept of form in poetry so well that his parody of Spenser beautifully integrates with his subject. Traditional forms in these cases liberated the poet.

The reader will discover, finally, that there are four primary uses of the Spenserian stanza: (1) for narration or action; (2) for description; (3) for reflection; and (4) for analysis, either of character or of theme. Not every one of the following passages or poems demonstrates all of these usages, but in each passage will be found at least one of them. The reader should also note that the predominant use of the Spenserian stanza is for narration. Spenser, Byron, Keats, and even Shelley understood that the first injunction of the form was that of action, of a forward motion that most often reveals itself as narrative.

GEORGE GORDON, LORD BYRON (1788-1824)

from *Canto II of Childe Harold's Pilgrimage*

1

Come, blue-eyed Maid of Heaven!—but Thou, alas!
Didst never yet one mortal song inspire—
Goddess of Wisdom! here thy temple was,
And is, despite of war and wasting fire,
And years, that bade thy worship to expire:
But worse than steel, and flame, and ages slow,
Is the dread sceptre and dominion dire
Of men who never felt the sacred glow
That thoughts of thee and thine on polish'd breasts bestow.

2

Ancient of days! august Athena! where,
Where are thy men of might? thy grand in soul?
Gone—glimmering through the dream of things that were:
First in the race that led to Glory's goal,
They won, and pass'd away—is this the whole?
A schoolboy's tale, the wonder of an hour!
The warrior's weapon and the sophist's stole
Are sought in vain, and o'er each mouldering tower,
Dim with the mist of years, gray flits the shade of power.

3

Son of the Morning, rise! approach you here!
Come—but molest not yon defenceless urn:
Look on this spot—a nation's sepulchre!
Abode of gods, whose shrines no longer burn.
Even gods must yield—religions take their turn;
'Twas Jove's—'tis Mahomet's, and other creeds
Will rise with other years, till man shall learn

Vainly his incense soars, his victim bleeds,—
Poor child of Doubt and Death, whose hope is built on reeds.

4

Bound to the earth, he lifts his eye to Heaven—
Is't not enough, unhappy thing! to know
Thou art? Is this a boon so kindly given,
That, being, thou wouldst be again, and go,
Thou know'st not, reck'st not to what region, so
On earth no more, but mingled with the skies?
Still wilt thou dream on future joy and woe?
Regard and weigh yon dust before it flies:
That little urn saith more than thousand homilies.

5

Or burst the vanish'd Hero's lofty mound;
Far on the solitary shore he sleeps:
He fell, and falling nations mourn'd around;
But now not one of saddening thousands weeps,
Nor warlike worshipper his vigil keeps
Where demi-gods appear'd, as records tell.
Remove yon skull from out the scatter'd heaps:
Is that a temple where a God may dwell?
Why ev'n the worm at last disdains her shatter'd cell!

6

Look on its broken arch, its ruin'd wall,
Its chambers desolate, and portals foul:
Yes, this was once Ambition's airy hall,
The dome of Thought, the palace of the Soul.
Behold through each lack-lustre, eyeless hole,
The gay recess of Wisdom and of Wit
And Passion's host, that never brook'd control:
Can all saint, sage, or sophist ever writ,
People this lonely tower, this tenement refit?

7

Well didst thou speak, Athena's wisest son!
"All that we know is, nothing can be known."
Why should we shrink from what we cannot shun?
Each hath his pang, but feeble sufferers groan
With brain-born dreams of evil all their own.
Pursue what Chance or Fate proclaimeth best;
Peace waits us on the shores of Acheron:

There no forced banquet claims the sated guest,
But Silence spreads the couch of ever welcome rest.

8

Yet if, as holiest men have deem'd, there be
A land of souls beyond that sable shore,
To shame the doctrine of the Sadducee
And sophists, madly vain of dubious lore;
How sweet it were in concert to adore
With those who made our mortal labours light!
To hear each voice we fear'd to hear no more!
Behold each mighty shade reveal'd to sight,
The Bactrian, Samian sage, and all who taught the right!

9

There, thou!—whose love and life, together fled,
Have left me here to love and live in vain—
Twined with my heart, and can I deem thee dead,
When busy Memory flashes on my brain?
Well—I will dream that we may meet again,
And woo the vision to my vacant breast:
If aught of young Remembrance then remain,
Be as it may Futurity's behest,
For me 'twere bliss enough to know thy spirit blest!

10

Here let me sit upon this massy stone,
The marble column's yet unshaken base;
Here, son of Saturn! was thy fav'rite throne,
Mightiest of many such! Hence let me trace
The latent grandeur of thy dwelling-place.
It may not be: nor ev'n can Fancy's eye
Restore what Time hath labour'd to deface.
Yet these proud pillars claim no passing sigh;
Unmoved the Moslem sits, the light Greek carols by.

Goddess of Wisdom (1. 3): Athena. *sophist's* (2. 7): sophists were philosopher-teachers prominent in the latter half of the fifth century B.C.— popularly identified with fallacious or specious reasoning. *stole* (2. 7): a long robe resembling a toga. *Mahomet's* (3. 6): Mohammed's. *shun* (7. 3): prevent. *Acheron* (7. 7): marshy region at the entrance to the underworld over which Charon had to ferry any arrivals. *sable shore* (8. 2): dark or mournful land; refers to the shores of Acheron. *Sadducee* (s) (8. 3): one of the principal Jewish religious parties during the period of Christ. It was composed of aristocratic and high-priestly families and advocated strict adherence to the ancient Mosaic laws, as opposed to the Pharisees, who favored a more liberal interpretation of Scripture.

from Canto III

21

There was a sound of revelry by night,
And Belgium's capital had gathered then
Her Beauty and her Chivalry, and bright
The lamps shone o'er fair women and brave men;
A thousand hearts beat happily; and when
Music arose with its voluptuous swell,
Soft eyes looked love to eyes which spake again,
And all went merry as a marriage bell—
But hush! hark! a deep sound strikes like a rising knell!

22

Did ye not hear it?—No; 'twas but the wind,
Or the car rattling o'er the stony street;
On with the dance! let joy be unconfined;
No sleep till morn, when Youth and Pleasure meet
To chase the glowing Hours with flying feet—
But hark!—that heavy sound breaks in once more,
As if the clouds its echo would repeat;
And nearer, clearer, deadlier than before!
Arm! Arm! it is—it is—the cannon's opening roar!

23

Within a windowed niche of that high hall
Sate Brunswick's fated chieftain; he did hear
That sound the first amidst the festival,
And caught its tone with Death's prophetic ear;
And when they smiled because he deemed it near,
His heart more truly knew that peal too well
Which stretched his father on a bloody bier,
And roused the vengeance blood alone could quell:
He rushed into the field, and, foremost fighting, fell.

24

Ah! then and there was hurrying to and fro,
And gathering tears, and tremblings of distress,
And cheeks all pale, which but an hour ago
Blushed at the praise of their own loveliness;
And there were sudden partings, such as press
The life from out young hearts, and choking sighs

Which ne'er might be repeated; who could guess
If ever more should meet those mutual eyes,
Since upon night so sweet such awful morn could rise!

25

And there was mounting in hot haste: the steed,
The mustering squadron, and the clattering car,
Went pouring forward with impetuous speed,
And swiftly forming in the ranks of war;
And the deep thunder peal on peal afar;
And near, the beat of the alarming drum
Roused up the soldier ere the morning star;
While thronged the citizens with terror dumb,
Or whispering, with white lips—"The foe! They come! they come!"

26

And wild and high the "Cameron's gathering" rose!
The war-note of Lochiel, which Albyn's hills
Have heard, and heard, too, have her Saxon foes—
How in the noon of night that pibroch thrills,
Savage and shrill! But with the breath which fills
Their mountain pipe, so fill the mountaineers
With the fierce native daring which instills
The stirring memory of a thousand years,
And Evan's, Donald's fame rings in each clansman's ears!

27

And Ardennes waves above them her green leaves,
Dewy with nature's teardrops, as they pass,
Grieving, if aught inanimate e'er grieves,
Over the unreturning brave—alas!
Ere evening to be trodden like the grass
Which now beneath them, but above shall grow
In its next verdure, when this fiery mass
Of living valor, rolling on the foe
And burning with high hope, shall molder cold and low.

28

Last noon beheld them full of lusty life,
Last eve in Beauty's circle proudly gay,
The midnight brought the signal-sound of strife,
The morn the marshaling in arms—the day
Battle's magnificently-stern array!

The thunderclouds close o'er it, which when rent
The earth is covered thick with other clay,
Which her own clay shall cover, heaped and pent,
Rider and horse—friend, foe—in one red burial blent!

The lamps shone o'er fair women and brave men (21. 4): this is a reference to the ball given by the Duchess of Richmond on the eve of the Battle of Quatre Bras. *Brunswick's fated chieftain* (23. 2): the Duke of Brunswick, who was to be killed in the Battle of Quatre Bras. *father* (23. 7): the Duke of Brunswick's father had been killed in 1806 while commanding the Prussian army against Napoleon. *Lochiel* (26. 2): chief of the clan Cameron. *Albyn('s)* (26. 2): Scotland. *pibroch* (26. 4): bagpipe music, most often of a warlike character. *Evan's, Donald's fame* (26. 9): Sir Evan and Donald Cameron were famous warriors of the seventeenth and eighteenth centuries in the Stuart cause.

from Canto IV

1

I stood in Venice, on the Bridge of Sighs,
A palace and a prison on each hand:
I saw from out the wave her structures rise
As from the stroke of the enchanter's wand:
A thousand years their cloudy wings expand
Around me, and a dying Glory smiles
O'er the far times, when many a subject land
Looked to the wingéd Lion's marble piles,
Where Venice sate in state, throned on her hundred isles!

2

She looks a sea Cybele, fresh from ocean,
Rising with her tiara of proud towers
At airy distance, with majestic motion,
A ruler of the waters and their powers:
And such she was—her daughters had their dowers
From spoils of nations, and the exhaustless East
Poured in her lap all gems in sparkling showers:
In purple was she robed, and of her feast
Monarchs partook, and deemed their dignity increased.

3

In Venice Tasso's echoes are no more,
And silent rows the songless gondolier;

Her palaces are crumbling to the shore,
And music meets not always now the ear:
Those days are gone—but Beauty still is here;
States fall, arts fade—but Nature doth not die,
Nor yet forget how Venice once was dear,
The pleasant place of all festivity,
The revel of the earth, the masque of Italy!

. . . . . .

178

There is a pleasure in the pathless woods,
There is a rapture on the lonely shore,
There is society where none intrudes,
By the deep sea, and music in its roar:
I love not Man the less, but Nature more,
From these our interviews, in which I steal
From all I may be, or have been before,
To mingle with the Universe, and feel
What I can ne'er express, yet can not all conceal.

179

Roll on, thou deep and dark blue Ocean—roll!
Ten thousand fleets sweep over thee in vain;
Man marks the earth with ruin—his control
Stops with the shore; upon the watery plain
The wrecks are all thy deed, nor doth remain
A shadow of man's ravage, save his own,
When, for a moment, like a drop of rain,
He sinks into thy depths with bubbling groan,
Without a grave, unknelled, uncoffined, and unknown.

Bridge of Sighs (1. 1): a covered bridge between the Doge's Palace and the prison of San Marco. *wingéd Lion's* (1. 8): the emblem of St. Mark, the patron saint of Venice. *Cybele* (2. 1): the great goddess of the land, whose cult was orgiastic, often violent, and therefore associated with the cult of Dionysius. *Tasso's* (3. 1): Torquato Tasso, famous poet of the Italian Renaissance and author of the epic poem *Jerusalem Delivered*. It was the custom of the gondoliers to chant stanzas of *Jerusalem Delivered* as they rowed. *unknelled* (179. 9): with no ceremony (tolling of bells).

1. The four passages above indicate the uses to which Byron put the Spenserian stanza in this long poem, the first two cantos of which appeared in 1812. Byron was the first Romantic poet to use the form,

and the extraordinary originality of his choice can be seen in his subject. Harold (or Byron himself) is a great prototype of modern rootlessness. The passages above reveal some of the problems of this modern consciousness, and—with a powerful irony—Byron chooses an ancient form for this contemporary revelation. In his preface to the first edition of the poem, Byron remarks that "the stanza of Spenser admits of every variety." How does each of these passages reflect this variety, the complexity of living in "the lonely crowd" of the modern world?

2. Byron's remarkable feat consists in adapting the stanza form to his subject—that is, to Harold's "pilgrimage" to the ancient root-centers of European vitality. From countless English and American Victorians on down to the modern consciousness of such figures as Hemingway and Durrell, this search for vitality in Europe has been our own. The landscape in this poem is thereby crucial to its very structure; the power of description inherent in the stanza form becomes absolutely necessary to the entire poem. For example, what is the meaning of Venice for Harold? Through whose eyes is he really seeing Venice?

3. In the first passage (from Canto II), there is a long meditation on the Acropolis before the Parthenon. Harold explicitly refers to the monument dedicated to Athena. Why is the tone here pessimistic? What is the source of Harold's cosmic despair? How do the Spenserian stanzas support this cosmic despair? Look especially at stanzas 5 and 6, in which the broken skull and the ruined Parthenon are compared. In stanza 9, there is reference to a friend who gives some hope. What kind of hope? Does it matter in the poem itself if we do not know who the friend is? Explain.

4. The second passage (from Canto III) describes the battle of Waterloo and its effect on Brussels. Which of the four general uses of the Spenserian stanza (see p. 259) does it demonstrate? Note that in stanza 28 of this passage the alexandrine is broken by dashes, punctuation that indicates caesuras. Compare the effect of this alexandrine with the success of other alexandrines in the excerpts from Byron. Is Byron always successful in employing the unitive effects of the alexandrine? Explain. Does the alexandrine here summarize and look forward, as it does so magnificently in Spenser? Comment.

5. Compare Byron's rhyme schemes with those of Spenser in the fight scene of *The Faerie Queene* (p. 248). Does Byron's rhyme

scheme serve consistently to emphasize action through interlocking, or is it used merely to fill out the form? Is the complex rhyme scheme or even the alexandrine important to Byron's use of the form? Why *does* Byron use the form? To decide this fundamental purpose, you must turn to the matter of narrative, and of the stanza form as narrative. Do the stanzas themselves sustain suspense or progressing action? Cite examples to support your answer.

6. Byron's poem is full of landscape descriptions, but are you invited to remain on the Acropolis? In Brussels? In Venice? Are these descriptions in the third passage (from Canto IV, st. 1–3) therefore the great static displays that most definitions of the Spenserian stanza would indicate they might be? Why is the ocean passage (Canto IV, st. 178–179 from the end of the poem) so symbolic of the flux implied through the poem? Is the concept of momentum basic to understanding the poem? Why? What is the great source of this momentum? Explain in a paragraph. How much does Byron depend on the reader's natural curiosity as to narrative development?

If Byron's poem concerns the modern ego in search of itself, how does the form of the poem lend immediacy to this theme? That is, if the Spenserian stanzas both enclose the story line by focusing on an incident, scene, or theme (and even linger there) and, at the same time, free the narrative by the momentum of the form itself, how is this form suited to such a search or quest? Write an essay to determine this relationship of content and form.

PERCY BYSSHE SHELLEY (1792–1822)

from Adonais

1

I weep for Adonais—he is dead!
O, weep for Adonais! though our tears
Thaw not the frost which binds so dear a head!
And thou, sad Hour, selected from all years
To mourn our loss, rouse thy obscure compeers,
And teach them thine own sorrow, say: "With me

268   *The Spenserian Stanza*

Died Adonais; till the Future dares
Forget the Past, his fate and fame shall be
An echo and a light unto eternity!"

2

Where wert thou, mighty Mother, when he lay,
When thy Son lay, pierced by the shaft which flies
In darkness? where was lorn Urania
When Adonais died? With veiléd eyes,
'Mid listening Echoes, in her Paradise
She sate, while one, with soft enamored breath,
Rekindled all the fading melodies,
With which, like flowers that mock the corse beneath,
He had adorned and hid the coming bulk of Death.

3

Oh, weep for Adonais—he is dead!
Wake, melancholy Mother, wake and weep!
Yet wherefore? Quench within their burning bed
Thy fiery tears, and let thy loud heart keep
Like his, a mute and uncomplaining sleep;
For he is gone, where all things wise and fair
Descend—oh, dream not that the amorous Deep
Will yet restore him to the vital air;
Death feeds on his mute voice, and laughs at our despair.

. . . . . .

[In stanzas 4–6 Urania, mother of Adonais, is invoked to "lament anew."]

7

To that high Capital, where kingly Death
Keeps his pale court in beauty and decay,
He came; and bought, with price of purest breath,
A grave among the eternal.—Come away!
Haste, while the vault of blue Italian day
Is yet his fitting charnel-roof! while still
He lies, as if in dewy sleep he lay;
Awake him not! surely he takes his fill
Of deep and liquid rest, forgetful of all ill.

8

He will awake no more, oh, never more!—
Within the twilight chamber spreads apace

The shadow of white Death, and at the door
Invisible Corruption waits to trace
His extreme way to her dim dwelling place;
The eternal Hunger sits, but pity and awe
Soothe her pale rage, nor dares she to deface
So fair a prey, till darkness, and the law
Of change, shall o'er his sleep the mortal curtain draw.

. . . . . .

[Stanzas 9–17, employing a device derived from the pastoral tradition, recount the procession of mourners. The first mourners consist mainly of personifications (e.g., Dreams and Splendours) associated with Adonais or Keats; but Morning, Echo, and Spring also weep along with the nightingale and with the eagle who represents England or Albion.]

18

Ah, woe is me! Winter is come and gone,
But grief returns with the revolving year;
The airs and streams renew their joyous tone;
The ants, the bees, the swallows reappear;
Fresh leaves and flowers deck the dead Seasons' bier;
The amorous birds now pair in every brake,
And build their mossy homes in field and brere;
And the green lizard, and the golden snake,
Like unimprisoned flames, out of their trance awake.

19

Through wood and stream and field and hill and Ocean
A quickening life from the Earth's heart has burst
As it has ever done, with change and motion,
From the great morning of the world when first
God dawned on Chaos; in its stream immersed,
The lamps of Heaven flash with a softer light;
All baser things pant with life's sacred thirst,
Diffuse themselves, and spend in love's delight,
The beauty and the joy of their renewéd might.

20

The leprous corpse, touched by this spirit tender,
Exhales itself in flowers of gentle breath;
Like incarnations of the stars, when splendor
Is changed to fragrance, they illumine death

And mock the merry worm that wakes beneath;
Nought we know, dies. Shall that alone which knows
Be as a sword consumed before the sheath
By sightless lightning?—the intense atom glows
A moment, then is quenched in a most cold repose.

21

Alas! that all we loved of him should be,
But for our grief, as if it had not been,
And grief itself be mortal! Woe is me!
Whence are we, and why are we? of what scene
The actors or spectators? Great and mean
Meet massed in death, who lends what life must borrow.
As long as skies are blue, and fields are green,
Evening must usher night, night urge the morrow,
Month follow month with woe, and year wake year to sorrow.

. . . . . .

[Stanzas 22–29 show the central mourning of Urania as she comes to the grave of her son. Stanzas 30–35 present contemporary poets as mourners, with Shelley himself as a major mourner.]

36

Our Adonais has drunk poison—oh!
What deaf and viperous murderer could crown
Life's early cup with such a draught of woe?
The nameless worm would now itself disown:
It felt, yet could escape, the magic tone
Whose prelude held all envy, hate, and wrong,
But what was howling in one breast alone,
Silent with expectation of the song,
Whose master's hand is cold; whose silver lyre unstrung.

37

Live thou, whose infamy is not thy fame!
Live! fear no heavier chastisement from me,
Thou noteless blot on a remembered name!
But be thyself, and know thyself to be!
And ever at thy season be thou free
To spill the venom when thy fangs o'erflow;
Remorse and Self-contempt shall cling to thee;
Hot Shame shall burn upon thy secret brow,
And like a beaten hound tremble thou shalt—as now.

38

Nor let us weep that our delight is fled
Far from these carrion kites that scream below;
He wakes or sleeps with the enduring dead;
Thou canst not soar where he is sitting now.—
Dust to the dust! but the pure spirit shall flow
Back to the burning fountain whence it came,
A portion of the Eternal, which must glow
Through time and change, unquenchably the same,
Whilst thy cold embers choke the sordid hearth of shame.

39

Peace, peace! he is not dead, he doth not sleep—-
He hath awakened from the dream of life—
'Tis we, who lost in stormy visions, keep
With phantoms an unprofitable strife,
And in mad trance, strike with our spirit's knife
Invulnerable nothings.—We decay
Like corpses in a charnel; fear and grief
Convulse us and consume us day by day,
And cold hopes swarm like worms within our living clay.

40

He has outsoared the shadow of our night;
Envy and calumny and hate and pain,
And that unrest which men miscall delight,
Can touch him not and torture not again;
From the contagion of the world's slow stain
He is secure, and now can never mourn
A heart grown cold, a head grown gray in vain;
Nor, when the spirit's self has ceased to burn,
With sparkless ashes load an unlamented urn.

41

He lives, he wakes—'tis Death is dead, not he;
Mourn not for Adonais.—Thou young Dawn,
Turn all thy dew to splendor, for from thee
The spirit thou lamentest is not gone;
Ye caverns and ye forests, cease to moan!
Cease, ye faint flowers and fountains, and thou Air,˙
Which like a mourning veil thy scarf hadst thrown
O'er the abandoned Earth, now leave it bare
Even to the joyous stars which smile on its despair!

42

He is made one with Nature: there is heard
His voice in all her music, from the moan
Of thunder, to the song of night's sweet bird;
He is a presence to be felt and known
In darkness and in light, from herb and stone,
Spreading itself where'er that Power may move
Which has withdrawn his being to its own;
Which wields the world with never-wearied love,
Sustains it from beneath, and kindles it above.

43

He is a portion of the loveliness
Which once he made more lovely: he doth bear
His part, while the one Spirit's plastic stress
Sweeps through the dull dense world, compelling there
All new successions to the forms they wear;
Torturing th' unwilling dross that checks its flight
To its own likeness, as each mass may bear;
And bursting in its beauty and its might
From trees and beasts and men into the Heaven's light.

44

The splendors of the firmament of time
May be eclipsed, but are extinguished not;
Like stars to their appointed height they climb,
And death is a low mist which cannot blot
The brightness it may veil. When lofty thought
Lifts a young heart above its mortal lair,
And love and life contend in it, for what
Shall be its earthly doom, the dead live there
And move like winds of light on dark and stormy air.

45

The inheritors of unfulfilled renown
Rose from their thrones, built beyond mortal thought,
Far in the Unapparent. Chatterton
Rose pale—his solemn agony had not
Yet faded from him; Sidney, as he fought
And as he fell and as he lived and loved
Sublimely mild, a Spirit without spot,
Arose; and Lucan, by his death approved:
Oblivion as they rose shrank like a thing reproved.

46

And many more, whose names on Earth are dark,
But whose transmitted effluence cannot die
So long as fire outlives the parent spark,
Rose, robed in dazzling immortality.
"Thou art become as one of us," they cry,
"It was for thee yon kingless sphere has long
Swung blind in unascended majesty,
Silent alone amid an Heaven of Song.
Assume thy wingéd throne, thou Vesper of our throng!"

47

Who mourns for Adonais? Oh, come forth,
Fond wretch! and know thyself and him aright.
Clasp with thy panting soul the pendulous Earth;
As from a center, dart thy spirit's light
Beyond all worlds, until its spacious might
Satiate the void circumference: then shrink
Even to a point within our day and night;
And keep thy heart light lest it make thee sink
When hope has kindled hope, and lured thee to the brink.

48

Or go to Rome, which is the sepulcher,
Oh, not of him, but of our joy: 'tis nought
That ages, empires, and religions there
Lie buried in the ravage they have wrought;
For such as he can lend—they borrow not
Glory from those who made the world their prey;
And he is gathered to the kings of thought
Who waged contention with their time's decay,
And of the past are all that cannot pass away.

49

Go thou to Rome—at once the Paradise,
The grave, the city, and the wilderness;
And where its wrecks like shattered mountains rise,
And flowering weeds, and fragrant copses dress
The bones of Desolation's nakedness
Pass, till the spirit of the spot shall lead
Thy footsteps to a slope of green access
Where, like an infant's smile, over the dead
A light of laughing flowers along the grass is spread;

50

And gray walls molder round, on which dull Time
Feeds, like slow fire upon a hoary brand;
And one keen pyramid with wedge sublime,
Pavilioning the dust of him who planned
This refuge for his memory, doth stand
Like flame transformed to marble; and beneath,
A field is spread, on which a newer band
Have pitched in Heaven's smile their camp of death,
Welcoming him we lose with scarce extinguished breath.

51

Here pause: these graves are all too young as yet
To have outgrown the sorrow which consigned
Its charge to each; and if the seal is set,
Here, on one fountain of a mourning mind,
Break it not thou! too surely shalt thou find
Thine own well full, if thou returnest home,
Of tears and gall. From the world's bitter wind
Seek shelter in the shadow of the tomb.
What Adonais is, why fear we to become?

52

The One remains, the many change and pass;
Heaven's light forever shines, Earth's shadows fly;
Life, like a dome of many-colored glass,
Stains the white radiance of Eternity,
Until Death tramples it to fragments.—Die,
If thou wouldst be with that which thou dost seek!
Follow where all is fled!—Rome's azure sky,
Flowers, ruins, statues, music, words, are weak
The glory they transfuse with fitting truth to speak.

53

Why linger, why turn back, why shrink, my Heart?
Thy hopes are gone before: from all things here
They have departed; thou shouldst now depart!
A light is passed from the revolving year,
And man, and woman; and what still is dear
Attracts to crush, repels to make thee wither.
The soft sky smiles—the low wind whispers near:
'Tis Adonais calls! oh, hasten thither,
No more let Life divide what Death can join together.

The Followers of Spenser   275

54

That Light whose smile kindles the Universe,
That Beauty in which all things work and move,
That Benediction which the eclipsing Curse
Of birth can quench not, that sustaining Love
Which through the web of being blindly wove
By man and beast and earth and air and sea,
Burns bright or dim, as each are mirrors of
The fire for which all thirst, now beams on me,
Consuming the last clouds of cold mortality.

55

The breath whose might I have invoked in song
Descends on me; my spirit's bark is driven,
Far from the shore, far from the trembling throng
Whose sails were never to the tempest given;
The massy earth and spheréd skies are riven!
I am borne darkly, fearfully, afar;
Whilst, burning through the inmost veil of Heaven,
The soul of Adonais, like a star,
Beacons from the abode where the Eternal are.

Adonais (title): Adonis (from which the name "Adonais" is derived) was in Greek mythology a handsome youth loved by Aphrodite and eventually killed by a wild boar. *dead* (1. 1): John Keats, whom Shelley had called "among the writers of the highest genius who have adorned our age," died in Rome on February 23, 1821, and was buried in the Protestant Cemetery there. *mighty Mother* (2. 1): Shelley alters the myth, making Urania—an epithet for Aphrodite—the mother rather than the lover of Adonais. *one* (2. 6): the echo of Keats's own poems. *corse* (2. 8): corpse. *Capital* (7. 1): Rome. *brake* (18. 6): thicket. *brere* (18. 7): briar. *nameless worm* (36. 4): unnamed reviewer of Keats's poem *Endymion*. *thou* (37. 1): the reviewer of Keats's *Endymion* who, in accordance with the journalistic custom of that time, remained nameless. *Chatterton, Sidney, Lucan* (45. 3,5,8): poets whose early and violent deaths prevented their fulfilling the promise of their genius. *slope of green access* (49. 7): the cemetery where Keats is buried.

1. To recognize how the Spenserian stanza contributes to creating unity in this 1821 pastoral elegy on the death of Keats, note how the stanzas break into distinct units. How do these units relate to the conventions of a *pastoral elegy* (see p. 346)? What is the contrast presented in stanzas 18–21? Three stanzas (36, 37, 38) attack the English reviewers who had condemned Keats's poem *Endymion*. Why is it necessary to read these stanzas in the light of the myth of

Adonis? Do stanzas 39–44 constitute the climax of the poem? Why, or why not? Explain. What specifically does Shelley mean by the references to immortality, a theme that reaches its height in stanza 52? In the poem's conclusion, how does the mourning poet find himself renewed? Write a short essay, developing your answer from these last stanzas.

2. Here, as in all successful poems using the Spenserian stanza, you are constantly moving forward; although you do not find a story as in Keats's own "The Eve of St. Agnes," you are led to ask this question: "What happens next?" What passages particularly have this quality of suspense? Are there passages that do not go forward? Explain.

3. The pastoral conventions are rather muted in this poem except for the recurring procession of mourners, which, as much as any other device, unifies the poem. Yet Shelley intended to keep something of the old pastoral form, and clearly the Spenserian stanza—with its deliberate echo of an earlier age in which the pastoral had a meaning—was the right form in which to do this. Yet compare the stanzas of "Adonais" with Byron's stanzas, which lack the pastoral conventions. What similarities are there? In both there are sharp dramatic scenes, but notice how those scenes always merge into the reflective consciousness. Could you argue that "Adonais" itself presents a stream of consciousness? Explain by writing a short essay showing what philosophical themes occur in the elegy.

4. The very loose employment of the pastoral conventions in "Adonais" contrasts with the precise, profound employment of those conventions in the greatest of all pastoral elegies in English, Milton's "Lycidas" (p. 341). How does Shelley's subject limit his particular use of those conventions, as Milton's did not? Do you see any other relationships between Milton's elegy and Shelley's?

5. The alexandrine is a good illustration of the success or failure of the Spenserian stanza as it supports Shelley's philosophical subject. Compare the alexandrines in the following stanzas: 1, 3, 42, 51, 52, and 55. How are the caesuras used in each? Does each line tend to stand alone, or is it integrated with the rest of the stanza? Where are there examples of enjambment? Are they successful? Does any of these alexandrines look forward to the next stanza? In any of the alexandrines, do the twelve syllables appear oppressive? Why? Is the rhyme of the alexandrines in each of the stanzas adequately or

meaningfully related to the other *c* rhymes? Is the rhyme scheme in each stanza really interlocking enough to give the stanza a cohesion? Illustrate your answer, and note how one of the real difficulties of the Spenserian stanza—the finding of a few rhymes for nine lines—can be a means of gaining greater unity.

6. There are several stanzas in this work that illustrate the "imitative harmony" discussed in the Spenser section (see p. 255). Compare stanza 19 and the alexandrines of stanzas 20 and 21. Then look at the climactic stanza 43, especially at the concluding lines. What do the alliteration and the exact iambic rhythm give to the meaning of the stanza?

<hr/>

QUESTIONS – KEATS

JOHN KEATS (1795–1821)

The Eve of St. Agnes

1

St. Agnes' Eve—Ah, bitter chill it was!
The owl, for all his feathers, was a-cold;
The hare limped trembling through the frozen grass,
And silent was the flock in woolly fold:
Numb were the Beadsman's fingers, while he told
His rosary, and while his frosted breath,
Like pious incense from a censer old,
Seemed taking flight for heaven, without a death,
Past the sweet Virgin's picture, while his prayer he saith.

2

His prayer he saith, this patient, holy man;
Then takes his lamp, and riseth from his knees,
And back returneth, meager, barefoot, wan,
Along the chapel aisle by slow degrees:
The sculptured dead, on each side, seem to freeze,
Imprisoned in black, purgatorial rails:
Knights, ladies, praying in dumb orat'ries,

He passeth by; and his weak spirit fails
To think how they may ache in icy hoods and mails.

3

Northward he turneth through a little door,
And scarce three steps, ere Music's golden tongue
Flattered to tears this aged man and poor;
But no—already had his deathbell rung:
The joys of all his life were said and sung:
His was harsh penance on St. Agnes' Eve:
Another way he went, and soon among
Rough ashes sat he for his soul's reprieve,
And all night kept awake, for sinner's sake to grieve.

4

That ancient Beadsman heard the prelude soft;
And so it chanced, for many a door was wide,
From hurry to and fro. Soon, up aloft,
The silver, snarling trumpets 'gan to chide:
The level chambers, ready with their pride,
Were glowing to receive a thousand guests:
The carvéd angels, ever eager-eyed,
Stared, where upon their heads the cornice rests,
With hair blown back, and wings put cross-wise on their breasts.

5

At length burst in the argent revelry,
With plume, tiara, and all rich array,
Numerous as shadows haunting fairily
The brain, new stuffed, in youth, with triumphs gay
Of old romance. These let us wish away,
And turn, sole-thoughted, to one Lady there,
Whose heart had brooded, all that wintry day,
On love, and winged St. Agnes' saintly care,
As she had heard old dames full many times declare.

6

They told her how, upon St. Agnes' Eve,
Young virgins might have visions of delight,
And soft adorings from their loves receive
Upon the honeyed middle of the night,
If ceremonies due they did aright;

As, supperless to bed they must retire,
And couch supine their beauties, lily white;
Nor look behind, nor sideways, but require
Of Heaven with upward eyes for all that they desire.

7

Full of this whim was thoughtful Madeline:
The music, yearning like a God in pain,
She scarcely heard: her maiden eyes divine,
Fixed on the floor, saw many a sweeping train
Pass by—she heeded not at all: in vain
Came many a tiptoe, amorous cavalier,
And back retired; not cooled by high disdain;
But she saw not: her heart was otherwhere:
She sighed for Agnes' dreams, the sweetest of the year.

8

She danced along with vague, regardless eyes,
Anxious her lips, her breathing quick and short:
The hallowed hour was near at hand: she sighs
Amid the timbrels, and the thronged resort
Of whisperers in anger, or in sport;
'Mid looks of love, defiance, hate, and scorn,
Hoodwinked with faery fancy; all amort,
Save to St. Agnes and her lambs unshorn,
And all the bliss to be before tomorrow morn.

9

So, purposing each moment to retire,
She lingered still. Meantime, across the moors,
Had come young Porphyro, with heart on fire
For Madeline. Beside the portal doors,
Buttressed from moonlight, stands he, and implores
All saints to give him sight of Madeline,
But for one moment in the tedious hours,
That he might gaze and worship all unseen;
Perchance speak, kneel, touch, kiss—in sooth such things have been.

10

He ventures in: let no buzzed whisper tell:
All eyes be muffled, or a hundred swords
Will storm his heart, Love's fev'rous citadel:
For him, those chambers held barbarian hordes,

Hyena foemen, and hot-blooded lords,
Whose very dogs would execrations howl
Against his lineage: not one breast affords
Him any mercy, in that mansion foul,
Save one old beldame, weak in body and in soul.

11

Ah, happy chance! the aged creature came,
Shuffling along with ivory-headed wand,
To where he stood, hid from the torch's flame,
Behind a broad hall-pillar, far beyond
The sound of merriment and chorus bland:
He startled her; but soon she knew his face,
And grasped his fingers in her palsied hand,
Saying, "Mercy, Porphyro! hie thee from this place;
They are all here tonight, the whole bloodthirsty race!

12

"Get hence! get hence! there's dwarfish Hildebrand;
He had a fever late, and in the fit
He curséd thee and thine, both house and land:
Then there's that old Lord Maurice, not a whit
More tame for his gray hairs—Alas me! flit!
Flit like a ghost away."—"Ah, Gossip dear,
We're safe enough; here in this armchair sit,
And tell me how"—"Good Saints! not here, not here;
Follow me, child, or else these stones will be thy bier."

13

He followed through a lowly archéd way,
Brushing the cobwebs with his lofty plume,
And as she muttered "Well-a—well-a-day!"
He found him in a little moonlight room,
Pale, latticed, chill, and silent as a tomb.
"Now tell me where is Madeline," said he,
"O tell me, Angela, by the holy loom
Which none but secret sisterhood may see,
When they St. Agnes' wool are weaving piously."

14

"St. Agnes! Ah! it is St. Agnes' Eve—
Yet men will murder upon holy days:
Thou must hold water in a witch's sieve,

And be liege lord of all the Elves and Fays,
To venture so: it fills me with amaze
To see thee, Porphyro!—St. Agnes' Eve!
God's help! my lady fair the conjuror plays
This very night: good angels her deceive!
But let me laugh awhile, I've mickle time to grieve."

15

Feebly she laugheth in the languid moon,
While Porphyro upon her face doth look,
Like puzzled urchin on an aged crone
Who keepeth closed a wondrous riddle-book,
As spectacled she sits in chimney nook.
But soon his eyes grew brilliant, when she told
His lady's purpose; and he scarce could brook
Tears, at the thought of those enchantments cold,
And Madeline asleep in lap of legends old.

16

Sudden a thought came like a full-blown rose,
Flushing his brow, and in his painéd heart
Made purple riot: then doth he propose
A stratagem, that makes the beldame start:
"A cruel man and impious thou art:
Sweet lady, let her pray, and sleep, and dream
None with her good angels, far apart
From wicked men like thee. Go, go!—I deem
Thou canst not surely be the same that thou didst seem."

17

"I will not harm her, by all saints I swear,"
Quoth Porphyro: "O may I ne'er find grace
When my weak voice shall whisper its last prayer,
If one of her soft ringlets I displace,
Or look with ruffian passion in her face:
Good Angela, believe me by these tears;
Or I will, even in a moment's space,
Awake, with horrid shout, my foemen's ears,
And beard them, though they be more fanged than wolves and bears."

18

"Ah! why wilt thou affright a feeble soul?
A poor, weak, palsy-stricken, churchyard thing,

Whose passing bell may ere the midnight toll;
Whose prayers for thee, each morn and evening,
Were never missed."—Thus plaining, doth she bring
A gentler speech from burning Porphyro;
So woeful and of such deep sorrowing,
That Angela gives promise she will do
Whatever he shall wish, betide her weal or woe.

19

Which was, to lead him, in close secrecy,
Even to Madeline's chamber, and there hide
Him in a closet, of such privacy
That he might see her beauty unespied,
And win perhaps that night a peerless bride,
While legioned faeries paced the coverlet,
And pale enchantment held her sleepy-eyed.
Never on such a night have lovers met,
Since Merlin paid his Demon all the monstrous debt.

20

"It shall be as thou wishest," said the Dame:
"All cates and dainties shall be storéd there
Quickly on this feast night: by the tambour frame
Her own lute thou wilt see: no time to spare,
For I am slow and feeble, and scarce dare
On such a catering trust my dizzy head.
Wait here, my child, with patience; kneel in prayer
The while: Ah! thou must needs the lady wed,
Or may I never leave my grave among the dead."

21

So saying, she hobbled off with busy fear.
The lover's endless minutes slowly passed:
The dame returned, and whispered in his ear
To follow her; with aged eyes aghast
From fright of dim espial. Safe at last,
Through many a dusky gallery, they gain
The maiden's chamber, silken, hushed, and chaste;
Where Porphyro took covert, pleased amain.
His poor guide hurried back with agues in her brain.

22

Her falt'ring hand upon the balustrade,
Old Angela was feeling for the stair,

When Madeline, St. Agnes' charméd maid,
Rose, like a missioned spirit, unaware:
With silver taper's light, and pious care,
She turned, and down the aged gossip led
To a safe level matting. Now prepare,
Young Porphyro, for gazing on that bed;
She comes, she comes again, like ringdove frayed and fled.

23

Out went the taper as she hurried in;
Its little smoke, in pallid moonshine, died:
She closed the door, she panted, all akin
To spirits of the air, and visions wide:
No uttered syllable, or, woe betide!
But to her heart, her heart was voluble,
Paining with eloquence her balmy side;
As though a tongueless nightingale should swell
Her throat in vain, and die, heart-stifled, in her dell.

24

A casement high and triple-arched there was,
All garlanded with carven imag'ries
Of fruits, and flowers, and bunches of knot-grass,
And diamonded with panes of quaint device,
Innumerable of stains and splendid dyes,
As are the tiger moth's deep-damasked wings;
And in the midst, 'mong thousand heraldries,
And twilight saints, and dim emblazonings,
A shielded scutcheon blushed with blood of queens and kings.

25

Full on this casement shone the wintry moon,
And threw warm gules on Madeline's fair breast,
As down she knelt for heaven's grace and boon;
Rose-bloom fell on her hands, together pressed,
And on her silver cross soft amethyst,
And on her hair a glory, like a saint:
She seemed a splendid angel, newly dressed,
Save wings, for heaven—Porphyro grew faint:
She knelt, so pure a thing, so free from mortal taint.

26

Anon his heart revives: her vespers done,
Of all its wreathéd pearls her hair she frees;

Unclasps her warméd jewels one by one;
Loosens her fragrant bodice; by degrees
Her rich attire creeps rustling to her knees:
Half-hidden, like a mermaid in sea-weed,
Pensive awhile she dreams awake, and sees,
In fancy, fair St. Agnes in her bed,
But dares not look behind, or all the charm is fled.

27

Soon, trembling in her soft and chilly nest,
In sort of wakeful swoon, perplexed she lay,
Until the poppied warmth of sleep oppressed
Her soothéd limbs, and soul fatigued away;
Flown, like a thought, until the morrow-day;
Blissfully havened both from joy and pain;
Clasped like a missal where swart Paynims pray;
Blinded alike from sunshine and from rain,
As though a rose should shut, and be a bud again.

28

Stol'n to this paradise, and so entranced,
Porphyro gazed upon her empty dress,
And listened to her breathing, if it chanced
To wake into a slumberous tenderness;
Which when he heard, that minute did he bless,
And breathed himself: then from the closet crept,
Noiseless as fear in a wide wilderness,
And over the hushed carpet, silent, stepped,
And 'tween the curtains peeped, where, lo!—how fast she slept.

29

Then by the bedside, where the faded moon
Made a dim, silver twilight, soft he set
A table, and, half anguished, threw thereon
A cloth of woven crimson, gold, and jet—
O for some drowsy Morphean amulet!
The boisterous, midnight, festive clarion,
The kettledrum, and far-heard clarinet,
Affray his ears, though but in dying tone—
The hall door shuts again, and all the noise is gone.

30

And still she slept an azure-lidded sleep,
In blanchéd linen, smooth, and lavendered,

While he from forth the closet brought a heap
Of candied apple, quince, and plum, and gourd;
With jellies soother than the creamy curd,
And lucent syrups, tinct with cinnamon;
Manna and dates, in argosy transferred
From Fez; and spicéd dainties, every one,
From silken Samarcand to cedared Lebanon.

31

These delicates he heaped with glowing hand
On golden dishes and in baskets bright
Of wreathéd silver: sumptuous they stand
In the retired quiet of the night,
Filling the chilly room with perfume light.—
"And now, my love, my seraph fair, awake!
Thou art my heaven, and I thine eremite:
Open thine eyes, for meek St. Agnes' sake,
Or I shall drowse beside thee, so my soul doth ache."

32

Thus whispering, his warm, unnervéd arm
Sank in her pillow. Shaded was her dream
By the dusk curtains: 'twas a midnight charm
Impossible to melt as icéd stream:
The lustrous salvers in the moonlight gleam;
Broad golden fringe upon the carpet lies:
It seemed he never, never could redeem
From such a steadfast spell his lady's eyes;
So mused awhile, entoiled in wooféd fantasies.

33

Awakening up, he took her hollow lute—
Tumultuous—and, in chords that tenderest be,
He played an ancient ditty, long since mute,
In Provence called "*La belle dame sans merci*":
Close to her ear touching the melody;
Wherewith disturbed, she uttered a soft moan:
He ceased—she panted quick—and suddenly
Her blue affrayéd eyes wide open shone:
Upon his knees he sank, pale as smooth-sculptured stone.

34

Her eyes were open, but she still beheld,
Now wide awake, the vision of her sleep:

There was a painful change, that nigh expelled
The blisses of her dream so pure and deep,
At which fair Madeline began to weep,
And moan forth witless words with many a sigh;
While still her gaze on Porphyro would keep,
Who knelt, with joinéd hands and piteous eye,
Fearing to move or speak, she looked so dreamingly.

35

"Ah, Porphyro!" said she, "but even now
Thy voice was at sweet tremble in mine ear,
Made tunable with every sweetest vow;
And those sad eyes were spiritual and clear:
How changed thou art! how pallid, chill, and drear!
Give me that voice again, my Porphyro,
Those looks immortal, those complainings dear!
Oh leave me not in this eternal woe,
For if thou diest, my Love, I know not where to go."

36

Beyond a mortal man impassioned far
At these voluptuous accents, he arose,
Ethereal, flushed, and like a throbbing star
Seen mid the sapphire heaven's deep repose;
Into her dream he melted, as the rose
Blendeth its odor with the violet—
Solution sweet: meantime the frost-wind blows
Like Love's alarum pattering the sharp sleet
Against the windowpanes; St. Agnes' moon hath set.

37

'Tis dark; quick pattereth the flaw-blown sleet:
"This is no dream, my bride, my Madeline!"
'Tis dark: the icéd gusts still rave and beat:
"No dream, alas! alas! and woe is mine!
Porphyro will leave me here to fade and pine.—
Cruel! what traitor could thee hither bring?
I curse not, for my heart is lost in thine,
Though thou forsakest a deceivéd thing—
A dove forlorn and lost with sick unprunéd wing."

38

"My Madeline! sweet dreamer! lovely bride!
Say, may I be for aye thy vassal blest?

Thy beauty's shield, heart-shaped and vermeil dyed?
Ah, silver shrine, here will I take my rest
After so many hours of toil and quest,
A famished pilgrim—saved by miracle.
Though I have found, I will not rob thy nest
Saving of thy sweet self; if thou think'st well
To trust, fair Madeline, to no rude infidel.

39

"Hark! 'tis an elfin-storm from faery land,
Of haggard seeming, but a boon indeed:
Arise—arise! the morning is at hand—
The bloated wassaillers will never heed—
Let us away, my love, with happy speed;
There are no ears to hear, or eyes to see—
Drowned all in Rhenish and the sleepy mead:
Awake! arise! my love, and fearless be,
For o'er the southern moors I have a home for thee."

40

She hurried at his words, beset with fears,
For there were sleeping dragons all around,
At glaring watch, perhaps, with ready spears—
Down the wide stairs a darkling way they found.—
In all the house was heard no human sound.
A chain-drooped lamp was flickering by each door;
The arras, rich with horseman, hawk, and hound,
Fluttered in the besieging wind's uproar;
And the long carpets rose along the gusty floor.

41

They glide, like phantoms, into the wide hall;
Like phantoms, to the iron porch, they glide;
Where lay the Porter, in uneasy sprawl,
With a huge empty flagon by his side:
The wakeful bloodhound rose, and shook his hide,
But his sagacious eye an inmate owns:
By one, and one, the bolts full easy slide:
The chains lie silent on the footworn stones;
The key turns, and the door upon its hinges groans.

42

And they are gone: aye, ages long ago
These lovers fled away into the storm.

That night the Baron dreamt of many a woe,
And all his warrior-guests, with shade and form
Of witch, and demon, and large coffin-worm,
Were long be-nightmared. Angela the old
Died palsy-twitched, with meager face deform;
The Beadsman, after thousand aves told,
For aye unsought for slept among his ashes cold.

St. *Agnes' Eve* (1. 1): January 21. St. Agnes is the patron saint of virgins. According to legend, a girl who is virtuous and carries out the proper rituals will dream of her future husband on St. Agnes' Eve. *Beadsman's* (1. 5): one who is paid to pray. *dumb orat'ries* (2. 7): chapels that are silent because the praying knights and ladies are sculptures. *To think* (2. 9): while thinking. *amort* (8. 7): dead. *beldame* (10. 9): old lady. *wand* (11. 2): cane. *Gossip* (12. 6): godmother. *mickle* (14. 9): much. *plaining* (18. 5): arguing. *Merlin . . . Demon* (19. 9): By using magic he had taught her, Lady Vivien locked Merlin in a rock. *cates* (20. 2): fancy food. *amain* (21. 8): much. *frayed* (22. 9): afraid. *gules* (25. 2): red. *swart Paynims* (27. 7): dark pagans. *Morphean amulet* (29. 5): charm to bring sleep. *eremite* (31. 7): religious recluse, or worshipper. *wooféd* (32. 9): weaved. *"La belle . . . merci"* (33. 4): "The Lovely Lady Without Pity." *flaw-blown* (37. 1): windblown. *wassaillers* (39. 4): drunks.

1. Keats's romance is famous for its descriptive stanzas, but it should be remembered that it is primarily a narrative. What, for example, is the larger conflict? What is the smaller but central conflict around which the episode of the bedroom is built?

2. Reading this long poem allows the reader to see again how the Spenserian stanza, by its very repetition, builds momentum. The alexandrine is again focal in establishing this sense of forward motion. It functions somewhat like a wave, cresting with a look backward—a moment of poise in which the meaning of the previous stanza is assimilated—and then sweeping forward. "The Eve of St. Agnes" shows the clearest and most sensitive understanding of this power of the alexandrine. Of all the imitators of Spenser, Keats seems best to have understood how the interlocking of the difficult rhyme scheme can crest in the alexandrine and then how the alexandrine operates as a transition into the next stanza. The twelve crucial stanzas of the poem—24 to 35—exhibit this genius of Keats in using the instrument of the Spenserian stanza. How, for example, is the caesura used in each of the alexandrines in these twelve stanzas? Where is it muted? Where is it heightened? In each case, does the technical device support the narrative? Explain. In each stanza, how does the alexandrine look forward to the next stanza? Are there actual words

repeated? Sensual details? Images? Is there a deliberate use of the pause or silence between stanzas?

3. "The Eve of St. Agnes" has moments of stasis or pictorial units that do not, however, disturb the larger rhythm of forward motion; rather, they propel that momentum. Stanzas 24–35, for instance, offer superb examples of what we found in Spenser, "imitative harmony" (see p. 255). As an extension of this technique, Keats's stanzas also offer what Flaubert was later to call the "sensual complex," in which one sensual detail acts on another. What is remarkable here is that the very tensions brought about by the described sensations are the means by which we feel the suspense and excitement—as well as the very sexual presence—of Porphyro and his plot. Stanzas 29 and 30 concentrate this atmosphere and simultaneously this momentum. Look carefully at the sensations described. What senses are referred to? What is the effect of the allusions in stanza 30? How does Keats's skillful but limited use of enjambment support the sensual and exotic atmosphere?

4. The early modern critic George Saintsbury says that a more conscious use of assonance in English poetry begins with Keats; and Walter Jackson Bate, a recent biographer of the poet, has brilliantly demonstrated how Keats, in this poem and others of the same period, varies the long and short vowels with almost mathematical regularity. Consider the interlocking rhymes used in stanzas 29 and 30. Notice the variation in the vowels of these rhymes, especially in 29. How heavily does Keats depend on assonance and alliteration in stanza 29? What aspect of Porphyro's character do these devices solidify? Explain.

5. At the end of these crucial twelve stanzas occurs the climax of the poem, Madeline's awakening and accepting of Porphyro. This scene repeats the pattern of dream and reality, a favorite theme of Keats that surrounds the romance. Critics have pointed out that such use of contrast is the very essence of this poem. The beadsman and Angela are counterforces to the young lovers. Similarly, there are contrasts of music and silence, of outer cold and inner warmth, and of the narrative and descriptive passages themselves—all of which are unified by the repetitive patterns of the Spenserian stanza. Cite specific examples of such contrasts. The apex of these contrasts is the awakening of Madeline. How does the legend of St. Agnes dramatically function at this moment? What has Porphyro, however, been

preparing all along? What is the irony in this scene? Look carefully in the crucial twelve stanzas for the effects of this contrast of religion and eroticism. Does this contrast relate to the larger complex pattern of dream and reality? Does it relate to their ironic mingling? Explain in a long paragraph.

6. In this poem Keats imitated not only Spenser's stanzaic form, but also his diction. Words like the repeating "saith" in stanzas 1 and 2, like "returneth" in 2, "argent" in 5, "amort" in 8, "beldame" in 10, "espial" in 21, and "azure-lidded" in 30 are all either archaic, exotic, or highly artificial. Find other examples of such diction. Neither in subject matter (one must remember how very exotic the Catholic custom of a saint's day would have been in early nineteenth-century England) nor in diction does Keats adhere to Wordsworth's famous dictum about the proper subject and the proper diction for poetry (see p. 3). Yet the poem is manifestly successful. Clearly Keats's instinctive choice of the form as well as of the subject and diction acts as a kind of serious parody (see p. 259)—a parody of the past that operates for us symbolically, offering to the present a unified work of art in which the very form expresses human aspiration, a dream of love, but a dream firmly established in the continuing momentum of sensual reality. How does this dream / reality tension relate to Keats's odes (see p. 228)?

QUESTIONS – LOWELL

ROBERT LOWELL (1917–)

Christmas Eve Under Hooker's Statue

Tonight a blackout. Twenty years ago
I hung my stocking on the tree, and hell's
Serpent entwined the apple in the toe
To sting the child with knowledge. Hooker's heels
Kicking at nothing in the shifting snow,   5
A cannon and a cairn of cannon balls
Rusting before the blackened Statehouse, know
How the long horn of plenty broke like glass
In Hooker's gauntlets. Once I came from Mass;

Now storm-clouds shelter Christmas, once again   10
Mars meets his fruitless star with open arms,
His heavy sabre flashes with the rime,
The war-god's bronzed and empty forehead forms
Anonymous machinery from raw men;
The cannon on the Common cannot stun   15
The blundering butcher as he rides on Time—
The barrel clinks with holly. I am cold:
I ask for bread, my father gives me mould;

His stocking is full of stones, Santa in red
Is crowned with wizened berries. Man of war,   20
Where is the summer's garden? In its bed
The ancient speckled serpent will appear,
And black-eyed susan with her frizzled head.
When Chancellorsville mowed down the volunteer,
"All wars are boyish," Herman Melville said;   25
But we are old, our fields are running wild:
Till Christ again turn wanderer and child.

Statue (title): a statue in Boston of General Joseph Hooker (1814–79).

1. Few contemporary poets have attempted nine-line stanzas, and practically none has written them successfully. Robert Lowell is the exception. "Christmas Eve Under Hooker's Statue" is, of course, not a pure Spenserian stanza. Why? What is conspicuously lacking? What is the rhyme scheme in each stanza? The important point here is that the poem, like many modern sonnets, is a significant variation on an old form. Irregularities are expected in the extraordinary individuality of modern poetry; the echo of an old form is startling.

2. Does this poem fit into any one of the four general uses of the Spenserian stanza (see p. 259)? If so, consider its dramatic setting in determining which use. Both time and place are in the title, and —since this poem is about history—they must be immediately apprehended. How does this poem relate to the passage from Canto II of Byron's "Childe Harold" (p. 260)? How are the dramatic settings of the two pieces similar? What does this form allow that couplets or quatrains would not?

3. Each stanza ends with a couplet. What is the function of these couplets? How does each summarize and anticipate, thus performing some of the same work as the missing alexandrine? Is there a

crest before the silence between stanzas? Note that the last couplet provides a magnificent conclusion, the very last line performing something of the epigrammatic twist of the couplet in the Shakespearean sonnet.

4. The volume in which this poem appeared, *Lord Weary's Castle*, has many variations on traditional forms. A poet like Lowell did not merely use these forms, but explored their new possibilities in a modern world. The conscious (serious) parody was part of a philosophical orientation in his book, in which the past operating in the present made it only natural that old forms should be renewed with contemporary rhythms. How do the enjambment and the marked caesura in the poem set up a contemporary prose rhythm that the generally regular rhymes control? Must one stop at the end of these lines? Would the assumption that the poem is a dramatic monologue clarify the meaning of the caesuras? Explain. What devices for momentum does Lowell employ? How do they differ or correspond to devices employed by Shelley and Keats?

5. In the poem, it would seem that the Civil War, like the Christmas "Twenty years ago," was a loss of innocence. World War II, the "present," is a continuation of that loss: the present is a result of the failures of the past, both Hooker's and the speaker's father's. The only way out of the present "blackout" is to seek "the summer's garden" far away from the December snows. But it too has "The ancient speckled serpent"; youth and human innocence are not enough, and no place is secure. "All wars are boyish" (and it should be noted that perhaps the very germ of the poem is in this quotation from Melville). No, continues the final couplet, there is no solution to the present destruction until the reader becomes, as Christ, wanderer *and* child. Thus the poem moves on three levels: personal, national, and spiritual. How are all three integrated in the final four lines? As an exercise, consider each stanza and list the allusions for each level. How does this exercise demonstrate unity in the poem?

6. But the poem contains infinitely more than a skeleton reading will give. Its structural beauty is that its complex details are unified into the last lines, and its three levels blended yet kept in tension with each other, as Lowell's rhyme scheme is kept in tension with his prose rhythms. Using Lowell's poem as illustration, write an essay justifying or refuting the following statement: such complexity of content and form as that found in Lowell's "Christmas Eve Under Hooker's Statue" is only possible in the unit of the long stanza.

Chapter 9

Other Stanzaic Forms

In certain of the earlier chapters of this book, recurrent and dominant stanzaic forms have been explored at some length. In addition to those already treated, a number of others deserve attention, most notably these six: two varieties of three-line stanzas (the tercet and *terza rima*); two varieties of four-line stanzas (quatrains rhyming *abab* and *abba*); the seven-line stanza known as *rhyme royal*; and the eight-line stanza known as *ottava rima*. Altogether, the study of these various forms should serve to demonstrate one of the most significant features of rhyme—its function as a structural element in the organization of the verses of a poem.

THE TERCET (TRIPLET STANZA)

Rhyming *aaa*, the three-line tercet proper (or triplet stanza) is most commonly composed in lines of equal length. So Shakespeare uses the form in the *Threnos* section of his "The Phoenix and the Turtle":

> Beauty, truth, and rarity,
> Grace in all simplicity,
> Here enclos'd in cinders lie.

And so, almost two hundred years later (in 1797), Philip Freneau uses it in his "On Passing by an Old Church-Yard":

> Pensive, on this green turf I cast my eye,
> And almost feel inclined to muse and sigh:
> Such tokens of mortality so nigh.

But occasionally poets have chosen to write their tercets in lines of varying length, as in this example from Richard Crashaw's "Wishes for the Supposed Mistress" (1646):

> Whoe'er she be,
> That not impossible She
> That shall command my heart and me;

Generally, however, the three consecutive rhymes of the tercet have struck most poets as too conspicuous for extended employment; and aside from its use in short poems (and occasionally in those of moderate length, such as Tennyson's "The Two Voices"), the tercet has been best used not as a separate stanza but as a conscious variation within a long poem written almost wholly in couplets. This, indeed, is one of the characteristic devices of a poet like John Dryden, who —as the following passage from "Absalom and Achitophel" (1681) demonstrates—breaks up the potentially monotonous flow of the long couplet poem's *aabbcc . . .* rhyme scheme with an unexpected tercet:

> Of these the false Achitophel was first;
> A name to all succeeding ages cursed:
> For close designs, and crooked counsels fit;
> Sagacious, bold, and turbulent of wit;
> Restless, unfixed in principles and place;   5
> In power unpleased, impatient of disgrace:
> A fiery soul, which, working out its way,
> Fretted the pygmy body to decay,
> And o'er-informed the tenement of clay.

ROBERT HERRICK (1591–1674)

Upon Julia's Clothes

Whenas in silks my Julia goes,
Then, then, methinks, how sweetly flows
That liquefaction of her clothes.

Next, when I cast mine eyes, and see
That brave vibration, each way free,   5
O , how that glittering taketh me!

1. The word "liquefaction" (l. 3) is clearly an unusual one, but Herrick prepares for it in the second line. How? What image is suggested by the first three lines? What is the image suggested in lines 4–6?

2. Compare Herrick's poem to this remark of Mohammed's: "Silk was invented so that women could go naked in clothes." What are the essential differences between the two "statements"? Does Herrick's, when compared to Mohammed's prose one, reveal something significant about the nature of poetry. How does the simplicity of the triplet stanza contribute to the tone?

ALFRED, LORD TENNYSON (1809–92)

The Eagle

He clasps the crag with crooked hands;
Close to the sun in lonely lands,
Ringed with the azure world, he stands.

The wrinkled sea beneath him crawls;
He watches from his mountain walls,   5
And like a thunderbolt he falls.

1. One of the potential functions of rhyme is to suggest, by a change in its pattern, a shift in the development of the thought of a poem. (Consider, for example, the change in rhyme introduced in the ninth line of a Petrarchan sonnet.) What shift in the direction of the thought in Tennyson's poem is suggested by the rhyme change introduced in the second stanza?

ROBERT BROWNING (1812–89)

A *Toccata of Galuppi's*

1

Oh, Galuppi, Baldassaro, this is very sad to find!
I can hardly misconceive you; it would prove me deaf and blind;
But although I take your meaning, 'tis with such a heavy mind!

2

Here you come with your old music, and here's all the good it brings.
What, they lived once thus at Venice where the merchants were the
    kings,   5
Where Saint Mark's is, where the Doges used to wed the sea with rings?

3

Aye, because the sea's the street there; and 'tis arched by . . . what you
    call
. . . Shylock's bridge with houses on it, where they kept the carnival:
I was never out of England—it's as if I saw it all.

4

Did young people take their pleasure when the sea was warm in May?   10
Balls and masks begun at midnight, burning ever to midday,
When they made up fresh adventures for the morrow, do you say?

5

Was a lady such a lady, cheeks so round and lips so red—
On her neck the small face buoyant, like a bellflower on its bed,
O'er the breast's superb abundance where a man might base his
    head?   15

6

Well, and it was graceful of them—they'd break talk off and afford
—She, to bite her mask's black velvet—he, to finger on his sword,
While you sat and played toccatas, stately at the clavichord?

7

What? Those lesser thirds so plaintive, sixths diminished, sigh on sigh,
Told them something? Those suspensions, those solutions—"Must we
die?"   20
Those commiserating sevenths—"Life might last! we can but try!"

8

"Were you happy?"—"Yes."—"And are you still as happy?"—"Yes. And
you?"
—"Then, more kisses!"—"Did I stop them, when a million seemed so
few?"
Hark, the dominant's persistence till it must be answered to!

9

So, an octave struck the answer. Oh, they praised you, I dare say!   25
"Brave Galuppi! that was music; good alike at grave and gay!
I can always leave off talking when I hear a master play!"

10

Then they left you for their pleasure: till in due time, one by one,
Some with lives that came to nothing, some with deeds as well undone,
Death stepped tacitly and took them where they never see the sun.   30

11

But when I sit down to reason, think to take my stand nor swerve,
While I triumph o'er a secret wrung from nature's close reserve,
In you come with your cold music till I creep through every nerve.

12

Yes, you, like a ghostly cricket, creaking where a house was burned:
"Dust and ashes, dead and done with, Venice spent what Venice
earned.   35
The soul, doubtless, is immortal—where a soul can be discerned.

13

"Yours for instance: you know physics, something of geology,
Mathematics are your pastime; souls shall rise in their degree;
Butterflies may dread extinction—you'll not die, it cannot be!

"As for Venice and her people, merely born to bloom and drop,   40
Here on earth they bore their fruitage, mirth and folly were the crop:
What of soul was left, I wonder, when the kissing had to stop?

15

"Dust and ashes!" So you creak it, and I want the heart to scold.
Dear dead women, with such hair, too—what's become of all the gold
Used to hang and brush their bosoms? I feel chilly and grown old.   45

Galuppi (1): Baldassaro Galuppi was an eighteenth-century Venetian composer.
The occasion for the poem is a performance of one of Galuppi's works to which
the speaker (or meditator) in the poem is listening. *Doges* . . . *with rings* (6):
Venice, "Queen of the Adriatic," held an annual ceremony in which its chief
executive, the Doge, threw a ring into the water as a mark of the city's marriage
to the sea. *Shylock's bridge* (8): the Rialto, a bridge leading to the commercial
center of Venice.

1. Stanzas 7–9 contain references to the musical devices used by
Galuppi in his composition to attain certain effects. How effective
is Browning in suggesting the rhythm of the music itself in these
stanzas? Is there an overall rhythmical effect produced by the poem
from beginning to end? What does the triplet rhyme of each stanza
contribute?

2. As the speaker of the poem listens to Galuppi's piece, and as it
starts in him a series of reflections, we learn much about him. What
is his profession, for example? How does his life contrast to the lives
of the people who once listened to Galuppi play his own music? Are
we to think of him as superior to the Venetians of Galuppi's time? as
pathetic in comparison to them? Is Galuppi—as artist—the real
"hero" of the poem?

TERZA RIMA

Unlike the tercet, *terza rima* is a form designed to promote the
continuous flow of the verses of a poem. Based on a conscious imita-
tion of Dante's metrical scheme in the *Divine Comedy*, it can be de-
fined most simply as a series of tercets connected by an interlinking
rhyme—that is, as *aba, bcb, cdc, ded,* and so forth. Its earliest ap-
pearance in English poetry is in the sixteenth century, in the work of
Sir Thomas Wyatt, where, as in this example from "Mine Own John

Poins" (c. 1536), the great potential of *terza rima* to flow freely and rapidly is well suggested:

> Mine own John Poins, since ye delight to know
> The cause why that homeward I me draw, $\qquad$ 5½
> And flee the press of courts, whereso they go,
> Rather than to live thrall, under the awe
> Of lordly looks, wrapped within my cloak,
> To will and lust learning to set a law;
> It is not for because I scorn and mock
> The power of them to whom Fortune hath lent
> Charge over us, of right to strike the stroke.

And since Wyatt's time, despite the inherent difficulties of transposing an Italian metrical scheme into English, such major poets as Milton, Byron, Shelley, and Browning have made use of the form.

QUESTIONS – TERZA RIMA

PERCY BYSSHE SHELLEY (1792–1822)

Ode to the West Wind

I

O wild West Wind, thou breath of autumn's being,
Thou, from whose unseen presence the leaves dead
Are driven, like ghosts from an enchanter fleeing,

Yellow, and black, and pale, and hectic red,
Pestilence-stricken multitudes: O thou, $\qquad$ 5
Who chariotest to their dark wintry bed

The wingèd seeds, where they lie cold and low,
Each like a corpse within its grave, until
Thine azure sister of the spring shall blow

Her clarion o'er the dreaming earth, and fill $\qquad$ 10
(Driving sweet buds like flocks to feed in air)
With living hues and odors plain and hill;

Wild Spirit, which art moving everywhere;
Destroyer and preserver; hear, oh hear!

II

Thou on whose stream, mid the steep sky's commotion,   15
Loose clouds like earth's decaying leaves are shed,
Shook from the tangled boughs of Heaven and Ocean,

Angels of rain and lightning: there are spread
On the blue surface of thine aery surge,
Like the bright hair uplifted from the head   20

Of some fierce Maenad, even from the dim verge
Of the horizon to the zenith's height,
The locks of the approaching storm. Thou dirge

Of the dying year, to which this closing night
Will be the dome of a vast sepulchre,   25
Vaulted with all thy congregated might

Of vapors, from whose solid atmosphere
Black rain, and fire, and hail will burst: oh hear!

III

Thou who didst waken from his summer dreams
The blue Mediterranean, where he lay,   30
Lulled by the coil of his crystàlline streams,

Beside a pumice isle in Baiae's bay,
And saw in sleep old palaces and towers
Quivering within the wave's intenser day,

All overgrown with azure moss and flowers   35
So sweet, the sense faints picturing them! Thou
For whose path the Atlantic's level powers

Cleave themselves into chasms, while far below
The sea-blooms and the oozy woods which wear
The sapless foliage of the ocean, know   40

Thy voice, and suddenly grow gray with fear,
And tremble and despoil themselves: oh hear!

If I were a dead leaf thou mightest bear;
If I were a swift cloud to fly with thee;
A wave to pant beneath thy power, and share   45

The impulse of thy strength, only less free
Than thou, O uncontrollable! If even
I were as in my boyhood, and could be

The comrade of thy wanderings over Heaven,
As then, when to outstrip thy skiey speed   50
Scarce seemed a vision; I would ne'er have striven

As thus with thee in prayer in my sore need.
Oh, lift me as a wave, a leaf, a cloud!
I fall upon the thorns of life! I bleed!

A heavy weight of hours has chained and bowed   55
One too like thee—tameless, and swift, and proud.

V

Make me thy lyre, even as the forest is:
What if my leaves are falling like its own!
The tumult of thy mighty harmonies

Will take from both a deep, autumnal tone,   60
Sweet though in sadness. Be thou, Spirit fierce,
My spirit! Be thou me, impetuous one!

Drive my dead thoughts over the universe
Like withered leaves to quicken a new birth!
And, by the incantation of this verse,   65

Scatter, as from an unextinguished hearth
Ashes and sparks, my words among mankind!
Be through my lips to unawakened earth

The trumpet of a prophecy! O Wind,
If winter comes, can spring be far behind?   70

1. In an essay, discuss thematic progression in the poem by answering the following questions: Why is the West Wind character-

ized paradoxically as "Destroyer and preserver" (l. 14) in section I? How does the simile in line 16 clarify the relationship between sections I and II? What relationship do the waves of section III hold to the clouds of section II and the leaves of section I? What cumulative effect results from the use of the symbol of the West Wind in sections I–III? Since each of the first three verses of section IV (ll. 43–45) refers to one of the preceding three sections of the poem, is there the suggestion that a new subject or subject emphasis will be introduced? How does this new subject relate directly to the poem's persona? In section IV how does the poet contrast his boyhood with his present? Explain the closing couplet in section IV. Why does the reference to "mighty harmonies" (l. 59) in section V suggest hopefulness? How is the image of hope solidified by the concluding couplet?

2. Shelley's poem is perhaps the best example of an English poet's use of *terza rima*. An obvious innovation in the poem is the use of the five couplets to close the poem's sections. What is the particular purpose of the couplets? That is, do they further thematic development? explicate symbols? summarize?

3. Does Shelley's poem achieve greatest success from a perceptively intellectual statement or from use of richly sensuous images? Explain.

WILLIAM EMPSON (1906–)

The Scales

The proper scale would pat you on the head
But Alice showed her pup Ulysses' bough
Well from behind a thistle, wise with dread;

And though your gulf-sprung mountains I allow
(Snow-puppy curves, rose-solemn dado band)   5
Charming for nurse, I am not nurse just now.

Why pat or stride them, when the train will land
Me high, through climbing tunnels, at your side,
And careful fingers meet through castle sand.

Claim slyly rather that the tunnels hide   10
Solomon's gems, white vistas, preserved kings,
By jackal sandhole to your air flung wide.

Say (she suspects) to sea Nile only brings
Delta and indecision, who instead
Far back up country does enormous things.   15

1. Through highly compressed allusions Empson suggests the sub-
ject of his poem. In line 2, for example, "Alice" and "Ulysses' bough"
both suggest transport to a kind of wonderland (*Alice in Wonder-
land,* and the association of Ulysses' bough with Nausicaa, a princess
who led Ulysses to her father's palace). At the same time, both allu-
sions also suggest a journey underground—Alice through a hole, and
"Ulysses' bough" suggesting the journey to the underworld of an-
other classical hero, Aeneas, who made use of a golden bough. "By
jackal sandhole" (1. 12) reverses the idea of a journey downward by
its reference to the avenue of escape for the heroes in Rider Hag-
gard's *King Solomon's Mines.* As for Empson's own comments on
his poem, he has told us that "the tunnels . . . stand for difficulties
of communication" and that "the Nile takes on the tunnel symbolism
as being for long unknown up country." What, then, *is* the subject
of Empson's poem? Childhood (because of the reference to Alice)?
The "underworld" in an adult (i.e., his buried nature and the past
which only he himself knows)? The difficulty of a close relationship
between two adults when so much—including the childhood of each
—remains hidden? (In this connection is the "castle" of line 9 a
real castle?) But what, then, of the second stanza? Is it a description
of a woman's breasts? Is the poem really about sexuality? Write a
long paragraph in which you present the prose "meaning" of Emp-
son's poem.

2. Does the *terza rima* contribute to balancing meanings in the
poem? Write a long paragraph on the value of a formal rhyme
scheme in defining such complex meaning.

THE QUATRAIN STANZA

Although the rhyme scheme of the quatrain is capable of a great
many variations, three variations in particular have been important
in English poetry. The first, the ballad stanza rhyming *abcb,* has al-

ready been discussed (see Chapter 2). A second important quatrain is the one rhyming *abab*. When all four lines of this stanza are written in iambic pentameter, the quatrain is often called "heroic" or "elegiac" (the second name has its origin from Thomas Gray's use of the *abab* stanza for his "Elegy Written in a Country Churchyard"). Here is an example of John Dryden's use of the heroic quatrain in "Annus Mirabilis" (1666):

> The Duke, less numerous, but in courage more,
> On wings of all the winds to combat flies:
> His murdering Guns a loud defiance roar,
> And bloody Crosses on his Flag-staffs rise.

Although the pentameter quatrain rhyming *abab* has earned for itself a special name, *abab* quatrains in various other line lengths comprise one of the most frequently found stanzas in English and American poetry. Consider, for example, the following variations:

> As virtuous men pass mildly away,
> And whisper to their souls to go,
> Whilst some of their sad friends do say
> The breath goes now, and some say, No . . . (*Donne*)

> Gather ye rosebuds while ye may,
> Old time is still a-flying;
> And this same flower that smiles today
> Tomorrow will be dying. (*Herrick*)

> I heard a thousand blended notes,
> While in a grove I sate reclined,
> In that sweet mood when pleasant thoughts
> Bring sad thoughts to the mind. (*Wordsworth*)

> I built my soul a lordly pleasure-house,
> Wherein at ease for aye to dwell.
> I said, "O Soul, make merry and carouse,
> Dear soul, for all is well." (*Tennyson*)

> Miniver Cheevy, child of scorn,
> Grew lean while he assailed the seasons:
> He wept that he was ever born,
> And he had reasons. (*E. A. Robinson*)

Perhaps something of the attraction the *abab* quatrain has held for poets can be explained by the seeming compromise it effects between the potentially excessive insistence of consecutive rhymes and the potentially excessive subtlety of rhymes more than a single line apart or connected by a more complex pattern than simple alternation.

The third major quatrain is characterized by a rhyme scheme of *abba*. Although it too, like the *abab* quatrain, is susceptible of numerous variations of line length, the most successful variation has been a four-line pattern of iambic tetrameter. Here is an example of Tennyson's use of it in his "In Memoriam" (1850), a poem which so successfully employed the *abba* four-stress quatrain that it has been known ever since as the "In Memoriam" stanza:

> Yet if some voice that man could trust
>   Should murmur from the narrow house,
>   "The cheeks drop in, the body bows;
> Man dies, nor is there hope in dust":
>
> Might I not say? "Yet even here,
>   But for one hour, O Love, I strive
>   To keep so sweet a thing alive."
> But I should turn mine ears and hear
>
> The moanings of the homeless sea,
>   The sound of streams that swift or slow
>   Draw down Aeonian hills, and sow
> The dust of continents to be . . .

Note that the separation of the *a* rhyme by the intervening *b* couplet (and this is perhaps the most important single feature of the "In Memoriam" quatrain) allows a greater potential for flow between the stanzas than does the *abab* rhyme scheme, where the *b* rhyme of the fourth line falls with a more noticeable suggestion of conclusion.

THOMAS GRAY (1716–71)

Elegy Written in a Country Churchyard

The curfew tolls the knell of parting day,
The lowing herd wind slowly o'er the lea,
The plowman homeward plods his weary way,
And leaves the world to darkness and to me.

Now fades the glimmering landscape on the sight, 5
And all the air a solemn stillness holds,
Save where the beetle wheels his droning flight,
And drowsy tinklings lull the distant folds;

Save that from yonder ivy-mantled tower
The moping owl does to the moon complain 10
Of such, as wandering near her secret bower,
Molest her ancient solitary reign.

Beneath those rugged elms, that yew tree's shade,
Where heaves the turf in many a moldering heap,
Each in his narrow cell forever laid, 15
The rude forefathers of the hamlet sleep.

The breezy call of incense-breathing Morn,
The swallow twittering from the straw-built shed,
The cock's shrill clarion, or the echoing horn,
No more shall rouse them from their lowly bed. 20

For them no more the blazing hearth shall burn,
Or busy housewife ply her evening care;
No children run to lisp their sire's return,
Or climb his knees the envied kiss to share.

Oft did the harvest to their sickle yield, 25
Their furrow oft the stubborn glebe has broke;
How jocund did they drive their team afield!
How bowed the woods beneath their sturdy stroke!

Let not Ambition mock their useful toil,
   Their homely joys, and destiny obscure;   30
Nor Grandeur hear with a disdainful smile
   The short and simple annals of the poor.

The boast of heraldry, the pomp of power,
   And all that beauty, all that wealth e'er gave,
Awaits alike the inevitable hour.   35
   The paths of glory lead but to the grave.

Nor you, ye proud, impute to these the fault,
   If Memory o'er their tomb no trophies raise,
Where through the long-drawn aisle and fretted vault
   The pealing anthem swells the note of praise.   40

Can storied urn or animated bust
   Back to its mansion call the fleeting breath?
Can Honor's voice provoke the silent dust,
   Or Flattery soothe the dull cold ear of Death?

Perhaps in this neglected spot is laid   45
   Some heart once pregnant with celestial fire;
Hands that the rod of empire might have swayed,
   Or waked to ecstasy the living lyre.

But Knowledge to their eyes her ample page
   Rich with the spoils of time did ne'er unroll;   50
Chill Penury repressed their noble rage,
   And froze the genial current of the soul.

Full many a gem of purest ray serene,
   The dark unfathomed caves of ocean bear:
Full many a flower is born to blush unseen,   55
   And waste its sweetness on the desert air.

Some village Hampden, that with dauntless breast
   That little tyrant of his fields withstood;
Some mute inglorious Milton here may rest,
   Some Cromwell guiltless of his country's blood.   60

The applause of listening senates to command,
   The threats of pain and ruin to despise,
To scatter plenty o'er a smiling land,
   And read their history in a nation's eyes,

Their lot forbade: nor circumscribed alone 65
    Their growing virtues, but their crimes confined;
Forbade to wade through slaughter to a throne,
    And shut the gates of mercy on mankind,

The struggling pangs of conscious truth to hide,
    To quench the blushes of ingenuous shame, 70
Or heap the shrine of Luxury and Pride
    With incense kindled at the Muse's flame.

Far from the madding crowd's ignoble strife,
    Their sober wishes never learned to stray;
Along the cool sequestered vale of life 75
    They kept the noiseless tenor of their way.

Yet even these bones from insult to protect
    Some frail memorial still erected nigh,
With uncouth rhymes and shapeless sculpture decked,
    Implores the passing tribute of a sigh. 80

Their name, their years, spelt by the unlettered Muse,
    The place of fame and elegy supply:
And many a holy text around she strews,
    That teach the rustic moralist to die.

For who to dumb Forgetfulness a prey, 85
    This pleasing anxious being e'er resigned,
Left the warm precincts of the cheerful day,
    Nor cast one longing lingering look behind?

On some fond breast the parting soul relies,
    Some pious drops the closing eye requires; 90
Even from the tomb the voice of Nature cries,
    Even in our ashes live their wonted fires.

For thee, who mindful of the unhonored dead
    Dost in these lines their artless tale relate;
If chance, by lonely contemplation led, 95
    Some kindred spirit shall inquire thy fate,

Haply some hoary-headed swain may say,
    "Oft have we seen him at the peep of dawn
Brushing with hasty steps the dews away
    To meet the sun upon the upland lawn. 100

"There at the foot of yonder nodding beech
    That wreathes its old fantastic roots so high,
His listless length at noontide would he stretch,
    And pore upon the brook that babbles by.

"Hard by yon wood, now smiling as in scorn,   105
    Muttering his wayward fancies he would rove,
Now drooping, woeful wan, like one forlorn,
    Or crazed with care, or crossed in hopeless love.

"One morn I missed him on the customed hill,
    Along the heath and near his favorite tree;   110
Another came; nor yet beside the rill,
    Nor up the lawn, nor at the wood was he;

"The next with dirges due in sad array
    Slow through the churchway path we saw him borne.
Approach and read (for thou canst read) the lay,   115
    Graved on the stone beneath yon aged thorn."

THE EPITAPH

Here rests his head upon the lap of Earth
    A youth to Fortune and to Fame unknown.
Fair Science frowned not on his humble birth,
    And Melancholy marked him for her own.   120

Large was his bounty, and his soul sincere,
    Heaven did a recompense as largely send:
He gave to Misery all he had, a tear,
    He gained from Heaven ('twas all he wished) a friend.

No farther seek his merits to disclose,   125
    Or draw his frailties from their dread abode
(There they alike in trembling hope repose),
    The bosom of his Father and his God.

glebe (26): soil. *Hampden* (57): one of the heroes of the Puritan Revolution
against the autocracy of Charles I.

1. An *elegy* may be defined most simply as a poem of lamentation
for the dead. Whose death is the true subject of Gray's "Elegy"?
The common man's? All mankind's? The poet's own, in prospect?

2. At the exact midpoint of Gray's poem (ll. 64–65), there is a marked enjambment between stanzas. In how many other places does Gray make use of a suspension of thought between stanzas? Would it be more accurate to describe Gray's use of the heroic (or elegiac) stanza in this poem as free-flowing or self-contained? How does the presence or lack of enjambment within quatrains influence your answer?

3. Describe Gray's diction and imagery. Is the diction elevated or natural? Explain. Does the imagery appear strikingly original or conventional? (In answering this last question, recall the imagery of other eighteenth-century poems you have read.)

WILLIAM BLAKE (1757–1827)

The Little Black Boy

My mother bore me in the southern wild,
And I am black, but O! my soul is white;
White as an angel is the English child:
But I am black as if bereav'd of light.

My mother taught me underneath a tree,   5
And sitting down before the heat of day,
She took me on her lap and kisséd me,
And pointing to the east, began to say:

"Look on the rising sun: there God does live,
And gives his light, and gives his heat away;   10
And flowers and trees and beasts and men receive
Comfort in morning, joy in the noon day.

"And we are put on earth a little space,
That we may learn to bear the beams of love,
And these black bodies and this sun-burnt face   15
Is but a cloud, and like a shady grove.

"For when our souls have learn'd the heat to bear,
The cloud will vanish; we shall hear his voice,
Saying: 'Come out from the grove, my love & care,
And round my golden tent like lambs rejoice.' "   20

Thus did my mother say, and kisséd me;
And thus I say to little English boy:
When I from black and he from white cloud free,
And round the tent of God like lambs we joy,

I'll shade him from the heat till he can bear   25
To lean in joy upon our father's knee;
And then I'll stand and stroke his silver hair,
And be like him, and he will then love me.

1. This is one of Blake's "Songs of Innocence" (1789), poems that, beneath a childlike simplicity of surface, sometimes carry a barbed implication. What are we to make of this poem? Is the persona, the little black boy, a victim of the sense of racial inferiority? Does he unwittingly reveal, in his childlike fashion, his moral superiority to the white child? Has Blake really written a poem that condemns the white man for his racial attitudes? Explain.

2. How closely do Blake's quatrains resemble Gray's? Are the poems alike in diction? imagery? Explain.

ALFRED, LORD TENNYSON (1809–92)

from In Memoriam

28

The time draws near the birth of Christ.
   The moon is hid; the night is still;
   The Christmas bells from hill to hill
Answer each other in the mist.

Four voices of four hamlets round,   5
   From far and near, on mead and moor,
   Swell out and fail, as if a door
Were shut between me and the sound;

Each voice four changes on the wind,
   That now dilate, and now decrease,
   Peace and goodwill, goodwill and peace,   10
Peace and goodwill, to all mankind.

This year I slept and woke with pain,
   I almost wished no more to wake,
   And that my hold on life would break   15
Before I heard those bells again.

But they my troubled spirit rule,
   For they controlled me when a boy;
   They bring me sorrow touched with joy,
The merry merry bells of Yule.   20

29

With such compelling cause to grieve
   As daily vexes household peace,
   And chains regret to his decease,
How dare we keep our Christmas Eve;

Which brings no more a welcome guest   25
   To enrich the threshold of the night
   With showered largess of delight
In dance and song and game and jest?

Yet go, and while the holly boughs
   Entwine the cold baptismal font,   30
   Make one wreath more for Use and Wont,
That guard the portals of the house;

Old sisters of a day gone by,
   Gray nurses, loving nothing new;
   Why should they miss their yearly due   35
Before their time? They too will die.

30

With trembling fingers did we weave
   The holly round the Christmas hearth;
   A rainy cloud possessed the earth,
And sadly fell our Christmas Eve.   40

At our old pastimes in the hall
   We gamboled, making vain pretense
   Of gladness, with an awful sense
Of one mute Shadow watching all.

The Quatrain Stanza   313

We paused. The winds were in the beech;   45
   We heard them sweep the winter land;
   And in a circle hand-in-hand
Sat silent, looking each at each.

Then echo-like our voices rang;
   We sung, though every eye was dim,   50
   A merry song we sang with him
Last year; impetuously we sang.

We ceased; a gentler feeling crept
   Upon us: surely rest is meet.
   "They rest," we said, "their sleep is sweet,"   55
And silence followed, and we wept.

Our voices took a higher range;
   Once more we sang: "They do not die
   Nor lose their mortal sympathy,
Nor change to us, although they change;   60

"Rapt from the fickle and the frail
   With gathered power, yet the same,
   Pierces the keen seraphic flame
From orb to orb, from veil to veil."

Rise, happy morn, rise, holy morn,   65
   Draw forth the cheerful day from night;
   O Father, touch the east, and light
The light that shone when Hope was born.

31

When Lazarus left his charnel-cave,
   And home to Mary's house returned,   70
   Was this demanded—if he yearned
To hear her weeping by his grave?

"Where wert thou, brother, those four days?"
   There lives no record of reply,
   Which telling what it is to die   75
Had surely added praise to praise.

From every house the neighbors met,
   The streets were filled with joyful sound,

A solemn gladness even crowned
The purple brows of Olivet.   80

Behold a man raised up by Christ!
   The rest remaineth unrevealed;
   He told it not; or something sealed
The lips of that Evangelist.

32

Her eyes are homes of silent prayer,   85
   Nor other thought her mind admits
   But, he was dead, and there he sits,
And he that brought him back is there.

Then one deep love doth supersede
   All other, when her ardent gaze   90
   Roves from the living brother's face,
And rests upon the Life indeed.

All subtle thought, all curious fears,
   Borne down by gladness so complete,
   She bows, she bathes the Savior's feet   95
With costly spikenard and with tears.

Thrice blest whose lives are faithful prayers,
   Whose loves in higher love endure;
   What souls possess themselves so pure,
Or is there blessedness like theirs?   100

33

O thou that after toil and storm
   Mayst seem to have reached a purer air,
   Whose faith has center everywhere,
Nor cares to fix itself to form,

Leave thou thy sister when she prays,   105
   Her early Heaven, her happy views;
   Nor thou with shadowed hint confuse
A life that leads melodious days.

Her faith through form is pure as thine,
   Her hands are quicker unto good;   110

Oh, sacred be the flesh and blood
To which she links a truth divine!

See thou, that countest reason ripe
   In holding by the law within,
     Thou fail not in a world of sin,   115
And ev'n for want of such a type.

34

My own dim life should teach me this,
   That life shall live for evermore,
     Else earth is darkness at the core,
And dust and ashes all that is;   120

This round of green, this orb of flame,
   Fantastic beauty; such as lurks
     In some wild poet, when he works
Without a conscience or an aim.

What then were God to such as I?   125
   'Twere hardly worth my while to choose
     Of things all mortal, or to use
A little patience ere I die;

'Twere best at once to sink to peace,
   Like birds the charming serpent draws,   130
     To drop head-foremost in the jaws
Of vacant darkness and to cease.

35

Yet if some voice that man could trust
   Should murmur from the narrow house,
     "The cheeks drop in; the body bows;   135
Man dies, nor is there hope in dust"—

Might I not say, "Yet even here,
   But for one hour, O Love, I strive
     To keep so sweet a thing alive"?
But I should turn mine ears and hear   140

The moanings of the homeless sea,
   The sound of streams that swift or slow

Draw down Æonian hills, and sow
The dust of continents to be;

And Love would answer with a sigh,   145
   "The sound of that forgetful shore
   Will change my sweetness more and more,
Half-dead to know that I shall die."

O me, what profits it to put
   An idle case? If Death were seen   150
   At first as Death, Love had not been,
Or been in narrowest working shut,

Mere fellowship of sluggish moods,
   Or in his coarsest Satyr-shape
   Had bruised the herb and crushed the grape,   155
And basked and battened in the woods.

.   .   .   .   .

48

If these brief lays, of Sorrow born,
   Were taken to be such as closed
   Grave doubts and answers here proposed,
Then these were such as men might scorn.   160

Her care is not to part and prove;
   She takes, when harsher moods remit,
   What slender shade of doubt may flit,
And makes it vassal unto Love;

And hence, indeed, she sports with words,   165
   But better serves a wholesome law,
   And holds it sin and shame to draw
The deepest measure from the chords;

Nor dare she trust a larger lay,
   But rather loosens from the lip   170
   Short swallow-flights of song, that dip
Their wings in tears, and skim away.

49

From art, from nature, from the schools,
   Let random influences glance,

Like light in many a shivered lance   175
That breaks about the dappled pools.

The lightest wave of thought shall lisp,
    The fancy's tenderest eddy wreathe,
    The slightest air of song shall breathe
To make the sullen surface crisp.   180

And look thy look, and go thy way,
    But blame not thou the winds that make
    The seeming-wanton ripple break,
The tender-penciled shadow play.

Beneath all fancied hopes and fears   185
    Ay me, the sorrow deepens down,
    Whose muffled motions blindly drown
The bases of my life in tears.

1. *In Memoriam* (1850) grew out of Tennyson's grief over the death by apoplexy of his closest friend, Arthur Henry Hallam, on September 15, 1833, in Vienna. The poem is best regarded as a kind of poetic diary that Tennyson kept over the course of almost twenty years, reflecting in it the various moods and meditations aroused in him by Hallam's death. The selection printed here opens with the first Christmas (1833) after Hallam's death. Note that the religious associations of the season (especially evident in the last stanza of section 30) lead to reflections on Christ's raising Lazarus from the dead (sections 31 and 32). But Tennyson is too much a product of the mid-nineteenth century to be able to rest in a traditional faith in Hallam's immortality (although in section 33 he warns against disturbing those who believe in Christianity simply and sincerely). As the selection proceeds, Tennyson exhibits various reactions to the questions raised by a beloved individual's death. In section 34, for example, what emotional conviction does he offer? In sections 48–49 Tennyson describes his manner of composition. How does he reveal his intentions?

2. Compare Tennyson's use of the "In Memoriam" stanza in sections 32 and 33 with Gray's use of heroic quatrains in the "Elegy." What is the most striking difference between the effects achieved by the two poets? What might Tennyson's problem have been if he had employed Gray's rhyme scheme?

WILLIAM BUTLER YEATS (1865–1939)

The Lake Isle of Innisfree

I will arise and go now, and go to Innisfree,
And a small cabin build there, of clay and wattles made;
Nine bean rows will I have there, a hive for the honey bee,
    And live alone in the bee-loud glade.

And I shall have some peace there, for peace comes dropping slow,   5
Dropping from the veils of the morning to where the cricket sings;
There midnight's all a glimmer, and noon a purple glow,
    And evening full of the linnet's wings.

I will arise and go now, for always night and day
I hear lake water lapping with low sounds by the shore;   10
While I stand on the roadway, or on the pavements gray,
    I hear it in the deep heart's core.

1. What implicit contrast runs throughout "The Lake Isle of In-
nisfree"? Does the poem have a larger significance, or is it merely
one man's desire to escape to a particular island? Does each of us, in
reality, have an "Innisfree"? Explain in a paragraph or two.

When You Are Old

When you are old and grey and full of sleep,
And nodding by the fire, take down this book,
And slowly read, and dream of the soft look
Your eyes had once, and of their shadows deep;

How many loved your moments of glad grace,   5
And loved your beauty with love false or true;
But one man loved the pilgrim soul in you,
And loved the sorrows of your changing face;

And bending down beside the glowing bars,
Murmur, a little sadly, how Love fled   10
And paced upon the mountains overhead
And hid his face amid a crowd of stars.

The Quatrain Stanza   319

JOHN CROWE RANSOM (1888–   )

Blue Girls

Twirling your blue skirts, travelling the sward
Under the towers of your seminary,
Go listen to your teachers old and contrary
Without believing a word.

Tie the white fillets then about your lustrous hair   5
And think no more of what will come to pass
Than bluebirds that go walking on the grass
And chattering on the air.

Practise your beauty, blue girls, before it fail;
And I will cry with my loud lips and publish   10
Beauty which all our power shall never establish,
It is so frail.

For I could tell you a story which is true;
I know a lady with a terrible tongue,
Blear eyes fallen from blue,   15
All her perfections tarnished—and yet it is not long
Since she was lovelier than any of you.

KARL SHAPIRO (1913–   )

The Intellectual

What should the wars do with these jigging fools?

The man behind the book may not be man,
His own man or the book's or yet the time's,
But still be whole, deciding what he can
In praise of politics or German rimes;

But the intellectual lights a cigarette   5
And offers it lit to the lady, whose odd smile
Is the merest hyphen—lest he should forget
What he has been resuming all the while.

He talks to overhear, she to withdraw
To some interior feminine fireside   10
Where the back arches, beauty puts forth a paw
Like a black puma stretching in velvet pride,

Making him think of cats, a stray of which
Some days sets up a howling in his brain,
Pure interference such as this neat bitch   15
Seems to create from listening disdain.

But talk is all the value, the release,
Talk is the very fillip of an act,
The frame and subject of the masterpiece
Under whose film of age the face is cracked.   20

His own forehead glows like expensive wood,
But back of it the mind is disengaged,
Self-sealing clock recording bad and good
At constant temperature, intact, unaged.

But strange, his body is an open house   25
Inviting every passerby to stay:
The city to and fro beneath his brows
Wanders and drinks and chats from night to day.

Think of a private thought, indecent room
Where one might kiss his daughter before bed!   30
Life is embarrassed; shut the family tomb,
Console your neighbor for his recent dead;

Do something! die in Spain or paint a green
Gouache, go into business (Rimbaud did),
Or start another Little Magazine,   35
Or move in with a woman, have a kid.

Invulnerable, impossible, immune,
Do what you will, your will will not be done
But dissipate the light of afternoon
Till evening flickers like the midnight sun,   40

And midnight shouts and dies: I'd rather be
A milkman walking in his sleep at dawn

Bearing fat quarts of cream, and so be free,
Crossing alone and cold from lawn to lawn.

I'd rather be a barber and cut hair   45
Than walk with you in gilt museum halls,
You and the puma-lady, she so rare
Exhaling her silk soul upon the walls.

Go take yourselves apart, but let me be
The fault you find with everyman. I spit,   50
I laugh. I fight; and you, *l'homme qui rit*,
Swallow your stale saliva, and still sit.

What . . . *fools?* (motto): see Shakespeare's *Julius Caesar*, IV, iii. 137.
l'homme qui rit (51): the man who laughs.

RICHARD WILBUR (1921–   )

Mind

Mind in the purest play is like some bat
That beats about in caverns all alone,
Contriving by a kind of senseless wit
Not to conclude against a wall of stone.

It has no need to falter or explore;   5
Darkly it knows what obstacles are there,
And so may weave and flitter, dip and soar
In perfect courses through the blackest air.

And has this simile a like perfection?
The mind is like a bat. Precisely. Save   10
That in the very happiest intellection
A graceful error may correct the cave.

1. Explain the last stanza of Wilbur's poem.
2. Compare Wilbur's concept of intellectual activity to Karl Shapiro's, in the preceding poem. Which poem holds more meaning for you? Explain.

RHYME ROYAL

Rhyme royal is the most common name for a five-stress, seven-line stanza rhyming *ababbcc*. Because of its close association with Chaucer (who wrote approximately 14,000 lines in this form), *rhyme royal* is frequently called the "Chaucer" or "Troilus" stanza. Here is Chaucer's use of it in the opening of "Troilus and Criseyde" (c. 1385):

> The double sorwe of Troilus to tellen,
> That was the kyng Priamus sone of Troye,
> In lovynge, how his aventures fellen
> From wo to wele, and after out of joie,
> My purpos is, er that I parte fro ye.
> Thesiphone, thow help me for t'endite
> Thise woful vers, that wepen as I write.

And here is John Masefield's use of the same stanza, more than five hundred years later, in his long poem "Dauber" (1912):

> "Whales!" said the Mate. They stayed there all night long
> Answering the horn. Out of the night they spoke,
> Defeated creatures who had suffered wrong,
> But were still noble underneath the stroke.
> They filled the darkness when the Dauber woke;
> The men came peering to the rail to hear,
> And the sea sighed, and the fog rose up sheer.

But although Chaucer showed superbly how well suited *rhyme royal* is to the composition of a long poem, and although Shakespeare may be said to have confirmed Chaucer's use of the stanza by his own "The Rape of Lucrece" (1594), *rhyme royal* has been used only rarely since the seventeenth century. Aside from Masefield in our own century and William Morris in the nineteenth, the poets who have best succeeded with the stanza (Milton, Thomas Chatterton, and Wordsworth) have effected in a sense a compromise between *rhyme royal* and the Spenserian stanza (see Chapter 8), extending the seventh line of Chaucer's stanza into an alexandrine, as in this example from Milton's unfinished "The Passion" (1630):

For now to sorrow must I tune my song,
And set my harp to notes of saddest woe
Which on our dearest Lord did seize ere long,
Dangers, and snares, and wrongs, and worse than so,
Which he for us did freely undergo.
   Most perfect Hero, tried in heaviest plight
   Of labors huge and hard, too hard for human wight.

<hr />

QUESTIONS – RHYME ROYAL

WILLIAM SHAKESPEARE (1564–1616)

from The Rape of Lucrece

From the besieged Ardea all in post,
Borne by the trustless wings of false desire,
Lust-breathed Tarquin leaves the Roman host
And to Collatium bears the lightless fire
Which, in pale embers hid, lurks to aspire   5
   And girdle with embracing flames the waist
   Of Collatine's fair love, Lucrece the chaste.

Haply that name of 'chaste' unhap'ly set
This bateless edge on his keen appetite;
When Collatine unwisely did not let   10
To praise the clear unmatched red and white
Which triumph'd in that sky of his delight,
   Where mortal stars, as bright as heaven's beauties,
   With pure aspects did him peculiar duties.

For he the night before, in Tarquin's tent,   15
Unlock'd the treasure of his happy state:
What priceless wealth the heavens had him lent
In the possession of his beauteous mate;
Reck'ning his fortune at such high proud rate
   That kings might be espoused to more fame,   20
   But king nor peer to such a peerless dame.

O happiness enjoy'd but of a few,
And, if possess'd, as soon decay'd and done
As is the morning's silver-melting dew
Against the golden splendour of the sun!   25
An expir'd date, cancell'd ere well begun.
   Honour and beauty, in the owner's arms,
   Are weakly fortress'd from a world of harms.

Beauty itself doth of itself persuade
The eyes of men without an orator.   30
What needeth then apology be made
To set forth that which is so singular?
Or why is Collatine the publisher
   Of that rich jewel he should keep unknown
   From thievish ears, because it is his own?   35

Perchance his boast of Lucrece' sov'reignty
Suggested this proud issue of a king;
For by our ears our hearts oft tainted be.
Perchance that envy of so rich a thing
Braving compare, disdainfully did sting   40
   His high-pitch'd thoughts that meaner men should vaunt
   That golden hap which their superiors want.

But some untimely thought did instigate
His all too timeless speed, if none of those.
His honour, his affairs, his friends, his state,   45
Neglected all, with swift intent he goes
To quench the coal which in his liver glows.
   O rash false heat, wrapp'd in repentant cold,
   Thy hasty spring still blasts and ne'er grows old!

---

bateless (9): not to be dulled. *that sky* (12): Lucrece's face. *suggested* (37): tempted. *liver* (47): the liver was supposed to be the center of desire.

1. During his lifetime, Shakespeare's literary fame rested securely on his two long narrative poems, *Venus and Adonis* (1593) and *The Rape of Lucrece* (1594), as well as on his plays. In this excerpt from *The Rape of Lucrece*, Sextus Tarquin (son of the king of Rome) secretly leaves the Roman military camp near Ardea to hurry to the home of Collatine, intent on possessing Collatine's wife Lucrece in her husband's absence. As the last line of the first stanza makes clear,

Lucrece is noted for her chastity, and it is probably this reputation that motivates Tarquin more than anything else (ll. 8–42). That is, in Shakespeare's conception Tarquin is one of those personalities who must seek constant reassurance of his own superiority and uniqueness. How does the diction or imagery of this section contribute to Shakespeare's characterization?

2. What stanzaic form does Shakespeare employ? Why is the form appropriate—or inappropriate—to revealing the nuance of character?

WILLIAM WORDSWORTH (1770–1850)

Resolution and Independence

1

There was a roaring in the wind all night;
The rain came heavily and fell in floods;
But now the sun is rising calm and bright;
The birds are singing in the distant woods;
Over his own sweet voice the stock dove broods;
The jay makes answer as the magpie chatters;
And all the air is filled with pleasant noise of waters.

2

All things that love the sun are out of doors;
The sky rejoices in the morning's birth;
The grass is bright with raindrops; on the moors
The hare is running races in her mirth;
And with her feet she from the plashy earth
Raises a mist; that, glittering in the sun,
Runs with her all the way, wherever she doth run.

3

I was a Traveler then upon the moor;
I saw the hare that raced about with joy;
I heard the woods and distant waters roar;
Or heard them not, as happy as a boy:
The pleasant season did my heart employ:
My old remembrances went from me wholly;
And all the ways of men, so vain and melancholy.

But, as it sometimes chanceth, from the might
Of joy in minds that can no further go,
As high as we have mounted in delight
In our dejection do we sink as low;
To me that morning did it happen so;
And fears and fancies thick upon me came;
Dim sadness—and blind thoughts, I knew not, nor could name.

5

I heard the skylark warbling in the sky;
And I bethought me of the playful hare:
Even such a happy Child of earth am I;
Even as these blissful creatures do I fare;
Far from the world I walk, and from all care;
But there may come another day to me—
Solitude, pain of heart, distress, and poverty.

6

My whole life I have lived in pleasant thought,
As if life's business were a summer mood;
As if all needful things would come unsought
To genial faith, still rich in genial good;
But how can he expect that others should
Build for him, sow for him, and at his call
Love him, who for himself will take no heed at all?

7

I thought of Chatterton, the marvelous Boy,
The sleepless Soul that perished in his pride;
Of him who walked in glory and in joy
Following his plow, along the mountainside;
By our own spirits are we deified:
We Poets in our youth begin in gladness,
But thereof come in the end despondency and madness.

8

Now, whether it were by peculiar grace,
A leading from above, a something given,
Yet it befell that, in this lonely place,
When I with these untoward thoughts had striven,
Beside a pool bare to the eye of heaven

I saw a Man before me unawares:
The oldest man he seemed that ever wore gray hairs.

9

As a huge stone is sometimes seen to lie
Couched on the bald top of an eminence;
Wonder to all who do the same espy,
By what means it could thither come, and whence;
So that it seems a thing endued with sense:
Like a sea beast crawled forth, that on a shelf
Of rock or sand reposeth, there to sun itself;

10

Such seemed this Man, not all alive nor dead,
Nor all asleep—in his extreme old age;
His body was bent double, feet and head
Coming together in life's pilgrimage;
As if some dire constraint of pain, or rage
Of sickness felt by him in times long past,
A more than human weight upon his frame had cast.

11

Himself he propped, limbs, body, and pale face,
Upon a long gray staff of shaven wood;
And, still as I drew near with gentle pace,
Upon the margin of that moorish flood
Motionless as a cloud that old Man stood,
That heareth not the loud winds when they call,
And moveth all together, if it move at all.

12

At length, himself unsettling, he the pond
Stirred with his staff, and fixedly did look
Upon the muddy water, which he conned,
As if he had been reading in a book;
And now a stranger's privilege I took,
And, drawing to his side, to him did say,
"This morning gives us promise of a glorious day."

13

A gentle answer did the old Man make,
In courteous speech which forth he slowly drew;
And him with further words I thus bespake,
"What occupation do you there pursue?

This is a lonesome place for one like you."
Ere he replied, a flash of mild surprise
Broke from the sable orbs of his yet-vivid eyes.

14

His words came feebly, from a feeble chest,
But each in solemn order followed each,
With something of a lofty utterance dressed—
Choice word and measured phrase, above the reach
Of ordinary men; a stately speech;
Such as grave livers do in Scotland use,
Religious men, who give to God and man their dues.

15

He told, that to these waters he had come
To gather leeches, being old and poor:
Employment hazardous and wearisome!
And he had many hardships to endure:
From pond to pond he roamed, from moor to moor;
Housing, with God's good help, by choice or chance;
And in this way he gained an honest maintenance.

16

The old Man still stood talking by my side;
But now his voice to me was like a stream
Scarce heard; nor word from word could I divide;
And the whole body of the Man did seem
Like one whom I had met with in a dream;
Or like a man from some far region sent,
To give me human strength, by apt admonishment.

17

My former thoughts returned: the fear that kills;
And hope that is unwilling to be fed;
Cold, pain, and labor, and all fleshly ills;
And mighty Poets in their misery dead.
—Perplexed, and longing to be comforted,
My question eagerly did I renew,
"How is it that you live, and what is it you do?"

18

He with a smile did then his words repeat;
And said that, gathering leeches, far and wide
He traveled, stirring thus about his feet

The waters of the pools where they abide.
"Once I could meet with them on every side,
But they have dwindled long by slow decay;
Yet still I persevere, and find them where I may."

19

While he was talking thus, the lonely place,
The old Man's shape, and speech—all troubled me:
In my mind's eye I seemed to see him pace
About the weary moors continually,
Wandering about alone and silently.
While I these thoughts within myself pursued,
He, having made a pause, the same discourse renewed.

20

And soon with this he other matter blended,
Cheerfully uttered, with demeanor kind,
But stately in the main; and, when he ended,
I could have laughed myself to scorn to find
In that decrepit Man so firm a mind.
"God," said I, "be my help and stay secure;
I'll think of the Leech Gatherer on the lonely moor!"

Chatterton (St. 7): Thomas Chatterton (1752–70), perhaps the greatest instance of precocity in English poetry, committed suicide at the age of seventeen, when poverty and misunderstanding were about to overwhelm him. *Of him . . . mountainside* (St. 7): Robert Burns (1757–96), whose untimely death was also hastened by the pressures of poverty.

WILLIAM MORRIS (1834–96)

June

O June, O June, that we desired so,
Wilt thou not make us happy on this day?
Across the river thy soft breezes blow,
Sweet with the scent of beanfields far away;
Above our heads rustle the aspens gray;   5
Calm is the sky with harmless clouds beset—
No thought of storm the morning vexes yet.

See, we have left our hopes and fears behind
To give our very hearts up unto thee;
What better place than this, then, could we find   10
By this sweet stream that knows not of the sea,
That guesses not the city's misery—
This little stream whose hamlets scarce have names,
This far-off, lonely mother of the Thames?

Here then, O June, thy kindness will we take;   15
And if indeed but pensive men we seem,
What should we do? Thou wouldst not have us wake
From out the arms of this rare happy dream
And wish to leave the murmur of the stream,
The rustling boughs, the twitter of the birds,   20
And all thy thousand peaceful happy words.

OTTAVA RIMA

Ottava rima is a five-stress, eight-line stanza rhyming *ababab cc*. Although it was introduced into English poetry in the sixteenth century by Sir Thomas Wyatt, the undoubted master of the form is George Gordon, Lord Byron, who belongs to the early nineteenth century. It was Byron who, more than any other poet before or since, seized upon the potential whiplash effect of the final *cc* couplet (after six lines of alternating *ab* rhyme) and transformed what had been an essentially romantic stanza into one of the greatest vehicles for satire in English poetry. The following stanza from Byron's "Don Juan" illustrates:

Sagest of women, even of widows, she
    Resolved that Juan should be quite a paragon,
And worthy of the noblest pedigree:
    (His sire was of Castile, his dame from Aragon).
Then for accomplishments of chivalry,
    In case our lord the king should go to war again,
He learned the arts of riding, fencing, gunnery,
And how to scale a fortress—or a nunnery.

Ottava rima can, however, be used for purposes other than the satirical. John Keats did so while Byron was still alive, and in our own century William Butler Yeats has used the form for one of his greatest poems, "Sailing to Byzantium." But since Byron appropriated the stanza, the term *ottava rima* has evoked by association both his name and the concepts of Byronic wit and irony. Moreover, the form —like any other stanzaic form—can be inserted into a nonstanzaic poem for the purpose of achieving a structural force. For this reason, we have included Milton's "Lycidas" in this chapter. Although it is not a stanzaic poem, it ends with a stanza-like eight lines in *ottava rima*.

QUESTIONS – OTTAVA RIMA

GEORGE GORDON, LORD BYRON (1788–1824)

from Canto I of Don Juan

133

Man's a phenomenon, one knows not what,
    And wonderful beyond all wondrous measure;
'T is pity though, in this sublime world, that
    Pleasure's a sin, and sometimes sin's a pleasure;
Few mortals know what end they would be at,
    But whether glory, power, or love, or treasure,
The path is through perplexing ways, and when
The goal is gained, we know, you know—and then——

134

What then?—I do not know, no more do you—
    And so good night.—Return we to our story:
'T was in November, when fine days are few,
    And the far mountains wax a little hoary,
And clap a white cape on their mantles blue;
    And the sea dashes round the promontory,
And the loud breaker boils against the rock,
And sober suns must set at five o'clock.

135

'T was, as the watchmen say, a cloudy night;
    No moon, no stars, the wind was low or loud

By gusts, and many a sparkling hearth was bright
  With the piled wood, round which the family crowd;
There's something cheerful in that sort of light,
  Even as a summer sky's without a cloud;
I'm fond of fire, and crickets, and all that,
A lobster salad, and champagne, and chat.

136

'T was midnight—Donna Julia was in bed,
  Sleeping, most probably,—when at her door
Arose a clatter might awake the dead,
  If they had never been awoke before,
And that they have been so we all have read,
  And are to be so, at the least, once more;—
The door was fastened, but with voice and fist
First knocks were heard, then "Madam—Madam—hist!

137

"For God's sake, Madam—Madam—here's my master,
  With more than half the city at his back—
Was ever heard of such a curst disaster!
  'T is not my fault—I kept good watch—Alack!
Do pray undo the bolt a little faster—
  They're on the stair just now, and in a crack
Will all be here; perhaps he yet may fly—
Surely the window's not so *very* high!"

138

By this time Don Alfonso was arrived,
  With torches, friends, and servants in great number;
The major part of them had long been wived,
  And therefore paused not to disturb the slumber
Of any wicked woman, who contrived
  By stealth her husband's temples to encumber:
Examples of this kind are so contagious,
Were *one* not punished, *all* would be outrageous.

139

I can't tell how, or why, or what suspicion
  Could enter into Don Alfonso's head;
But for a cavalier of his condition
  It surely was exceedingly ill-bred,

Without a word of previous admonition,
  To hold a levee round his lady's bed,
And summon lackeys, armed with fire and sword,
  To prove himself the thing he most abhorred.

140

Poor Donna Julia! starting as from sleep
  (Mind—that I do not say—she had not slept),
Began at once to scream, and yawn, and weep;
  Her maid, Antonia, who was an adept,
Contrived to fling the bed-clothes in a heap,
  As if she had just now from out them crept:
I can't tell why she should take all this trouble
To prove her mistress had been sleeping double.

141

But Julia mistress, and Antonia maid,
  Appeared like two poor harmless women, who
Of goblins, but still more of men afraid,
  Had thought one man might be deterred by two,
And therefore side by side were gently laid,
  Until the hours of absence should run through,
And truant husband should return, and say,
"My dear, I was the first who came away."

142

Now Julia found at length a voice, and cried,
  "In heaven's name, Don Alfonso, what d' ye mean?
Has madness seized you? would that I had died
  Ere such a monster's victim I had been!
What may this midnight violence betide,
  A sudden fit of drunkenness or spleen?
Dare you suspect me, whom the thought would kill?
Search, then, the room!"—Alfonso said, "I will."

143

He searched, *they* searched, and rummaged everywhere,
  Closet and clothes-press, chest and window-seat.
And found much linen, lace, and several pair
  Of stockings, slippers, brushes, combs, complete,
With other articles of ladies fair,
  To keep them beautiful, or leave them neat:

Arras they pricked and curtains with their swords,
And wounded several shutters, and some boards.

144

Under the bed they searched, and there they found—
  No matter what—it was not that they sought;
They opened windows, gazing if the ground
  Had signs of footmarks, but the earth said nought;
And then they stared each other's faces round:
  'T is odd, not one of all these seekers thought,
And seems to me almost a sort of blunder,
Of looking *in* the bed as well as under.

145

During this inquisition Julia's tongue
  Was not asleep—"Yes, search and search," she cried,
"Insult on insult heap, and wrong on wrong!
  It was for this that I became a bride!
For this in silence I have suffered long
  A husband like Alfonso at my side;
But now I'll bear no more, nor here remain,
If there be law or lawyers in all Spain.

146

"Yes, Don Alfonso! husband now no more.
  If ever you indeed deserved the name,
Is 't worthy of your years?—you have three-score—
  Fifty, or sixty, it is all the same—
Is 't wise or fitting, causeless to explore
  For facts against a virtuous woman's fame?
Ungrateful, perjured, barbarous Don Alfonso,
How dare you think your lady would go on so?

147

"Is it for this I have disdained to hold
  The common privileges of my sex?
That I have chosen a confessor so old
  And deaf, that any other it would vex,
And never once he has had cause to scold,
  But found my very innocence perplex
So much, he always doubted I was married—
How sorry you will be when I've miscarried!

148

"Was it for this that no Cortejo e'er
    I yet have chosen from out the youth of Seville?
Is it for this I scarce went anywhere,
    Except to bull-fights, mass, play, rout, and revel?
Is it for this, whate'er my suitors were,
    I favored none—nay, was almost uncivil?
Is it for this that General Count O'Reilly,
Who took Algiers, declares I used him vilely?

149

"Did not the Italian Musico Cazzani
    Sing at my heart six months at least in vain?
Did not his countryman, Count Corniani,
    Call me the only virtuous wife in Spain?
Were there not also Russians, English, many?
    The Count Strongstroganoff I put in pain,
And Lord Mount Coffeehouse, the Irish peer,
Who killed himself for love (with wine) last year.

150

"Have I not had two bishops at my feet?
    The Duke of Ichar, and Don Fernan Nunez?
And is it thus a faithful wife you treat?
    I wonder in what quarter now the moon is:
I praise your vast forbearance not to beat
    Me also, since the time so opportune is—
Oh, valiant man! with sword drawn and cocked trigger,
Now, tell me, don't you cut a pretty figure?

151

"Was it for this you took your sudden journey,
    Under pretence of business indispensable,
With that sublime of rascals your attorney,
    Whom I see standing there, and looking sensible
Of having played the fool? though both I spurn, he
    Deserves the worst, his conduct's less defensible,
Because, no doubt, 't was for his dirty fee,
And not from any love to you nor me.

152

"If he comes here to take a deposition,
    By all means let the gentleman proceed;

You've made the apartment in a fit condition:—
　　There's pen and ink for you, sir, when you need—
Let everything be noted with precision,
　　I would not you for nothing should be fee'd—
But as my maid's undrest, pray turn your spies out."
"Oh!" sobbed Antonia, "I could tear their eyes out."

153

"There is the closet, there the toilet, there
　　The antechamber—search them under, over;
There is the sofa, there the great arm-chair,
　　The chimney—which would really hold a lover.
I wish to sleep, and beg you will take care
　　And make no further noise, till you discover
The secret cavern of this lurking treasure—
And when 't is found, let me, too, have that pleasure.

154

"And now, Hidalgo! now that you have thrown
　　Doubt upon me, confusion over all,
Pray have the courtesy to make it known
　　Who is the man you search for? how d' ye call
Him? what's his lineage? let him but be shown—
　　I hope he's young and handsome—is he tall?
Tell me—and be assured, that since you stain
Mine honor thus, it shall not be in vain.

155

"At least, perhaps, he has not sixty years,
　　At that age he would be too old for slaughter,
Or for so young a husband's jealous fears—
　　(Antonia! let me have a glass of water.)
I am ashamed of having shed these tears,
　　They are unworthy of my father's daughter;
My mother dreamed not in my natal hour,
That I should fall into a monster's power.

156

"Perhaps 't is of Antonia you are jealous,
　　You saw that she was sleeping by my side,
When you broke in upon us with your fellows;
　　Look where you please—we've nothing, sir, to hide;

Only another time, I trust, you'll tell us,
  Or for the sake of decency abide
A moment at the door, that we may be
Dressed to receive so much good company.

157

"And now, sir, I have done, and say no more;
  The little I have said may serve to show
The guileless heart in silence may grieve o'er
    The wrongs to whose exposure it is slow:—
I leave you to your conscience as before,
  'T will one day ask you, *why* you used me so?
God grant you feel not then the bitterest grief!
Antonia! where's my pocket-handkerchief?"

158

She ceased, and turned upon her pillow; pale
  She lay, her dark eyes flashing through their tears,
Like skies that rain and lighten; as a veil,
    Waved and o'ershading her wan cheek, appears
Her streaming hair; the black curls strive, but fail,
  To hide the glossy shoulder, which uprears
Its snow through all;—her soft lips lie apart,
And louder than her breathing beats her heart.

159

The Senhor Don Alfonso stood confused;
  Antonia bustled round the ransacked room,
And, turning up her nose, with looks abused
    Her master, and his myrmidons, of whom
Not one, except the attorney, was amused;
  He, like Achates, faithful to the tomb,
So there were quarrels, cared not for the cause,
Knowing they must be settled by the laws.

160

With prying snub-nose, and small eyes, he stood,
  Following Antonia's motions here and there,
With much suspicion in his attitude;
    For reputations he had little care;
So that a suit or action were made good,
  Small pity had he for the young and fair,

And ne'er believed in negatives, till these
Were proved by competent false witnesses.

161

But Don Alfonso stood with downcast looks,
    And, truth to say, he made a foolish figure;
When, after searching in five hundred nooks,
    And treating a young wife with so much rigor,
He gained no point, except some self-rebukes,
    Added to those his lady with such vigor
Had poured upon him for the last half hour,
Quick, thick, and heavy—as a thunder-shower.

162

At first he tried to hammer an excuse,
    To which the sole reply was tears and sobs,
And indications of hysterics, whose
    Prologue is always certain throes, and throbs,
Gasps, and whatever else the owners choose:
    Alfonso saw his wife, and thought of Job's;
He saw too, in perspective, her relations,
And then he tried to muster all his patience.

163

He stood in act to speak, or rather stammer,
    But sage Antonia cut him short before
The anvil of his speech received the hammer,
    With "Pray, sir, leave the room and say no more,
Or madam dies."—and Alfonso muttered, "D—n her."
    But nothing else, the time of words was o'er;
He cast a rueful look or two, and did,
He knew not wherefore, that which he was bid.

164

With him retired his *"posse comitatus,"*
    The attorney last, who lingered near the door
Reluctantly, still tarrying there as late as
    Antonia let him—not a little sore
At this most strange and unexplained *"hiatus"*
    In Don Alfonso's facts, which just now wore
An awkward look; as he revolved the case,
The door was fastened in his legal face.

165

No sooner was it bolted, than—Oh shame!
Oh sin! Oh sorrow! and Oh womankind!
How can you do such things and keep your fame,
    Unless this world, and t' other too, be blind?
Nothing so dear as an unfilched good name!
    But to proceed—for there is more behind:
With much heartfelt reluctance be it said,
Young Juan slipped, half-smothered, from the bed.

166

He had been hid—I don't pretend to say
    How, nor can I indeed describe the where—
Young, slender, and packed easily, he lay,
    No doubt, in little compass, round or square;
But pity him I neither must nor may
    His suffocation by that pretty pair;
'T were better, sure, to die so, than be shut
With maudlin Clarence in his Malmsey butt.

167

And, secondly, I pity not, because
    He had no business to commit a sin,
Forbid by heavenly, fined by human laws,
    At least 't was rather early to begin;
But at sixteen the conscience rarely gnaws
    So much as when we call our old debts in
At sixty years, and draw the accompts of evil,
And find a deuced balance with the devil.

168

Of his position I can give no notion:
    'T is written in the Hebrew Chronicle,
How the physicians, leaving pill and potion,
    Prescribed, by way of blister, a young belle,
When old King David's blood grew dull in motion,
    And that the medicine answered very well;
Perhaps 't was in a different way applied,
For David lived, but Juan nearly died.

---

temples to encumber (st. 138): a reference to the imaginary horns that grow
from a cuckold's forehead. *Cortejo* (st. 148): the acknowledged lover of a
married woman. *maudlin Clarence* (st. 166): the lachrymose Duke of Clarence is

first stabbed and then stuffed into a butt (or large cask) of Malmsey wine in Shakespeare's *Richard III*, I. iv. *Hebrew Chronicle* (st. 168): see I Kings I: 1–3.

1. How successful is Byron in stanzas 145–157 in suggesting the rhythms of an actual speaking voice? Does his use of *ottava rima* ever seem strained or artificial? If so, where? Is the entire excerpt "poetry," or is it simply good prose that rhymes? Explain.

2. How many human foibles does Byron satirize in this excerpt? In what fashion might stanza 135 be considered a satirical comment on the long episode that follows? Explain.

3. Locate at least three places where the narrator intrudes into the story and show how each intrusion enlarges the total effect. Characterize the narrator.

JOHN MILTON (1608–74)

Lycidas

In this monody the author bewails a learned friend, unfortunately drowned in his passage from Chester on the Irish seas, 1637. And by occasion foretells the ruin of our corrupted clergy, then in their height.

> Yet once more, O ye laurels, and once more
> Ye myrtles brown, with ivy never sere,
> I come to pluck your berries harsh and crude,
> And with forced fingers rude,
> Shatter your leaves before the mellowing year.   5
> Bitter constraint, and sad occasion dear,
> Compels me to disturb your season due;
> For Lycidas is dead, dead ere his prime,
> Young Lycidas, and hath not left his peer.
> Who would not sing for Lycidas? He knew   10
> Himself to sing, and build the lofty rhyme.
> He must not float upon his watery bier
> Unwept, and welter to the parching wind,
> Without the meed of some melodious tear.
>   Begin then, sisters of the sacred well   15
> That from beneath the seat of Jove doth spring,
> Begin, and somewhat loudly sweep the string.
> Hence with denial vain, and coy excuse;
> So may some gentle Muse

With lucky words favor my destined urn, 20
And as he passes turn,
And bid fair peace be to my sable shroud.
For we were nursed upon the selfsame hill,
Fed the same flock, by fountain, shade, and rill.
   Together both, ere the high lawns appeared 25
Under the opening eyelids of the morn,
We drove afield, and both together heard
What time the grayfly winds her sultry horn,
Battening our flocks with the fresh dews of night,
Oft till the star that rose at evening bright 30
Toward Heaven's descent had sloped his westering wheel.
Meanwhile the rural ditties were not mute,
Tempered to th' oaten flute,
Rough satyrs danced, and fauns with cloven heel
From the glad sound would not be absent long, 35
And old Damoetas loved to hear our song.
   But O the heavy change, now thou art gone,
Now thou art gone, and never must return!
Thee, shepherd, thee the woods and desert caves,
With wild thyme and the gadding vine o'ergrown, 40
And all their echoes mourn
The willows and the hazel copses green
Shall now no more be seen,
Fanning their joyous leaves to thy soft lays.
As killing as the canker to the rose, 45
Or taint-worm to the weanling herds that graze,
Or frost to flowers that their gay wardrobe wear,
When first the white thorn blows;
Such, Lycidas, thy loss to shepherd's ear.
   Where were ye, nymphs, when the remorseless deep 50
Closed o'er the head of your loved Lycidas?
For neither were ye playing on the steep,
Where your old Bards, the famous Druids lie,
Nor on the shaggy top of Mona high,
Nor yet where Deva spreads her wizard stream: 55
Ay me! I fondly dream—
Had ye been there—for what could that have done?
What could the Muse herself that Orpheus bore,
The Muse herself, for her inchanting son
Whom universe Nature did lament, 60
When by the rout that made the hideous roar,
His gory visage down the stream was sent,

Down the swift Hebrus to the Lesbian shore?
   Alas! What boots it with incessant care
To tend the homely slighted shepherd's trade,   65
And strictly meditate the thankless Muse?
Were it not better done as others use,
To sport with Amaryllis in the shade,
Or with the tangles of Neaera's hair?
Fame is the spur that the clear spirit doth raise   70
(That last infirmity of noble mind)
To scorn delights, and live laborious days;
But the fair guerdon when we hope to find,
And think to burst out into sudden blaze,
Comes the blind Fury with th' abhorréd shears,   75
And slits the thin spun life. "But not the praise,"
Phoebus replied, and touched my trembling ears;
"Fame is no plant that grows on mortal soil,
Not in the glistering foil
Set off to th' world, nor in broad rumor lies,   80
But lives and spreads aloft by those pure eyes,
And perfect witness of all-judging Jove;
As he pronounces lastly on each deed,
Of so much fame in Heaven expect thy meed."
   O fountain Arethuse, and thou honored flood,   85
Smooth-sliding Mincius, crowned with vocal reeds,
That strain I heard was of a higher mood.
But now my oat proceeds,
And listens to the herald of the sea
That came in Neptune's plea.   90
He asked the waves, and asked the felon winds,
"What hard mishap hath doomed this gentle swain?"
And questioned every gust of rugged wings
That blows from off each beakéd promontory;
They knew not of his story,   95
And sage Hippotades their answer brings,
That not a blast was from his dungeon strayed,
The air was calm, and on the level brine,
Sleek Panope with all her sisters played.
It was that fatal and perfidious bark   100
Built in th' eclipse, and rigged with curses dark,
That sunk so low that sacred head of thine.
   Next Camus, reverend sire, went footing slow,
His mantle hairy, and his bonnet sedge,
Inwrought with figures dim, and on the edge   105

Like to that sanguine flower inscribed with woe.
"Ah! who hath reft," quoth he, "my dearest pledge?"
Last came and last did go
The pilot of the Galilean lake,
Two massy keys he bore of metals twain   110
(The golden opes, the iron shuts amain).
He shook his mitered locks, and stern bespake:
"How well could I have spared for thee, young swain,
Enow of such as for their bellies' sake,
Creep and intrude, and climb into the fold!   115
Of other care they little reckoning make,
Than how to scramble at the shearers' feast,
And shove away the worthy bidden guest.
Blind mouths! That scarce themselves know how to hold
A sheep-hook, or have learned aught else the least   120
That to the faithful herdsman's art belongs!
What recks it them? What need they? They are sped;
And when they list, their lean and flashy songs
Grate on their scrannel pipes of wretched straw.
The hungry sheep look up, and are not fed,   125
But swoln with wind, and the rank mist they draw,
Rot inwardly, and foul contagion spread,
Besides what the grim wolf with privy paw
Daily devours apace, and nothing said.
But that two-handed engine at the door   130
Stands ready to smite once, and smite no more."
    Return, Alpheus, the dread voice is past,
That shrunk thy streams; return, Sicilian muse,
And call the vales, and bid them hither cast
Their bells and flowerets of a thousand hues.   135
Ye valleys low where the mild whispers use,
Of shades and wanton winds, and gushing brooks,
On whose fresh lap the swart star sparely looks,
Throw hither all your quaint enameled eyes,
That on the green turf suck the honeyed showers,   140
And purple all the ground with vernal flowers.
Bring the rathe primrose that forsaken dies.
The tufted crow-toe, and pale jessamine,   ·
The white pink, and the pansy freaked with jet,
The glowing violet,   145
The musk-rose, and the well attired woodbine.
With cowslips wan that hang the pensive head,
And every flower that sad embroidery wears:

Bid amaranthus all his beauty shed,
And daffadillies fill their cups with tears, 150
To strew the laureate hearse where Lycid lies.
For so to interpose a little ease,
Let our frail thoughts dally with false surmise.
Ay me! Whilst thee the shores and sounding seas
Wash far away, where'er thy bones are hurled, 155
Whether beyond the stormy Hebrides,
Where thou perhaps under the whelming tide
Visit'st the bottom of the monstrous world;
Or whether thou, to our moist vows denied,
Sleep'st by the fable of Bellerus old, 160
Where the great vision of the guarded mount
Looks toward Namancos and Bayona's hold;
Look homeward angel now, and melt with ruth:
And, O ye dolphins, waft the hapless youth.
Weep no more, woeful shepherds, weep no more, 165
For Lycidas your sorrow is not dead,
Sunk though he be beneath the watery floor,
So sinks the day-star in the ocean bed,
And yet anon repairs his drooping head,
And tricks his beams, and with new-spangled ore, 170
Flames in the forehead of the morning sky:
So Lycidas sunk low, but mounted high,
Through the dear might of him that walked the waves,
Where other groves, and other streams along,
With nectar pure his oozy locks he laves, 175
And hears the unexpressive nuptial song,
In the blest kingdoms meek of joy and love.
There entertain him all the saints above,
In solemn troops and sweet societies
That sing, and singing in their glory move, 180
And wipe the tears forever from his eyes.
Now, Lycidas, the shepherds weep no more;
Henceforth thou art the genius of the shore,
In thy large recompense, and shalt be good
To all that wander in that perilous flood. 185
Thus sang the uncouth swain to th' oaks and rills,
While the still morn went out with sandals gray;
He touched the tender stops of various quills,
With eager thought warbling his Doric lay:
And now the sun had stretched out all the hills, 190
And now was dropped into the western bay;

At last he rose, and twitched his mantle blue:
Tomorrow to fresh woods, and pastures new.

blind Fury (75): Atropos, one of the three Fates. *foil* (79): gaudy metal. *scrannel* (124): harsh. *swart star* (138): Sirius. *rathe* (142): early. *tricks* (170): dresses. *quills* (188): the stalks of the pipes the "swain" (186) has been playing on. *Doric* (189): simple. (See also additional notes under item 3 below.)

1. "Lycidas" (1637) is a *pastoral elegy*, a poem which assumes a pastoral frame in order to mourn the death of an individual. Significant conventions of the pastoral elegy are these: (1) the mourner is a shepherd-poet bemoaning the loss of one who was himself a shepherd-poet; (2) the mourner is joined by all nature in bemoaning the loss; (3) the guardians of the dead one are asked where they were when the death occurred; (4) there is a procession of mourners; (5) the chief mourner resumes his domination of the lament and questions Divine Providence in allowing so good a shepherd to die; (6) in a resolution that is also a consolation, sorrow gives way to joy as the mourner realizes that the apparent defeat by death is actually a victory. In "Lycidas," locate an example of each of these conventions.

2. Although "Lycidas" is characterized for the most part by a free and varied use of rhyme, the poet chooses to conclude the poem with a formal stanzaic pattern. What is that pattern? What is its structural significance to the rest of "Lycidas"?

3. One of the major obstacles to a full enjoyment of Milton's poetry is the extraordinary density of learning and allusion in it (see p. 5). In the first two lines of "Lycidas," for example, reference is made to "laurels," "myrtles," and "ivy." The first is sacred to Apollo, the second to Venus, the third to Bacchus. Thus the young man being mourned is associated, singly, with learning, beauty, and joy—and, compositely, with poetic activity. But further, since all three of these plants are evergreens, the idea of immortality is also suggested. "Damoetas" (l. 36), "Amaryllis," and "Neaera" (ll. 68–69) are typical names found in pastoral poetry. "Arethuse" (l. 85) is a fountain in Sicily; "Mincius" (l. 86), a river in Italy: each is associated with a famous pastoral poet—Theocritus and Virgil. In line 58 reference is made to Orpheus, son of the muse of epic poetry (Calliope). Since Orpheus was torn to pieces by a "rout" (l. 61), or mob of priestesses of Bacchus, and his head and harp were thrown into the river Hebrus, it would seem that the idea of a pervasive cruelty in Nature towards

the young gifted poet is being suggested. Yet since Orpheus was transformed into a swan after his death, the idea of immortality or resurrection is also implied. The "pilot of the Galilean lake" (l. 109) is St. Peter. "Bellerus" (l. 160) is a legendary giant supposedly buried in Cornwall, at the western tip, near St. Michael's Mount ("the guarded mount"). "Namancos" and "Bayona" (l. 162) are envisioned by Milton as being in a direct line of vision from St. Michael's Mount, across the Atlantic and the Bay of Biscay. The "angel" of line 163 is St. Michael.

Does such a wealth of allusion and elaborate knowledge run counter to the professed intention of "Lycidas"? That is, is it incongruous in a poem ostensibly lamenting someone to find such an extraordinary amount of literary sophistication? Does the supposed grief become suspect? Dr. Johnson, in the following comments, suggests that it does: "It is not to be considered as the effusion of real passion; for passion runs not after remote allusions and obscure opinions. Passion plucks no berries from the myrtle and ivy, nor calls upon Arethuse and Mincius, nor tells of rough *satyrs* and *fauns with cloven heal.* Where there is leisure for fiction there is little grief." What answer can be made to Johnson? Has he missed the point of the poem? Is Milton primarily interested in suggesting "passion"? Does Johnson's criticism become irrelevant if "Lycidas" is read not as a lament for someone already dead, but rather as Milton's probing into the question of his own destiny in life? Explain.

Chapter 10

Modern Poetry

Modern poetry began with a search for forms. The innovations of Walt Whitman, Robert Browning, and Gerard Manley Hopkins were the keystones of that search; thus, even though what we call modern poetry really emerged in the years just before World War I, the roots of its achievement are in the nineteenth century. Like their contemporaries Marx and Freud—and like the symbolist poets in France—Whitman, Browning, and Hopkins were concerned with the discovery of new forms for the clearly new experiences that were confronting modern man. As poets, in highly individual ways, they sought to liberate the startling effects of modern life in new verse forms.

THE SEARCH FOR FORMS

Typically, each of the three turned to the past for the sources of these new forms, a truer past—or so it seemed to them—than that of their nineteenth century. Walt Whitman had less theory than the other two about what he did; and his tremendous achievement, giving us our first great nonmetrical prosody in English, has thus appeared both so simple and complete that the subtlety of the connection between it and its sources (especially the Bible, in which syntax, as music, is substituted for meter) has often been ignored. Browning was thinking of the Renaissance poet John Donne when he rather consciously shaped his dramatic monologues, adapting blank verse to modern speech cadences. Hopkins returned to the experiments of Milton and to the very first prosody in English, the stress rhythms of Anglo-Saxon. The question naturally arises: why this extraordinary concern with form? Again, the answer takes us to the heart of modern poetry: the very urgency of the life of modern man has required this search for genuinely expressive form. Or, as Ezra Pound put it in "Hugh Selwyn Mauberly":

> The age demanded an image
> Of its accelerated grimace,
> Something for the modern stage,
> Not, at any rate, an Attic grace;
>
> Not, not certainly, the obscure reveries   5
> Of the inward gaze;
> Better mendacities
> Than the classics in paraphrase!
>
> The "age demanded" chiefly a mould in plaster,
> Made with no loss of time,   10
> A prose kinema, not, not assuredly, alabaster
> Or the "sculpture" of rhyme.

The result is that an almost obsessive search for the right form has characterized modern poetry from its very beginnings with Ezra Pound and the Imagists, to the very latest issue of *Poetry* magazine. Never before in the history of English and American literature has there been poetry for which there was literally no established standard from which to deviate. The significant long poems of modern poetry—surely a good place to test a controlling form—reveal no intrinsic similarity of form, *except* the individuality of the form of the poem itself. Is there anything distinctly similar about the forms of William Carlos Williams' "Paterson," Ezra Pound's "The Cantos," Hart Crane's "The Bridge," and T. S. Eliot's "Four Quartets" in the way that Byron's "Childe Harold's Pilgrimage," Shelley's "Adonais," and Keats's "The Eve of St. Agnes" all use the Spenserian stanza as a basic form? The answer, of course, is no.

Most modern poets have felt that the image that the "age demanded" had to be—consistently and constantly—varying. Otherwise, poetry could not truly or honestly reveal modern life as poets have seen it. The past forms have helped, of course, as already pointed out in the cases of Whitman, Browning, and Hopkins; and poets like W. H. Auden and the early Robert Lowell have demonstrated again, more recently, how the forms of the past can be renewed. But it is the present that those past forms serve, the immediate flux "made with no loss of time," to quote Ezra Pound again. If there is a permanence beyond this flux, the forms of modern poetry have not been especially concerned with it.

The problem that such varying forms present to a student of poetic forms is obvious. Where can any order be found which might permit some kind of generalization about modern forms? After all, understanding forms means grasping abstract terms that can take us back —hopefully enlightened—to the concrete context of poems. But if the only law is lawlessness, where does one start?

Fortunately, human nature being what it is, even modern poets tend to repeat and imitate each other. The result is that certain large formal patterns tend to appear and, although such patterns may appear arbitrary, they are valuable guides through some difficult terrain. There are certainly at least three of these guides, and examining the dimensions of each will give us some directions for the exploration of a modern poem. These guides are the following: (1) the startling image, (2) the emphasis on a visual line, and (3) the particular variations of modern prosody. All three can be found, more or less, in every important modern poem. They appear, however, in formal patterns essentially different from the images, visual lines, or prosodies of previous ages of poetry.

THE STARTLING IMAGE

Imagery in a modern poem does not mean merely the use of metaphor or simile (or the other figures of speech), but the concreteness of world evoked in the poem. It is a concreteness that generally builds on surprise, and through shock, compresses the poetic effect. The startling images in a modern poem give, therefore, both a visual and temporal completeness that reminds readers of the precisely rendered (although less compressed) world of modern fiction. In Pound's terms, the "image"—not "the inward gaze"—is all important; but if this image is to be of "accelerated grimace" and "made with no loss of time," it must be startling. The special qualities of time natural to the medium of poetry are thus combined with the concreteness natural to the world of fiction.

In fact, when Ezra Pound said that a modern poem should be at least as good as modern prose, he was thinking of the richly detailed world of Henry James, and also of the fictional technique of novelists like Gustave Flaubert, especially of Flaubert's use of the "sensual complex," in which the description of a scene builds on sensual responses so intricately interwoven that the reader feels the immediate reality of the action as his own. Consequently, in contrast to the moralizing, abstracting, and generalizing responses of much Victorian verse, the Imagists in the early twentieth century—T. E. Hulme, Ezra Pound, Amy Lowell, H. D., and D. H. Lawrence, to name a few— developed the technique of revealing a poem through brief objective descriptions which in themselves offered the reality of the poem. The subjective response of the poet was barely, if at all, visible. In their desire to build a poem through seemingly dissociated and startling images, these poets were working toward the kind of "thingness" which the modern German poet Rainer Maria Rilke had called for. They were giving to modern poetry its characteristic hard, objective surface—the toughness of texture that the best modern poems display.

A logical step from building a poem through deliberate use of disparate images was to return to one of the favorite devices of early poets like John Donne: free association of thought and image. The influence of Freud and Jung and of modern novelists like Joyce and Dos Passos reinforced this associative formal tendency of the Imagists. Thus, the intricate associative imagery of poems like Dylan Thomas' "Among Those Killed in the Dawn Raid" (p. 132) or Hart Crane's "At Melville's Tomb" (p. 7) arises naturally out of such an early Imagist poem as "Along the Yellow Sand" by H. D. (Hilda Doolittle), in which images are disparate, ultimately associated not by grammatical connections, but by the feeling, the voice, which sustains the *whole context* of the poem.

In the following H. D. poem, "Along the Yellow Sand," as in so many poems building on this concept of disparate images, the subject seems blurred. The reader, as in great short stories, must work by indirection. What is going on? More important to a poem, who is speaking? The reader must seek the action in the various images that brilliantly appeal to the senses and give objective surface. If there is "emotion," the reader will have to look between the lines or, significantly in this poem, between the parentheses. It is also important to realize that the almost jagged texture of images is revealed through a dramatic monologue—a form inherited from Browning and frequently used in modern poetry. In this case the device is perfectly right for the stream-of-consciousness perceptions of a young girl who, in a group of Greek votive maidens, brings an offering to Aphrodite and recalls her own boyfriend. Because of the dramatic monologue, the reader knows that all these seemingly objective, "hard" images belong to a personality and a voice, and therefore contain feeling—a feeling to be found beyond the sum total of all the seemingly disparate images, in a unity that we call the context of the poem.

H[ILDA] D[OOLITTLE] (1886–1961)

Along the Yellow Sand

Along the yellow sand
above the rocks,
the laurel-bushes stand.

Against the shimmering heat,
each separate leaf   5
is bright and cold,
and through the bronze
of shining bark and wood,
run the fine threads of gold.

Here in our wicker-trays,   10
we bring the first faint blossoming
of fragrant bays:

Lady, their blushes shine
as faint in hue,
as when through petals   15
of a laurel-rose,
the sun shines through,
and throws a purple shadow
on a marble vase.

(Ah, love,   20
so her fair breasts will shine
with the faint shadow above.)

EMPHASIS ON A VISUAL LINE

The manipulation of the *visual line* in poetry is, of course, quite old. But the hallmark of most modern poems—as "Along the Yellow Sand" illustrates—is the varied use of visual space. Lack of capitals, breaking up of a word, heavy spacing between lines, inverted punctuation: these visual devices and more have been used by the best modern poets to tell us something about our own experience in the modern world. Indeed, they have taught us the meaning of silence as well as sound. Often, modern poets combine startling disparate images, as described above, with the shocking visual line; or they use visual space to give an image Haiku-like brevity, as in this poem of Ezra Pound's:

In a Station of the Metro

The apparition of these faces in the crowd:
Petals on a wet, black bough.

It is interesting to note that Pound took this concept of image combined with visual space and built it into the predominant form of his long and controversial unfinished poem, "The Cantos": the ideogram. This is perhaps the extreme of the method of the visual in English, approaching as it does—at least in theory—to Chinese characters. And, before the extreme is reached, the enduring works of T. S. Eliot and William Carlos Williams stand as vivid testaments to the dictum of T. E. Hulme at the beginning of the Imagist movement: "This new verse resembles sculpture rather than music: it appeals to the eye rather than to the ear."

Yet, even before the Imagists or the Symbolists in France, Walt Whitman had boldly explored the possibilities of visual prosody. In fact, in verse that establishes no formal metric, the use of the line unit demands something other than repetition: it demands the variations that visual rhythm can give. With the invention of the typewriter, poets discovered another source for shaping meaning. What happened in modern poetry was akin to the innovations of Stravinsky and Picasso: a line unit was broken down for greater expressiveness, for new harmonies to emerge. As in modern painting and modern music, sometimes these innovations in the visual line helped to produce magnificently complex poems like Eliot's "Four Quartets," and sometimes the innovations produced disasters.

The most dynamic variations of the visual line, as in Whitman's poetry, have been in long modern poems. But a great many poets have been able to combine lyric effects with visual manipulation of the line, and perhaps none more poignantly than E. E. Cummings, who can reshape simple words like "a leaf falls" and "loneliness" into a visual melody far more expressive than conventional lines or metaphor. Through visual means, Cummings creates, in fact, the hard objective reality of a "thing." Indeed, the line saves the poem from sentimentality by giving a kind of picture or emblem of nostalgia and loss.

E. E. CUMMINGS (1894–1962)

l from 95 Poems

l(a

le
af
fa

ll

s)
one
l

iness

VARIATIONS OF MODERN PROSODY

It was Gerard Manley Hopkins who most dramatically introduced the possibilities of *stress rhythm* into modern poetry. Before the publication of Hopkins, however, this basic meter of Anglo-Saxon verse had been explored by Ezra Pound and others in the first years of the century; and the range of Hopkins' influence on prosody could only have been possible in an atmosphere already created by other influences. Browning himself had sought to adapt the rhythms of speech into the prosody of his dramatic monologues. Whitman had deliberately eschewed any attempt at formal metric, preferring to build by line unit, catalogue, parallelism, repetition, absolute constructions, and other devices for unity such as he might have read in the King James translation of the Psalms.

Most of all, modern poetry had begun, like Romantic poetry, as an attempt to bring the language of men into the language of poetry (see p. 3). Wordsworth and Ezra Pound thus stand as figureheads in two great, sympathetic quests for poetic forms. But their different ages demanded different images and different sounds; for what was happening to the eyes of poets was also happening to their ears. Mozart, as one famous musician has commented, never heard a telephone. As a result, new harmonies of sound, often blending with the variations of visual line, were the only way to capture the new sounds of contemporary life. There were four such new harmonies of sound, prosodies built on *syllable-stress; stress; syllable;* and *no formal metric* at all. But these patterns of prosody were, in fact, not new. All had ties with the prosodies of the past; it was merely their *modern renewal in the mainstream of English and American verse* that made them seem so innovative.

Syllable-stress. A prosody built on syllable-stress or the counting of syllables *and* of accents or stresses is the most familiar of all English prosodies (see p. 47). This is the prosody one can find in iambic pentameter, with its requirement of ten syllables per line, every other syllable accented with the result of five stresses per line. How, one might ask, does this old standard find its way into modern poetry? It is, after all, a prosody used by poets from Chaucer on. The answer is twofold: first, syllable-stress prosody is renewed by the rhythmic variations of modern poets and, secondly, the prosody itself reflects something constant in the way the English language is constructed— a fact that not even modern poets can ignore if they are to use sounds. Indeed, studies have shown that syllable-stress remains more the basic metric of modern poems than any other pattern of prosody. A complex modern poem like T. S. Eliot's "Gerontion," for example, certainly has variations in its musical structure, but it builds on an iambic line.

Of all important modern poets, Robert Frost has most frequently used syllable-stress to gain his effects. In the following poem, the use of iambic stress—the medium of Shakespeare and Milton—seems almost unbelievably right for the "thingness" of the subject. As a master of rhythm, Frost knows where to vary the standard prosody through the slight use of caesura and inverted stresses in order to keep his conversational tone and speech cadence. The result is that the whole poem has, despite its pastoral subject, the tough separateness of objective reality.

ROBERT FROST (1874–1963)

Stopping by Woods on a Snowy Evening

Whose woods these are I think I know.
His house is in the village though;
He will not see me stopping here
To watch his woods fill up with snow.

My little horse must think it queer   5
To stop without a farmhouse near
Between the woods and frozen lake
The darkest evening of the year.

He gives his harness bells a shake
To ask if there is some mistake.   10
The only other sound's the sweep
Of easy wind and downy flake.

The woods are lovely, dark and deep,
But I have promises to keep,
And miles to go before I sleep,   15
And miles to go before I sleep.

Stress. The return to stress rhythm in modern poetry, its most spectacular feature prosodically, has simply meant a return to the kind of prosody one finds in the alliterative line of *Beowulf* (i.e., four stresses or accents to a line with any number of unaccented syllables).

This kind of prosody differs from syllable-stress prosody, obviously, in the freedom of syllables that it may have. Immediately one can see how this freedom suited the modern need for full expressiveness. Ironically stress prosody was the oldest in English; and this irony demonstrates once more that all prosodies ultimately build on the permanent features of language. There have even been attempts, as in Auden's "Age of Anxiety," to use the exact alliteration and the heavy caesura in the middle of the line characteristic of Anglo-Saxon verse. But more frequently, the modern form of stress prosody has simply meant the use of stresses, either three or four (sometimes more or less), scattered throughout a line of uncounted syllables.

William Butler Yeats used this prosody of three stresses in his poem "Easter, 1916"; and this line, using brilliant variations of rhyme to strengthen the stresses, has proved one of the most popular and successful in modern poetry. Its very brevity and yet freedom of stress render the terrible reality of the revolutionary moment, as this first stanza reveals:

WILLIAM BUTLER YEATS (1865–1939)

from *Easter, 1916*

I have met them at close of day
Coming with vivid faces
From counter or desk among grey
Eighteenth-century houses.
I have passed with a nod of the head   5
Or polite meaningless words,
Or have lingered awhile and said
Polite meaningless words,
And thought before I had done
Of a mocking tale or a gibe   10
To please a companion
Around the fire at the club,
Being certain that they and I
But lived where motley is worn:
All changed, changed utterly: 15
A terrible beauty is born.

But stress rhythm has also been incorporated in successful long modern poems, and nowhere more powerfully for its musicality than in T. S. Eliot's "Four Quartets." Working in a different context, Eliot's rhythms tend to be more jagged than Yeats's. In both, however, one can hear the beats, the more pronounced syllables, amid the looser rhythms of the line, the less pronounced syllables. Sometimes, as in Eliot's lines, or in Pound's "Hugh Selwyn Mauberly" (p. 349) there seems to be more than a basic pattern of three or four accented syllables. The result is that in "Four Quartets" (or in any poem consistently using this prosody) one can hear the meditation of a modern consciousness—as in Yeats's poem—seeking meaning in the change, the revolution, characteristic of modern life.

Syllable. A prosody based on counting the number of syllables in a line and ignoring the stresses or accents is characteristic of many modern poems, especially those of Marianne Moore, Dylan Thomas, and W. H. Auden. Here there is freedom in reverse: the poet may use any number of stresses but he must count syllables, allowing only so many per line. In a poem like "Fern Hill" by Dylan Thomas, this method is a formal metric that unites the whole poem through repetition of varying lines, each with fixed numbers of syllables. Such a counting of syllables and ignoring of stresses has not, however, been universally popular, for the simple reason that our language, as the examination of stress prosody has just shown, is fundamentally spoken by stressing some syllables above others. The advantage of a syllable prosody for modern poetry, however, lies in its freedom. It allows a more conversational rhythm to enter. It has the flavor of prose; and, if combined with powerful devices like rhyme, assonance, and alliteration as it so frequently is in the great modern poems that use this prosody, the result is a controlled ease and fluency that expresses, as beautifully and subtly as any other prosody, the new harmonies of sound demanded by the modern world. In "Silence" by Marianne Moore, the anecdotal, the aphoristic, and—above all—the sense of personal voice and consciousness are revealed in this prosody, which here builds on a simple but controlled contrast between a basic line of generally seven or eight syllables and an occasional longer line of generally thirteen or fourteen syllables.

MARIANNE MOORE (1887–   )

Silence

My father used to say,
'Superior people never make long visits,
have to be shown Longfellow's grave
or the glass flowers at Harvard.
Self-reliant like the cat—   5
that takes its prey to privacy,
the mouse's limp tail hanging like a shoelace from its mouth—
they sometimes enjoy solitude,
and can be robbed of speech
by speech which has delighted them.   10
The deepest feeling always shows itself in silence;
not in silence, but restraint.'
Nor was he insincere in saying, 'Make my house your inn.'
Inns are not residences.

No formal metric. Finally, we turn to the no-man's land of modern
prosody, the poem without a formal metric. Here, and we have al-
ready seen examples of this, the sense of the visual line is all impor-
tant. One must read such poems as William Carlos Williams' "The
Bull" (p. 37) or "To a Dog Injured in the Street" (p. 243) with
eye as well as ear. But the line unit is not the only formal element
that, by its very repetition, provides us with a shape in these poems.
Like Whitman, Williams uses parallelism and anaphora (i.e., repeat-
ing words or phrases at the beginning of successive clauses or sen-
tences); alliteration and assonance; and a consistent diction that
celebrates more than it describes. Wisely, Williams avoids rhyme
(only a bad poet would suddenly insert a fixed order of sound where
the prevailing rhythm is open). Yet Williams seems to gain the
concentration characteristic of most rhyme by the use of sudden brief
images that underline the "thingness" of both poems. Thus, what is
lacking in a formal metric is compensated for by a formal attitude
toward the subject (especially revealed in the diction) and by other
formal devices of rhetoric. There is, in short, no lack of form. There
is only a new kind of expressiveness to render the new sounds, sub-
jects, and attitudes of contemporary life.
After reading even the best modern poems, however—written in a

verse as free as, say, Walt Whitman's—one might still logically ask: what can prevent this freedom from becoming the most terrible kind of prison? Not having an established pattern in any aspect of life—modern or otherwise—can be exhilarating; but it can also ultimately be destructive of life itself. The law of human nature is that some form must settle in—right or wrong. But how does the poet settle for the true form and not the false in this kind of poetry? Where is the standard?

The response to these questions can best be found in the poet who has successfully abandoned formal metric for a greater expressiveness; that is, in the depth of the poet himself. It is the voice, the questing consciousness in the poem, that will ultimately determine the success of this kind of poem. For verse without a formal metric finally demands an almost heroic voice from a poet to be fully expressive; and unfortunately these poets—or perhaps, their poems—are few and far between. Two modern poems abandoning a formal metric but succeeding through the very depth of their expression are Robert Lowell's "Skunk Hour" (p. 386) and Theodore Roethke's "Elegy for Jane." It is significant that both of them are celebratory in highly individual ways. They are laments in an almost classic sense, and the loss that each concerns is vividly revealed in the very freedom of the lines. Lowell's loss is his own and the society's that surrounds him. Roethke, on the other hand, sees a loss outside himself that equates itself with the most intimate aspects of nature; in that equation, echoed by the surprising images and parallelism of the poem, the poet finds the loss of Jane capable of being celebrated. As Roethke's free verse probes the mysterious and irrational experience of both nature and his own loss, the very freedom of the form allows for that equation of mysteries to produce a lament or poetic experience itself as mysterious as the workings of nature and of death. For Roethke, neither can be captured in a system, and so his form expressing the lament must be free and probing. In this way it allows a true elegy for the young girl.

THEODORE ROETHKE (1908–1963)

Elegy for Jane

(My student, thrown by a horse)

I remember the neckcurls, limp and damp as tendrils;
And her quick look, a sidelong pickerel smile;
And how, once startled into talk, the light syllables leaped for her,
And she balanced in the delight of her thought,
A wren, happy, tail into the wind,   5
Her song trembling the twigs and small branches.
The shade sang with her;
The leaves, their whispers turned to kissing;
And the mold sang in the bleached valleys under the rose.

Oh, when she was sad, she cast herself down into such a pure depth,   10
Even a father could not find her:
Scraping her cheek against straw;
Stirring the clearest water.

My sparrow, you are not here,
Waiting like a fern, making a spiny shadow.   15
The sides of wet stones cannot console me,
Nor the moss, wound with the last light.

If only I could nudge you from this sleep,
My maimed darling, my skittery pigeon.
Over this damp grave I speak the words of my love: 20
I, with no rights in this matter,
Neither father nor lover.

What we call modern poetry does, therefore, possess a shape. Like the Greek god Proteus, though, it cannot be easily captured; and even in captivity, its form may be something so new that it cannot be recognized. But these three guides—the startling image, the visual line, and the variations in prosody—will allow a reader to see the outlines of modern poetry, if not the full shape. Yet there are no guarantees. The reader must work hard in discovering the form of a modern poem. Unfortunately in modern poetry we do not have sufficient historical distance to allow us to distinguish between the major and the trivial forms. The abstract forms themselves, as in every age, are no guides; for bad poets can write in both established or original forms.

The following poems should help the student to make that final act of discrimination without which he cannot function as a reader. But this act of discrimination is difficult because each good modern poem, like all forms ultimately, must be seen in that uniqueness that characterizes all true life. Such difficulty, as A. R. Ammons asserts in "Corsons Inlet" (p. 388), the last poem in this book, is merely the pain of discovery. Thus, what can be discovered finally is form *transforming*—that is, the experience of the poem becoming your experience.

QUESTIONS – ELIOT

T. S. ELIOT (1888–1965)

The Love Song of J. Alfred Prufrock

S'io credesse che mia risposta fosse
A persona che mai tornasse al mondo,
Questa fiamma staria senza piu scosse.
Ma perciocche giammai di questo fondo
Non torno vivo alcun, s'i'odo il vero,
Senza tema d'infamia ti rispondo.

Let us go then, you and I,
When the evening is spread out against the sky
Like a patient etherised upon a table;
Let us go, through certain half-deserted streets,
The muttering retreats   5
Of restless nights in one-night cheap hotels
And sawdust restaurants with oyster-shells:
Streets that follow like a tedious argument
Of insidious intent
To lead you to an overwhelming question . . .   10
Oh, do not ask, "What is it?"
Let us go and make our visit.

In the room the women come and go
Talking of Michelangelo.

The yellow fog that rubs its back upon the window-panes,   15
The yellow smoke that rubs its muzzle on the window-panes
Licked its tongue into the corners of the evening,
Lingered upon the pools that stand in drains,
Let fall upon its back the soot that falls from chimneys,
Slipped by the terrace, made a sudden leap,   20
And seeing that it was a soft October night,
Curled once about the house, and fell asleep.

And indeed there will be time
For the yellow smoke that slides along the street,
Rubbing its back upon the window-panes;   25
There will be time, there will be time
To prepare a face to meet the faces that you meet;
There will be time to murder and create,
And time for all the works and days of hands
That lift and drop a question on your plate;   30
Time for you and time for me,
And time yet for a hundred indecisions,
And for a hundred visions and revisions,
Before the taking of a toast and tea.

In the room the women come and go   35
Talking of Michelangelo.

And indeed there will be time
To wonder, "Do I dare?" and, "Do I dare?"
Time to turn back and descend the stair,
With a bald spot in the middle of my hair—   40
[They will say: "How his hair is growing thin!"]
My morning coat, my collar mounting firmly to the chin,
My necktie rich and modest, but asserted by a simple pin—
[They will say: "But how his arms and legs are thin!"]
Do I dare   45
Disturb the universe?
In a minute there is time
For decisions and revisions which a minute will reverse.

For I have known them all already, known them all:—
Have known the evenings, mornings, afternoons,   50

I have measured out my life with coffee spoons;
I know the voices dying with a dying fall
Beneath the music from a farther room.
    So how should I presume?

And I have known the eyes already, known them all—   55
The eyes that fix you in a formulated phrase,
And when I am formulated, sprawling on a pin,
When I am pinned and wriggling on the wall,
Then how should I begin
To spit out all the butt-ends of my days and ways?   60
    And how should I presume?

And I have known the arms already, known them all—
Arms that are braceleted and white and bare
[But in the lamplight, downed with light brown hair!]
Is it perfume from a dress   65
That makes me so digress?
Arms that lie along a table, or wrap about a shawl.
    And should I then presume?
    And how should I begin?

          .   .   .   .   .

Shall I say, I have gone at dusk through narrow streets   70
And watched the smoke that rises from the pipes
Of lonely men in shirt-sleeves, leaning out of windows? . . .

    I should have been a pair of ragged claws
Scuttling across the floors of silent seas.

          .   .   .   .

And the afternoon, the evening, sleeps so peacefully!   75
Smoothed by long fingers,
Asleep . . . tired . . . or it malingers,
Stretched on the floor, here beside you and me.
Should I, after tea and cakes and ices,
Have the strength to force the moment to its crisis?   80
But though I have wept and fasted, wept and prayed,
Though I have seen my head [grown slightly bald] brought in upon a
    platter,
I am no prophet—and here's no great matter;
I have seen the moment of my greatness flicker,

And I have seen the eternal Footman hold my coat, and snicker,   85
And in short, I was afraid.

   And would it have been worth it, after all,
After the cups, the marmalade, the tea,
Among the porcelain, among some talk of you and me,
Would it have been worth while,   90
To have bitten off the matter with a smile,
To have squeezed the universe into a ball
To roll it toward some overwhelming question,
To say: "I am Lazarus, come from the dead,
Come back to tell you all, I shall tell you all"—   95
If one, settling a pillow by her head,
    Should say: "That is not what I meant at all.
    That is not it, at all."

   And would it have been worth it, after all,
Would it have been worth while,   100
After the sunsets and the dooryards and the sprinkled streets,
After the novels, after the teacups, after the skirts that trail along the
    floor—
And this, and so much more?—
It is impossible to say just what I mean!
But as if a magic lantern threw the nerves in patterns on a screen: 105
Would it have been worth while
If one, settling a pillow or throwing off a shawl,
And turning toward the window, should say:
    "That is not it at all,
    That is not what I meant, at all."   110

              . . . . .

No! I am not Prince Hamlet, nor was meant to be;
Am an attendant lord, one that will do
To swell a progress, start a scene or two,
Advise the prince; no doubt, an easy tool,
Deferential, glad to be of use,   115
Politic, cautious, and meticulous;
Full of high sentence, but a bit obtuse;
At times, indeed, almost ridiculous—
Almost, at times, the Fool.

   I grow old . . . I grow old . . .   120
I shall wear the bottoms of my trousers rolled.

Shall I part my hair behind? Do I dare to eat a peach?
I shall wear white flannel trousers, and walk upon the beach.
I have heard the mermaids singing, each to each.

I do not think that they will sing to me.   125

  I have seen them riding seaward on the waves
Combing the white hair of the waves blown back
When the wind blows the water white and black.

We have lingered in the chambers of the sea
By sea-girls wreathed with seaweed red and brown   130
Till human voices wake us, and we drown.

S'io . . . rispondo (epigraph): From Dante's *Inferno*, Canto XXVII. "If I
thought that my answer were to a person who ever might return to the world,
this flame would be without further shaking. But since no one alive ever returned
from this bottom—if I hear the truth—I reply to you without fear or infamy."
(trans. Philip Mankin)

1. This poem, published in 1917, stands at the beginning of
modern poetry. Its influence has been enormous, and commentary
on it almost as immense. It exhibits all three of our general guides:
startling imagery; a visual line; and a prosody that reflects the rhythms
of prose and conversation. In these ways the poem shows the in-
fluence of Browning, Hopkins, and Whitman. How is the poem a
dramatic monologue like Browning's? Who is speaking? Where is he?
Does the occasion seem recognizable? What time of year is it? In
short, what is the dramatic situation that frames the psychological
conflict of the speaker?

2. How does this monologue differ from Browning's "My Last
Duchess" (p. 154)? How does it relate to the stream-of-consciousness
novels being written about the same time? Notice especially the
ending of the poem, where reality fades into fantasy. The water
imagery here begins to function like symbolism (see p. 27). But
symbolism of what? If the meaning is ambiguous, is the poem
necessarily bad? Explain. If the meaning cannot be precisely para-
phrased, can it be approximated? Explain.

3. As in much modern fiction, the reader must work by indirection
to get into the dramatic situation. He must depend not on generaliza-
tions, but on succinct descriptions of things to lead him on. In short,

he must depend on images and, as here, a vivid series of images. Often these images are seemingly unrelated. However, as in H. D.'s "Along the Yellow Sand" (p. 352), the personality of the speaker unites them. Look, for example, at the image in lines 2 and 3 of "The Love Song of J. Alfred Prufrock." Is it possible to imagine this surprising combination outside of a consciousness or personality? Line 3 has been called the most famous figure of speech in modern poetry. What kind is it? Explain its vehicle and tenor. What is its shock value? How does its irony help us to understand the personality of Mr. Prufrock? How does its contrast relate to the paradox in the title? Does the Dante quotation from the beginning of the poem reinforce the startling image in the third line? Explain.

4. To what is the fog in lines 15–22 compared? Such imagery dramatizes the scene, but what does it also tell us about the character of Prufrock in whose consciousness this poem is taking place? What is the difference between the fog imagery and the water imagery at the end? Why is the latter more clearly symbolic? In a short essay, trace the most important images of the poem from the fog passage to the water passage, showing the counterpoint between the actual scene of the afternoon party with its "things" and the revery of Prufrock with its "things." Does this counterpoint indicate a musical structure? A psychological struggle? Is there a rising of action? How do the images contribute to this growing intensity? Incorporate your answers in your essay.

5. The psychological conflict of Prufrock is reflected in images. Note that some of them (e.g., "butt-ends of my days and ways") are as violent and heterogeneous as the imagery of the metaphysical poets. Their content, however, is strikingly modern. Also, there are allusions, parodies, and even quotations from great works of the past in the poem. Identify as many of these as possible. How do they add to the irony and mock-heroic atmosphere? Why might such allusions naturally be in the consciousness of Prufrock? Eliot's texture of images is tough and objective; and, as a result, the "thingness" of Prufrock's world makes the conflict of Prufrock—his search for meaning and identity—all the more alive for the reader. Or does this conflict seem alive to you? Explain in a short essay whether or not you believe there is a real search for identity in this poem.

6. The indirection of the poem is not only the result of disparate images but also of a manipulation of the visual line. Particularly

notice the spacing of the couplet in lines 13–14. For the first time the reader is in the outside world, yet how does the irony (women discussing the mighty Michelangelo) reflect back to the title, the image of line 3, and thus the character of Prufrock? How does this recurring image of the women coming and going add to the musical and psychological counterpoint that is at the structural base of the poem? Notice that, as the poem progresses, the lines begin to break up. Why? What do the spacing and elipsis periods at the end of the poem tell us about Prufrock himself?

7. There is a basic iambic rhythm in the poem, but its prosody is too varied to call it syllable-stress. There is no obvious pattern of stresses either, and certainly no counting of syllables alone. But is the poem free verse, verse without formal metric? Look at the insistence of the iambic line throughout. Scan, for example, any ten consecutive lines, allowing for some natural variations. Does the iambic rhythm seem too constant to be accidental? Furthermore, what about the recurring use of rhyme throughout the poem? Is its pattern as haphazard as it appears, or does the rhyme punctuate important moments of Prufrock's psychological dilemma? Locate some of these moments. Why, for example, is there so much rhyme in the final water passage? Does the rhyme reinforce the symbolism? If so, how? Where, then, can a student place the prosody of this poem? Answer in a long paragraph by contrasting this prosody with other modern types.

QUESTIONS – SANDBURG · FROST · YEATS

CARL SANDBURG (1878–1967)

Grass

Pile the bodies high at Austerlitz and Waterloo.
Shovel them under and let me work—
    I am the grass; I cover all.

And pile them high at Gettysburg
And pile them high at Ypres and Verdun.   5

Shovel them under and let me work.
Two years, ten years, and passengers ask the conductor:
     What place is this?
     Where are we now?

     I am the grass.   10
     Let me work.

1. How does this poem illustrate the three guides for modern poetry suggested in the opening of this chapter? Are they used successfully? If so, why? If not, why?

2. Of the four types of modern prosody discussed in this chapter, which does this poem use? How do you know? Illustrate by analyzing several consecutive lines. Are there poetic devices here that can be found in other poems using this prosody?

3. Are the allusions here used well—that is, are they suited to the context of the whole poem? Or do they seem accidental? Explain in a short paragraph.

ROBERT FROST (1874–1963)

Mending Wall

Something there is that doesn't love a wall,
That sends the frozen-ground-swell under it,
And spills the upper boulders in the sun;
And makes gaps even two can pass abreast.
The work of hunters is another thing: 5
I have come after them and made repair
Where they have left not one stone on a stone,
But they would have the rabbit out of hiding,
To please the yelping dogs. The gaps I mean,
No one has seen them made or heard them made,   10
But at spring mending-time we find them there.
I let my neighbour know beyond the hill;
And on a day we meet to walk the line
And set the wall between us once again.
We keep the wall between us as we go.   15
To each the boulders that have fallen to each.
And some are loaves and some so nearly balls

We have to use a spell to make them balance:
"Stay where you are until our backs are turned!"
We wear our fingers rough with handling them.   20
Oh, just another kind of out-door game,
One on a side. It comes to little more:
There where it is we do not need the wall:
He is all pine and I am apple orchard.
My apple trees will never get across   25
And eat the cones under his pines, I tell him.
He only says, "Good fences make good neighbours."
Spring is the mischief in me, and I wonder
If I could put a notion in his head:
"Why do they make good neighbours? Isn't it   30
Where there are cows? But here there are no cows.
Before I built a wall I'd ask to know
What I was walling in or walling out,
And to whom I was like to give offence.
Something there is that doesn't love a wall,   35
That wants it down." I could say "Elves" to him,
But it's not elves exactly, and I'd rather
He said it for himself. I see him there
Bringing a stone grasped firmly by the top
In each hand, like an old-stone savage armed.   40
He moves in darkness as it seems to me,
Not of woods only and the shade of trees.
He will not go behind his father's saying,
And he likes having thought of it so well
He says again, "Good fences make good neighbours."   45

1. This poem has a distinct dramatic situation and a distinct
dramatic structure. It can be called a drama in three acts: the first,
lines 1–11; the second, 12–27; and the third, 28–45. How is each
section different in its emphasis from the other two? Is there a
dramatic conflict in the poem? Is there a resolution of any kind? Who
is affected by it? What do the first and third sections have in com-
mon? Could the poem be called a dramatic monologue? If so, why?
If not, is there a personal voice uniting the poem?

2. There is no manipulation of the visual line in this poem, but
the poem is centered around the image of a wall and its being mended
in spring. There is also a very concrete world presented in the poem.
Identify some of the natural and human processes that go on in the

action of the poem. Contrast the processes here with the one in Frost's sonnet "Mowing" (p. 129). Is the local color of the New England setting integrated into the objective texture of both poems? Explain in a long paragraph. In each case, does the setting fit the theme of the poem? That is, is it part of the poem and not just added realism? How does Frost achieve this natural use of New England landscape even in the last section of "Mending Wall," when the poem obviously rises to philosophic statement?

3. In the last section of "Mending Wall," the wall is no longer just a concrete image; it also exists in the realm of symbolism. It is the same wall, but is now enlarged in significance because of a new relationship to the world of ideas. Look at the word "stone" (ll. 39–40). Used denotatively in the two earlier sections, how does it now expand in meaning? Watch the natural intensity of feeling at the end of the poem and especially the deliberate shift in tone at the beginning of the third section. Identify this shift in tone. Paraphrase in a few sentences the literal argument in lines 28–34. How does that argument relate to the heightened use of "stone" (ll. 39–40), to the related "darkness" (l. 41), and to "his father's saying" (l. 43)? How does the use of "Elves" (l. 36) subtly contrast with the new meaning of "stone"? Is the neighbor turned "old-stone savage" in line 40 related in any way to the activities in lines 8–9? Explain by looking at the progression in the poem. Has Frost so skillfully established the hard, objective texture of the first sections of his. poem, with their almost completely denotative language and seeming prose statements, that the reader might fail to see the tight interrelationships operating in the poem, many of them functioning ironically? Notice that Frost uses repetition of phrase or line several times in this poem, a new meaning emerging with the repetition. Look at the last line in this poem, for example. What is its new meaning? Do you understand this meaning better if you know that the poem was written in 1914? Explain by writing a short essay on this meaning and its relationship to the subject and progression of the poem.

4. The first line of "Mending Wall" reminds us that the prosody is modern. The inverted sentence structure echoes the novelistic stream of consciousness. Allowing, however, for the initial trochee traditionally to be found in many iambic lines, does the whole line scan regularly? Continue scanning the next five lines. What seems to be the dominant prosody? How can you account for the irregulari-

ties in accent or syllables? Identify the caesuras in lines 9, 17, 22, 30, 36, and 38. Why are they used? What is the dominant prosody trying to approximate? How does the humor (as in lines 19 and 28) help to establish a voice? How does diction like "frozen-ground-swell" (l. 2) or "spell" (l. 18) or "all pine" (l. 24) also help to establish the presence of the New England farmer without resorting to dialect? Notice that, when the conflict actually begins in line 12, the rhythm tightens. Why? Now compare the irregular accents of line 28, in which we return, as in the first section of the poem, to the speaker's own consciousness. Why is the basic line irregular here? What is the traditional name for this unrhymed verse? (Look both at Chapter 5 and Frost's "Birches" [p. 205]—and also Stevens' "Sunday Morning" [p. 207].) In both of these poems has Frost succeeded in adapting this old form to modern content? Or is the rhythm in the two poems so natural that the question of adaptation is irrelevant? Write an essay explaining your answer and justifying Frost's success (or failure) with this old form.

WILLIAM BUTLER YEATS (1865–1939)

Sailing to Byzantium

1

That is no country for old men. The young
In one another's arms, birds in the trees
—Those dying generations—at their song,
The salmon-falls, the mackerel-crowded seas,
Fish, flesh, or fowl, commend all summer long
Whatever is begotten, born, and dies.
Caught in that sensual music all neglect
Monuments of unaging intellect.

2

An aged man is but a paltry thing,
A tattered coat upon a stick, unless
Soul clap its hands and sing, and louder sing
For every tatter in its mortal dress,
Nor is there singing school but studying
Monuments of its own magnificence;

And therefore I have sailed the seas and come
To the holy city of Byzantium.

3

O sages standing in God's holy fire
As in the gold mosaic of a wall,
Come from the holy fire, perne in a gyre,
And be the singing-masters of my soul.
Consume my heart away; sick with desire
And fastened to a dying animal
It knows not what it is; and gather me
Into the artifice of eternity.

4

Once out of nature I shall never take
My bodily form from any natural thing,
But such a form as Grecian goldsmiths make
Of hammered gold and gold enamelling
To keep a drowsy Emperor awake;
Or set upon a golden bough to sing
To lords and ladies of Byzantium
Of what is past, or passing, or to come.

1. Critics of modern poetry often complain that contemporary
poets expect too much of their readers. It might be helpful at this
point—before analyzing Yeats's "Sailing to Byzantium"—to consider
this accusation in some detail. Too often, such critics say, there seem
to be too many learned allusions, parodies, or even quotations in the
body of a modern poem. In our own poems for discussion, for ex-
ample, Robert Lowell in line 35 of "Skunk Hour" (p. 386) inserts a
parody of Milton amid the insistent realism of a New England resort
of the 1950's; Marianne Moore in "Poetry" (p. 379) resorts to quota-
tions from Tolstoy and Yeats; and Eliot in "Prufrock," as we have
seen, helped to establish the whole pattern. What is often worse, say
these same critics, is that these allusions, parodies, and quotations
can be only understood within a context of the poet's personal em-
phases; and, worst of all, that there are allusions which are completely
personal and incapable of being apprehended in any objective sense
outside of the poet's private scheme of things. "Sailing to Byzantium"
illustrates this characteristic of modern poetry and will perhaps offer
some answers to this complaint of critics.

First of all, where or what is Byzantium? The specific references to "sages" and "mosaic" in lines 17–18 become more alive when one knows that Byzantium (or Constantinople or Istanbul) was the holy city of Greek Orthodox Christianity in the early Middle Ages (the place and time that together constituted for Yeats the greatest moment in two thousand years) and that its greatest church, Hagia Sophia or Holy Wisdom, contained magnificent mosaics. But what about the strange phrase in line 19 "perne in a gyre"? Here the problem of allusions becomes most difficult, for "perne in a gyre" is an invention out of Yeats's own contrived cosmology and refers to two spirals which symbolized for Yeats cycles of European history.

One may well question whether there can be any justification for such erudite and highly personal references. Before answering, you should recall the use of allusion in the sonnets of Milton (p. 115), Wordsworth (p. 118), and Keats (p. 121). Compare these with Yeats's allusions. Can you see a difference between the two sets of allusions? If you can, look ahead to Wallace Stevens' "Of Modern Poetry" (p. 380), especially to the lines about the changing of the theater and the constructing of a new stage. The modern poet must become, says Stevens, "A metaphysician in the dark" and therefore must construct, however obliquely, his own frames of reference; there are no objective world-pictures that seem to fit contemporary life in the way that the Elizabethan world-picture clearly provided a base for Shakespeare, Spenser, and Milton. The poetic search then is forced to be intellectual; the poet must search, as Yeats says in line 8, for "Monuments of unaging intellect" like Byzantium; the modern poem must be, as Stevens says in the last line of his poem, "The poem of the act of the mind." A poet's scheme of belief or cosmology can thus be as privately created as Yeats's own, with modern poetry therefore growing out of this personal, highly subjective world-picture. The old, largely Judaic-Christian or scientific, world-view does not seem, for better or for worse, to operate for most modern poets unless, as with poets like T. S. Eliot, it is personally renewed in modern terms. Modern poetry, therefore, is finding images of "satisfaction," as Stevens says, and that "satisfaction" is wholly determined by the poet, as in Yeats's personal use of Byzantium or "perne in a gyre."

Is this fair? says the beginning student of modern poetry. Is modern life fair? one might reply. The answer is, however, more complex than simple justice. Again, Stevens gives us the clue in "Of Modern

Poetry": modern poetry "has to be living, to learn the speech of the place. / It has to face the men of the time . . ." A good poet therefore cannot lie. He must express those subjects and rhythms that are truly expressive of contemporary life, of his own life. The result is often difficulty because, for everybody in the modern world, poet and reader, communication is difficult. There is no objectively accepted world-picture to facilitate communication anywhere. What, then, is to distinguish the excellence of one modern poem from another as it absorbs the allusions, parodies, and quotations that filter in through the poet's consciousness? The response is the perennial answer of form: the success, the excellence, with which these allusions are integrated into the whole context of the poem. Successful integration of allusions may not make the modern poem any easier, but it does focus all of these allusions into the right place—that is, into the living voice of the poem.

After this long introduction to our analysis of the poem "Sailing to Byzantium," with its problem of allusion, you can now ask yourself the central question: does Yeats succeed in focusing his allusions? Does Byzantium or "perne in a gyre" get in the way of the voice of the old man speaking? Could the poem exist without either allusion? If not, which one could be discarded first? Why? Does the voice, in fact, have a progression all its own that the allusions reinforce but do not create? Elaborate your answers to all these questions in an essay which will justify your sense of the values (if any) of allusion in this poem (or any other poem).

2. The progression in "Sailing to Byzantium" is clearly dramatic; it is built on a simple contrast. What is that contrast? How do we know that the persona or speaker is an old man? How do the details of animal copulation develop the dramatic situation in the first stanza? What is the pun on "dying"? To what is the old man compared in the beginning of stanza two? How does the comparison emphasize his aging? His ironic self-deprecation? The use of "therefore" in line 15 gives the poem a major shift in its progression. Can you justify the "therefore" at this stage of the poem? The ironic tone disappears at the beginning of stanza three. Why? How does the carefully chosen diction of "artifice of eternity" in line 24 look backwards and look forwards at the same time? To what does it relate (largely through contrast) in the first two stanzas? In the last two stanzas? Do the phrases "Once out of nature" and "any

natural thing" in lines 25–26 of the climactic final stanza make the animal imagery in the first stanza more meaningful? Explain in a short paragraph. Is there a contrast of nature and art throughout the poem? The golden bird is eternal if it can tell past, present, and future. Does Byzantium therefore become symbolic of the heavenly city or the eternal city of art? Is this kind of symbolism arrived at naturally? Or has such a progression violated the limits of the speaker's consciousness? Could you call this poem a dramatic monologue? How does its progression of voice differ from that in "The Love Song of J. Alfred Prufrock"? Answer in a short essay.

3. Although the poem is rich in images and symbols, there is no manipulation of visual line. In fact, the poem reveals itself to us in a steady series of stanzas with a very regular rhyme scheme. What is this traditional rhyme scheme? On the surface, it would seem that the prosody is also regular syllable-stress and that, in fact, the whole metric is traditional. Yeats, however, is a master of prosody, and the contrast that marks the progression of theme in the poem also marks the prosody. Scan, for example, the first stanza. Is it regular iambic pentameter? If not, what is it? Is it syllable-stress at all? Can you locate four stresses in each line? How does the diction in this first stanza support the jagged rhythm? Now scan the last stanza. What has happened to the rhythm? Also watch the progression of the rhymes in the poem. Where are they most exact? Why is the last stanza so balanced and "golden" in tone and rhythm? Does the contrast in prosody support the thematic development of the poem? How does the steady repetition of one stanza form and of the regular rhyme scheme support this very contrast? The thematic development? Does the prosody show how the old man has learned to sing in the poem as he so fervently wished in the beginning? Explain. As in all great poetry, can you here really distinguish form from content? Can you understand what Yeats says in "Among School Children": "How can we know the dancer from the dance?" Write an essay on this relationship of form and content.

4. In "Sailing to Byzantium," Yeats takes an historical allusion— the Greek city of Byzantium—and turns it into a symbol of eternity. The poem progresses from realism or naturalism to symbolism. How does this process contrast with the progression in "Mending Wall"? Yeats begins with his own private "satisfaction," Byzantium, hardly as tangible as a stone wall in New England. His symbol does not

develop out of a scene but out of his reading. Is it therefore less successful? For an answer, pose this crucial question: is the symbol natural in the context of the poem? Write an essay, justifying your answer.

WILLIAM BUTLER YEATS (1865–1939)

Leda and the Swan

A sudden blow: the great wings beating still
Above the staggering girl, her thighs caressed
By the dark webs, her nape caught in his bill,
He holds her helpless breast upon his breast.

How can those terrified vague fingers push   5
The feathered glory from her loosening thighs?
And how can body, laid in that white rush,
But feel the strange heart beating where it lies?

A shudder in the loins engenders there
The broken wall, the burning roof and tower   10
And Agamemnon dead.
                              Being so caught up,
So mastered by the brute blood of the air,
Did she put on his knowledge with his power
Before the indifferent beak could let her drop?

1. Identify the allusions in this poem. What is the relationship of the story of Agamemnon to the rape of Leda? Why do you think the poet chooses such violent allusions? Are these allusions meaningful? What is the real subject of the poem? Is it a modern one? Look back to the beginning of Yeats's "Easter, 1916" (p. 357).

2. How does the beginning of this poem resemble that of "Mending Wall"? Is the poem merely description? What is the psychological effect of the use of questions to develop meaning? What is the effect of the visual shift in the last six lines of the poem? Or of the rather unusual space between the parts of the sonnet? Write a short essay, pointing out how the vivid images of the rape—the "thingness" of the description—and the other technical devices create a context for

the allusions so that Yeats's poem has a theme that is an experience and not a statement.

3. What is the form of this poem? After looking back to Chapter 3, compare how Yeats uses the form in terms of rhythm and rhyme scheme. Do you see any relationship between the poet's choice of an old form which he varies and his use of a classical myth to express a contemporary subject? Explain in a long paragraph.

QUESTIONS – JEFFERS · MOORE · STEVENS

ROBINSON JEFFERS (1887–1962)

Boats in a Fog

Sports and gallantries, the stage, the arts, the antics of dancers,
The exuberant voices of music,
Have charm for children but lack nobility; it is bitter earnestness
That makes beauty; the mind
Knows, grown adult.   5
                    A sudden fog-drift muffled the ocean,
A throbbing of engines moved in it,
At length, a stone's throw out, between the rocks and the vapor,
One by one moved shadows
Out of the mystery, shadows, fishing-boats, trailing each other   10
Following the cliff for guidance,
Holding a difficult path between the peril of the sea-fog
And the foam on the shore granite.
One by one, trailing their leader, six crept by me,
Out of the vapor and into it,   15
The throb of their engines subdued by the fog, patient and cautious,
Coasting all round the peninsula
Back to the buoys in Monterey harbor. A flight of pelicans
Is nothing lovelier to look at;
The flight of the planets is nothing nobler; all the arts lose virtue   20
Against the essential reality
Of creatures going about their business among the equally
Earnest elements of nature.

1. Unlike the two poems by Yeats, this poem has no allusions that become symbolic of human experience. Does it have, however, a symbol? What is it? Does it arise naturally from the realistic landscape of the California coast?

2. Write a short essay, showing how the rhythm of "Boats in a Fog" suits the subject and its progression to the thematic statements of the last lines.

To the Stone-Cutters

Stone-cutters fighting time with marble, you foredefeated
Challengers of oblivion,
Eat cynical earnings, knowing rock splits, records fall down,
The square-limbed Roman letters
Scale in the thaws, wear in the rain. The poet as well   5
Builds his monument mockingly;
For man will be blotted out, the blithe earth die, the brave sun
Die blind, his heart blackening:
Yet stones have stood for a thousand years, and pained thoughts found
The honey of peace in old poems.

MARIANNE MOORE (1887–   )

Poetry

I, too, dislike it: there are things that are important beyond all this fiddle.
   Reading it, however, with a perfect contempt for it, one discovers in
   it after all, a place for the genuine.
      Hands that can grasp, eyes
      that can dilate, hair that can rise   5
         if it must, these things are important not because a

high-sounding interpretation can be put upon them but because they are
   useful. When they become so derivative as to become unintelligible,
   the same thing may be said for all of us, that we
      do not admire what   10
      we cannot understand: the bat
         holding on upside down or in quest of something to

eat, elephants pushing, a wild horse taking a roll, a tireless wolf under
    a tree, the immovable critic twitching his skin like a horse that feels a
        flea, the base-
    ball fan, the statistician—   15
        nor is it valid
            to discriminate against 'business documents and

school-books'; all these phenomena are important. One must make a dis-
    tinction
    however: when dragged into prominence by half poets, the result is not
        poetry,
    nor till the poets among us can be   20
        'literalists of
        the imagination'—above
            insolence and triviality and can present

for inspection, "imaginary gardens with real toads in them," shall we have
    it. In the meantime, if you demand on the one hand,   25
    the raw material of poetry in
        all its rawness and
        that which is on the other hand
            genuine, then you are interested in poetry.

WALLACE STEVENS (1879–1955)

Of Modern Poetry

    The poem of the mind in the act of finding
    What will suffice. It has not always had
    To find: the scene was set; it repeated what
    Was in the script.
                   Then the theatre was changed   5
    To something else. Its past was a souvenir.
    It has to be living, to learn the speech of the place.
    It has to face the men of the time and to meet
    The women of the time. It has to think about war
    And it has to find what will suffice. It has   10
    To construct a new stage. It has to be on that stage
    And, like an insatiable actor, slowly and
    With meditation, speak words that in the ear,
    In the delicatest ear of the mind, repeat,
    Exactly, that which it wants to hear, at the sound   15

Of which, an invisible audience listens,
Not to the play, but to itself, expressed
In an emotion as of two people, as of two
Emotions becoming one. The actor is
A metaphysician in the dark, twanging   20
An instrument, twanging a wiry string that gives
Sounds passing through sudden rightnesses, wholly
Containing the mind, below which it cannot descend,
Beyond which it has no will to rise.
                    It must   25
Be the finding of a satisfaction, and may
Be of a man skating, a woman dancing, a woman
Combing. The poem of the act of the mind.

1. The three preceding poems deal with the subject of poetry itself: Robinson Jeffers' "To the Stone-Cutters"; Marianne Moore's "Poetry"; and Wallace Stevens' "Of Modern Poetry." As you have read in the previous discussion, Stevens' poem particularly deals with the problems of the modern poet. Both Jeffers and Moore, on the other hand, are concerned with the enduring reality of poetry itself. Yet all three share some of the same attitudes toward the art of making verses. Especially, they find it difficult. What is the point, for example, of Jeffers' overall analogy? How does the rest of the Jeffers poem after line 6 support that line? Similarly, as has been observed, Stevens probes the whole problem of the metaphysical basis for modern poetry and the poet's almost overwhelming problem in the face of shifting "stages." Marianne Moore recognizes all these difficulties, too. Her poem represents the focusing of an attitude toward the reality of poetry amidst these inevitable difficulties, an attitude of irony that accepts all the painful negations but, beyond these, affirms the essential truth of "imaginary gardens with real toads in them."

Marianne Moore's "Poetry" is, therefore, a poem that builds with a progression of structure (see p. 36) toward the definition of poetry in line 24, an ironic definition that blends imagination and reality. This structure begins with the natural colloquial opening that, characteristically for Miss Moore, involves the title in the poem. The tone is casual, light; and the reader feels that he is in for some good conversation. How does the diction further support this idiomatic, unrhetorical tone? Look especially at "all this fiddle" (1. 1), "perfect" (1. 2), and "after all" (1. 3). Despite the abstract subject, then, there is a voice here, not dramatized as Mr. Prufrock's or the New England farmer's in "Mending Wall" or Yeats's old man's. But a consciousness is probing amid "things" for a reality, for a definition that will not come easily because it is honest and true. Even the structure of the lines on the pages and the prosody support the indirection and difficulty of search. How does the attitude of the speaker in the first three lines establish this difficulty of understanding poetry? In a long paragraph, explain how such an attitude sets up an irony of effect.

2. With the images in lines 4 and 5, the voice of the probing consciousness becomes distinctly intense. What are these images? Notice how "eyes" appearing as the end of the visual line has a much more dramatic effect than it would within a line. In fact, how is the dramatic shift in the voice helped by these two short visual lines appearing after the first three longer ones and before the last longer line in stanza one? Does the rhyming of these two lines also help this shift? Explain. The voice in the poem, however, never loses its wit, its ironic awareness. Here the manipulation of the visual line supports the wit. "Rise" has the same kind of dramatic effect as "eyes" does, and this effect is increased by the exact rhyme. But after the lingering drama of "rise" we read the modifying phrase "if it must" and the heroic becomes mock-heroic.

In the same surprising way, although Marianne Moore's grammar is always correct, it sometimes is as deliberately twisted as in a stream of consciousness. Can you justify the comma after "must" (l. 6)? Notice that the first three stanzas end with an ironic flatness. How is this accomplished? Why? Why do you think that the last two stanzas end with words that have a firm rhetorical and grammatical stress? What are these words? How are they crucial to the progression and structure of the poem?

3. The second and third stanzas of "Poetry" develop the concept that "all these phenomena are important" (l. 18). The result is a brief catalogue of "things" that poetry should not exclude, "things" that seem "unpoetic," at least in the conventional sense. The use of the quotation by Tolstoy ("business documents and schoolbooks") emphasizes this necessity for inclusion. But does this prose quotation function well here? Why or why not?

How many of the "things" in these stanzas are animals? Why do you think the poet includes them? Does an animal appear in the final definition of poetry in this poem? Look ahead to Robert Lowell's detailed description of the skunks in "Skunk Hour" (p. 386). Are the skunks also important in the theme and personal lament of that poem? Also compare the animal imagery of "Sailing to Byzantium" and "Mending Wall." In Marianne Moore's poem, where is there a simile using an animal? Is its figurative use just as denotative as the rest of the language in this part of the poem? What is the advantage in this kind of poem in creating the rough texture of an objective world? Is such a world necessary to the climax of the poem in line 24? Write an essay explaining the value (or lack of it) of involving such a created world in a definition of poetry.

4. The last two stanzas progress from the arguments of the first three. Poetry does tend to be "all this fiddle," but it can be "genuine." Yet it must include all of concrete reality; it must not abstract and generalize life. But, says the fourth stanza, phenomena in themselves are not enough. Why do you think Miss Moore uses the Yeats quotation here ("literalists of the imagination")? What does it mean in the poem? How does it prepare for the definition of line 24? Why, in stanza four, is the phrase "insolence and triviality" used? Why is "present" used? Why "inspection"? The choice of diction (see p. 4) is crucial at this stage of the poem. Does the diction fit the tone (see p. 65) of the poem thus far? How does the diction, the very image, of the climactic definition suit the irony that has governed the poem throughout? What exactly is the irony in this definition? Why do you think that this image is the only metaphor in the poem? Is the language here highly connotative?

The last five lines are a kind of coda or conclusion to this carefully structured poem. In a paragraph, give a paraphrase of these lines. How do they summarize the theme of the poem and its various stages of progression? Review the types of progression discussed in Chapter 1 and identify the type used in this poem. Which is more vivid to you, this last discursive analysis of the ideas of the poem or the brief definition itself? Why? Does this last stanza—in its entirely different rhythm—have the same sense of "golden" completion as the last stanza of "Sailing to Byzantium"? Write a short essay, justifying your answer.

5. Marianne Moore may have deliberately worked to avoid what she calls a "high-sounding interpretation." As we have seen, however, her carefully structured progression and the modulated revelation of

her ideas have the formality, even the ceremony, of the highest rhetoric. Like Yeats, she has a steady progression of stanzas. There are five, and with the exception of the third, each stanza has six lines. (You must remember that what sometimes looks like a half-line after the first and second lines of each stanza is often the continuation of the line before.) This controlled stanzaic base for her rhythm supports her dominant metric: the counting of syllables per line. The first stanza sets the pattern, which is followed in the other four stanzas as regularly as iambic pentameter or any pattern of syllable-stress. This pattern is 19 syllables in the first line; 19 in the second; 11 in the third; 5 in the fourth; 8 in the fifth; and 13 in the sixth line. Of course, Marianne Moore's prosody has variations, just as any iambic pattern has. Some lines have more or less syllables than the pattern in the first stanza. But the stanza pattern is roughly the same, and its repetition helps to establish the formality of structure. Take each stanza, counting the syllables in each line, and discover where there are variations. What you will find is what this prosody of counting syllables offers: a speaking voice developing flexible natural rhythms.

Furthermore, does Marianne Moore use rhyme and half-rhyme (see p. 56) to accentuate her rhythms? Miss Moore is considered one of the modern masters of rhyme. Looking at this usage, do you agree? Do the rhymes seem natural? Poets who use this prosody and neglect rhyme often use the very repetition of syllables in varying lines to have the force of rhyme. Look back at Robinson Jeffers' "To the Stone-Cutters" and see if the pattern of syllables in that poem—14, 7, 14, 7, 12, 8, 14, 8, 13, 8—have the effect of rhyme and near-rhyme. Now look ahead to Dylan Thomas' "A Refusal to Mourn the Death, by Fire, of a Child in London." Thomas' dominant metric is that of syllables, but with variations. However, the essential pattern is a contrast of long and short lines, with a mean of nine syllables in the long lines. The result is a rather regular metric. Strengthening the formality of prosody is the exact rhyme scheme of the poem. What is this rhyme scheme? How do Thomas' nearly perfect rhymes strengthen this prosody that does not move by stresses or accents at all? Do you find it significant that all three poems using the prosody of syllables without stresses ("To the Stone-Cutters," "Poetry," and "A Refusal to Mourn the Death") are quite ceremonial in their attitudes toward respective subjects?

Write an essay showing how a traditional attitude and content can be revealed in modern form, using any of the following as examples: the last three poems of this chapter; Allen Tate's "Ode to the Confederate Dead" (p. 240); William Carlos Williams' "To a Dog Injured in the Street" (p. 243); or Dylan Thomas' "Among Those Killed in a Dawn Raid was a Man Aged a Hundred" (p. 132).

QUESTIONS – THOMAS · LOWELL · AMMONS

DYLAN THOMAS (1914–1953)

A Refusal to Mourn the Death, by Fire, of a Child in London

Never until the mankind making
Bird beast and flower
Fathering and all humbling darkness
Tells with silence the last light breaking
And the still hour   5
Is come of the sea tumbling in harness

And I must enter again the round
Zion of the water bead
And the synagogue of the ear of corn
Shall I let pray the shadow of a sound   10
Or sow my salt seed
In the least valley of sackcloth to mourn

The majesty and burning of the child's death.
I shall not murder
The mankind of her going with a grave truth   15
Nor blaspheme down the stations of the breath
With any further
Elegy of innocence and youth.

Deep with the first dead lies London's daughter,
Robed in the long friends,   20
The grains beyond age, the dark veins of her mother,

Secret by the unmourning water
Of the riding Thames.
After the first death, there is no other.

1. The last three poems in this book deal with specific scenes which give a kind of narrative situation to each poem. Dylan Thomas celebrates the death of a young girl in a London air raid during World War II; Robert Lowell laments a loss of identity in a New England summer resort; and A. R. Ammons describes a walk by the sea and an inlet shore in New Jersey. Is this use of scene characteristic of modern poetry? Relate your answer to the discussion in the introduction of this chapter about the origins of modern poetry.

2. Dylan Thomas employs a highly elaborate diction to develop his scene and situation. If there are allusions like Zion and Thames, are they immediately symbolic? The language is also highly associative (see the discussion of Thomas, p. 384) and concentrated in its use of figures of speech, particularly in adding metaphor to metaphor (one term of which often seems to be only in the poet's mind). Given the subject of the poem, do you find it meaningful that you must stop constantly to unravel the connotative values of such language? Is the rhythm of this language colloquial? Biblical? Why? Write a paragraph, contrasting the use of idiom in Thomas' poem and in Lowell's "Skunk Hour."

3. In all of these last three poems, tone (see p. 65) is a key to understanding the poem because it expresses the individual voice probing the situation in each. Write an essay, showing how the theme in each poem can only be understood by the establishment of this tone.

ROBERT LOWELL (1917–)

Skunk Hour

Nautilus Island's hermit
heiress still lives through winter in her Spartan cottage;
her sheep still graze above the sea.
Her son's a bishop. Her farmer
is first selectman in our village;   5
she's in her dotage.

Thirsting for
the hierarchic privacy
of Queen Victoria's century,
she buys up all   10
the eyesores facing her shore,
and lets them fall.

The season's ill—
we've lost our summer millionaire,
who seemed to leap from an L. L. Bean   15
catalogue. His nine-knot yawl
was auctioned off to lobstermen.
A red fox stain covers Blue Hill.

And now our fairy
decorator brightens his shop for fall;   20
his fishnet's filled with orange cork,
orange, his cobbler's bench and awl;
there is no money in his work,
he'd rather marry.

One dark night,   25
my Tudor Ford climbed the hill's skull;
I watched for love-cars. Lights turned down,
they lay together, hull to hull,
where the graveyard shelves on the town. . . .
My mind's not right.   30

A car radio bleats,
"Love, O careless Love. . . ." I hear
my ill-spirit sob in each blood cell,
as if my hand were at its throat. . . .
I myself am hell;   35
nobody's here—

only skunks, that search
in the moonlight for a bite to eat.
They march on their soles up Main Street:
white stripes, moonstruck eyes' red fire   40
under the chalk-dry and spar spire
of the Trinitarian Church.

I stand on top
of our back steps and breathe the rich air—
a mother skunk with her column of kittens swills the garbage pail.   45
She jabs her wedge-head in a cup
of sour cream, drops her ostrich tail,
and will not scare.

A. R. AMMONS (1926–   )

Corsons Inlet

I went for a walk over the dunes again this morning
to the sea,
then turned right along
        the surf

                        rounded a naked headland   5
                        and returned

        along the inlet shore:

it was muggy sunny, the wind from the sea steady and high,
crisp in the running sand,
        some breakthroughs of sun   10
    but after a bit

continuous overcast:

the walk liberating, I was released from forms,
from the perpendiculars,
        straight lines, blocks, boxes, binds   15
of thought
into the hues, shadings, rises, flowing bends and blends
        of sight:

                        I allow myself eddies of meaning:
yield to a direction of significance   20
running
like a stream through the geography of my work:
        you can find
in my sayings

<pre>
            swerves of action   25
            like the inlet's cutting edge:

                there are dunes of motion,
    organizations of grass, white sandy paths of remembrance
    in the overall wandering of mirroring mind:

    but Overall is beyond me: is the sum of these events   30
    I cannot draw, the ledger I cannot keep, the accounting
    beyond the account:

    in nature there are few sharp lines: there are areas of
    primrose
            more or less dispersed;   35
    disorderly orders of bayberry; between the rows
    of dunes,
    irregular swamps of reeds.
    though not reeds alone, but grass, bayberry, yarrow, all . . .
    predominantly reeds: 40

    I have reached no conclusions, have erected no boundaries,
    shutting out and shutting in, separating inside
            from outside: I have
            drawn no lines:
            as   45

    manifold events of sand
    change the dune's shape that will not be the same shape
    tomorrow,

    so I am willing to go along, to accept
    the becoming   50
    thought, to stake off no beginnings or ends, establish
            no walls:

    by transitions the land falls from grassy dunes to creek
    to undercreek: but there are no lines, though
            change in that transition is clear   55
            as any sharpness: but "sharpness" spread out,
    allowed to occur over a wider range
    than mental lines can keep:
</pre>

the moon was full last night: today, low tide was low:
black shoals of mussels exposed to the risk   60
of air
and, earlier, of sun,
waved in and out with the waterline, waterline inexact,
caught always in the event of change:
     a young mottled gull stood free on the shoals   65
     and ate
to vomiting: another gull, squawking possession, cracked a crab,
picked out the entrails, swallowed the soft-shelled legs, a ruddy
turnstone running in to snatch leftover bits:

risk is full: every living thing in   70
siege: the demand is life, to keep life: the small
white blacklegged egret, how beautiful, quietly stalks and spears
     the shallows, darts to shore
               to stab—what? I couldn't
     see against the black mudflats—a frightened   75
     fiddler crab?

       the news to my left over the dunes and
reeds and bayberry clumps was
     fall: thousands of tree swallows
     gathering for flight: 80
     an order held
     in constant change: a congregation
rich with entropy: nevertheless, separable, noticeable
     as one event,
         not chaos: preparations for   85
flight from winter,
cheet, cheet, cheet, cheet, wings rifling the green clumps,
beaks
at the bayberries:
     a perception full of wind, flight, curve,   90
     sound:
     the possibility of rule as the sum of rulelessness:
the "field" of action
with moving, incalculable center:
in the smaller view, order tight with shape: 95
blue tiny flowers on a leafless weed: carapace of crab:
snailshell:

                pulsations of order
                in the bellies of minnows: orders swallowed,
broken down, transferred through membranes   100
to strengthen larger orders: but in the large view, no
lines or changeless shapes: the working in and out, together
                and against, of millions of events: this,
                        so that I make
                        no form of   105
                        formlessness:

orders as summaries, as outcomes of actions override
or in some way result, not predictably (seeing me gain
the top of a dune,
the swallows   110
could take flight—some other fields of bayberry
                        could enter fall
                        berryless) and there is serenity:

                no arranged terror: no forcing of image, plan,
or thought: 115
no propaganda, no humbling of reality to precept:

terror pervades but is not arranged, all possibilities
of escape open: no route shut, except in
                the sudden loss of all routes:

                I see narrow orders, limited tightness, but will   120
not run to that easy victory:
                still around the looser, wider forces work:
                I will try
                to fasten into order enlarging grasps of disorder, widening
scope, but enjoying the freedom that   125
Scope eludes my grasp, that there is no finality of vision,
that I have perceived nothing completely,
                that tomorrow a new walk is a new walk.

Author-Title Index

Author-Title Index   **395**

Author-Title Index   397

Index to Critical Terms

Couplet (*Continued*)
  Hudibrastic couplet, 140–141
  iambic pentameter, 136–138
  mnemonic character of, 136–137
  octosyllabic, 136–138
  open couplet, 135–136
  pace of, 137
Cowleyan ode, 215–216

Dactyl, 48
Decorum, 5
  Pope's attitude toward, 5
Denotation, 5
Diction, 3–5
  analysis of, 5
  Coleridge's attitude toward, 4
  definition of, 3
  Dr. Johnson's attitude toward, 3
  in arousing aesthetic imagination, 4
  levels of diction, 4
  relationship to audience, 3
  Wordsworth's use of terms, 3–4,
    239–246
Dimeter, 49
Dramatic blank verse, 160–165
  stages in development of, 164
Dramatic irony, 24
Dramatic monologue, 204

Elegiac (or heroic) stanza, 305
Elegy, 310
  See also Pastoral elegy, 346
End rhyme, 56–58
End-stopped line, 50
English ode, 215–216
English sonnet, 98–99
Enjambment, 50
Epic, 192
Epigram, 99–100
Euphony, 57, 223–224
Extended figure, 18

Falling meter, 52
Feminine rhyme, 57
Figurative irony, 24
Figurative language, 14–24
  apostrophe, 21–22
  extended figure, 18
  irony, 24
  metaphor, 15, 16–19
  metonymy, 20–21

Figurative language (*Continued*)
  overstatement (or hyperbole), 19–
    20
  paradox, 23–24
  personification, 22–23
  simile, 15–16
  synecdoche, 20–21
  understatement, 19–20
Figures of speech, 14 ff.
Foot, metrical, 47
Free verse, 359–360

Heptameter, 49
Heroic couplet, 138–140
Heroic (or elegiac) stanza, 305
Hexameter, 49
Homostrophic (or Horatian) ode,
  213–215
Horatian (or homostrophic) ode,
  213–215
Hudibrastic couplet, 140–141
Hyperbole (or overstatement), 19–20

Iamb, 47–48
Image, 12
  as total sensory response, 12
  See also Imagery
Imagery, 8–14
  as distinct from conceptual imagery,
    8–9
  auditory imagery, 10
  definition of, 8
  distinction between literal and figur-
    ative, 8–10
  gustatory imagery, 11
  in modern poetry, 350–352
  kinesthetic imagery, 10
  olfactory imagery, 11
  organic imagery, 10
  tactile imagery, 10
  to evoke a total sensory response, 12
  visual imagery, 10
"In Memoriam" stanza, 306
Inversion, 224
Invocation, 227
Irony, 23–24
  as figure of speech, 24
  four concepts of, 24
Irony of situation, 24
Irony of statement, 24
Irregular ode, 215–216

Italian (or Petrarchan) sonnet, 98, 100–101

Literary ballad, 90

Masculine rhyme, 59
Metaphor, 15, 16–19
  cliche metaphor, 18
  dead metaphor, 18
  decorative metaphor, 17–18
  mixed metaphor, 18
  tenor of, 17
  used to include all figurative expressions, 15
  vehicle of, 17
Metaphysical poetry, 180, 182, 110–114, 145–146, 148–149
Meter, 46–55
  anapestic, 48
  dactylic, 48
  definition of, 47
  dimeter, 49
  falling, 52
  heptameter, 49
  hexameter, 49
  iambic, 47–48
  metrical foot, 47
  monometer, 49
  number of feet in, 49
  octometer, 49
  pentameter, 49
  pyrrhic, 49
  rising, 52
  spondaic, 48
  tetrameter, 49
  trimeter, 49
  trochaic, 48
  variety in, 49
Metonymy, 20–21
Metrical foot, 47
Miltonic blank verse, 180–182, 192–194
Mimetic forms, 36, 40–41
Modern poetry, 348–362
  emphasis on a visual line in, 353–354
  individuality of form in, 348–350
  no formal metric in, 359–362
  presence of order in, 348–350
  relationship to modern life, 349–350
  relationship to past, 348–349
  search for forms in, 348–350

Modern poetry (*Continued*)
  startling image in, 350–353
  stress rhythm in, 354–358
  syllable metric in, 358–359
  syllable-stress rhythm in, 355–356
  variations of modern prosody, 354–362
Monometer, 49

Narrator
  See Persona, 34–36
Nonce symbol, 29–30

Occasional piece (or poem), 212
Octameter, 49
Octet (octave), 99
Ode, 212–218
  as mode for philosophical reflection, 212
  as occasional piece, 212
  classical antecedents of, 212–215
  definition of, 212
  English (irregular or Cowleyan), 215–216
  general characteristics of, 212
  Horatian (homostrophic), 213–215
  modern, 240
  Pindaric, 213–215
  use of apostrophe and personification in, 217
  use of periodic sentence in, 217
Onomatopoeia, 60–61
Open couplet, 135–136
Ottava rima, 331–332
Overstatement (or hyperbole), 19–20

Pace, 137
Paradox, 23–24
Paragraph, 45
  as opposed to stanza, 45–46
Parody, 259
Pastoral elegy, 346
Pentameter, 49
Persona, 34–36
Personification, 22–23
Petrarchan (or Italian) sonnet, 98, 100–101
  early adaptation of, 100–101
  Shakespeare's adaptation of patterns, 108
Pindaric ode, 213–215
Poetic license, 5

Poetry
corporeal truth and purpose of, 2–3
definition of, 1
inspired truth and purpose of, 2
language of, 3
mimetic truth and purpose of, 2
pragmatic truth and purpose of, 2
relationship of language to everyday
usage, 3
Progression, 36–43
in argumentative forms, 36, 42–43
in associational forms, 36, 41–42
in mimetic forms, 36, 40–41
in static forms, 36–38
in temporal forms, 36, 38–39
Prosody, 46
Pyrrhic, 49

Quatrain stanza, 304–306
ballad stanza, 73, 304–305
heroic (or elegiac) stanza, 305
"In Memoriam" stanza, 306
use of masculine and feminine
rhymes in, 57

Refrain, 73–74
Rhetoric of poetry, 36 ff.
Rhyme, 56 ff.
apocapated rhyme, 56–57
approximate rhyme, 56
end rhyme, 56–58
feminine, 57
half rhyme, 56
identical rhyme, 56
internal rhyme, 57, 58 ff.
leonine rhyme, 57–58
masculine, 59
near rhyme, 56
rich rhyme, 56
rime riche, 56
slant rhyme, 56
Rhyme royal, 323–324
Rhythm, 46 ff.
definition of, 47
Rich rhyme, 56
Rising meter, 52
Run-on line, 50

Satire, 42, 140–141
Scansion, 49 ff.
as descriptive process, 49, 51
definition of, 49

Scansion (Continued)
in determining line length, 49
learning to scan, 51–54
reasons for, 53–54
Sestet, 99
Shakespearean sonnet, 98–99
Simile, 15–16
Socratic irony, 24
Sonnet, 97–101
challenge of, 97–98
English (or Shakespearean), 98–99
evolution of form, 100–101
Italian (or Petrarchan), 98, 100–
101
Octet (or octave), 99
periods in English, 100–101
role of structure in, 99–100
sequence, 98
sestet, 99
similarity to epigram, 99–100
tone in, 100
Sonnet sequence, 98
Spenserian stanza, 246–248
advantages of form, 247–248
definition of, 246
followers of Spenser, 256–259
uses of form, 259
Spondee, 48
Stanza, 45
as opposed to verse paragraph, 45–
46
Static forms, 36–38
Stichic, 212–213
Strophic (or stanzaic), 212
Symbolism, 27–30
definition of, 27
degree of complexity in, 28
distinguished from sign, 28
nonce symbol, 29–30
relation to metaphor, 27
traditional symbol, 29–30
Synecdoche, 20–21

Temporal forms, 36, 38–39
Tenor of metaphor, 17
Tercet (or triplet) stanza, 294–295
Terza rima, 299–300
Tetrameter, 49
Theme, 64–65
definition of, 64–65
distinguished from moral, 65

Tone, 65–66
  definition of, 65
  relationship to theme, 65–66
Traditional ballad, 70–74
Traditional symbol, 29–30
Trimeter, 49
Triplet (or tercet) stanza, 294–295
Trochee, 48

"Troilus" stanza, 323–324

Understatement, 19–20

Vehicle of metaphor, 17
Verse paragraph, 45
  as opposed to stanza, 45–46
Verse, 137